W9-AWG-529

ROAD&TRACK's

USED·CAR
CLASSICS

A Guide To Affordable Exciting Cars.

Edited by Peter Bohr

John Muir Publications
Santa Fe, New Mexico

Cover photo credits:
Camaro / John Lamm
Alfa Romeo / Richard Baron
Corvette / Joe Rusz
Volkswagen / Jeff Anderson
Austin-Healey / John Lamm
Ferrari / Larry Crane
Datsun / Jon Thompson
Porsche / Scott Malcom
Jaguar XJ6 / Jaguar International

Road & Track is a registered trademark of CBS Inc.

Drawings that appear in this book are based on illustrations in *Reader's Digest Complete Car Care Manual,* ©1981 The Reader's Digest Association, Inc., and have been adapted by permission of the publisher.

Copyright © 1987 by Peter Bohr
Cover design copyright ©1987 by John Muir
    Publications
All rights reserved.
No part of this book may be reproduced in any
    form without written permission of the
    publisher.
Printed in the United States of America.

Book design by Ted Rose
Cover design by Jeff Anderson
Published by John Muir Publications
            P.O. Box 613
            Santa Fe, NM 87504

Library of Congress Catalogue
    Card No. 85-72198

ISBN 0-912528-69-9

Second Edition April 1987

CONTENTS

Preface

When Thoreau remarked that most men live lives of quiet desperation, he obviously foresaw freeways and expressways jammed with twentieth-century citizens slogging through rush-hour traffic in gas-guzzling Impalas. It's no wonder that a great many people today find driving tedious and cars about as fascinating as refrigerators.

That's a pity because driving cars does take a lot of our time. We Americans annually put a total of some 1.2 trillion miles on our speedometers. And if each of us drove only one hour a day, we would spend the equivalent of fifteen solid days a year behind the steering wheel.

Now if you subscribe to the notion that any activity requiring so much time should be organized for maximum pleasure, then you'll want a car that will deliver it. Indeed, the right car can transform a mundane experience into an intoxicating one.

Of course, the cost of new cars, especially exciting new cars, has exploded beyond the bounds of decency in recent years. You'll need nearly $6,000 to buy even one of the most basic (and boring) new models if you include a radio, fees and taxes.

But with all due consideration to Mr. Thoreau, don't despair. Just buy a used car. A virtual cornucopia of interesting cars awaits you in the used-car market, many at prices that are a fraction of the cost of the cheapest new cars. And even if you can afford a boxy new econo-car, you can get more excitement for your buck by purchasing the kind of car this book is all about — a *used enthusiast car* — like a sexy convertible or perhaps a sports sedan.

There is, however, one catch. There's always a chance of buying someone else's heap of trouble. When shopping for a new car, you can assume some correlation between cost and performance. But with used cars the correlation becomes muddied when you consider that a used car's price is a measure of performance diminished by age and use — and often misuse. The challenge then is to find a car that can deliver high levels of performance with as little risk as possible for a given price.

If you're determined to maximize your car-buying dollar with a used car, yet minimize the risk, then you've got the right book. In Part One, I'll give you the basic information you'll need to become a smart used-car buyer. And don't worry if you can't distinguish a dipstick from a popsicle stick; Part One is written under the assumption that you're neither a lifelong reader of *Road & Track* nor a mechanical engineer.

But if you do know that the Stirling Moss isn't a vintage wine, Part Two will be of special interest to you. There you'll find profiles of some 70 enthusiast cars. Most of the profiles are updated versions of the popular "Used Car Classic" series of articles that have appeared in *Road & Track* over the past decade. Written by editors of *Road & Track*, these descriptions present the strengths and drawbacks of each car, not only in terms of its handling characteristics, but in terms of its maintenance requirements as well. It's the kind of detailed information that's hard to find in any other source and is invaluable to the used-car buyer.

The profiled cars range from economical family sedans to exotic sports cars; from cars with simple 4-cylinder engines to cars with complex 12-cylinder engines; from cars that sell in the used-car market in good condition for as little as $2,500 to cars that can sell for as much as $25,000. But despite the variety, they all have one thing in common. Each car described in Part Two has a personality that makes it fun to drive.

So if you'd like to indulge in a little automotive hedonism and save money too, then just turn the page and discover the world of used enthusiast cars.

—*Peter Bohr*

PART ONE

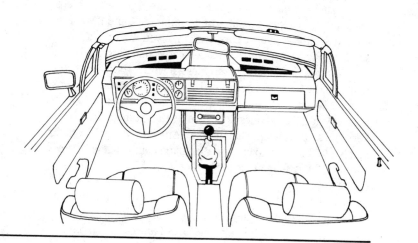

Chapter One:

Come on,
Try an Enthusiast Car!

When I approached the Ferrari Berlinetta Boxer with its fresh red paint glistening in the warm Italian sunshine, I felt a mixture of anticipation and awe. As the factory mechanics hovered around the virgin sports car, preening it for its maiden drive, it looked as if it were in motion though it didn't move an inch. The graceful swoop of the front fenders, the purposeful bluntness of the rear end, and the sheer massiveness of the tires and wheels bestowed the Boxer with a sensuous though sinister beauty.

After introducing myself to the test driver, I slid into the bucket seat beside him and fastened the safety harness. He twisted the key and that unmistakable Ferrari sound — a symphony of valves, camshafts and twelve pistons — filled the cockpit. In an instant we were tearing up the narrow mountain road outside Modena. I felt transmogrified; no longer a mere mortal, I was at one with the machine. My body was now a 360-horsepower projectile capable of traveling 175 miles per hour (mph).

Flying past trucks, buses and ordinary cars as they wheezed their way uphill, we rounded curves at speeds twenty or thirty miles faster than seemed possible. Yet the car remained flat and composed, as if a gyroscope hid in the engine compartment. Suddenly a *bambino* on a bicycle wobbled in the midst of our intended path. Simultaneously downshifting and braking, the driver decelerated with nary a screech or a swerve. Moving rapidly once more, we soon reached the summit where the driver pronounced the Ferrari *"bene."* The brief test was over, but my ear-to-ear grin lasted for hours.

The Sporting Difference

If you have blood flowing in your veins, if you are perceptive enough to appreciate life's better moments, and if you are endowed with just a little craziness, then you'll soon discover a secret known only to the enthusiast-car initiate: driving is a kick — plain ol' fun! A person blessed with a good car, a good road and the enthusiasm to use them can have one of the most heart-thumping, soul-stirring good times found in this frequently dreary age. And it doesn't have to be the ultimate $100,000 Ferrari on a picturesque Italian road. An eight-year-old $2,500 Fiat Spider blasting down a New England country lane in the summer, top down and picnic basket stowed in the trunk, is exhilarating too.

And just what is an "enthusiast car?" That's a question certain to provoke a lively discussion. After all, there are people who can become enamored by just about any car, even ones that are widely acknowledged as disasters — Edsels, for example. Did you know there are folks who have vast collections of Edsels, a car that has come to be a generic symbol for failed products?

As for my colleagues at *Road & Track* and me, we usually equate enthusiast cars with the various types of sports cars and sports sedans. In a recent issue of the magazine, the editor asked staff members to give his or her own "subjective, biased, maybe unreasonable view of what a sports car should be." Though the topic was sports cars, the staff members' comments could just as well have applied to enthusiast cars in general. A sampling:

"A sports car should be nimble, small; make me feel special, give a rakish, exhilarated feeling; have a personality that agrees with mine . . . ." —Dorothy Clendenin, managing editor

"A sports car is one in which I never felt the urge to smoke. It occupies my hands—not to say my feet, eyes, ears and balance mechanism—in an immensely more pleasurable manner . . . ." —Dennis Simanaitis, engineering editor

'Its sole purpose is to give the enthusiast the feeling of driving a car that is designed for entertainment . . . . a sports car also has to have romance, an aura of history that ties it to the classics of old . . . ." —Thos. L. Bryant, executive editor

"Above all else, a sports car must have character and be downright fun. It must beckon you to drive down your favorite twisty mountain road on that beautiful spring morning, leaving you with a lasting memory of that journey. It should entertain you with mechanical sounds and burbling exhaust notes. It must be a machine that becomes a part of you, like a good friendship . . . ." —Richard M. Baron, associate art director

"I suppose any car that makes me want to drive it even when I have nowhere I need to go is a sports car. But the complete joy of the sports car is in its appeal to the senses—the beauty of the bodywork, the touch of the controls, the sound of the engine . . . ." —Jonathan Thompson, associate editor

". . . Some of the best cars in getting you quickly from point A to B are often the dullest. I like a sports car to have quick, accurate steering, a precise gearbox . . . . good brakes, proper pedal placement, a relatively firm ride . . . . and a nuts-and-bolts mechanical directness that make a machine rather than a collection of plastic and rubber bushings . . . ." —Peter Egan, senior editor

"Incredible handling, breathtaking performance, striking good looks and exclusively with a capital X (as in rated) . . . [that's] the ultimate embodiment of all that is good and holy in an enthusiast automobile . . . ." —Joe Rusz, motor sports editor

"A sports car needs to exhibit a balance and blend of performance, ride, handling, steering, braking and ergonomic characteristics. Most of all it must be fun to drive . . . ."

—John Dinkel, editor

When you ask these staff members to name a favorite car, or when you look at the enthusiast cars we've selected as Used Car Classics in Part Two of this book, you'll find there's quite a variety. Some purists on the staff may insist that the only proper enthusiast car is a 2-seat roadster. But for most of us, a car's configuration isn't what counts. A 4-door sedan, a convertible, a coupe can all fit the definition of an enthusiast car. And for most of us, a high price, a big engine or even a manual transmission doesn't necessarily define an enthusiast car either.

What does make an enthusiast car different from an ordinary car is simple — emotion. Ordinary cars are designed by committees of anonymous executives and engineers whose prime concerns are cost accounting, market share and mass consumer appeal. But enthusiast cars are frequently the highly personal — and emotional — statement of one individual. Consider Enzo Ferrari, for example. Since the 1920s, his passion has been race cars. And when he builds a road car, it will always reflect that interest. "Racing remains the final test," he says. "It constitutes a useful test bed for the technical solutions we adopt." If there should be a conflict between handling and performance, and comfort and convenience, then there will be a search for an engineering solution (though it may be costly) that won't compromise the former qualities. Not infrequently, the solutions show up on mass produced Detroit sedans years later.

Like Ferrari, Zora Arkus-Duntov (Corvette), Sir William Lyons (Jaguar), and Ferdinand Porsche, among others, were also connoisseurs of the uncompromising characteristics of race cars. Sometimes quirky, often innovative, and always entertaining, their road cars may not always appeal to the typical American car buyer. But if you buy one of their cars, you immediately become a participant in the genius of a superior mind. That genius is manifested in cars that do three things very well: they handle, they're quick, and they look indecently beautiful.

Above all, an enthusiast car must communicate the feel of the road to the driver. Friction, mushiness and anything that disturbs that communication is minimized. Every driving function, from steering to braking to gearshifting, is crisp and precise. This is in contrast to the traditional Detroit sedan that isolates its occupants from the driving environment and anesthetizes their senses with a marshmallow ride and vague steering.

Though enthusiast cars are usually fast, it isn't top speed that's most important. In these days of double-nickle speed limits, whether a car is capable of reaching 120 mph or 135 mph is quite academic. What counts is the responsiveness ("pickup") of the engine in the normal range of everyday driving speeds — power to move away smartly from traffic lights, power to pass poky traffic and power to zip up mountain roads.

Ideally, an enthusiast car's body should have elegance that stands apart from committee-design sedans, as different as

Sophia Loren from the girl next-door. But that sleek shape will be born out of function; aerodynamic efficiency enhances fuel economy and quietness while cruising, as well as top speed and stability.

In fact, some enthusiast cars are imbued with enough creativity, beauty, and innovative design to qualify as works of art. If you doubt this, just walk through New York City's Museum of Modern Art, where you'll find a 1947 Italian Cisitalia designed by Pininfarina, one of the most renowned automotive designers. And lest you think that such cars are highly unusual, consider the work of Giorgetto Giugiaro, another great automotive stylist: the Alfa Romeo GTV, the Lotus Esprit, the Maserati Ghibli, the Volkswagen Scirocco, among others. Just think, for as little as $3,000 — the price of a good used Scirocco — you can have your very own Giugiaro original.

Though he speaks especially of his own cars, Enzo Ferrari sums up the enthusiast-car experience well: "Owning a Ferrari is a symbol of distinction. It is not just a matter of money; it is a great passion for cars, a love of uncommon engineering, and a taste for very exclusive design."

"Love" and "Passion" — the quintessential expressions of emotion.

Chapter Two:

The Dollars and Sense of Used-Car Buying

There it is lurking in the dealer's showroom, sleek, shiny and powerful. Like a child yearning to play with the puppy in a pet-shop window, you peer through the showroom glass at the new car and fantasize about the great times you could have together. Naturally, you think of all the good reasons why you should buy a new car:

- You'll be the first. You can break in the car's engine properly and carefully. And you don't have to worry about finding an old wad of bubblegum or the remains of a fast-food feast under the seat.
- Because they haven't had the chance to fatigue or be abused, the car's mechanical parts should work perfectly and reliably. And if they don't, you'll be protected by a warranty.
- You can pick just the right color and the exact options you want.
- You'll be the star of the neighborhood with your new car.
- Besides, it's gorgeous and it has *you* written all over it.

Indeed, the pristine beauty of a brand-new car could easily cause almost anyone to temporarily forget mundane matters like budget-busting monthly payments. But when you can no longer resist and you wander inside the showroom to peek at your dream car's sticker price, another feeling suddenly grips you. It's such a common feeling these days that there's even a term for it: *sticker shock*.

Fortunately, sticker shock doesn't have to be terminal to your dreams of owning an enthusiast car. You can instead turn to the used-car market, as two out of three car buyers do each year. And there are some very rational reasons for doing so:

• You don't have to pay new-car prices. That's the best reason of all.

• You have a wider choice of cars, including all the out-of-production cars which, in some cases, are more attractive and exciting than their new-car replacements.

• You don't have to get caught up in the new-car dealer's tiresome sales pitch, one of the more degrading rituals our society has to offer. Instead, you can buy a used car from a private individual.

• You can sidestep the brunt of depreciation. In the first years of a car's life, depreciation costs can be more than insurance, loan interest, maintenance or fuel. (See Table A)

The Magic of Depreciation

For the money-wise individual, avoiding the big depreciation costs of a new car is reason enough to buy used. Today, the average price of a new domestic car is around $12,000 while a mid-range Mercedes is about $35,000. Twenty years ago 12 grand would have bought a top-of-the-line Mercedes and $35,000 a house.

Table A
Driving Costs in Cents Per Mile

	New Car	2-year-old Car	6-year-old Car
Depreciation:	$.15	$.09	$.03
Insurance, Licenses & Fees:	.10	.06	.05
Loan Interest:	.09	.04	.01
Maintenance:	.03	.04	.05
Gasoline & Oil:	.08	.09	.09
Total:	$.45	$.32	$.23

(Table based on data collected by the Hertz Corporation. The data is for an American-made compact car that is driven 10,000 miles a year.)

For most of us, buying a car is the largest investment we'll ever make except for buying a house. But while most houses become more valuable over time, most cars lose their value like Christmas tree ornaments on December 26. Many new-car buyers purchase on impulse and are too easily swayed by a rebate check, slightly discounted financing or some other creative marketing gimmick. All too many new-car buyers cheerfully hand over $10,000 for a new Chevy and don't even wince as the car immediately plunges $2,000 in value as soon as it's driven off the dealer's lot.

That's bad news for the new-car buyer, but it's great news for the used-car buyer. Through the magic of depreciation, the unobtainable car becomes obtainable. If you don't have $6,000 or so—the price of an inexpensive new car—you can still buy a decent used car for half that or less. And if you can afford a new economy car, for the same amount of money you can buy a more exciting used car. For the price of a new Toyota Corolla, you could buy an older Jaguar XJ6, for instance.

Now choosing between a Jaguar and a Toyota is like trying to decide whether to go on a date with Bo Derek or Joan Rivers (or for you female readers, between Tom Selleck and Boy George perhaps). Both have their attributes, but they are very different indeed.

It all depends on what you want. If you value above all else reliable, low-maintenance, hassle-free transportation, and if you can afford a new car, then I strongly advise you to head straight off for your local new-car dealer. However if you want to save money or if you want to put a little fun into your driving and can't afford a new enthusiast car, then you'll undoubtedly find the used cars described in Part Two mighty tempting.

"Oh sure," you say, "I'd like some fun, but I also need a reliable car to get me to work on time. And besides, even though a new Toyota and used Jaguar may cost the same initially, won't the maintenance costs of an old Jag drive me straight into personal bankruptcy?"

But What About Maintenance?

It's true that an older car, especially one that's been mistreated, is sort of like the aging beauty queen behind the cosmetics counter — it takes a lot of work to keep her in shape. New-car buyers don't just blithely absorb thousands of dollars in depreciation costs for the thrill of tearing the protective plastic off the seats. Most expect freedom from breakdowns and repairs as well.

So if you're stupid about buying a used Jaguar, then you may indeed find your accountant suggesting bankruptcy court. But if you're careful about buying a good used Jaguar, you might discover that after a few years of ownership it really hasn't cost you much more than if you had bought a new Toyota.

Let's translate that last statement into an example. Suppose you had bought a new front-wheel-drive Toyota Corolla LE in

1985 that had a list price of about $7,500. By the time you added air conditioning and a few other options, you could have easily spent $9,000. For the Corolla's list price of $7,500, you could have bought a very nice used 1975 or 1976 Jaguar XJ6. Because the Jag was nine or ten years old, it had already suffered its worst depreciation. And unlike more ordinary cars, which are practically worthless after ten years or so, the Jag will probably continue to be worth about $7,000 well into the future, just as long as it's properly maintained.

According to trade-in values compiled by the National Automobile Dealers Association, a 1979 Toyota Corolla lost 44.2 percent of its value between 1979 and 1983. If we extrapolate into the future using that figure, by 1989 a 1985 Corolla that originally cost $9,000 will be worth about $5,000. In other words, you could spend about $4,000 for repairs on the Jaguar over the four years and be no worse off than if you had bought the new Corolla and absorbed its depreciation. Meanwhile you would have had the pleasure of driving the Jaguar.

To be fair, we should add in other operating costs as I've done in Table B. The total operating costs of the XJ6 will be a little higher than the Corolla's not only because of the Jag's higher maintenance and repair costs, but because of its relatively high fuel consumption.

However, keep in mind that I've contrasted two extremes here; the Jaguar is one of the most troublesome cars while the Toyota is one of the least. Many of the cars profiled in Part Two aren't nearly as expensive to maintain and get much better fuel economy than the Jag. In Table C, I've compared the Toyota with a 1974 Alfa Romeo GTV, a sexy Italian coupe. In this example I'm assuming we only had $4,500 cash, which would have bought outright an excellent 1974 GTV. If we had bought the Toyota, we'd have had to finance half the car's total purchase price of $9,000 at 14 percent for four years. In this comparison, our total operating costs are substantially less for the used Alfa than the new Toyota.

Which Cars Hold Their Value Best?

Depreciation is most devastating to a car's value in the first five years of the car's life. After that, most cars continue to lose their value, though at a slower rate, until they're almost worthless and ready for the eternal junkyard.

But smart buyers know that some cars retain their value better than others. Which cars? Enthusiast cars like the ones described in Part Two. According to National Automobile Dealers Association trade-in values as reported in the August 1983 issue of *Money* magazine, the Chevrolet Corvette, the Mercedes-Benz 450SL and the Volkswagen Beetle convertible, as examples, all retain a higher percentage of their value after four years than any American sedan.

Using the NADA figures, I've calculated that enthusiast cars generally maintain about 70 percent of their value after four years. By contrast, ordinary cars that most people consider more sensible and "economical" retain only about 55 percent of their value after four years. But more important to the used-car buyer, the sportier enthusiast cars seem to reach a plateau after four or five years when they stop depreciating, while ordinary cars just keep on falling.

Table B

	Used Jaguar	New Toyota
Price	$7,500	$7,500
Options, Dealer prep, etc.	— 0 —	1,500
Sales tax, License for 4 years	650	850
Maintenance and Repairs	4,400	1,200
Gasoline	3,350	1,650
Total	$15,900	$12,700
Resale Value at end of 1989	7,000	5,000
Total Cost	$8,900	$7,700

Table C

	Used Alfa Romeo	New Toyota
Price	$4,500	$7,500
Options, Dealer prep, etc.	— 0 —	1,500
Sales tax, License for 4 years	450	850
Finance Charges	— 0 —	1,400
Maintenance and Repairs	3,200	1,200
Gasoline	2,000	1,650
Total	10,150	14,100
Resale Value at end of 1989	4,000	5,000
Total Cost	$6,150	$9,100

And why do enthusiast cars hold their value better? As discussed in Chapter One, enthusiast cars perform and handle exceptionally well and are usually visually attractive. In addition, they often possess superior technology, show fine craftsmanship, and are frequently fuel efficient as well. They may also be relatively uncommon. The more of these attributes a particular car has, the less it will depreciate.

Grounds For Appreciation

Some highly esteemed enthusiast cars actually have appreciated in value as they've gotten older. Back in 1970, a sporty, black Mercedes-Benz 190SL roadster came into my life for a mere $800. The car was eleven years old at the time. The convertible top was tatty and the paint lackluster, but everything else was sound. I replaced the top for $75 and sold the car three years later for $1,200. A nice profit? Yes, but if I'd kept the car a few years longer, I could have sold it for about $8,000, or ten times my original investment! And the Mercedes is not a freak example.

You could have doubled your money if you had bought a 1972 Ferrari 365 GTC/4 for $17,500 in 1975. Today the car would sell for over $40,000. In 1972, $10,000 would have purchased a pristine two-year-old Mercedes-Benz 280SL. Now, a decade later, you could easily find a buyer for that car — if you had kept it in good condition — for $16,000 or more. Few stocks would have done so well. And unlike stocks, you would have used and enjoyed your investment while it appreciated.

What happened to cause such a wild escalation in prices? And more to the point, is it still possible to speculate in enthusiast cars and expect such a return?

If we look back over the years since World War II, the mid- to late-1970s must be considered an aberrant period. Before then, wealthier people bought new enthusiast cars, used them for a few years, and then resold them at a substantial loss to those people who couldn't afford new-car prices. They were resold at a discount because the years of use by the first owner imposed wear and tear and diminished their useful lives. It was a system that ensured almost anyone with a few dollars could have an enthusiast car.

But this depreciation phenomenon only worked as long as new-car prices held fairly steady and as long as new cars were perceived as being superior to older models. In the mid-1970s both those conditions failed. The declining value of the dollar relative to other currencies around the world especially affected the price of enthusiast cars, since most are imported. The torrid pace of inflation caused not only by the declining dollar but by other economic woes such as government deficit spending, industry's low productivity and high-priced foreign oil, pushed up car prices in general during the 1970s.

The consequences of a plethora of government regulations also became clear during that decade. The variety of car models diminished, remaining models lost performance and sometimes aesthetic appeal, and the cost of required antipollution and safety equipment only added to already rising new-car prices.

With all these forces conspiring to boost new-car prices dramatically, fewer people could afford new cars. This meant people held onto their old cars longer, which diminished the number of used cars coming onto the market; shortages, of course, meant higher prices. Moreover, older cars were often more desirable anyway. Who wanted ugly 5-mph crash bumpers or performance-robbing smog-control devices?

Soon the hot action in used enthusiast cars had attracted the attention of speculators. These weren't motorists looking for personal transportation or even enthusiasts who wanted the cars for personal enjoyment; they were folks who smelled easy bucks. New enthusiast-car dealers, brokers, auctioneers and restorers suddenly sprang up like weeds after the first spring rain. Overnight, Ferraris, Porsches, and even innocuous sports cars like my Mercedes commanded astronomical prices.

Whether this madness will continue depends upon your personal assessment of the future. It's my judgment that if you didn't buy several years ago, you've probably missed out. Remember the two conditions that must hold: escalating new-car prices and diminished desirability of new cars. Although new-car prices are still rising, the pace of government regulation has slowed dramatically. After stumbling around cobbling up old designs to meet new regulations, automakers are now rapidly introducing fresh, innovative cars. And finally, people have gotten wise—to the point that every owner of a clapped-out old roadster thinks he has a "classic" worth a fortune.

All this doesn't mean, however, that enthusiast cars aren't going to be good investments in the future; it only means that quick, high profits will be harder to come by. For truly desirable cars, prices won't decline. And almost any enthusiast car that is very old and in mint, original condition will undoubtedly appreciate, though chances are you wouldn't want to drive such a veteran every day. As for enthusiast cars of fairly recent vintage suitable for daily use, appreciation would be the exception rather than the rule. So. . . . think of an enthusiast car as a hedge against depreciation.

Taking Advantage of Depreciation

Here are a few rules for making the most of the depreciation phenomenon:

Rule Number 1: Buy a used car and let the previous owner(s) absorb the brunt of the depreciation.

Rule Number 2: Buy an enthusiast car. As I just explained, they hold their value best.

Rule Number 3: If you buy a used enthusiast car and wish to remain financially solvent, buy a car that's in good shape. Some of the cars profiled in Part Two, such as the BMWs, Ferraris, Jaguars and Mercedes, can be frightfully expensive to repair — for both parts and labor. You could probably buy a couple of new Honda Civics for the price of rebuilding an old Ferrari from stem to stern.

With the cost of repairs so high these days, you're generally better off to spend top dollar to buy a used car in perfect condition than to spend too little on "a bargain," only to be faced with costly repairs later.

But don't make the mistake of overestimating an older car's worth. A seller will often value his car by taking the price he paid for the car and then adding on what he's spent for repairs or restoration. A car is only worth the going rate for similar cars, no matter how much the owner has spent.

Rule Number 4: Don't blow your entire budget to buy the car. You may find a seemingly perfect used car, but you can bet that something will need attention, even if it's nothing more than a major service. So keep a little money left over to get the car in top shape as soon as you buy it and then be religious about keeping it that way. Preventive maintenance is the secret to having an older car that's reliable. Moreover, when it comes time to sell, you'll have the best chance of recouping your investment if the car is in mint condition.

Chapter 3:

Choices, Choices, Choices

Back in the early 1950s, an enthusiast car meant only one thing — a two-seat convertible sports car, probably of British make.

Though automotive historians might say the sports car made its debut in the early 1900s with the likes of Mercer Raceabouts and Hispano-Suiza Alfonsos, it was the British who started the modern sports-car phenomenon in this country after World War II. A few homeward-bound GIs brought with them MG TCs. Compared to the domestic-built cars Americans were driving at the time, the MG was different, to say the least. A 1947 Ford was just under 200 inches long, weighed nearly 3,200 pounds, and was powered by a V-8 engine. The TC was 25 percent shorter, weighed 40 percent less, and had half as many cylinders. But it was low and open, and beautifully proportioned with high fenders, a long square hood and a spare wheel jauntily stuck on the rear. And in contrast to the wallowing American behemoths, the MG's ability to take a corner was sensational.

Of course by today's standards the MG drove like a truck and was about as reliable as a politician's campaign promise. Its open cockpit was noisy and its stiff, unsophisticated suspension, though good at rounding corners, gave a Mexican-jumping-bean quality to the ride. Altogether, a journey in the MG was not unlike tumbling down a cobblestone street in an aluminum garbage can.

The MG, and other British roadsters that followed, came to symbolize the sports car to post-World War II Americans. To this day some purists insist that the only true sports car is an MG TC-like roadster with side curtains (roll-up windows came later), a "rag" top that was really meant to stay stowed away in the garage, and absolutely no other frills that added weight or complexity. A TC in 1947, by the way, cost under $2,000. A pristine example would go for nearly ten times that today.

However, their very lack of amenities, together with their unreliability and their underwhelming horsepower (the poor MG was no match for a 1950s Caddy V-8 in stoplight drag racing), caused the little roadsters to be looked upon as amusing playthings rather than as serious threats to Detroit's scheme of things.

But in the ensuing twenty years or so, the sports car underwent a transformation. The first blow to its primitive image came from the British themselves. The Jaguar XK-120 was a truly revolutionary car. Unlike the MG, which was basically a design handed down from the 1930s, the XK was Thoroughly Modern Millie. It still drove like a truck, but a very fast one. It could easily cruise at speeds in excess of 100 mph and quite reliably too. But though the 6-cylinder Jaguar engine was quiet, the XK-120 lacked the basic comfort features we expect today.

The next step in the evolution of the open sports car came with roll-up windows, a top that really attempted to keep out the rain, and a suspension that was more pliant. The Mercedes-Benz 190SL of 1955 and the Alfa Romeo Giulietta Spider of 1956 were examples of the "soft" sports car, a car not altogether different from current convertible sports cars in its concept of handling, performance and modest comfort. (The term "Spider" or "Spyder" has come to designate 2-seat convertible sports cars. The original Spider was a light 2-seat, horse-drawn carriage. In addition to Alfa Romeo, Ferrari, Fiat, Porsche and Triumph have used the name.)

But while the wind-in-the-face crowd were bashing recalcitrant SU electric fuel pumps on their Jaguars and were wiping the rain off the seats of their MGs, the Italians were busy developing enclosed coupe versions of sports cars especially suited for scooting over long distances at high speed. *Ecco-la*: the Grand Touring car, or GT. The Lancia Aurelia B20 of 1951 was the first modern GT car to be produced in quantity. It combined graceful flowing lines with the performance of a thoroughbred sports car and the comfort of a sedan. Based on the idea that it's less tiring to travel in an enclosed car than in an open one, the designation GT has come to mean a sleek coupe that satisfies all the performance requirements of a sports car. In recent years Ferrari has become perhaps the preeminent GT car, though it has a number of worthy competitors. Any Ferrari, with its ample engine, outstanding roadability and luxurious interior can travel cross country safely and comfortably hour after hour at twice our national speed limit.

In the mid-1950s, Alfa Romeo and Jaguar started producing hybrids — crosses between upright four-passenger sedans and sports cars. More precisely, they were true sedans with such sports-car features as bucket seats, 4-speed transmissions and fairly stiff suspensions. In fact, Alfa and Jaguar took many of the same basic chassis and drivetrain components of their sports cars and merely covered them with sedan bodies. In recent years sports sedans like those from BMW have been a rapidly growing part of the enthusiast-car market.

In June of 1974, *Road & Track* compared the handling and performance of three sports cars to three sports sedans. The Triumph Spitfire, a somewhat dated design, clearly lost to a Chevrolet Vega equipped with a "handling package" that included stiffer than normal suspension and wider radial tires. The editors found that the more modern Fiat X1/9 sports car and a Volkswagen Dasher were equal competitors. However, a Jensen-Healey convertible did win out over a BMW 2002tii sedan. The editors concluded: "Perhaps that business of sitting low, of feeling at unity with a compact machine, is the most important thing about sports cars these days. . . ."

Meanwhile, back in the States, Detroit virtually ignored sports cars, grand touring cars and sports sedans. The only exceptions were Chevrolet's Corvette and perhaps Ford's original 2-seat Thunderbird, both built in very low production numbers compared to the rest of Detroit's fare.

During the early 1960s, Detroit had embarked upon a horsepower race that especially appealed to young Americans. The automakers were stuffing monstrous engines in otherwise plain-Jane sedans. In 1962, Chevrolet, Ford, Plymouth and Pontiac all offered production engines that produced over 400 horsepower (compared, for example, to a 1962 Alfa Romeo Spider's 80 horsepower). Perhaps most famous of these American "muscle cars" was Pontiac's GTO. The GTO moniker, meaning *Gran Turismo Omologato* in Italian, was swiped from one of Ferrari's models in order to lend the Pontiac a little European pizzazz.

With the mid-1964 introduction of the Ford Mustang, however, the muscle cars suddenly had competition for youthful American car buyers from the sporty-looking coupes that came to be known as as "pony cars." Following Ford's lead, General Motors, Chrysler and American Motors came out with pony cars of their own. Some, like the Camaro Z-28 and the Barracuda 340-S, had high-horsepower engines too.

Compared to European sports cars, GTs and sports sedans, the muscle/pony cars were quite crude in the handling department. But they were certainly fast in a straight line and the big engines made a ferocious growl.

However, as the 1970s dawned with their high fuel prices and emissions regulations, the big-engine cars rapidly turned into the dinosaurs of automotivedom and became extinct.

Their place was taken by a group of cars with sporty pretentions. Some of these were revamped and detuned versions of the 1960s pony cars — the Mustang, Camaro and Firebird. These American sporty coupes were joined by slightly smaller versions from Europe and Japan, like Ford-of-Europe's Capri and Toyota's Celica. With their zoomy styling, the sporty coupes of the 1970s often fit the popular conception of a sports car. But in general, they didn't have the crisp handling characteristics of a true sports or GT car, nor did they have the gut-wrenching performance of a 1960s-style muscle car. (As a footnote, however, for the 1980s Detroit has once again put hunky V-8s in some of their sporty cars, which give them acceleration approaching that of the muscle cars of yore.)

So where does all this leave you in your search for a suitable used enthusiast car? To summarize, you have a choice among the open, 2-seat sports cars, either of a traditional roadster or a more modern "soft" convertible (technically, a roadster has a soft top that is completely removed from the car when not needed, while a convertible has a soft top that folds down into a compartment or area behind the seats; most modern open cars are convertibles). Then there are the enclosed GT cars which are also basically two-passenger vehicles. There are the full 4-seat sports sedans. There are the muscle / pony cars from the 1960s. And finally, there are the mild-mannered, fun cars, including the 2-door sporty coupes from the 1970s. Here's how I would classify the cars profiled in Part Two:

Traditional Sports Cars:
Austin-Healey 100-4, 100-6, 3000
Austin-Healey Sprite
MGA
MGB
MG Midget
Triumph Spitfire
Triumph TR2, TR3, TR4, TR6

More Modern Sports Cars:
Alfa Romeo Spider: Duetto, 1750, 2000
Chevrolet Corvette Sting Ray convertible
Datsun SPL-310, 1600, 2000
Fiat Spider 124, 2000
Fiat X1-9
Jaguar E-type convertible
Jensen-Healey
Mercedes Benz 350SL, 450SL
Sunbeam Alpine, Tiger

Grand Touring (GT) Cars:
Alfa Romeo GT: Sprint, GTV, 1750 GTV, 2000 GTV
BMW 2800CS, 3.0CS
Chevrolet Corvette Sting Ray coupe
Datsun 240Z
Ferrari 250GTE 2+2, 330GT 2+2
Fiat 124 Sport Coupe
Ford/DeTomaso Pantera

Jaguar E-type coupe
MGB GT
Opel GT
Porsche 912, 911, 914, 914/6
Triumph GT6
Volkswager Scirocco
Volvo P 1800

Sports Sedans:
BMW 1600, 2002
BMW 2500, 2800, Bavaria, 3.0
Datsun 510
Jaguar XJ6
Mercedes-Benz SE/SEL 3.5/4.5
Volvo 122-S

Muscle / Pony Cars:
Chevrolet Camaro Z-28
Ford Mustang Boss 302
Plymouth Barracuda 340-S
Pontiac Firebird Trans-Am

Sporty Fun Cars:
Chevrolet Camaro
Fiat 850 Spider
Ford Capri 2600
Toyota Celica GT
Volkswagen Beetle convertible
Volkswagen Karmann-Ghia

To help you decide which of these cars might best fit your needs, here are some general questions you should consider:

Vintage 1950s, 1960s or 1970s?

In this gadget-laden society of ours, we're often forced to ask ourselves if some new-fangled product is truly worth an expenditure of our hard-earned cash. The question is usually easier to answer if we don't already own a product that does essentially the same task. In that case, the issue is then whether the improvements in the new product are genuine or whether they are merely marketing gimmicks.

Take, for example, the task of putting words to paper. For those who type proficiently, a typewriter is a far more efficient tool for the task than a pencil or pen. An electric typewriter is more efficient than a manual typewriter, while a computer can be the most efficient of all.

From my point of view, the newest product (the computer) makes the task (writing) easier to perform and even enjoyable, and thus is certainly worth an expenditure of my very hard-earned bucks. Besides, it's tax-deductible. Nevertheless, under certain circumstances — for instance, when I'm out on an interview and I can't lug my computer with me — the original word processor, the pencil or pen, becomes once again the most efficient product.

Now a primary premise of this book is that the task of driving should be enjoyable and that the right product, an enthusiast car, will help accomplish that objective. And when you consider that automotive technology has moved at a dizzying pace in the past decade and a half, you would think that the most recent automotive designs would be vastly superior and thus preferable to older ones. If you followed this logic, you'd be nuts to buy one of the cars profiled in Part Two that date back to the 1950s or early 1960s, like an Austin-Healey or MGA, even if you found one in mint condition with low mileage or one that's been beautifully restored.

Well, automobiles are very complex products, and a newer car is *not* always preferable to an older car. Here are some of my own observations:

Observation Number One: In terms of comfort, ride, braking, safety, reliability, automatic transmissions, power-assisted steering and, in some cases, cornering ability, the newer cars — cars designed in the late 1960s or during the 1970s — are light-years ahead of older cars.

But in terms of aesthetics, engine performance and ease of maintenance, the older cars are often as good if not better.

Many of the disadvantages of the newer cars are a result of the triple tribulations of pollution, fuel shortages and government regulations that hit with a fury in the 1970s. First came unleaded, low-octane gas; automakers were forced to lower engine compression ratios, which often took the edge off high-performance cars. Emissions regulations tightened each year as well. In the early 1970s, it became unusual for a car to run properly; hard starting, stumbling, pinging and surging were too common. Catalytic converters, introduced mid-decade, allowed manufacturers to tune engines for better performance. But they have the disadvantages of adding weight to the car, increasing maintenance requirements (the catalytic converters usually need replacement every 50,000 miles or so, and they're not cheap) and in some cases they decrease engine performance by restricting the exhaust flow.

Then there was the infamous Arab oil embargo of late 1973 and the cutoff of Iranian oil in early 1979. The ensuing shortages of gas were rude shocks not only because they threatened our cherished mobility, but they left us with two unwelcome legacies: higher gas prices and the 55 mph national speed limit.

In addition, they caused Congress to legislate fuel economy standards for cars built in the years to come. This legislation has forced the automakers to reduce engine sizes, to reduce overall size of their cars and to reduce their weight.

Light weight and small size are usually desirable in an enthusiast car. But in their effort to reduce weight, the automakers have often substituted "tinny," cheap-feeling materials for more substantial ones, making the cars less emotionally appealing. Moreover, other government regulations having to do with energy-absorbing bumpers and various safety requirements have often made modern cars less aesthetically pleasing.

Finally, the on-board computers, electronic black boxes, digital instrument displays, exhaust-gas recirculation systems and other devices found on late-model cars for the purposes of reducing emissions, improving fuel economy or just plain marketing can be expensive and frustrating maintenance headaches.

Observation Number Two: To make a sweeping generalization, it seems the more common family sedans and "econoboxes" have benefited the most from the advances in automotive technology, while the more exclusive, higher performance cars have been diminished the most by government regulation.

Let's return to those two examples used in the last chapter, the ubiquitous Toyota Corolla and the elegant Jaguar XJ6. If you compare a Corolla from the early 1970s with a 1985 Corolla, the differences are astounding. From braking ability to cornering ability, from air conditioning to the shapes of the seats, the improvements are real. Of course like everything else, it became more expensive over the years—a 1985 Corolla cost about three times more than a Corolla from the early 1970s.

Then consider a much less common car, the Jaguar XJ6. An early 1970 model is basically the same car as a 1985 model. When *Road & Track* tested an XJ6 in 1972, the editors found it to be one of the most comfortable, best handling and best riding sedans in the world. And today, a decade and a half later, it still is. Jaguar made a number of improvements in the car, but there were some less welcome changes as well. The XJ6 became heavier, longer, more complicated and far more expensive— a new 1985 XJ6 was about four times more expensive than the 1972 model we tested.

Observation Number Three: When it comes to selecting a tool for putting words on paper, few people would dispute the advantages of the new product (a computer) over the old product (a pencil). But when it comes to selecting an enthusiast car, it's your own individual values that count most.

Right now my everyday car is a 24-year-old Jaguar MK2 sedan. Its ride is terrible on anything but a smooth surface; its steering is heavy when I try to park and too light at high speed; its primitive carburetors are a constant source of trouble; its heater is just adequate enough to warm my right foot on a cold day, while "air conditioning" consists of rolling down the windows. But it has beautifully formed, real chrome bumpers, not big ugly rubber ones; its dash is a vast expanse of genuine polished walnut, not cheap plastic; there's no catalytic converter or smog-control equipment to worry about (in fact, the car is old enough to be exempt from my state's smog inspections); the engine is powerful, giving 0-to-60 mph times that'll beat the vast majority of new cars; and its styling....well, it's classic.

To me, my Jaguar's virtues outweigh its deficiencies. But if you value a well-controlled ride and air conditioning more than a walnut dash and classic styling, then clearly you should be looking for a more modern car.

Soft-Top or Hardtop?

No question about it, convertibles are the most fun. There is nothing quite like a bright day, an uncrowded country road and a sports car with the top down. The warmth of the sun, the smell of freshly cut hay and the wind ruffling your hair are sensations missed in an enclosed car.

But unfortunately, few of us are lucky enough to spend much of our driving time on country roads. Instead we are often forced to grind along on a congested three-lane highway through a metropolis, with a Peterbilt on one side and a noisome motorcycle on the other. Under circumstances like that, a coupe with a good air-conditioning system is far more comfortable.

Aside from considerations of comfort, convertibles have other disadvantages. A convertible is a tempting target for vandals or thieves. Just a quick slash of the top, and any valuables inside (including the expensive stereo system) are there for the taking. Of course an accomplished thief can break into any locked car, convertible or not, in a matter of seconds. But instead of a jimmied lock or at worst a broken window, with a convertible you'll have to replace the whole top, which can cost from $500 to $1,000 on most sports cars. And even if it's not slashed, the sun and elements can decay the top so that after a few years it will need replacement anyway.

Moreover, unless you install a roll bar in your convertible, you stand a good chance of decapitation if you should ever flip over. And finally, convertibles have an annoying propensity to leak. For all of these reasons most of the newer sports-car designs are GTs.

But there is a compromise solution to the problems of rag tops. Sunroofs and targa tops are designed to give you some of the sensation of the convertible without the hassles. A sliding metal sunroof is usually the most leakproof and practical, too — simply unlock and slide it back (or even more simply, just push a button, for some are electrically operated). But some small GT cars don't have enough roof area for sliding sunroofs; the BMW CS and several models of Porsches are a few that do. For cars without the room, there is the removable sunroof. Volkswagen offers a metal, removable sunroof on the Scirocco.

Targa tops are a nifty alternative to completely open convertibles. Back in the late 1960s, Porsche popularized this configuration on its 912 and 911 models. A targa incorporates a metal roll bar (much wider than the usual roll bars installed in convertibles) and a plastic or metal section that fits between the roll bar and the windshield frame. A removed targa top lets in a lot of fresh air, but there's the problem of finding room for it in the trunk. They are also prone to leaking and squeaking.

Finally, some GT cars have a lift-up tailgate or "hatchback" instead of a trunk. It's a convenient arrangement for loading and unloading stuff, but anything lying in the rear of the car could easily attract the attention of thieves.

Two, Four or 2+2 Seats?

The sports sedans profiled in Part Two, like typical American family sedans, have rear seats capable of comfortably carrying two adults. And some, like the Jaguar XJ6, the Mercedes-Benz SELs and the larger BMWs, have four doors as well.

But most of the sports and GT cars will have two seats, two doors and trunk space for a small amount of luggage. The pony cars and some of the sporty coupes and GT cars are so-called "2+2s." Ferrari was the first to use that designation back in 1960. The company knew that its customers basically wanted 2-seat GT cars, but on occasion they needed to carry two more passengers as well. By no stretch of the imagination can the rear seats of 2+2s be considered comfortable on long passages, except for small children.

Four, Six, Eight or Twelve Cylinders?

Big engines with lots of cylinders and gobs of power are exciting. But with the importance of fuel economy these days, the wise enthusiast-car buyer must carefully consider whether or not he can afford to operate a gas guzzler, no matter how attractive its performance may be. If you drive 10,000 miles a year, a 15-mpg car will cost you about $400 more than a 30-mpg car each year when gas costs $1.25 a gallon.

Because many enthusiast cars are lightweight, 4- or 6-cylinder affairs, they're quite fuel-efficient. But Ferraris with twelve cylinders, or Corvettes with eight, can be gas guzzlers of the first order, in the 8-to-15-mpg range.

Four-cylinder cars will of course be the most thrifty, but a lightweight 6-cylinder car can do almost as well. Generally a 6-cylinder engine in a small car will be less stressed than a 4-cylinder engine in the same car, which means greater durability. On the negative side, the larger engine requires more spark plugs, oil and other items at tune-up time.

Front-, Rear- or Mid-Engine?

Engines aren't always in the front. Sometimes they're in the back, and sometimes they're even in the middle (see illustration). Where a car designer places the engine has major implications for handling, comfort and styling.

Traditionally, cars had an engine in the front and a drive shaft running down the center line that transferred the engine's power to the rear wheels. Well, unless you've spent the last few years on a remote desert island, you're undoubtely aware that the trendy setup nowadays is front-wheel drive. The engine is still in front, but the front wheels get the power through a rather tricky axle / gear setup. Front-wheel drive is nifty because the designer can turn the engine sideways and eliminate the long drive shaft; this means there's more room left for passengers in-

Engine Layouts

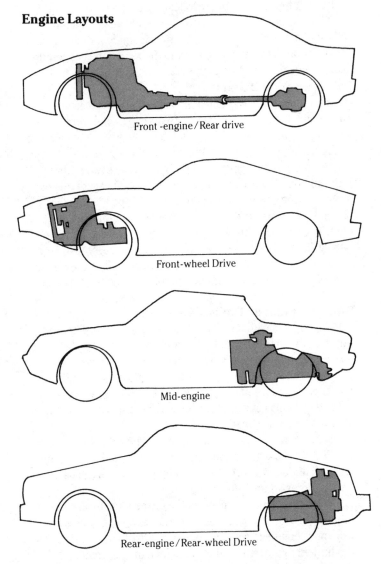

Front -engine / Rear drive

Front-wheel Drive

Mid-engine

Rear-engine / Rear-wheel Drive

side, and the engine compartment can be shortened, thus making the car smaller on the outside. That's why so many econoboxes are pulled around by their front wheels.

Because front-wheel drive cars can be quite nose-heavy with all those components up front, front tire wear may be excessive. But having the weight of the engine over the wheels that supply the motive power also gives the front-wheel drive car better traction in snow or rain than conventional front-engine / rear-drive cars.

Handling tends to be different, too. Most American sedans with front-engine/rear-wheel drive are said to understeer, which means the car is reluctant to change direction when the driver turns the steering wheel. The average driver is less likely to get into trouble if he enters a corner too fast in an understeering car. Oversteering, on the other hand, means that during hard cornering the car's tail wants to swing out and cause a spin. Older front-wheel drive designs understeered as long as

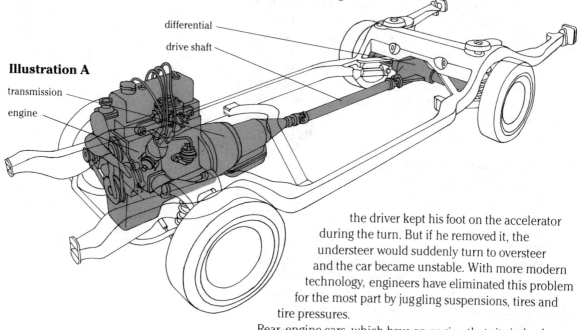

Illustration A

differential

drive shaft

transmission

engine

the driver kept his foot on the accelerator during the turn. But if he removed it, the understeer would suddenly turn to oversteer and the car became unstable. With more modern technology, engineers have eliminated this problem for the most part by juggling suspensions, tires and tire pressures.

Rear-engine cars, which have an engine that sits in back and drives the rear wheels, have been known for wild oversteering tendencies. Once again, they have been tamed in modern design, but rear-engine cars still tend to be unusually susceptible to being pushed around by side winds. However, they do have advantages; like front-wheel drive cars, there's no need for a drive-shaft tunnel inside the passenger compartment, and traction in slippery conditions is excellent.

There's one other combination to consider: a design that places the engine more or less in the center of the car, in front of the rear axle, but just behind the driver and passenger. Because the weight of the engine, which drives the rear wheels, is distributed equally over the four wheels, these "mid-engine" cars are the darlings of the racing fraternity. But they also demand a fair degree of driver competence; they may not break away in a tight turn as quickly as other configurations, but when they do, they go with little warning.

The vast majority of enthusiast cars, including the ones profiled in Part Two, have the traditional front-engine/rear-wheel drive arrangement, and these cars offer no compelling advantages or disadvantages in handling and ride over other designs. Of the cars in Part Two, these are the exceptions:

Fiat X1-9 (mid-engine)
Fiat 850 (rear-engine)
Ford / DeTomaso Pantera (mid-engine)
Porsche 912, 911 (rear-engine)
Porsche 914, 914 / 6 (mid-engine)
Volkswagen Beetle Convertible and Karmann-Ghia (rear-engine)
Volkswagen Scirocco (front-wheel drive)

Automatic or Manual Transmission?

To go forth automatically or not is an important considera-tion these days. Many Americans don't even know how to shift gears manually. That's one reason why many of the cars discussed in Part Two of this book are available with automatics.

Of course the sports-car purist will have nothing but a 4-speed, or even better, a 5-speed manual transmission (the fifth forward speed allows the engine to relax a little during straight and level cruising, providing better fuel economy and less noise). Manual transmissions are preferred because they give more control and allow more involvement in the driving process.

But automatic transmissions have come a long way in the past ten years. They used to be clunky, especially combined with the 4- or 6-cylinder engines found in sports cars. And they used to extract quite a fuel-economy penalty as well. But today automatics are much more precise and economical. According to the U.S. Environmental Protection Agency, the difference in mileage between a VW Scirocco with a manual tranny and one with an automatic is a mere one mile per gallon. So if you ex-pect to do battle with bumper-to-bumper traffic every evening on your way home from work, or if you frequently ascend or descend the hills of San Francisco, then don't pay attention to what the purists think: buy an automatic and be assured that no one will demand that you surrender your driving gloves.

Chapter Four:

Enthusiast Cars From Around the World

Because enthusiast cars are built in several countries around the world, they reflect the diverse natures of the peoples who build them. Americans are indeed fortunate to have such a smorgasbord of choices; we can buy enthusiast cars from Great Britain, Germany, Italy, Japan, or the United States.
(And on occasion, the Swedes and French have exported en-thusiast cars to the U.S., as well.)

The unique philosophy of design behind every car is an amalgam of two criteria: the driving conditions found in a par-ticular country and the temperament of that country's people. The first point is easy to understand. If a nation has mile after mile of superhighways, its automakers will build cars that emphasize long-legged comfort and reliability. But if a nation imposes high fuel taxes and has narrow mountain roads, then its automakers will build nimble, fuel-efficient cars.

National temperament, however, is less easily defined. The slightly tongue-in-cheek answers to the question, "What happens when a motorist gets a flat tire?" reveal some aspects of national character: If the driver is British, he'll patch the tire by the roadside with a kit he always carries in his car. If he's American, he'll throw the old tire away and buy two new ones on a charge card. The German, well....German tires wouldn't dare go flat. The Japanese motorist would change the tire and expect an apology from the tire maker. And the Italian? He'd change governments.

In your search for an enthusiast car that satisfies your emotional and practical needs, keep in mind that the conservatism of the Englishman, the extravagance of the American, the perfectionism of the German, and so on, all influence the designs of their respective cars.

British Charm

Contradictory. That pretty well describes the British auto industry. No country is home to as many eminent race-car constructors as Britain. The roster includes Brabham, Lotus, McLaren and Tyrrell, all of whom are among the best in a branch of automotive technology that demands state-of-the-art design. Yet the British auto industry is possibly the most moribund in the world.

In the early 1960s, an American seeking a popular-priced sports car would probably have turned to the British, who could have offered him his choice of at least nine roadsters representing six marques. They ranged from powerful Jaguar E-types and Austin-Healey 3000s, to nimble MG Midgets and Lotus Elans. Today, nearly all of them are gone. Most of the marques simply quit doing business in this country or went under altogether instead of developing modern replacements for their aging designs. Lotus moved way upscale into the ranks of exotic cars. Morgan still makes a car that was designed in the 1930s but hasn't actively exported it since the late 1960s. Austin-Healey went out of business in 1968. MG — the car that started it all in this country — gave up in 1980, as did Triumph in 1981. The recent strength of Jaguar is the only major bright spot in the British auto industry, though Jaguars could hardly be called "popular-priced" cars.

Contradictions also characterize British cars. The British Isles abound with homely sedans, stubby-looking vehicles with strange humps and bulges. But the British are just as capable of aesthetic success; the Jaguar XJ6 is perhaps the most handsome sedan built since World War II. British sports cars also tend to be inconsistent — they're either traditional designs like the MGB or rather wild trend setters like Jaguar E-types.

But never mind all this, because British cars are charming.

Despite suffering what must be some of the dampest, dankest weather any nation offers, the British adore open convertibles, certainly the most endearing kind of car. They even design convertible tops that are nearly impossible to raise once they're down; just don the tweeds and damn the drizzle! The British are also exceedingly fond of wire wheels and genuine leather seats, two wonderful Old World features. And they usually make their cars easy to understand. The mechanically simple MGs and Triumphs are the perfect cars for the weekend tinkerer.

Of course, it's not all tea and crumpets. Removing a Jaguar starter motor or getting a row of SU carburetors to work together is considered great sport by the British. And though British engines and transmissions are largely unbreakable, everything else on old British sports (especially electrical systems) seems to self-destruct.

Anachronistic yet advanced. Steadfast but cantankerous. Beautiful and frumpy. As I said, British cars are incongruous. But they are lovable cars you can get involved with — and you'll have to if you want to keep them running.

German Precision

It's difficult to think of similarities between Germans and Italians. But they do have one thing in common, the Alps. These mountains profoundly shape the characters of the cars that come from both countries. Blasting along the treacherous roads through the St. Bernard Pass, with precipitous drops on one side and rocks on the other, requires smooth-pulling engines, accurate steering, and capable brakes. And once descended onto the German *autobahnen* or the Italian *autostradas*, free of the ridiculously slow speed limits that plague motorists in the U.S., the cars must withstand the rigors of flat-out driving. It's not uncommon to travel down a German *autobahn* for several hours at a stretch going 130 mph. The pace keeps you awake, but it's not as terrifying as it sounds because the cars are designed to take it.

No wonder then, that the world's best-handling cars are built within a hundred miles or so of Alpine roads. Alfa Romeo, BMW, Ferrari, Maserati and Porsche are proof of the statement.

Beyond building cars that are expected to be driven to their limits, any similarity between the two nationalities ends. The stereotyped proud, disciplined, efficient and somewhat Spartan German is a fair characterization of German cars as well. Never flashy or frivolous like some American cars, and never silly or ill-conceived like some British cars, the German car is, above all, functional. The styling is prudently pleasing but rarely is it sensuously sleek. Interiors are comfortable but austere. The feel of the German car, from the way the door clicks, not slams, as it shuts, to the well-controlled suspension, is one of precision. And German cars have a well-deserved reputation for stoutness.

But heaven forbid that a German car break down. Perhaps the most trying aspect of owning a German car — other than paying for it — is dealing with the German mechanic. This high priest of grease is as picky in choosing his customers as Club 21 in New York, and almost as expensive. However, he'll spare nothing to do the job right. I once owned a lovely Mercedes-Benz roadster, now considered something of a classic, with a cracked oil pan. My mechanic insisted on replacing the pan with a genuine made-in-the-Fatherland Mercedes pan, even if it meant that I wouldn't eat for a week. When I protested that there must be another solution, he grunted, "Vell, you could junk the car." I eventually had the pan heli-arced at a local gas station for $25.

Robert Stempel, a vice-president of General Motors and former general manager of Chevrolet, compared the attitudes of an American who buys a German car to an American who owns a Detroit-made car: "When a Corvette breaks, the owner blames GM for having built a defective product. But if a Porsche should break, the owner blames himself for having defiled fine German machinery."

Italian Style

Italians share the German blitzkrieg style of driving, and if anything, are even more aggressive. Every stoplight encounter calls for a demonstration of acceleration; even the smallest Fiats are flogged without mercy: popping clutches, screaming engines and all. A twist in the road is a test of the car's cornering power, and it doesn't matter to the Italian driver how much road he uses or which lane he's in, just as long as he doesn't hit anybody.

Despite what seems to us a disgraceful lack of manners, the average Italian driver is perhaps the most skillful in the world. Certainly he is more accomplished than the typical American, who floats down the highway in a Buick Dynaflo with both his car and his brain on cruise control. By contrast, the Italian knows his car, its limitations as well as its capabilities. He's not just a passenger in his car; he dominates it, and he expects it to obey.

Italians not only demand agile, responsive cars, but they want them to be beautiful. They are the undisputed masters in automotive styling, perhaps because of their tradition of the *carrozzeria*, or coach-builders. Most auto companies around the world design their bodies in-house. But in Italy, Fiat and Alfa Romeo as well as the exotic car makers like Ferrari routinely turn to outside design firms. And for very low-production cars like the exotics, the bodies are sometimes built in factories owned by the designer. Because such designers as Giugiaro, Bertone and Pininfarina have totally outclassed any others around the world, more and more non-Italian automakers have turned to the *carrozzeria* for expertise, and the automotive world is better for it. For when Italians are elegant, they are very elegant indeed.

Considering the Italians' spirited driving style, you'd think Italian cars would be built like tanks in order to withstand the stress of battle. On the contrary: they're rather fragile. As the prima donnas of the automotive world, they're a combination of high style and irascibility. The Italian sports car's high-strung nature demands constant attention. Usually it's just a matter of minor adjustments and fussing, not major repairs. But unless you buy your Italian beauty expecting this, the car may drive you to despair.

Italian cars have a few other quirks, too. As long as the car is responsive and shapely, the Italians don't give a piece of pasta about frivolities like air conditioning and heaters. Not that the Italians don't grudgingly offer such things; it's just that they're not nearly as efficient as those found on American, Japanese or German cars. Italian sports cars also invariably have what one automotive writer called the *ciao, Sophia* driving position — sort of laid back with arms out. After trying to get comfortable in an Italian car, most Americans will swear that Italians must be able to touch their toes without bending over. Either your arms reach the steering wheel and your knees stick up into your chin, or your legs are stretched out and you can't reach the wheel.

But these are trifling matters. Accept the Italian sports car on its own terms, and it will make you feel as smooth and graceful as Mario Andretti at a Monza Grand Prix.

American Muscle and Japanese Ingenuity

American enthusiast cars have traditionally been long on brawn and short on finesse. The older Corvettes from the 1960s and 1970s, like the ones profiled in Part Two, exemplify very nicely the traditional American approach to enthusiast cars. Take their engines. They're big, gas-guzzling V-8s. Certainly they have to be considered unsophisticated compared to those powering German and Italian enthusiast cars of the time. But you can be sure they're as durable as the Rock of Gibraltar and have good acceleration too. Moreover, any gas-station jockey could tear one down and put it back together. The styling of these Corvettes isn't very sophisticated either, though some consider them zoomy. But General Motors, like all American automakers, builds outstanding climate-control systems that will keep you toasty on a winter's night in the Arctic, or will put you in a deep freeze in the Mojave Desert. Straightforward and honest, but overdone and crude are the adjectives that come to mind in describing older 'Vettes.

The Japanese are the real newcomers to the world of enthusiast cars. Datsun produced the 1600/2000 convertible in the 1960s, but the Japanese didn't make a serious sports-car effort until the 240Z stormed the American sales charts in the early 1970s.

The most striking aspect of Japanese cars in general is that they're so American. They're the kind of cars that Detroit has only recently started to offer the American car buyer. While British, Italian and even German cars are an acquired taste, Japanese cars like the Z-car instantly strike a responsive chord in the average American. A 240Z has many of the admirable qualities of an early 1970s Corvette: the simplicity of the components, the relatively high level of creature comfort, a flashy-looking body, and long-legged dependability for crossing Kansas prairies. But unlike an older 'Vette, a 240Z is a fairly modern package designed for these times of expensive fuel.

The Europeans build cars primarily to suit themselves, and if some Americans with European taste want to buy them, then that's fine. But the Japanese, in an effort to provide secure employment for Japanese workers, design cars for export. And they did their homework well; they studied what American sports-car buyers wanted — and what Detroit was too unresponsive to provide — and then delivered it. Japanese enthusiast cars lack the sophisticated handling qualities of the best European cars (Japan is such a crowded little island, it's a wonder Japanese cars corner at all). Nor is their styling as fresh and innovative as the European cars. But overall they are well suited to the American driver.

Defining Quality

It was also the Japanese who turned the attention of American car buyers to the issue of quality. "Quality" is certainly one of the most amorphous of all the popular buzz words these days. Like a designer label on an article of clothing, everybody seems to want it, yet few people know for sure what it signifies. But whatever quality is, we're now aware that it's been absent for quite some time in Detroit's cars and that even the cheapest Japanese cars have it in abundance.

Quality as it relates to enthusiast cars can mean everything from workmanship to value-for-the-money, from reliability and engineering to the sincerity of materials. Sincerity of materials? Metal is sincere; thin plastic is not. Thin plastic may fool the buyer in the showroom, but it cracks and breaks after a little use. There is something honestly satisfying about sitting in the cockpit of a British sports car and inhaling the aroma of Connolly leather or running your fingers over a polished walnut dash — that's the aesthetic and sensual aspect of quality.

Workmanship is an obvious determinant of quality. In auto-industry jargon, it is called "fit and finish." Is the gap between the hood and fenders even on both sides, or is it wider on one than on the other? Are there drips in the paint? Are there smudges of glue on the interior? Do trim stripes line up? Are there rough edges inside the trunk? Several years ago, Ward's *Auto World* magazine conducted a poll of 569 American automotive engineers and found that nearly half gave top honors in workmanship to the Japanese, far ahead of runners-up Germany and the U.S.

Then there is the area of technology and engineering. Do the engineers who design the car demonstrate creative, innovative thinking? You don't have to be an engineer yourself to know; external signs can tell the tale. Does the convertible top lower and raise easily? Is there good vision all the way around? Are the controls convenient? Are there thoughtful touches like a grab handle for the passenger or a remote trunk release? If a car rates high in these areas, the chances are there will be examples of good design underneath sheet metal in the engine, suspension, and brakes as well.

Reliability is yet another indication of quality. J.D. Power & Associates, a highly respected market research firm in California, publishes annually a *Consumer Satisfaction Index* which is based on interviews with owners who have had their cars one year. In one recent index, Japanese marques dominated the top spots on the satisfaction index. Lincoln was the only American make in the top ten.

Chapter Five:

Some Automotive Technicalities to Know

If you think a MacPherson strut is something that Fred Astaire did with Ginger Rogers, and that rack and pinion is a medieval torture device, then this chapter is for you. Don't worry if you're easily confused or bored with engineering jargon. Rather than confound you with esoterica, I'll stick to unraveling some of the basic mysteries under the hood, with an emphasis on technical features that distinguish enthusiast cars from ordinary sedans.

It seems many Americans have no idea how a car works; "as long as it runs," they say. Well, ignorance may be bliss for a fortunate few. But for the rest it's often mighty expensive. These people are plump pigeons waiting to be plucked by the nearest smooth-talking salesman or unscrupulous mechanic. Think of the countless ignorance-is-bliss car owners who have been suckered into buying $250 "rollerized muffler bearings" or cars that turn out to be lemons.

But saving yourself from needless expense isn't the only reason to learn a little about sports cars' innards. There is the satisfaction of knowing why your costly Porsche outcorners, outruns and outbrakes a Pinto. And if you understand a few of the technicalities, you may even drive with more authority and skill.

As a prelude to this discussion of automotive technicalities, keep in mind this important point:

What's true with racing bikes, mail sent through the U.S. Postal Service and our own bodies is also true for enthusiast cars — excess weight is bad.

When it comes to cars, whether we're discussing their engines, their sheet metal or their wheels, the less weight the better a car will be in terms of handling, performance and fuel economy. In fact, a major distinction between ordinary cars and enthusiast cars is the lengths to which the cars' designers will go to reduce weight.

That said, let's start with the engine.

Quality of Older Enthusiast Cars by Nationality

	Workmanship	Materials	Value for Money	Reliability	Technology and Engineering
British	Above average on older British sports cars.	Wonderful. Lots of wood and leather as well as a heavy gauge of metal.	Good. Many British marques, like MG, are probably undervalued now.	The reliability of older British cars has been the subject of a vast repertoire of cruel jokes.	State of the art ....in 1949.
German	Consistently outstanding.	Functional but generally austere.	Only doctors and oil-rich Arabs can afford German cars.	It vill verk!	State of the art.
Italian	Good on Ferraris and hit-or-miss on Alfas and Fiats.	Like the British, Italians appreciate sensuous materials.	Excellent for Alfas and Fiats, but Ferraris always come dear.	Not bad if you have a good mechanic.	Contrary to the popular image in the U.S., Italian automotive engineering is a match for the Germans.
American	Lousy.	Not elegant, but durable.	Corvettes always command high prices.	Quite good for Corvettes and pony cars.	Crude.
Japanese	Perhaps better than the Germans.	Chintzy.	Very good.	Excellent.	Ingenious.
Swedish	Good.	Built like tanks.	Average.	In Sweden, Volvos last for 11 years, ja?	Simple and straight-forward.

Engine Basics

Of course the heart of any car is its engine. After some eighty years of continuous development and refinement, the piston engine has become a remarkably smooth and durable instrument.

Think of an engine as having two basic parts, a bottom half and a top half. The major portion of the bottom half is comprised of the *block* which, as its name implies, is a large chunk of metal. Depending upon how many cylinders the engine is to have, the block will have several holes bored through it, not unlike a piece of Swiss cheese. Inside each of these holes or *cylinders*, a *piston* will slide up and down producing the engine's power. Both the number and the volume of the cylinders indicate an engine's size — that is, a 6-cylinder, 2500-cubic-centimeter (cc) engine, for instance.

The top half of the engine is made up of the *cylinder head*. The cylinder head contains several important engine components — the *spark plugs* and the *valves* — and the bottom part of the cylinder head also helps form the *combustion chambers*. The cylinder head sits right on top the block, with only a thin *head gasket* in between.

Piston engines follow a four-part routine in order to produce power. First, a mixture of fuel and air flows through an intake valve and into the combustion chamber where it is tightly compressed by an upward stroke of a piston. Once the fuel-air mixture is compressed (the second part of the routine), the third stroke occurs when the highly combustible mixture is ignited by the spark plug. The ensuing explosion forces the piston down the cylinder, and as it goes, the other end of the piston, which is attached to a *connecting rod*, rotates the *crankshaft* sitting at the bottom of the engine block. The crankshaft, in turn, rotates *transmission gears*, the *drive shaft*, the *differential gears* and finally the wheels (see Illustration A, page 25). The number of rotations per minute made by the crankshaft (rpm) is a measure of the engine's rate of activity.

Back to the engine: after the downstroke, the piston rises again and forces the spent gases out of the combustion chamber through the exhaust valve, into an *exhaust manifold* and then (on most cars built since 1975) through a *catalytic converter*. The converter cleans the dirty exhaust gases before they exit the car through the tail pipe.

I should mention that with all those explosions going on, the pistons, cylinders and so on get pretty hot. That's why there's a cooling system — usually a *radiator*, *water pump*, a *fan* and other pieces of plumbing. There's also an *electrical system* that provides the spark for the plugs, as well as the juice for the lights and the stereo. Of course this system also keeps the battery charged for operating the *starter motor* when you want to get the whole shebang going in the morning.

That's all there is to it. In enthusiast cars, there aren't many variations on the basic theme. Certain Porsche and Volkswagen models have engines that rely on air instead of water for cooling. These Porsche engines have two banks of cylinders (each bank has two or three cylinders) that face each other. That's unusual because the cylinders on most engines are either in-line (i.e., they stand up vertically one in front of the other), or there are two banks canted toward each other, hence the so-called V-8 or V-6 engines.

Though they've been faithful servants for decades, Porsche's and VW's air-cooled horizontally opposed engines are probably the last of their type; this layout tends to generate noise and emissions that are difficult to control. Both Porsche and VW have gone to more conventional water-cooled engines in the latest models.

So aside from Porsche's and VW's air-cooled engines, the enthusiast cars profiled in Part Two will have water-cooled, in-

Illustration B

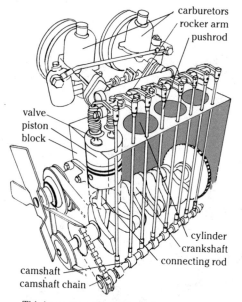

carburetors
rocker arm
pushrod

valve
piston
block

cylinder
crankshaft
connecting rod

camshaft
camshaft chain

This is a cutaway drawing of a basic 4-cylinder engine with pushrod-operated valves and a pair of carburetors.

Illustration C

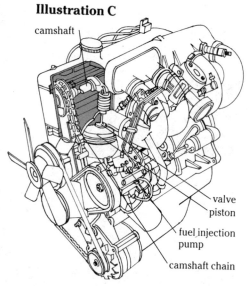

camshaft

valve
piston

fuel injection
pump

camshaft chain

This rather more complicated 4-cylinder engine has a single overhead camshaft instead of pushrods and a fuel injection system instead of carburetors.

line or V-type piston engines. Many enthusiast cars will have engines with blocks, cylinder heads and pistons made of aluminum instead of iron or steel. Aluminum is a good choice because it saves weight. And exhaust valves, which get very hot during the engine's operation, are sometimes filled with sodium to keep them cool. These will last longer, but they cost two or three times more than normal valves.

Perhaps the major difference between the engines of many enthusiast cars and those of common sedans has to do with the operation of the valves. Valves have to open and close exceedingly quickly; if there's any sort of lag, the whole engine operation can get fouled up. The cheapest way to operate the valves is with *pushrods* (see Illustration B). These rods go from near the bottom of the engine block, up the sides to the *rocker arms*. The rocker arms and the valves sit on top of the engine block in the cylinder head. At the bottom end of the pushrod there's a *camshaft* that causes the pushrod to go up and down. When this happens, the top end of the pushrod "rocks" the rocker arm, which opens and closes the valve.

All this works well at low rpm. But since enthusiast cars are meant to be driven fast, their engines must operate at relatively high rpm. In fact, the range between 3,000 rpm and the "redline" (the maximum "rev" limit, or number of revolutions, beyond which engine damage may occur) is where all the fun lives in an enthusiast car. Redlines on enthusiast-car engines are frequently as high as 6,500 or even 7,000 rpm, a limit that would cause quick destruction of most Detroit V-8s. Unfortunately, at high rpm all the pieces in a pushrod engine can easily become bent out of shape.

Wouldn't it be nice if we could eliminate the push rods and the rocker arms and put the camshaft in the cylinder head directly on top of the valves? Well, that's exactly what an "overhead cam" engine does (see Illustration C). Sometimes there's a *single overhead camshaft* (sohc) that operates both the set of intake valves and the set of exhaust valves.
Others have two overhead camshafts, one for the set of exhaust valves and one for the set of intake valves (dohc for *double overhead camshafts*). The drawback to ohc engines is their cost.

You may have wondered how the fuel and air get mixed. Good question, because that process also frequently distinguishes enthusiast-car engines from ordinary sedan engines. Normally, mixing is done in a *carburetor*. There are several brands of carbs found on cars, but two are worth special mention.

Because the SU carburetor is rather primitive and unsophisticated, it figures the British would love it. You'll find it on several older roadsters like Jaguar E-types and MGBs.
The other is the Weber, a carburetor found on several Italian sports cars. Sports-car enthusiasts love Webers because they are well made, straightforward to adjust and repair, and because they look terrific.

Though carburetors do their job well, *fuel injection* (FI) is generally more precise in delivering fuel to the combustion chamber; this means better engine response, increased fuel economy and improved emissions. All this comes at the price of added complication, with such devices as injectors and a metering unit. Though some Alfa Romeos and Mercedes-Benzes use a mechanical metering unit, most others use an electronic black box to regulate the fuel flow — hence the phrase "electronic fuel injection." The complexity of FI units puts them beyond the tinkering ability of backyard mechanics. And tired fuel injectors or metering units can be expensive to replace, more so than a carburetor overhaul.

What Is Performance?

So far, so easy. The concept of how an engine works isn't too difficult to understand, is it? It's simply a matter of a bunch of explosions pushing pistons up and down, and the paraphernalia that makes it all possible.

But in practice, the design details of an engine are complex and have a great deal to do with how it will perform. And at *Road & Track*, when we talk about a car's "performance," we're usually referring specifically to engine performance.

As you read the profiles of the cars in Part Two and examine their specification charts, you'll see a number of terms that tell you details about a particular engine, like "Bore x stroke," "Horsepower @ rpm," and "Torque, lb-ft @ rpm." Unless you love technical trivia, it's okay to just skip over that information. When you're judging the merits of one car versus another, what really counts is a car's performance data — the time it takes the car to reach 60 mph from a standing stop, or the time it takes the car to travel a quarter of a mile from a standing stop, or its fuel economy. This data represents the bottom line of a car's design.

Interpreting the practical significance of an engine's horsepower rating, for instance, can be tricky. There are several ways of measuring horsepower. *Brake horsepower* (bhp) is an indication of the power applied to the crankshaft and is measured on a device called a dynamometer. The question is whether you measure the power of a bare engine, one without an alternator, generator, water pump or other power-robbing-but-necessary devices attached, or do you measure it with these devices? In most of the profiles in Part Two, the horsepower is *net* which means the measurement is made with the devices. But in some cases, you'll find *gross horsepower ratings*, ones for just the bare engines. Keep in mind that for the same engine, a gross horsepower rating is higher than a net rating.

Like horsepower, *torque* is a measure of an engine's power. In practical terms, you can think of horsepower as an indication of a car's overall engine performance. Torque, however, is an indication of a car's low-speed acceleration ability. A car with a "torquey" engine is one that's good for jack-rabbit starts or stoplight drag racing. (Quick acceleration from a stop isn't just a function of an engine's torque, however; transmission and differential gearing are also involved. More on this later.)

Large-displacement engines generally produce more torque than small-displacement engines. *Displacement*, as I mentioned earlier, is a measure of an engine's size. If you take the amount of air displaced by the piston as it moves up to the top of its stroke from the bottom of its stroke, and then multiply it by the number of cylinders, you'll have the engine's displacement. *Road & Track* has traditionally measured the amount of displaced air in cubic centimeters, though American automakers often measure it in cubic inches. So on the specification charts you'll see a listing for displacement in cc's.

Just because a car doesn't have neck-snapping acceleration from a standing stop, and hence hasn't much low-end torque, doesn't necessarily mean the car lacks horsepower. Many high-performance European cars, including Alfa Romeos and even 12-cylinder Ferraris, are pretty sluggish when driven at low speed around town. But at higher speeds, when the engine's rpms start to climb, the cars suddenly seem to come alive and have lots of power. Other cars, like the Camaro Z-28, have gobs of torque and have lots of punch when you put your foot on the throttle pedal from a standing stop, but begin to run out of power at very high speeds, say 100 mph or more.

In the specification charts, horsepower and torque will always be given at a certain rpm. For instance, a Ferrari 250GTE 2+2 develops its maximum horsepower of 240 at 7,000 rpm and its maximum torque of 181 at 5,000 rpm. On the other hand, a Corvette with a V-8 might produce its maximum horsepower of 195 at 4,400 rpm and its maximum torque of 275 at 2,800 rpm.

From these specifications you can deduce a couple of things. First, the Corvette's maximum torque is relatively greater than its maximum horsepower (the Ferrari, by contrast, has relatively greater horsepower than torque), so the Corvette is a torquey engine. Second, the Ferrari produces both its maximum torque and horsepower at much higher rpms than the Corvette, and therefore has a higher revving engine.

Is a higher revving engine a good thing? For an enthusiast car, the answer is generally "yes". The higher revving engine is usually able to produce more horsepower for a given amount of displacement. Or to put it another way, you can get the same amount of power with a higher revving but smaller displacement engine as you can from a larger displacement but slower revving engine. And the smaller displacement engine may be preferable because it will often use less fuel and may even weigh less.

And what determines whether an engine is a high-revver or not? As I mentioned earlier, having overhead camshafts instead of pushrods helps. In addition, there's an engine *bore and stroke*. On the specification charts, you'll see an entry for "bore x stroke" in inches. In order to build an engine of a certain displacement, the engine's designers have the choice of making the cylinder bore wide while keeping its length (or stroke) short, or they can have a narrow bore and a longer stroke. Either way, the displacement remains the same.

So which should they choose? In general, a shorter stroke allows the engine to operate at higher rpms, thus producing more horsepower. But there's the disadvantage that a high-revving engine works harder and may not be as durable.

Like the ability of an engine to run at high rpms, a high *compression ratio* can mean higher horsepower. The difference between the volume inside a cylinder when the piston is at the bottom of its stroke and when it is at the top of its stroke is the compression ratio. It tells you how much the gas / air mixture is compressed before it's ignited by the spark plug. Unfortunately, high compression ratios like 9.5 or 10 can cause an increase in exhaust emissions.

When considering specifications as an indication of a car's performance, perhaps the most important of all is the relationship of the car's total weight to its power. While the specification tables in Part Two don't give a power-to-weight ratio, they do give the car's weight. By eyeballing a car's weight against its horsepower or torque rating, you can get a general idea of its performance. In other words, a heavy, two-ton car with a 98-horsepower engine is bound to be a slug. But a 2,000-pound car with a couple of hundred horsepower will be quite a performer.

If all this sounds confusing, don't worry. As I said earlier, what counts is a car's actual performance, not its bore and stroke, or horsepower or other specifications on paper. And what's good engine performance? If a car can accelerate from a standing stop to 60 miles per hour (0-60 mph) in less than 10 seconds, can travel a quarter of a mile from a standing stop in around 17 seconds, and can still deliver twenty or more miles per gallon of gas, it's doing very well.

Transmission Basics

As I've just noted in the examples of the Corvette and the Ferrari, automobile engines produce their useful power at relatively high rpms — in the case of the Ferrari's horsepower, 7,000 rpm. If the wheels turned once on the road for every turn of the crankshaft, cars could only travel at speeds over 50 mph or so. Automobile engines don't have sufficient low-rpm torque all by themselves to get several thousand pounds of metal moving from a standing stop. In other words, the engine needs to be "geared down."

Enter the *transmission* (often called the "gearbox") and *differential*. Remember, the up-and-down motion of the pistons turns the crankshaft at the bottom of the engine block. The crankshaft then turns the transmission gears, the driveshaft, the differential gears and finally the wheels. A gearbox, whether automatic or manual, will usually have either three or four forward gears and of course one reverse gear.

The gears in both the transmission and the differential (sometimes called the "rear end" because on all but front-wheel-drive cars, the differential is mounted underneath the rear of the car between the rear wheels) allow the driveshaft to run several times faster than the wheels. That's good because the faster the engine turns in rpms in relation to the wheels, the more torque it develops. And to get a mass of metal moving takes a lot of torque.

Automotive engineers select different gear ratios to match the characteristics of an engine: Is it a high-revving engine or a low-revving engine? Is it a torquey engine? They also choose the gear ratios according to how the car will be driven. For instance, if they're after neck-snapping acceleration in the 0-to-75 mph range, they'll choose different gear ratios than if they expect the car to do a lot of high-speed cruising over 100 mph.

In some of the profiles in Part Two you'll notice references to *final drive* ratios. The Sunbeam Alpine has a final drive ratio of 4.22:1, for instance. Final drive refers to the differential gearing. What's important to keep in mind is that high numerical ratios like the Alpine's are good for acceleration and pulling power, while low numerical ratios (2.22:1, for example) allow the engine to relax at cruising speed because the rpms drop, thus decreasing wear and tear on the engine, decreasing noise levels and increasing fuel economy.

The Alpine's final drive ratio may not be good for fuel economy and quiet cruising, but many Alpines are equipped with *overdrive*. An overdrive can be an electric unit operated by a special switch or lever on the steering column, as in the case of the Alpine, or it can be a fifth gear in the transmission. In either case an overdrive gearset is one with a ratio of less than 1:1 (0.8:1 in the case of the Alpine). An overdrive is wonderful for relaxing high-speed cruising, but while the overdrive is engaged, acceleration will usually be quite poor.

While we're on the subject of transmissions, there's one other term you should know — *synchromesh*. When changing gears, the teeth of the different gears have to disengage and then mesh again. On old cars, ones without a synchromesh system in the gearbox, the driver would just force the gears to mesh, often resulting in an irritating crunch. Most modern cars always have synchronizers on the upper gears, but some of the older sports cars profiled in Part Two lack a synchronizer in first gear, which can make the car a little more difficult to drive smoothly.

What is Handling?

From around 1957, I recall advertisements for a Chevrolet convertible that showed a leggy female sitting atop the seat back and steering the car with her toes. Aside from the fact that government regulators today would go into apoplexy over such disregard for safety, it wasn't really a demonstration of the car's good steering. Sure, it was easy to steer, but that doesn't mean control or good handling.

While a car's *performance* has to do with the engine and

drivetrain, *handling* is a function of four systems: *steering, suspension, brakes, wheels and tires.* How well these four systems each work and how well they all work together determines a car's handling characteristics. (Handling is also indirectly related to engine placement — see Chapter 3.)

Steering Systems

Consider the steering system. Nobody wants heavy steering, but driving enthusiasts want it to transmit the feel of the road. They also want it to be quick and precise. You've probably had the feeling when driving some cars that you could turn the steering wheel several inches from either side of center and nothing would happen. By contrast, a car with quick steering is one that changes direction in response to just a minor movement of the steering wheel. The front wheels should also center themselves after a turn without the driver having to crank the wheel consciously. Moreover, the feel of the road must always be apparent, especially at high speeds. Power-assisted steering is acceptable as long as it doesn't make the steering so light that you lose the sense of the road.

Many enthusiast cars have *rack-and-pinion* steering. It's a simple system with few parts in the steering linkage. Thus it tends to be very precise and quick. *Worm-and-roller* and *recirculating-ball* steering systems can also be precise and quick if they are well designed.

A Myriad of Suspensions

The design of an engine is a science, but the design of a suspension is an art. And to those not mechanically inclined, it's something of a black art. This feeling is underscored by the fact that the suspension sits there hidden by wheels and fenders and doesn't cause much bother until the shock absorbers wear out.

A car without a well-designed suspension loses a lot of appeal. A suspension combines *springs, shock absorbers, bushings* in various lengths and *rods* that connect each wheel to the car's frame or body. As the wheels jump over bumps, fall into potholes, suddenly swerve or come to a stop, the suspension's job is to keep the aplomb and stability of everyone and everything inside the car. The better the job the suspension does, the faster and more enthusiastically you can drive.

Technically, there is a vast array of suspension designs. For the sake of simplicity, the suspension universe may be divided four ways. First, think of the two front wheels and the two rear wheels as separate units. It's quite possible that the front wheels will have a different type of suspension than the rear wheels. Now consider that there are two basic suspension types: *independent* and *rigid.* This fact would seem to indicate four different combinations — independent front / rigid rear, independent front / independent rear, rigid front / independent rear, and rigid front / rigid rear.

But in practice the last two combinations don't exist because the front suspension of modern cars is always of the independent type. That leaves us with a choice of an independent or rigid type of suspension for the rear wheels.

Now what does independent mean? It indicates that each wheel of either the front or the rear pair of wheels can move without regard to what the other wheel is doing; that's because the wheels are not rigidly connected by an axle or axle housing. For instance, if the right wheel falls into a pothole, the left wheel will stay level without trying to pitch up in response to the right wheel. This avoids a loss of traction and possibly control, as well as a harsh ride.

So why doesn't every car maker use four-wheel independent suspension systems? Most would probably prefer to. But there's a disadvantage — you guessed it: cost and complexity. Moreover, rigid rear suspensions have been refined to the point that they are not always so bad. Alfa Romeo's convertibles and GT cars are examples of sports cars that have quite exemplary handling using rigid, *live axles*. (A live rear axle drives the rear wheels; if on a front-wheel-drive car the rear axle is part of a rigid suspension system, it will be called a *dead* or *beam axle*.)

There are myriad design variations for both rigid and independent suspension systems, each design carrying a different name. This chart will help you recognize whether a suspension is independent or rigid.

In the specification charts for the cars profiled in Part Two, you'll often find an entry that reads "Suspension, front / rear." For that entry, a typical car might be listed as having "ind coil / live leaf." Translated, this means the car's front suspension is of course independent and uses *coil springs*, while the rear has a rigid-type live axle combined with *leaf-type springs* (see Illustrations D and E).

Independent Suspension Systems

Front or Rear

Unequal length control arms or A-arm
MacPherson Strut
Swing axles

Rear Only

Chapman Strut
Pure trailing arm
Semitrailing arm

Rigid Suspension Systems

Hotchkiss
Link-type rigid axles
Rigid axle with trailing arms

Discs Versus Drums

Your car is only as fast as its brakes. That's right—unless you are suicidal, there's no point in going faster than the brakes are capable of safely stopping the car. The car's total braking power is a function of the brakes in combination with the tires and the suspension.

There are two types of brakes, *drum* and *disc*. Disc brakes are rapidly replacing drums on almost all cars, because they are more effective. Think of a brake as an engine

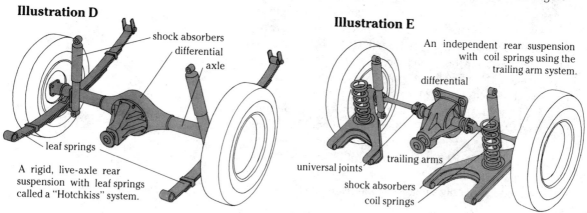

Illustration D

shock absorbers
differential
axle
leaf springs

A rigid, live-axle rear suspension with leaf springs called a "Hotchkiss" system.

Illustration E

An independent rear suspension with coil springs using the trailing arm system.

differential
trailing arms
universal joints
shock absorbers
coil springs

in reverse. The engine converts heat to power, and the brake converts power to heat. Problems with brakes appear when excessive heat diminishes their stopping power. Disc brakes dissipate heat buildup more readily than drum brakes, thus reducing brake "fade." The only reason drum brakes are still used is that they're cheaper to make and their linings last longer than those on disc brakes. As with steering, brakes on cars are frequently power assisted. Again, that's fine, as long as they're not overboosted, as they often are on American sedans. Brakes "as light as a feather" increase the probability of an uncontrolled skid in case of an emergency or sudden stop.

Fat Tires and Fancy Wheels

Perhaps no automotive component has changed so dramatically over the past few years as tires. Just compare the tall, skinny rubber on an old MG TC to the corpulent monsters on a late-model Ferrari or Corvette. Wider wheels and tires provide increased cornering power and traction, as well as improved braking because more rubber is on the ground.

Look closely and you'll also see that modern tires have a different tread pattern from the old *bias-ply* tire. These *radial* tires have completely taken over the enthusiast-car market. Compared to the bias tire, radials "squirm" less as they roll along the road. That translates into better traction on wet or dry pavement, increased fuel economy and longer tread life (50,000 miles is not uncommon).

Don't underestimate what a good set of tires can do for your car's handling. Any race driver will testify that the right tires — properly inflated — can make the winning difference.

As you investigate tires you'll notice a code on the sidewall like this: "P-195 / 60HR-14." The P stands for passenger-car tire and is a designation sometimes omitted on European-made tires. The 195 indicates the width of the tire (across the tread) in millimeters (mm), 60 is the ratio of height of the sidewall to width, the letter R means radial, and the number 14 is the wheel diameter in inches. The H is a speed rating. In Europe it is illegal to drive on tires that don't meet or exceed the performance capabilities of the car. European-made tires always carry a speed rating, as do Japanese-made tires and some American-made tires as well. A lot of drivers are beginning to recognize speed ratings as a sign of quality. Until recently, there have only been three: S (adequate for speeds up to 112 mph), H (for speeds up to 130 mph) and V (for speeds over 130 mph). Now, a couple of other ratings are also showing up: T (for speeds up to 118 mph) and U (speeds up to 124 mph).

You'll also find a "Uniform Tire Quality Grade" somewhere on the sidewall. A grade of 100 means the tire should last 30,000 miles, while a grade of 90 means it should last ten percent fewer miles, or 27,000 miles. Likewise, a rating of 120 means the tire should last 36,000 miles, or twenty percent longer. The rating is not a guarantee, but only a guide depending upon your driving habits.

On expensive sports cars like Ferraris and Mercedes-Benz SLs, aluminum or magnesium wheels (*alloys* or *mags*) are standard equipment. But on less pricy marques, they're usually extra-cost options for standard steel wheels. Alloys or mags are worth their cost on two counts. First, they save considerable weight. A normal steel wheel can weigh up to twenty pounds, while an alloy wheel weighs about half that. Of course reducing pounds on any part of the car means the engine has to work less hard and fuel economy improves. Moreover, when you reduce the weight of wheels and tires — so-called unsprung weight because these components are not supported by the car's springs but by the road — you achieve improvements in ride, handling and acceleration.

Second, alloy wheels usually look terrific; they'll provide the crowning touch to your car's appearance. Back in the days of the British roadster, *wire wheels* performed the same functions as modern alloy wheels, and many of the British cars profiled in Part Two have them. Though alloys are more prone to corrosion from road salt than steel wheels, they're not as difficult to maintain as wire wheels. Wire wheels are undeniably handsome, but spokes frequently bend or break, and it takes all Saturday morning to clean them.

Construction Methods

Years ago, cars almost always had a separate body and frame. The usual frame was built of two parallel, heavy, rectangular (or *box section*) steel tubes that were held together by some sort of cross-member arrangement. The engine would sit between the steel tubes and the body would then be lowered onto the frame and bolted to it (see Illustration F).

Over the last two or three decades, European automakers abandoned that construction method in favor of unit-body or *unibody* construction. With this method, there is no separate frame; instead body sheet metal is formed into some rather complex shapes and then welded together to form a single shell (see Illustration G). It may not seem as if this type of construction would be very strong, but in fact a unibody car is generally more rigid than a car built of a separate frame and body. Moreover, a unibody car is lighter because there is no heavy frame.

For these reasons, American automakers have followed the Europeans and switched to unibody construction in the last five years or so. But the American cars profiled in Part Two — the Camaro, the Corvette, etc. — do have separate bodies and frames, as do several of the older British cars like the MGA.

Volkswagen (the Karmann-Ghia and Beetle convertible) used a variation of the unibody method. Instead of a box-section type of frame, VW stamped out a complete floor pan, which served as a frame. The body then was bolted to the floor pan, and this made for quite a rigid vehicle as well.

Rigidity and light weight are important in high-performance enthusiast cars, so unibody construction is

Illustration F
Box section frame

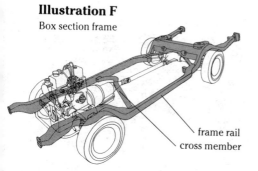

frame rail
cross member

Illustration G
Unit-body or "unibody"

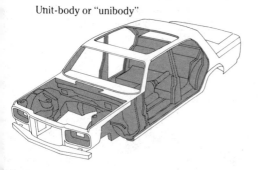

desirable. However, there are some important disadvantages of the method that especially pertain to older, used unibody cars. First, there's rust. In cars with separate frames, the heavy box section tubes take a long time to rust; the body panels may rust, but as long as the frame is uncorroded, the car will maintain its basic structural integrity. On unibody cars, if rust attacks the points where the engine, transmission or suspension are attached, you've got big trouble.

In addition, a minor accident can throw the entire alignment of a unibody car out of whack. Repairing collision damage on a unibody car often requires a good deal of expertise and special equipment, such as an expensive, sophisticated "bench" that forces the bent and damaged unibody back to the correct measurements so it can be welded.

All too often, severely damaged unibody cars are "clipped." If, for example, the front end of a car is severly bashed, a body shop might cut the car in half and then weld on the front half of another car, one presumably that was bashed in the rear. *Voila!* One unbent car made from two bashed ones. The only problem is that even in relatively minor accidents, clipped unibody cars have a tendency to split in half.

Ergonomics

Ergonomics has nothing to do with money supply, Laffer curves or John Maynard Keynes. Instead, it's a funny word used to describe the relationship between man and machine. An enthusiast car and its driver should feel a certain "at-oneness," as though the car is an extension of the driver's limbs and nervous system.

That feeling is diminished if you scrape your knuckles on the dashboard every time you shift into fifth gear, or if the steering-wheel rim blocks your view of the tachometer, or if the pedals are so close that you hit the clutch when you want to tap the brakes.

Good ergonomics dictate a proper array of instruments, including the tachometer and speedometer, plus oil pressure, water temperature and fuel gauges. Idiot lights without gauges won't do because they don't give you advance warning if anything goes wrong. Moreover, good ergonomics means that the instruments are arranged for quick viewing and are protected from glare. The shift lever should "fall readily to hand," as the British say. The steering wheel should be positioned so that the driver can find a comfortable yet efficient driving position. And any switches or buttons or levers should be logically arranged and well-identified (see Illustration H).

Summary of Important Technical Features

Now that wasn't so bad, was it? You may not be ready to rebuild a Maserati, but at least you might be able to understand the fine print in a car advertisement or perhaps fool a salesman into thinking you're a sharp customer. In case you forget, the following table summarizes the important mechanical bits and pieces found on a proper enthusiast car:

Illustration H

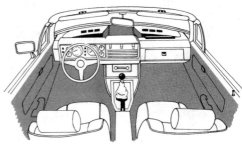

This is a proper sports-car cockpit with bucket seats that provide good support, a gear shift lever positioned for easy reach, a thick-rimmed 3-spoke steering wheel and a complete array of instruments directly in front of the driver.

Item	Advantages
Overhead Camshaft Engine	Gives smoother high-speed performance.
Fuel Injection	Provides better engine response, increased fuel economy and improved emission control.
Independent Rear Suspension (irs)	Provides a good combination of ride and handling.
Rack-and-Pinion Steering	Gives quick and accurate steering response.
Disc Brakes	Dissipate heat that causes brake fade.
Radial Tires	Provide better traction, longer tread life and increased fuel economy.
Alloy Wheels or Wire Wheels	Reduce weight and enhance the car's appearance.
Overdrive or Fifth Gear	Allows quieter, more fuel-efficient engine operation at cruising speeds.
Unit-Body (unibody)	Makes the car more rigid and light-weight.

Chapter Six:

Used Car Buying Strategy

In war, football games and used-car buying, a good strategy can make the winning difference. Here's a seven-part routine that will help you efficiently find and buy a used enthusiast car.

1. Take a vow of patience. If you want to buy a car *right now*, you'd better head over to your local dealership and buy a brand-new car. Too many used-car buyers hand over their cash for the first car they find that's the right make, model and color.

Keep in mind that most used cars, especially those that are ten or twenty years old like many of the cars profiled in Part Two, won't be spring chickens. The typical '65 sports car will have gone through three or four owners, a couple of crack-ups, an engine or two, 120,000 miles and basically will be a clapped-out heap.

Your mission then, is to find the exception — the older car that's had a life of tender-loving care — and that, friends, usually takes time. Be prepared to look at several cars before you buy.

2. Make a preliminary choice of cars. Narrow your selection down to one or two types of enthusiast cars that most appeal to you. As you get further involved in the buying process and actually drive one or two examples, you may of course want to change your selection.

Think about the general types of cars described in Chapter Three and, at the same time, your needs. Are you looking for a car to use as primary transportation? If you have a daily 100-mile commute through summer heat and winter snows, you need an old Austin-Healey like you need a social disease. Confine yourself instead to the cars in Part Two that are more modern and practical, like a Chevy Camaro or Datsun Z-car.

On the other hand, if you're looking for a weekend toy or the dream-car of your youth, let your emotions rule. As some sexist wag once said, "A woman is only a woman, but a Ferrari is a trip."

3. Educate yourself about the market. Classified advertisements are the usual source for most used cars. But word-of-mouth, if you're connected to the grapevine, can be the best source of all.

And what's the grapevine? Car clubs as well as mechanics who specialize in repairing a certain marque. There's a car club for almost every kind of car. Just look under the heading "Car Clubs" in the classified advertising section of any issue of *Road & Track* magazine for addresses. You'll find that car club members percolate with both enthusiasm and valuable information about their favorite cars. Members often know of good cars for sale. And most clubs publish newsletters that carry advertising for members who want to sell their cars. Prices for these cars may be on the high side, but the cars will usually be premium examples. Indeed, the best enthusiast cars are often just sold amongst members of a marque club.

Knowledgeable independent mechanics are another outstanding source. A mechanic will often know which of his clients want to sell their cars, and because the mechanic has cared for the cars, he can give you the straight scoop on their condition.

Your next best source is the classified advertising section of your local newspaper, especially if it's a large daily like the *New York Times* or *Los Angeles Times*. Other good sources are weekly tabloids available at convenience stores and newsstands in many areas of the country. They carry nothing but advertisements for used cars. One of these, the *Auto Trader*, runs a picture of each advertised car, a definite advantage over the usual newspaper classified ad. In newspapers and the tabloids, you'll find ads from both private parties and dealers. The following section of this chapter will give you the pros and cons of buying a car from a dealer or private party, and the section after that will translate some of the peculiar lingo of automotive classified advertising.

The trick to finding a car through the classifieds is to glean the ads every day for several weeks so that you'll get a feel for the prices and general availability of your chosen car in your area. You'll probably notice that some ads will appear for a day or two and then will be withdrawn, presumably because the car was sold. Others seem to stay in the paper day after day, most likely because the car is a dog or the price is too high.

4. In Step One I said you should have patience in your search. But when the right car does come along, be ready to act. As soon as you see an intriguing ad, especially if the price seems low, you must be ready to make an immediate inspection and a cash deposit. If you dally and the car is truly a good deal, you can be sure another buyer will beat you to the punch. However, if you judge the price to be too high, you may be better off to wait a day or two after the ad first appears. That'll give the seller a chance to become more anxious and more receptive to a lower offer. When a seller doesn't state a price at all in the ad, it almost always means he wants big bucks for the car.

When the right ad does appear, find out more about the car with a phone call. Keep in mind that you'll be conducting an interview, and the best interviewers always give the subject — in this case, the seller — plenty of opportunity to talk. That is, plenty of opportunity to hang himself. Ask tough questions, but in the friendliest tone of voice you have; you certainly don't want the seller to become overly defensive. Start with general questions. "How many owners has the car had?" "What's wrong with the car?" "What major repairs have been performed?" "How many accidents has it been in?" "Have you been happy with it?" If the general questions don't give you enough information, be more specific. Just be sure to cover all the major facets of the car: the paint and body work, the engine and transmission, the tires and brakes, and the interior. If the phone interview is a success, you'll have a good idea of whether or not the car is worth the time and effort to make a thorough inspection.

If you contact a dealer through an ad, he'll undoubtedly be quite adept at giving you responses over the phone that will lure you into his dealership. And he'll be less likely to volunteer any information in response to your general questions. Therefore, keep your questions to him specific: "Does the engine burn oil?" "Are the synchros in the transmission worn?" "Has the car been repainted?" "Is there any rust?"

When you conclude the interview, ask the salesman for his name and tell him you'll look for him if you should visit the dealership — he'll appreciate your assurance that you intend to be "his" customer.

5. Make your own inspection. If the car sounds good over the phone, you'll be ready for the most important step in your strategy, the inspection. (The following chapter will take you step by step through that process.)

6. Have a professional mechanic look at the car. If the car passes your own inspection, ask an independent mechanic to at least perform an engine compression test. It only takes a few minutes and will cost you little. If the seller objects, your response should be simple: stop considering the car.

With a compression gauge, the mechanic will measure the pressure in each cylinder. If the readings don't match up to the manufacturer's specifications or if the cylinders show uneven readings, you can be certain that the valves, rings or pistons need attention, an expensive proposition involving at minimum a valve job and perhaps an engine rebuild. A fairly complete overhaul of a simple MG or Triumph engine will cost around $1,500. Exotic cars like Ferraris could easily top $8,000.

7. Make an offer. Armed with a list of the car's problems and a rough idea of how much it will cost to have them repaired, you're now ready to negotiate a price with the seller, assuming of course you still want the car. When the seller is a dealer, you might simply hand over the list and tell him to fix everything on it. In return, you'll pay his asking price for the car. If he agrees, make sure that the sales contract specifically mentions each item to be repaired and that any replacement parts will be factory approved. A private-party owner usually expects to sell his car "as is." Your list of needed repairs then becomes a bargaining tool to knock down his asking price.

If you're willing to take a gamble on losing the car to another buyer, it's often good strategy to make the seller a very low offer, and when refused, leave a way of contacting you. Should the owner become desperate enough, you may get the car at a very low price. It won't usually work with dealers, however, because they are patient enough to wait for a fair offer

Once you've agreed on the price, expect to give the seller a nonrefundable cash down payment on the spot. When you pay the balance, don't expect the seller to take anything but cash or a bank check; any seller who accepts a personal check is a fool no matter how upstanding the buyer might appear.

A final note: if you buy from a private party, don't face your state's Department of Motor Vehicles alone when you go to reregister the car. If the seller accompanies you and problems arise — the car fails to pass smog inspection, for instance — you won't be forced to track him down.

Dealer or Private Party?

Not all private-party sellers are candidates for the priesthood, but they are less apt to employ the high-pressure sales tactics of the typical professional salesman. Buying a used sports car directly from an owner also allows you to get a firsthand idea of how the car was treated (or mistreated). Unlike a dealer's salesman, who probably knows nothing of the backgrounds of the cars he sells, the private-party seller can tell all about his car's peculiarities and may even be able to supply you with service records.

Of course the big advantage of buying from an individual is that you usually get a better price; private individuals don't have to cover the expenses of operating a dealership, salesmen's commissions or honoring warranties.

Nevertheless, dealers do offer you several benefits that could outweigh their premium prices. Used cars, especially the older ones, will invariably have parts that need fixing, and a dealer can correct any deficiencies at his cost. Does the car you want need tires? Pay the dealer his asking price and get him to throw in a new set. By contrast, you might pay less to a private party for a similar car, but after you buy the tires at their full retail price, you could easily end up spending more.

Then there are warranties. With a private party, what you see is what you get. But some dealers will offer a warranty on used cars. Usually they are 50-50 agreements (the buyer and the dealer split the cost of parts and labor) that cover the car for thirty, sixty, or ninety days. As of May 1985, the Federal Trade Commission started requiring used-car dealers to affix a "Buyer's Guide" sticker to the cars on their lots.

The sticker states whether the dealer offers a warranty or is selling the car "as is." (In addition, the stickers list a number of things that could go wrong with any used car, but they do not state any known defects about the specific car. You'll still have to discover the car's faults on your own, or have an independent mechanic inspect the car.)

Finally, when you buy from a dealer, you can avoid the dreadful, bureaucratic hassles of standing in line at your local Department of Motor Vehicles to change the registration and get clearance on smog and safety devices — the dealer will take care of all that for you.

If you should decide to buy from a dealer, select one that has a new-car franchise for the same marque that you want to buy. A Porsche dealer who takes a used Porsche on trade will know what he's buying. And he'll have the expert mechanics and factory parts readily available to put the car right either before the car goes on the lot or before you take possession. Moreover, he'll want to uphold his reputation as a worthy Porsche dealer by offering only good, clean cars. After all, he hopes you'll become a customer in either his service bays or, some day, in his new-car showroom.

For most of us, negotiating with a dealer is about as much fun as a trip to the dentist's chair. You should look upon it as a game. Unless you've been in training, don't expect to beat the dealer — he's a pro after all. When you emerge from the "closing room" (usually a cubicle with a desk and a couple of chairs), the best you can hope for is a fair deal to all the players.

Start the negotiating game by making an offer lower than the asking price. Assuming the dealer is willing to negotiate (and it's a rare one who isn't), you'll eventually wind up in the closing room with a salesman writing up a contract containing your offer. He'll then take the contract to a sales manager for approval. That's when the fun begins.

Though the sales manager makes the decision in an instant, the salesman will hang around the sales manager's office for quite a while in order to appear as if there's great deliberation. Undoubtedly, the salesman will return to you shaking his head and will make a counteroffer. You'll then counter the dealer's counteroffer, and the process will continue until you either threaten to walk out or everyone comes to terms. Here are some tips to keep in mind:

• The more time the salesman and dealer invest in you, the more they'll want to make a deal. Therefore, use up a lot of their time asking questions and taking test drives before you start negotiating price.

• Don't have a chip on your shoulder, but don't give the impression that you're married to the dealer. Be sure the salesman knows that you'll take a walk if you don't get a fair deal.

• In order to shorten the salesman's excursions into the sales manager's office, get up and wander around the dealership while he's out of the closing room. That'll make both the salesman and sales manager nervous about whether you're going to leave. And whatever you do, don't talk to anyone who may be with you about what you're *really* prepared to pay while the salesman is gone — sometimes the closing room is bugged.

• Once you've agreed on a price, be certain all repairs or any freebies are written into the contract before you sign it.

Interpreting the Ads

I was helping my friend Lisa the other day search for a used car. I thought she'd look terrific in an Alfa Romeo coupe. The task was to find one within her $4,000 budget. As we pored through the newspaper classified ads, I came across what looked like the perfect candidate. The ad read:

ALFA '74 Cpe. Alloys, stereo. Rblt eng.
Perfect cond. p / p $4200 / obo. 680-7300

"Too bad," she said. "I wish the owner wasn't so firm on the price."

"What do you mean 'firm'?" I asked. "The owner would probably jump at $4,000. After all, he says $4,200 'or best offer'. That's an invitation to dicker."

"Is that what 'obo' means? I thought it meant, 'I want $4,200 *or bug off.*' "

Automotive classified advertising in newspapers does have a lingo all its own. Like most languages, it was born of necessity; in this case, the need to cram as much information as possible into a couple of lines that can cost up to $15 each. Sometimes sellers are so adept with the jargon they just befuddle the poor prospective buyer. Here's a list of some frequently found abbreviations:

A / C = air conditioning
Alloys = special alloy or magnesium wheels
Alrm = alarm system to ward off thieves
AT = automatic transmission
Cond = condition (as in "good cond")
Conv = convertible

Cpe = coupe
Cyl = cylinders (as in "4-cyl")
K = thousands of miles (as in 32K)
Leath = leather upholstery
Lo mi = low mileage
Mags = special alloy or magnesium wheels
Met Pnt = metallic paint
Mi = miles (as in "low mi")
P/P = private party (the seller is not a dealer)
PS = power steering
Rblt = rebuilt engine
Rdls = radial tires
SP = speed (refers to the number of forward gears in a manual transmission - as in "5-sp")
S/R = sunroof
Stereo = usually means a combination AM/FM radio with tape player

Classified ad writers are also masters at turning the euphemistic phrase. Here are some popular examples and what they *really* mean:

Phrase	Translation
"Mechanics special"	It'll take a special mechanic to fix it.
"Concours condition"	Just waxed.
"Clean car"	Just washed.
"Sick, must sell"	Sick of this car.
"Low mileage"	Always in the shop for repairs.
"$6999.99"	Obviously $7,000 is too much.
"Rebuilt engine"	New plugs and points.
"Loaded"	With useless gadgets that break.
"A true classic"	Any heap over five years old.
"Priced to sell"	What else — priced to keep?
"Needs a little work"	Bring a tow truck.
"Must see to appreciate"	What a hard life it's had.
"Dealer demonstrator"	Been driven by every inept driver in town.

By the way, Lisa turned out to be a proficient bargainer. She bought the Alfa for $3,800. And I was right; the Alfa and Lisa are a stunning combination.

The Mileage Myth

Low mileage on a used car is usually considered a good thing. Well, it isn't necessarily so. The number of miles on the clock aren't as important as how the miles got there and how rigorously the car was maintained.

Any mechanic will tell you that around-town, stop-and-go driving is a punishing ordeal for a car's innards. The little old lady who dusts off her Mercedes three times a week to drive a couple of miles to the supermarket may have a cosmetically gorgeous car, but its drivetrain will probably be worse for the wear. That's because short trips don't allow the engine to reach peak operating temperatures, so the oil never warms up sufficiently to provide proper lubrication. In addition, carbon can build up during stop-and-go driving and congest the engine. And if the car sits too long without operating at all, rust deposits could begin to form inside the engine. Just like your body, cars need regular exercise.

Of course, the 200,000-mile car will probably be pretty tired no matter what. But the point is this: a car with especially low miles (less than 10,000 for each year of its age) may not be as good a buy as one with higher-than-average miles — especially if the high-mileage car did most of its traveling on freeways or expressways and was regularly serviced.

California Cars

For car enthusiasts who live in the snow belt, a trip to California (or any other arid state of the Southwest) can be something of a time warp. They'll see 10- or 15-year-old cars running around that look like they just left the showroom. Without any heavy rains, snow or road salt, California highways are kind to cars. And of course it's well known that Californians rate their cars' importance somewhere below health foods and above clean air. That interest translates into hundreds of used-car ads in the classified selection of the *Los Angeles Times* every Sunday, of which perhaps a third are for enthusiast cars.

So if you're looking for an especially clean, older used car, you might consider buying one in California. Unquestionably, a car that has never been exposed to conditions that cause rust makes the best investment.

Buying a Used Car in Europe

Because many of the older enthusiast cars discussed in Part Two are British, German or Italian, it may seem like a swell idea to fly to Europe to buy a used car. If you need an excuse for a European jaunt, it may well be a good idea just as long as you're aware of the risks involved in importing a car into the U.S.

The amount of risk needn't be great if the car you desire is quite old. But if the car is of a more recent vintage and wasn't intended for sale in the U.S., then be warned: The regulatory moat surrounding our shores abounds with danger for those who don't heed the rules.

To understand the rules, it's helpful to divide the universe of used European cars into two groups. The first group includes cars built prior to the 1968 model year. With a wave and a smile the ever-vigilant customs people will let these cars across our borders. That's because the Environmental Protection Agency's emissions control requirements didn't take effect until the 1968 model year, and because the Department of Transportation safety regulations weren't in force until January 1, 1968.

But with the second group, cars built after the 1967 model

year, customs agents become absolutely Draconian in their zeal to shut out imported cars. First, customs requires these cars to make what is called a "formal entry." That's bureaucrat talk for reams of paperwork, much of which is in triplicate. Formal entry also means that the importer must post a bond in the amount equal to the value of the car plus estimated duty.

If you can afford to post the bond and hire an authorized customs broker to take care of the paperwork, then you're free to tackle the most challenging part of the legalization procedure: modifying the car to meet EPA and DOT requirements applicable to the model year.

From the date of entry, you'll have 90 days to satisfy EPA requirements and 120 days to meet the DOT rules, with possible extension in either case to no more than 180 days. During that time the car will be released to you, but you'll have to take it to a specialist, who must determine what modifications are necessary, and then make the modifications.

After the work is completed you must return to customs and prove through more reams of paperwork, or through actual inspection, that the car conforms to the regulations. You may also be required to have the car tested in a qualified laboratory at a cost of $850 or more to see that it meets EPA standards. And what if the car doesn't pass muster? You're forced either to ship the car back from whence it came or turn it over to customs who will unceremoniously crush it. And if you don't return it, you will, of course, forfeit the bond. Moreover, the Feds will find you, impound the car and levy additional fines besides.

What modifications are involved? For some cars built in the early 1970s, DOT standards may be relatively easy to meet, especially if similar models were crash tested and certified for sale in the U.S. The standards involve things such as lighting, seatbelts, window glass and brake-failure warning systems. A European Porsche 911 and BMW CS Coupe are good examples. But cars built after the mid-1970s must be modified with impact-absorbing bumpers and door beams, items frequently expensive and complicated to engineer.

In some cases it may be easy to satisfy EPA regulations as well. Equipping a car to run on propane will usually meet EPA standards, though that's not an acceptable solution to most owners. Diesel-powered cars built prior to the 1975 model year are exempt from EPA rules altogether. But in general, cars built after 1967 must be retrofitted with various emissions control devices, or if built after 1975, with catalytic converters.

There is one loophole in all this that might make the legalization process a little easier. If the car you so desperately want to import is at least five years old, and if you promise that you've never before imported a nonconforming vehicle, and promise never to sell the car, then the car can be exempted from all EPA requirements. But note: The exemption only applies to EPA rules, not those of the DOT. Furthermore, the state of California doesn't recognize the EPA exemption and insists that all cars conform to emission regulations.

In sum, if the prospect of being swaddled in red tape doesn't frighten you, you probably can import a noncomplying car. But specialists who earn their living modifying European cars to meet U.S. regulations generally agree that it's only worth the effort if the car is high priced and unusually desirable—a Ferrari Boxer, BMW M1 or Porsche Turbo, for instance.

So what does that leave the less adventuresome buyer? Pre-1968 models, and the main problem with buying old cars in Europe is the same as buying them here at home, rust and deterioration. English weather may be perfect for the delicate complexions of young English maidens, but it renders automobile bodies into heaps of iron oxide in short order. And the same for the climes of most of Europe.

In addition, don't get caught up in the natives-don't-know-what-they've-got syndrome. The natives do know all about the worth of classic cars; in fact, an old Jaguar E-type or Ferrari often commands a higher price in Europe than in America.

Still, there are decent and interesting older cars available in Europe. Despite the miserable weather, England is probably your most fertile hunting ground. The English have a peculiar appreciation for old things and often take exceedingly good care of them. The island contains restoration shops and dealers galore who specialize in vintage cars. Moreover, a similarity in language will help the American tourist in his negotiations with a British car seller. Of course, the primary disadvantage is that most cars in England tend to be right-hand drive. That's dandy for your holiday tour of the English countryside, but it may be difficult to get used to at home. Nevertheless, plenty of people have imported right-hand-drive cars into the U.S. and seem to happily endure the startled stares of other drivers who don't think anyone is at the steering wheel.

For the names of English dealers, pick up copies of the British auto magazines, *Thoroughbred & Classic Cars* and *Classic And Sportscar*, available at many American newsstands. It's probably most efficient to shop with dealers who carry inventories of classic used cars rather than private parties selling a single example. In addition, dealers are usually better able to help arrange insurance, registration and shipping.

Unless you consider yourself an accomplished backyard mechanic, you'd do well to have a prospective automotive purchase checked by an authorized garage before you buy. Hotel personnel are often a good source of help in recommending mechanics. If you do make your own check, remember to pack a compression gauge in your suitcase. And keep a sharp eye for rust.

One other bit of advice: If the car you'd like to buy was built in 1967, be certain that it's a 1967 model, not a 1968 whose model run began in 1967. Otherwise you may have to go through all the nonsense of a formal customs entry for noncomplying cars. Customs agents have files of serial numbers against which your car's will be checked if there's any question.

Restoration Projects and Other Illusions

Let's say you don't have much money, but you fancy yourself good with tools. You also have half an empty garage and you'd like to get your hands dirty with a restoration project. What better way to learn mechanics and get a bargain enthusiast car at the same time than to buy a so-called basket case and fix it up yourself?

Well unfortunately it seems that 80 or 90 percent of these project cars never get finished. After a few weekends of organizing, cleaning and stripping parts, the basket-case buyer becomes a basket case himself when he realizes the magnitude of the task before him. The carcass and assorted bits and pieces then usually sit in the garage taking up space and collecting dust until the owner sells it all to some other starry-eyed, would-be restorer.

If, however, you buy a ratty car and want to have it professionally restored, expect to pay a small fortune. With the high price of labor these days, it's so easy to run up a bill that's higher than the car is really worth that restoration projects are best left to wealthy folk with true classic cars — the Bugattis, Duesenbergs and Packards. (People often spend $100,000 or more just to restore these cars, not including the price of the car!)

And what about buying a car that's already been restored? First, if it's less than ten years old, there's no reason why a car should need a true restoration (which would include rebuilding all the mechanical parts, new paint and upholstery) unless the car had been terribly abused or in a bad accident. But nothing lasts forever, and on a 30-year-old MGA for example, a restoration might be entirely reasonable. The already-restored car will often be a bargain compared to buying a ratty car and having it refurbished, as long as the restoration was a proper one. But finding a properly restored car can often be tricky. Was the body carefully prepared before it was painted? Was the engine completely overhauled with new pistons, valves, etc., or was it simply a case of throwing in some new rings? Does the new upholstery material closely match the original material as it came from the factory? If the answers to any of the questions are negative, then you could be buying a car that will give you trouble down the road, or one that won't be worth as much as you expect.

Your best bet, then, is to find a complete, well-running, unrestored car in as nearly original condition as possible, and preferably being sold by the original owner. That way you know exactly what you're getting. The car won't need so much work that it'll bankrupt you, but if it does need a little upholstery work or a paint respray, you can be sure to have it done right.

Chapter Seven:

Checking Out a Used Car

Becoming the new owner of a used car is like opening a box of Cracker Jacks: one never knows what surprises await inside. There are all the little goodies squashed under the carpets and seats — the bobby pins, gum wrappers, costume jewelry and spare change contributed by the former owner. And then there are the booby prizes — breakdowns and expensive repair bills.

Of course, the best way to avoid the booby prizes is to conduct your own thorough inspection of a used car, and to have a professional mechanic check the car over as well, before you buy. Some thoughts to keep in mind when you make an inspection:

- As mentioned in earlier chapters, you'll almost always be better off paying a high price (as long as it's not outrageous) for a used car in perfect condition than picking up a dog of a car cheap, only to be burdened with expensive repairs later on.
- Never examine a used car at night. Artificial light will hide a multitude of defects.
- Always drive the car yourself. You can't possibly judge a car until you take the wheel yourself; the owner may know how to drive his car in a way that minimizes its problems. For instance, if the second-gear synchro is bad, he can nurse it along so that the passenger never knows it's faulty.

If a certain car catches your fancy or if you become intrigued by a certain marque after reading the profiles in Part Two, you will actually be making two different inspections when you go to examine a used car. First, you'll be judging the make and model as to whether or not it meets your expectations and needs. And second, you'll be appraising that particular example for any cosmetic and mechanical problems. Though you'll actually be making both inspections simultaneously, I'll discuss them separately.

Appraising the Make and Model

Start by standing back from the car and taking a long look. Does the overall shape grab you? View it from all angles: from the sides, the rear, the front and as you stand up and as you crouch down. An enthusiast car's styling must stir the soul.

Now get a little closer and look for indications of good design as well as quality of construction. If the hood scoop is phony or if there are a lot of fussy, unneeded trim items, mentally mark the car down in your estimation. Look at the gaps between the hood and the fenders, notice how the doors hang: the spaces should be equidistant all the way around. This could be an indication of collision damage or it might just be sloppy workmanship at the factory. Look, too, at the paint. There shouldn't be much "orange peel" (sort of crinkly like the skin of an orange). And don't mistake orange peel for thickness; an outstanding paint job is as smooth to the eye and to the touch as glass.

Now pop the hood. Fine machinery is one reason you are buying an enthusiast car, so the engine and the engine compartment should be as well trimmed as the rest of the car. Run your hand along the inside edge of the hood. You won't find any spurs or jagged edges on a high-quality car. Notice, too, if there is at least a little space around the engine in which a mechanic could work. That will make his job easier and will cut down on repair costs — another objective of good design. The trunk also tells a story. Again, the edges should be smooth, and the overall finish should be suitable to receive your matched set of Gucci luggage. And check the shape of the trunk. Is it deep and wide enough to accommodate your luggage or bags of groceries?

If everything seems suitable so far, open the door and slide inside the driver's seat. It should fit as snugly as your favorite pair of jeans — a close fit keeps you from sliding around during brisk cornering. The seat should also give support at the small of the back and under the thighs. And don't be put off if the seat feels firm; it may not make a good impression in the showroom, but after several hours of driving, you'll feel less fatigued than if the seat is excessively cushy.

You should be able to move the seat back, as well as the steering wheel (if it's adjustable), so that your legs comfortably reach the pedals. And as you hold the steering wheel your arms should be nearly straight out, with just a slight bend at both elbows. The wheel, by the way, must be thick enough to afford a good grasp — a leather rim is ideal.

The low get-on-down seating of some sports cars may make you feel like Mario Andretti, but you'll drive like a demolition derby contestant if you can't see out the windows. Look all around for blind spots, and you should be able to tell where the hood ends even if it is fashionably long.

And finally, note the workmanship and the quality of the interior. Do the carpets fit? Does the glove-compartment door seem solid? Does the material used for the seats and headliner seem durable and well stitched?

Now you are ready to hit the road. The owner or dealer salesman will probably insist on accompanying you, but try to go alone if possible. And if he does come along ask him to keep quiet: you'll need to concentrate on the car without distracting chatter. And once you've tested the radio or stereo, keep it off. Don't forget to buckle the seat belt, making sure that it's comfortable.

Once on the road you'll probably notice the firm ride if it's a sports car, expecially if you're used to driving a large American car. But as long as it's not bad enough to require a kidney belt, you'll come to prefer a little tautness. Ride quality is always a compromise between comfort and handling. Soft springs mean softer riding, but they also allow the body to roll during hard cornering — obviously not desirable if you want to take curves without turning the world upside down. However, sports-car suspension designs are consistently improving. For example, anti-roll bars are now a common feature of car suspensions; they connect the two wheels at either end of the car so as to limit roll without limiting up-and-down movement.

On the test drive, try out a variety of roads. A car may corner and ride wonderfully down smooth blacktop, only to lose its aplomb over chuckholes or a series of undulations. Tar strips or lane-divider markers can also cause undue harshness in some cars.

An enthusiast car's steering should feel precise and well controlled, especially when compared to an American sedan's steering, which tends to be overly power assisted and inaccurate. Ditto for the brakes. At some point in the test drive, you might want to make a U-turn and note how much room it takes to perform the maneuver — the less room the better, of course.

Noise always diminishes driving comfort. It can emanate from a variety of sources: tires, exhaust, engine, differential and transmission. A virile-sounding growl from the engine is one thing, but wind leaks around the front doors, the convertible top or sunroof are quite another. They're so annoying because they are usually just about at ear level. As you take your test drive, note the noise level with the windows up and down, with the sunroof open and closed, and if the car is a convertible, with the top erected and stowed.

Appraising a Car's Condition

If the car seems to fit your requirements, you're ready to check out its condition. Your inspection is meant to uncover evidence of mechanical problems as well as rust, collisions, owner neglect and any untruths that the seller might profess. Rust is usually the most serious problem you could encounter. There are two types: surface rust that affects unpainted areas, and deeper rust that pervades a piece of metal from one side right through to the other. Surface rust can easily be removed with sanding, while deep rust requires that the affected area be completely cut away. If the car's rocker panels (the strips of metal that run the length of the car underneath the doors) or fenders show rust, it's possible (though expensive) to replace them with new ones. But when deep rust starts attacking the frame or even the floor pan, consider the car hopeless. It's all too common for unscrupulous body repairmen or owners to camouflage rusty areas with a little paint or body putty. Unfortunately, covering it up doesn't make it go away; it'll only spread and get worse.

A car that's had a minor collision or two isn't necessarily a bad deal. It depends on the extent of the damage and how it was repaired. A crunched fender that was completely replaced with a new one or was properly reworked with a minimum of body putty should cause no problems. But if the crash was serious enough to distort the frame or twist a unibody, watch out. (See

Chapter 5.)

Owner neglect can be difficult to uncover if the seller was smart enough to have the car properly cleaned up before putting it on the market. Otherwise, it's easy. If the seats are badly torn, the paint dull and the engine compartment filthy, you can bet the owner didn't care much about having the car properly serviced either.

An inspection should also confirm any statements about the car made by the seller. If he says the car was never repainted, yet you find overspray on the weather stripping, you should wonder about what else he's trying to hide.

The Exterior Inspection: Stand back and take a good look at the whole car. Does it stand upright and proud, or does it sag at one end or the other with fatigue? Sagging could mean a worn-out suspension. Now move to either the front or rear and crouch down. Examine the entire length of the car and look for straight bodywork. Compare both sides. If a style line is uneven, or if a crease that should be there isn't, then you've got a strong indication of shoddy repair work. If you're suspicious, take a small magnet and see if it sticks to the body. If it doesn't, then there's body putty under the paint — the less the better. (Obviously the magnet trick won't work on a fiberglass-bodied car like a Corvette.) The trunk will also frequently show evidence of a collision; body repairmen often leave telltale wrinkles and dents in the trunk floor or in the spare-tire well because they're out of sight and covered by carpeting or mats.

Now to the paint. The best used car will have the original paint, still in good condition of course. Original paint immediately tells you that the car was never in a serious accident, has never been rusted and then repaired, and that the owner cared enough to maintain the paint. To check for repainting, open the doors, trunk and hood, and look for paint overspray on the rubber weather stripping. Overspray will also frequently show up on the rubber gaskets around the rear window and windshield. If you find some, it either means that a portion of the car was repainted (because of a dent or a fenderbender perhaps) or that the entire car was repainted (because of a serious accident or simply because the paint was faded).

It's not unusual for an older car, five years or more, to need repainting even if the owner was fairly conscientious about maintenance. As long as it's a good job (no runs, drips or orange peel), don't worry, unless of course you think it covers up serious collision damage or rusting. The new paint should also exactly match the color of the original paint. Look underneath weather stripping, in the engine compartment and along the doorjambs to tell if the color was changed. Unless the car was completely stripped (including removal of the engine, interior and all chrome), a color change won't be satisfactory because the old paint will always show up somewhere. So if you want a good investment, avoid a used car that's had its color changed, and don't expect to change the color after you buy it.

Rust is usually easy to find. Look closely along the fenders, rocker panels and the bottoms of the doors for little bubbles or flaking paint. And by all means take a good look under the car (wear old clothes when you do an inspection) for more rust. While you're there, look for fresh, dripping oil around the engine, transmission and differential. Though it need not pass a white-glove test, a car's underside should be free of any flaking (from rust) of heavy buildups of grease (from oil leaks).

The Engine Compartment Inspection: A clean engine compartment can mean two things — either the owner was wonderfully meticulous about maintaining his car, or he just had it steam-cleaned to remove a dreadful accumulation of crud. The radiator water might provide a clue; if it's rusty-colored, that means the owner has neglected to flush out the cooling system (but don't confuse dirty liquid with the normal coloring of antifreeze). And if there's any trace of oil in the radiator, it could mean a blown head gasket or a cracked block. The color of the oil on the dipstick won't tell you much because modern detergent oil is supposed to get dirty as it picks up impurities in the engine. But you might check the reservoirs for the brakes, power steering and battery — a careful owner will keep them topped off. Moreover, extremely low fluid levels might mean a malfunctioning system.

The Road Test: A cold start is a good test of the engine's condition. Notice how long it takes to fire up, then how well it idles while still cold — a healthy engine will do both without fuss. Be sure that the oil-pressure gauge comes to life and that all the other idiot lights and gauges are functioning as they should. If the car has a manual transmission, put the gearshift lever in neutral and depress the clutch. Do you hear a marked increase in the noise level? That would indicate a worn clutch throw-out bearing. Now release the clutch. Excessive noise at this point means transmission problems.

Now while you're waiting for the engine to warm up, get out of the car and open the hood. It takes a trained ear to distinguish unusual engine noises from the normal valve-train and camshaft-chain clatter, but if the poor motor knocks like a diesel, something's seriously amiss. And while the engine will vibrate a little while it idles, it shouldn't jerk around convulsively. If it does, it could mean low compression or a broken engine mount.

Next, walk to the rear of the car, and if the engine is warmed up, ask the seller to gun it a time or two. If you see a copious amount of dark smoke, the car is either an oil burner or the fuel-air mixture is too rich. Oil burning is serious because it indicates that an engine may have to be rebuilt, or at least undergo a valve job. But a rich fuel mixture usually requires little more than an adjustment of the carburetor or fuel injection.

How can you tell the difference? With one of the niftiest — and easiest — tests of the engine's overall condition. Simply put your finger inside the tailpipe and rub it around a little. If you feel heavy deposits of grease and sludge, the engine is an oil burner. But if you only find soft, black carbon, then it's probably just a rich mixture. And if the engine is working as it should, you'll find that the tail pipe will be a light gray or even white inside.

And while you're at the rear of the car, place the palm of your hand lightly over the tailpipe as the engine idles. Do you feel a smooth, continuous stream of exhaust gas? If so, that's a sign of a healthy engine. An intermittent flow, however, means uneven combustion. Though a simple tune-up might solve the problem, it could also indicate the need for a complete overhaul; play it safe and have a mechanic check the car out before you buy.

Now get back in the driver's seat and check the clutch (if the car has a manual transmission, of course). Put the parking brake on and depress the clutch. Move the gearshift lever into first gear and rev up the engine to about 3,000 rpm. Now let out the clutch. The engine should stall immediately. But if the engine continues to run with the clutch out, then the clutch is slipping very badly indeed. You can also test the clutch by coming to a full stop on a steep hill and then trying to climb up the hill again; if the clutch is released and the engine revs up without much effect on forward motion, the clutch is slipping and will need replacement.

As you upshift and accelerate to highway speed and then decelerate and downshift, note how easily and quietly the gearshift moves through the gearbox. If there's any crunching, the transmission could need new synchros. As for an automatic transmission, it should shift smoothly but with authority as you accelerate. And with either a manual or an automatic transmission, don't forget to try out reverse.

Find an empty road so you can test the brakes. First, pump the brake pedal two or three times. Do you feel pressure build up? You shouldn't. If the pedal feels right, accelerate to 40 mph or so and then brake hard. The car should decelerate in a straight line without swerving. Problems with the brakes could indicate the need for anything from a simple replacement of the linings to a complete system overhaul. Swerving might also mean suspension problems such as worn ball joints or tie-rod ends — nothing terribly expensive on most cars.

On that same empty road, accelerate up to red line (check the tachometer so you don't exceed the red line!) in each gear. The engine should accelerate briskly and smoothly. If there's any stumbling or hesitation, it could mean something as innocent as fouled spark plugs or something as serious as poor compression.

Steering problems become obvious when you go over railroad tracks or any irregularities in the road and the steering wheel starts to jitter. And if you can move the wheel much more than an inch without any effect on the car's direction as you're driving a straight line, then there's too much play in the steering gear. Nor should the steering wheel pull to one side as you drive straight ahead. Steering irregularities mean problems in the so-called front end — tie rods, steering box, bushings and so on.

When you complete the test drive, but before you shut off the engine, glance at the gauges and check that there's adequate oil pressure and that the water temperature isn't too high.

If the car passes your inspection, now you're ready to make arrangements with the seller to take the car to an independent mechanic for a compression check.

Additional Items to Check in a Used-Sports-Car Inspection

Item	What to check
Exhaust System	Note any excessive noise or any holes (you can see 'em if you look underneath the car) in mufflers.
Shock Absorbers	Give a hard push on each corner of the car. Good shocks won't let the car bounce more than a couple of times.
Tires	First note the type of tires (radial or bias). Make sure that all four match. Mixing radial and bias-ply tires can give the car dangerous handling characteristics. Then check for general wear and for any unusual wear patterns. Uneven front-tire wear indicates front-end alignment problems.
Windshield	Cracks or heavy pitting could disqualify the car in some state safety inspections.
Convertible Top	Check for general condition of both the fabric and rear window.
Wire Wheels	Note missing, bent or broken spokes.
Upholstery	Check for tears and missing stitching. Don't forget to check the headliner — it's expensive to replace.
Controls and Switches	Operate every switch, button and control. And don't overlook the horn and lights.
Chrome	Check for pitting and corrosion — rechroming parts is very expensive.
Air Conditioning and Heater	Check for proper operation.
Windows	Do they go up and down easily?
Rear End	A whine while under way, or a clunk when you accelerate could mean worn gears or U-joints.

Making the Decision

Definitely avoid a car that has:

• Ever had anything but minor surface rust, even if the rust was supposedly repaired (often unrepairable).

- Had extensive collision damage, especially if there's a possibility of frame distortion (often unrepairable).
- A paint color different from the original color ($2,000 and up to strip car and repaint).
- An engine that burns or leaks heavy amounts of oil ($1,500 and up to rebuild engine).

Think twice about a car that has:

- A transmission with inoperative gears ($500 and up).
- A differential that is extremely noisy ($500 and up).
- A worn clutch ($300 and up).
- Need of a new paint job ($500 and up for simple respray).
- Inoperative or badly malfunctioning brakes ($300 and up to overhaul entire system).
- Need of a new convertible top ($500 and up).
- Badly torn upholstery or headliner ($300 and up).

Don't pass up a car just because it has:

- Worn shock absorbers.
- Worn tires.
- Inoperative instruments.
- Parking-lot rash or a minor dent or two.
- Brakes that simply need relining.
- An engine that only needs a tune-up.
- Need of a new exhaust system.
- Need of minor front-end work.

Chapter Eight:

Getting the Most from Your Car

It was an awful feeling. Foot to the floor and hardly any brakes. There I was, a new guy in New York City with an old foreign car that wouldn't stop. It was a perfect setup for a classic Big Apple rip-off.

Fearing exorbitant labor rates at a midtown dealership, I called a business associate who tentatively suggested a small independent shop in Queens. I should have known better when I saw what was scattered around the place — bashed-up veterans of Manhattan traffic, old tires, worn-out mufflers, half-assembled engines.

I should certainly have known better when I saw that the shop owner looked like an escapee from the maximum-security section of Rikers Island. But at least some of the cars in the shop were imported. Besides, I couldn't drive around without brakes looking for an alternative.

Every few days I'd hear the same words over the telephone: "Bad news. I've fixed your rollerized muffler bearing, but your portoflan opening is clogged. I've ordered a new one, but it'll take ten days to get here and it costs $295. Parts are sure expensive."

Two months passed until the car was finished. It ran well enough, but the bill? About $500 less than I originally paid for the car!

A week later I heard a strange popping noise, so back again I went to the same mechanic. Shaking his head mournfully, he was certain the engine needed an $800 valve job and that I shouldn't drive another mile without one.

Well, I did, straight to an authorized dealer in Manhattan. At a cost of fifteen minutes and $15, the dealer's mechanic replaced a defective exhaust gasket.

Spotter's Guide to Repair Shops

My woeful tale brings to mind several musings about repair shops. Among them:

Recommendations for repair shops from friends or associates are often useful. But consider carefully the source. Have your friends had firsthand experience with the shop? How well do they understand cars? Maybe they've been bilked and don't know it.

An independent mechanic isn't always cheaper, especially if he's a crook. Most dealership service departments charge top dollar, but they're less likely to out-and-out swindle you. After all, dealers usually have a big investment in facilities, and would like your business in their new-car showrooms as well. So they have a lot more to lose than a fly-by-night independent. Moreover, dealers often have quicker access to spare parts.

A competent and honest independent, however, can usually charge less because his overhead is lower. He'll also offer more personalized service. In most dealerships, the customer must speak to a service manager and never sees the mechanic who does the work. Throwing a middleman in the process risks a communications breakdown. Moreover, many dealers won't service cars more than ten years old; independents often welcome them.

If you select an independent shop, make sure it specializes in servicing your make of car, not just any car that wanders in. A mechanic familiar with the common quirks of your particular kind of car won't waste his time or your money on needless mechanical forays. And like a dealer, a specialist is more likely to have on hand any parts your car may need.

Steer clear of a messy shop. Good workmanship and cleanliness are highly correlated. A little grit or a few metal filings down the cylinders of a freshly rebuilt engine will quickly ruin the job. The best repair shops are as orderly and spotless as the kitchen of a fine restaurant.

Making A Friend of Your Mechanic

For many people, a visit to an auto repair shop is filled with all the joy and excitement of going for a tax audit.

There are, however, ways to make the visit less expensive. Above all, it's important to have a good relationship with a mechanic.

It's not simply a question of labor rates and time. The neatly printed shop sign that says, "Our labor rate is $35 an hour" means virtually nothing. An efficient mechanic who charges $45 an hour and does a job in half an hour is better than a bumbling idiot who takes three times as long at $25 an hour.

Mechanics have other ways to line their pockets. A dishonest mechanic says a part needs to be replaced when it's in fine shape. He won't touch a thing, but will charge you as if he did. Or he may replace a nondefective part with a new one, and take a 100 percent to 500 percent markup on the price of the new part.

A slightly less dishonest mechanic will replace a defective part with an inferior part and charge you for a high-quality one. Or he can install a new part when it would have been cheaper for you if he repaired or rebuilt the old one. The list goes on.

A knowledgeable mechanic with your interest at heart will do the job right — and efficiently — the first time. He'll use high-quality parts and will charge a fair markup on them. If you're a good, steady customer, he may even attend to small things without charge. So it pays to be nice to your mechanic. Here are some tips on how to ingratiate yourself:

A good mechanic will have grease on his overalls and dirt under his fingernails, but don't treat him like a stupid dirt-ball. To repair complex modern automobiles, a mechanic must be an engineer, machinist and electronics expert. If he owns his own shop, he has to be a smart businessman as well.

Keep your car clean. Any mechanic would rather work on a clean machine than a grease bucket. If he has to do a lot of cleaning to perform a repair, expect him to charge you for it.

Follow a trusted mechanic's repair recommendations; it may be false economy not to. A good mechanic will spot potential problems before they occur — and before they leave you stranded in rush-hour traffic on a rainy night.

If you're not sure whether to trust a mechanic, ask to watch while he works on your car. Some repair shops have legitimate rules against this (there could be lawsuits if you trip over a wrench, etc.).

But you should at least expect him to explain the problem and show you the defective part, preferably while it's still on the car. Even if you wouldn't know a defective rollerized muffler bearing from a telephone pole, the mechanic won't know that you don't know. A good mechanic will appreciate your interest.

It's proper business practice to ask for a written estimate before any work is performed. In some states, the mechanic must give you one by law. If you're not sure about the shop and the estimate seems high, don't hesitate to get a second opinion.

Understand that a car isn't a light bulb and that it's not always a simple question of whether it works or not. Some automotive ailments are difficult to diagnose without looking inside and poking around. Don't automatically assume a rip-off if your mechanic calls you back to revise an estimate upwards.

When talking to a mechanic, be as specific as possible. "There's a high-pitched squeal between 50 and 60 mph that seems to come from the right rear wheel," is a lot more helpful than, "The wheel makes funny noises."

When you do find an honest, competent mechanic, let him know you appreciate his work. Pay your bill on time, and don't take advantage of him by asking for freebies. Buy him a Christmas present.

Just remember, a deft mechanic can make a mangy mutt of a car run like a greyhound, and at a reasonable price, too.

Miscellaneous Maintenance Tips

A car is only as good as the mechanic who works on it. I hasten to add, however, that the car's owner plays an important role as well. Your mechanic may carefully tune your engine, but it won't matter one bit if the engine fries itself because you failed to notice that the radiator was out of coolant.

Performing even the most routine maintenance chores on our cars seems to be an un-American act. The Automotive Information Council surveyed one hundred cars at self-service gas stations and found fifty-six were a quart low on oil, thirty-four needed radiator coolant, twenty-nine needed power steering fluid, twenty-eight needed brake fluid, and twenty-seven needed battery water. Sure, a mechanic is supposed to check these things during a routine service. But due to malfunctions or evaporation or even normal operation, fluid levels can become dangerously low.

Long ago Detroit recognized America's laziness when it comes to car maintenance and gave the public big, brawny iron V-8s that ran and ran despite considerable neglect. But when the Europeans and Japanese design cars, their objectives don't include engines that run without oil or water. Instead, they design small engines that deliver high performance and high fuel-economy. To accomplish this, they use lightweight materials like aluminum. And because aluminum expands and contracts more than steel or iron as the temperature changes, aluminum engines will routinely burn or leak a little oil. Moreover, it stands to reason that small engines will have to work harder (and hotter) than large engines.

These small, high-revving engines will enjoy long lives with just a little consideration from their owners. Unfortunately, the attitude tends to be "if I didn't have to check the oil in my Cadillac, why should I check it in my Jaguar?" If you share that mind-set, you'll spare yourself anguish and expense by sticking to Cadillacs.

It really doesn't take much effort to check oil and coolant levels every time you fill the gas tank. Nor is it difficult to check tire pressure. Besides the fact that proper tire pressure makes an enormous difference in handling characteristics (and good handling is one reason you buy an enthusiast car, right?), tire pressure eight or ten pounds too low can cut tire life by 25 percent and fuel economy by 3 percent. For less than $5, you can buy a tire pressure gauge in any auto supply store. Check the tire pressure before you've driven far, while the tires are cold — otherwise you may get an inaccurate reading.

If you live in Southern California as I do, changing your car's smog-eaten windshield-wiper blades is about all you need to do to prepare for winter driving. But if you live in a colder northern climate, it's especially important to look after your car's needs in the wintertime. Your car will present you with three challenges on cold winter days: starting the beast, stopping it, and keeping wear and tear on chilled machinery to a minimum.

We'll start with the battery (pun intended). Batteries, like many car parts, don't work as well when cold. If you doubt your battery's ability to hold a charge, your mechanic can quickly check its condition. If necessary, and for good winter-driving insurance, replace it with a battery with 20 percent more cold-cranking power than the one recommended.

Batteries have it easier if the rest of the electrical system is up to snuff. In wet weather, regardless of how cold it is, worn points in the distributor, corroded battery terminals, frayed wires and dirty spark plugs will make for hard starting. Have your mechanic check them all.

You may think oil has nothing to do with starting a car. But when temperatures drop, the wrong oil will sit in the crankcase like a glob of cold oatmeal. Then the starter is forced to drag the pistons and assorted machinery through the mush, draining the battery's energy.

So you want an oil that stays thin. A multiviscosity 5W / 30 oil is good for northern climates. The "W" stands for "winter," not "weight," and means the oil will remain at the indicated viscosity in subfreezing temperatures — that is, it won't turn to mush.

If you live in a truly inhospitable climate where temperatures regularly plunge to minus 20 degrees, you might try a synthetic oil like Mobil 1, though it's more expensive. In mild Southern California, a 10W / 30 or 10W / 40 oil is fine for winter. (More on selecting the right oil in the next section of this chapter.)

If a powerful battery, healthy electrical system and thin oil aren't enough to arouse your car from a deep winter's sleep, an auxiliary heater might help. Some keep the battery toasty, while others warm the oil or cooling-system liquid. Or try an electrical device that automatically starts the engine every few hours; it may be disconcerting to hear your car start by itself in the middle of the night, but it'll be ready to go in the morning.

If snow is on the ground, warm the engine for three or four minutes before you drive off. But in warmer weather, idling the engine merely wastes time and gasoline. Just avoid jumping on the accelerator for a few miles until oil and other fluids have had a chance to reach normal operating temperature.

Want a thrill? Try to stop your car on an icy road when the

brakes are frozen and the tires worn. All-season radials, as long as tread remains, are OK for occasional drives in the snow. But if snow-covered roads are the norm, you'll need a full set of radial snow tires. Just don't mix any radials with cheaper bias-ply tires or you'll get quirky handling, even on dry roads.

When brake fluid absorbs too much water and the temperature drops — *voila!* — frozen brakes. Change the fluid in autumn. Avoid using your parking brake in freezing weather; drum-type parking brakes often ice up. Park in gear instead.

Water often condenses in the gas tank and then contaminates the fuel system. To prevent condensation, keep the tank fairly full and add a can of "fuel-line antifreeze" every so often.

Add antifreeze / detergent to your windshield-washer container. Washers are especially useful to clean the mud and slush of winter roads.

No matter what climate you live in, drain your car's cooling system every other year. Then add a 50-50 mix of antifreeze and water. If your winters are very cold, make it a 70-30 mix. Antifreeze, of course, lowers the freezing temperature of the water in the cooling system, but it has other purposes as well. Many European and Japanese cars have aluminum components in their engines. Aluminum is more prone to corrode and dissolve than iron, and antifreeze prevents this corrosion. Moreover, antifreeze is important in summertime driving too; it acts as a "coolant" by raising the boiling point of the water in the cooling system.

Even in California we rarely use a car's air conditioner in the winter. But exercise it a few minutes each month so it's in good order when the weather turns warm again.

Selecting the Right Oil

Blake Morris is one of the country's better mechanics. He's not just a parts-changer; like an engineer, he knows the theory behind the machinery.

He also has a genuine affection for fine cars. And he's emphatic when he addresses the recent trend for automakers to increase the time between recommended servicings, especially oil changes.

"Look," he says, "I've been working on the same make of car for twenty years. The cars still use the same basic engine, a design that goes back to the mid-1950s. Yet the manufacturer's recommended oil-change intervals have increased from 2,500 miles to 7,500 miles. Sure, oils are better today, but the real reason for the increase is competitive pressure from other manufacturers who are doing the same thing."

As evidence of his belief in frequent oil changes, he takes me to a bench where an engine is spread out in a zillion pieces.

"This engine is from an Italian car, and Italian cars are supposed to fall apart just sitting in your driveway, right? Well, this engine is ten years old, has 150,000 miles on it, and, until now, hasn't had any major repair. I've serviced it since it was new and its owner was religious about changing the oil every 3,000 miles. See those bearings? They still have 25,000 miles left on them," he says.

Oil is as important to your car's well-being as blood is to your body's health. Without blood, you'd expire quite rapidly, and without oil, so would your car's engine.

True enough, electronic ignitions on new cars have eliminated the need for changing points, and unleaded gas keeps spark plugs lasting longer. But automotive technology hasn't advanced so far that oil can be neglected for 10,000 miles, or even 7,000 miles in most people's cars.

Serenely propelling your car along the road, your car's engine is a veritable melting pot of ingredients. There's electricity, gasoline, water, air, various kinds of metals and, of course, oil.

Now add the heat generated by the combustion process to all these, and you're going to get some interesting chemical reactions, not all of which are beneficial to your engine's long life.

For instance, a high-speed run across the Mojave Desert in August or pulling a trailer up a steep grade may cause the oil to oxidize and form sludge. On the other hand, if the oil doesn't get a chance to warm up at all, fuel and condensed water contaminating the oil won't evaporate, which in turn can lead to the formation of rust and acids. That's why short trips of less than ten or fifteen miles can be cruel punishment for your car.

Moisture, acid, sludge and crud all wind up in the oil where they are lamentably ill-suited to assist the oil in its primary duty of lubricating all those pieces of metal that rub and work against each other as the engine operates. These contaminants can act as abrasives that will accelerate the wear of components like bearings.

But, you ask, the oil filter will remove contaminants from the oil, so why not just change the filter and keep the oil? The answer has to do with additives.

Additives in your cornflakes or peanut butter may be worrisome. But in motor oil, they're great stuff. Oil refiners take a base stock of oil and then blend in exotic things like viscosity index improvers, anti-oxidants, detergents, anti-wear agents, pour-point depressants, rust inhibitors and anti-foam agents.

They markedly increase the effectiveness of the oil, but only for a time. If they're too old, they'll break down and may even contribute to harmful engine deposits. This is especially true for viscosity index improvers found in multigrade oils (like 10W / 40 or 10W / 30 oils).

So if you plan on keeping your car alive for a long time, change your car's oil every 3,000 or 4,000 miles.

And what kind of oil should you use? If you have no idea, you're not alone. General Motors recently quizzed several hundred car owners and found nearly 95 percent couldn't pick the appropriate engine oil for their car.

Nevertheless, a surprisingly large number of car owners are daring enough to try to select an oil rather than leave the choice to professional mechanics. Oil company surveys show that 70 percent of all engine oil is sold directly to car owners either adding to or changing their car's oil themselves.

How do all these folks decide which oil to use? Many buy whatever is cheapest — "Oil is oil," they say. Many look at the numbers on the top of the can and think that they indicate quality, especially if they show a wide range. That is, oil labeled "SAE 10W / 40" is perceived to be of higher quality than a "SAE 10W / 30" or a straight "SAE 30" oil.

Both groups are wrong. All oils aren't alike, and the numbers have little to do with quality. Actually the "SAE" is short for "Society of Automotive Engineers," and the numbers refer to how thick or thin the oil is, or, in a word, its viscosity. A thin oil has a low number and a thick oil a higher one.

Equating viscosity with quality is like saying the beverage with the highest alcohol content is the best drink. Indeed, if it's your intention to get smashed, it may be. But on other occasions, wine might be more appropriate than whiskey.

So, too, with engine oil. A thin oil improves starting in cold weather, lubrication when the engine is cold and, to a slight degree, fuel economy and power. A thicker oil gives better lubrication on hot days, with some sacrifice to starting and fuel economy. A multiviscosity oil, such as a 10W / 30 or a 10W / 40, has a multiple personality; in cold weather it acts like a thin oil and in hot weather it acts like a thick oil.

So if it's not viscosity, then what does determine oil quality? Additives — ranging from detergents to rust inhibitors. As an oversimplifyied rule: the higher the quality of the additives and the more artfully mixed they are for a given engine, the better the oil.

Fortunately the oil industry has come up with a code that indicates the strength of the additive package. In addition to the SAE viscosity numbers, you'll also find several letters on an oil can. An "S" signifies an oil for gasoline engines, and a "C" signifies one for diesel engines. Following the "S" you'll also find a letter grading system ranging from A to F, and following the "C", you'll see a letter ranging from A to D.

An SA oil is basically straight (without many additives) and isn't much good for anything more than lubricating the hinges on your screen door. An oil marked SF / CD is one with the highest grade and is suitable for both gasoline and diesel engines. Few oils carry both designations; Exxon's Uniflo and Valvoline's Turbo V are two that do.

Where does this leave you in your search for a proper engine oil? Oil companies, automakers and professional mechanics all agree that using a high-quality oil is important if you want long life from your engine. For most gasoline engines, an SE- or SF-rated oil will do just fine.

As for viscosity, your car's owner's manual is your best guide. For most cars with engines in good condition, a multiviscosity oil is the right choice for year-round use. Pick one with a fairly narrow range, like a 10W / 30 or 10W / 40; the wider range multi-viscosity oils like a 10W / 50 often contribute to harmful deposits of sludge in the engine if the oil isn't changed frequently.

However, if your old clunker leaks oil and your garage floor is beginning to look like an opportunity for OPEC, or if the car burns too much oil, a thick, single-viscosity oil (like a 30 or a 40) might slow down oil consumption until you can replace engine seals and rings.

Selecting the Right Gasoline

Hype about "Lead-Free Super," "Ultra-High Test Unleaded," "Extra-Mile Regular," "Leaded Regular," "Irregular Regular," etc., can make buying gasoline a befuddling experience.

Perhaps you feel like a recent cartoon character; faced with all the choices, the fellow tells the gas station attendant, "Just surprise me!"

Well, that approach may be tempting, but not wise. It can even be illegal. If your car, like most built after 1974, has a catalytic converter, you're required to use unleaded gas. Lead ruins a converter and your car then spews out unhealthy emissions.

Although your car may need unleaded gas, you still must decide whether to use regular-grade or pay several cents more per gallon for a premium-grade. Which brings us to the nitty-gritty of gasoline buying: octane and knocking.

A car's engine develops power because a mixture of gasoline and air is burned in the combustion chamber in each cylinder. This mixture is supposed to burn rapidly, but not too rapidly or you'll get an explosion in the combustion chamber.

The engine won't fly apart, but the explosion will set up a vibration, which you'll hear as a ringing or "knocking" sound, especially when you accelerate. Inside the engine, the effect is not unlike a hammer blow to the top of the piston.

After a lot of these blows, the piston can be damaged. Moreover, heavy knocking indicates the engine isn't running efficiently.

By matching an engine's octane requirement with a gasoline's octane rating, you'll get a nice, even burn of the air-gas mixture. Your engine's octane requirement is listed in the owner's manual, and a gasoline's octane rating will be posted on the pump.

Sounds easy enough. Unfortunately, you may run into problems.

There are three methods to measure octane: the Motor method, the Research method, and a combination of the two. In recent years, oil and auto companies have agreed to use the combination method, which is the measurement on the gas pump and in the owners' manuals of late-model cars.

Manuals for older cars may specify an octane according to the Research method, which is generally three to five numbers higher than the combination number. Using the combination method, regular-grade gasolines are rated in the high 80s and premium-grades in the low 90s. So if the manual says to use a 98- or 100-octane gas (Research method, or sometimes abbreviated RON for "Research Octane Number"), a gasoline with a pump-posted number of 92 or 93 should do nicely.

There's another snag: Octane requirements change over time. For the first 20,000 miles or so, as deposits build up in the engine, the requirement slowly increases. Then it remains constant until the 80,000 or 100,000 mile mark, when engine wear often decreases the octane requirement.

This means you may have to experiment. If your owner's manual recommends a regular grade, and the engine doesn't knock, stick with it. Buying a higher octane gas wastes money and won't make your car run better. But if you hear knocking or if your engine continues to run in a jerky fashion after you've switched off the ignition, try several brands of premium until you find one that cures the malady.

What about pre-1974 cars designed to run on leaded gas?

The U.S. Environmental Protection Agency has reduced the amount of lead allowed in a gallon of gasoline to a tiny fraction of what it was in the 1960s. The EPA would like to eliminate leaded gas altogether. The agency is worried about the health problems associated with air-borne lead and about the 12 percent of motorists who are ruining their cars' smog-control systems by illegally using cheaper leaded gas in cars designed for unleaded, thus creating additional air pollution.

Getting the lead out may be a good thing for public health, but some fear it means the early demise of millions of automobiles that need leaded fuel to run properly.

Why do some cars require leaded gas? First, lead is used to increase the octane of gasoline. Fortunately, adding methanol or olefins instead of lead will also increase octane. So switching to a high-octane unleaded gas solves that problem.

But lead also protects certain engine parts. Over time, lead deposits itself inside the engine and forms a cushion between the valves and valve seats in the combustion chamber.

Without lead, the constant opening and closing of the valves would wear away the valve seats so that the valves would never quite close. If pressure or "compression" created by the normal combustion process escapes past an unclosed valve, the engine loses power. Escaping pressure may also burn a hole in the valve.

Lead also forms a protective cushion in the valve guides. Without lead, the guides wear and the valves wobble as they open and close. Oil then slips down the guides into the combustion chamber, and you've got a smoking, oil-burning car.

But a coating of lead is harmful to the catalytic converter. Just a few tankfuls of leaded gas can render a catalytic converter useless.

When automakers began to equip cars with catalytic converters around 1975, the oil industry began to offer unleaded gas. At the same time, American automakers started to build engines with harder materials for the valve seats and guides to compensate for the lack of lead. Some American companies, including General Motors, used these harder materials as early as 1971.

American automakers usually use iron cylinder heads, which require tougher materials for valve seats and guides only if lead is unavailable. But many European cars were unaffected by the switch to unleaded fuel, since they use aluminum cylinder heads, which have always required special hardened valve seats and guides anyway.

The change to unleaded gas came nearly a decade ago, but some 30 million lead-hungry cars still roam the roads. Will the EPA's lead ban turn all these cars into automotive dinosaurs?

Research engineers with GM and Union Oil say in most cases the answer is no. There's already a lot of lead deposited in their engines. Even when the owners of these older cars run them on a diet of unleaded gas, they can still avoid serious valve wear as long as they don't run at high speeds or pull a heavily loaded trailer.

But what if you own a prized high-performance car with an iron cylinder head and don't want to take any chances? It would be a pity to turn a beautiful '65 Corvette Sting Ray into a barely usable museum piece simply because leaded fuel is unavailable.

Well, there is a fix; you'll have to remove the cylinder head and insert special hardened valve seats and guides. And on some of the pony cars profiled in Part Two with extremely high compression ratios of 11:1, you might have to make other engine modifications to lower compression a bit. But once these changes are made, your high-performance car will coexist with unleaded gas of the highest octane rating.

Preventing Rust

My friend was merrily bouncing along the potholed streets of Manhattan one afternoon when the seat in his ancient Volkswagen Beetle suddenly plunged through the floor.

Fortunately, he kept his composure and brought the car safely to the side of the road. It seems the poor Beetle's floorpan was so riddled with rust that it could support neither my friend nor his seat any longer.

Like the Beetle, most cars are primarily made of steel. Steel is an iron oxide that's been heated up, combined with carbon and then cooled. However, the iron in the steel doesn't particularly like its new incarnation; it would prefer to regress back to simple iron oxide — rust — by mating with some oxygen.

Whether or not this liason takes place in your car depends on five factors: the quality of the steel, the way the car was designed, the extent of the car's antirust protection, its exposure to moisture and salt as well as how clean you keep your car.

There's not much you can do about your car's design or about the type of steel used in its construction. Certain older Italian cars used an inferior Italian steel and would start rusting away even before they got off the boat. The Japanese automakers have often used a thin gauge of steel that rusts easily. And then there were certain Porsche and BMW models that had places in their bodies that trapped moisture and salt, causing these cars to rust rapidly.

You see, moisture is an excellent marriage broker (or in technical talk, "electrolyte") for oxygen and iron. And if you add a dash of salt, be it sprinkled on roads to melt snow, or airborne from the ocean, you get a super, fast-acting electrolyte.

The rust begins as a reddish brown haze on the surface of the steel. Then it works its way deeper, until a hole appears, or the metal becomes a soft mass waiting to crumble.

Serious rust is often a terminal sentence for a car. You can almost always rebuild an engine or pound out a crunched fender, but if there's no steel left, well, about the only thing to do is weld in new steel; an expensive and sometimes impossible task.

At the factory, automakers can provide some sort of barrier so the electrolyte won't reach the steel. Paint is such a barrier, but it dries out and chips rather easily. Coating the steel with zinc or some type of plasticized vinyl gives a longer-lived barrier.

But once again, you don't have much control over what is done at the factory. You can, however, have your car treated by a professional rustproofer.

One of the most respected firms in the business is Ziebart. At a Ziebart franchise, a petroleum-based substance is injected or sprayed into all the nooks and crannies and along all the surfaces underneath the car that are most exposed to moisture. This will typically cost between $250 and $300.

There are do-it-yourself rustproofing kits available, but as you might expect, they're usually not as effective as a professional job.

If you live by the sea or in an area where salt is used on winter roads, and if you care about your car, some kind of rustproofing treatment is almost an imperative. But there are other steps you can take to avoid rust as well.

A warm garage makes your car easier to start on cold mornings, but the heat combined with melting snow and salt trapped underneath your car speeds up the rusting process; to retard rust, it's better to leave your car in the cold.

Most important, wash your car regularly, especially inside the wheel wells and behind the lower portions of the car. Clean out any leaves or dirt that may be clogging drain holes in the bottom of the doors and under the hood and trunk. Try to wash your car in the morning so the heat of the day's sun can dry the car thoroughly.

Topside, a good wax job protects the paint and chrome. And be sure to use touch-up paint on any scratches or chips before rust starts to form. Keeping your car dry and clean is the best way to prevent it from turning into a rust bucket.

Detailing Your Car

When Golda Meir, Israel's former leader, was troubled, she'd sit at her kitchen table and vigorously polish her teakettle, seemingly wiping away her problems along with the utensil's grime. In a similar way, I find cleaning my car good therapy. There's something very satisfying about making its paint and chrome glisten. (Besides, I don't have a teakettle and its more constructive than kicking the dog.)

But in addition to working off nervous energy and having the pleasure of driving a shiny car, cleaning your car frequently gives you an opportunity to spot potential problems. As you wash and wax all the painted surfaces and chrome, and clean inside the interior, the trunk and the engine compartment, you'll become intimately acquainted with your car. Moreover, your clean car will also impress your mechanic; chances are he'll do a better job if he knows you're a fastidious owner.

Unlike so many of the new "plasticky" feeling cars automakers are building today, many of the cars in Part Two were built with high-quality paint, chrome and upholstery that respond to a little elbow grease in ways plastic and aluminum won't. Whether you're moisturizing the leather seats of a Jaguar, waxing the paint of a Mercedes or polishing the chrome wire wheels of an MGB, your strenuous efforts will be rewarded by considerable beauty.

Of course many car owners have the idea that cleaning their car is simply a matter of running it through the $2.50 automated car wash. In fact, frequent visitations to such establishments are the surest way to destroy a fine paint job. Harsh detergents and rough brushes strip away protective wax and put minute scratches in the paint.

Keeping a car cosmetically beautiful is actually quite a skill, one known as "detailing" in the automotive jargon. For the February 1984 issue of *Road & Track*, Assistant Engineering Editor Kim Reynolds asked professional auto-detailer Steve Marchese of Steve's Detailing in Newport Beach, California, for some of his advice and secrets. Marchese, by the way, has quite an ardent following. Twice a year, one fellow ships a Porsche to Marchese for detailing — from Hawaii! Another client has flown Marchese from Newport Beach to Detroit just to detail his Mercedes. Here's part of Kim's report:

Steve begins with the engine compartment. It's best to clean up this messy area first so that its grime doesn't dirty other areas later. Here, cleaning can be handled in several ways, but as a rule, the least extreme measure is best. Steve prefers to avoid steam cleaning because he thinks that steam can dry out gaskets, perhaps causing them to leak, and that steam pressure can work loose or corrode delicate electrical connections. Instead, he prefers spray-on liquid degreasers, which generally have a less destructive effect. Cleaning the top of the battery is best done with a cloth and degreaser instead of a brush to avoid scattering corrosive debris onto the body's paint work. For a nice, finished appearance, Steve wipes all the hoses down with ArmorAll and lightly sprays WD-40 on most of the visible metal surfaces.

The wheels can be similarly cleaned with mild products such as Formula 409, Fantastik and ArmorAll cleaner. Naval Jelly is useful on chrome wheels in very poor condition, but because of its strength, it should not be left on too long. Steve uses soft toothbrushes to get at the nooks and crannies, always careful not to scatter the cleaning agent. When all the grime is broken loose from the wheels, they're liberally rinsed with water.

Next comes the car's washing. The aim here is to remove whatever dirt or grime is present with the least wear to the paint. Steve explains that he tested several brands of soaps by using them to clean his contact lenses. His reasoning was that if the product left a film residue, this would be the best way to see it. The winner was Ivory Liquid soap. Steve adds that unless you intend to wax your car every time you wash it, the soap you use must be easy on the existing wax coat, and here again Ivory does an excellent job. When washing the painted surfaces care must be taken not to rub or apply pressure and to use a soft lamb's wool mit or terrycloth towel. A chamois should be avoided because it will pull wax from the body, which is counter-productive. When drying, use a soft, clean bath towel.

If the car is due for waxing, the previous steps are followed, but in addition Steve uses R-M 900 Pre-Kleano degreaser (available through distributors in most cities) to remove any road tar or tenacious old bugs. It's simple to use: just wipe it on with a clean terrycloth towel. In areas where wax buildup is thick, such as door and lid jams), a soft toothbrush and degreaser will do the trick, but avoid brushing surrounding areas that don't actually need it. A note to the impatient who may follow these suggestions: don't skip the first washing and head straight for the degreaser. It's very important to follow a two-step procedure of washing with a gentle soap first to remove all dirt before using a degreaser.

Steve then rubs out the paint to give it luster. I'd always thought that paint was rubbed-out because of oxidation damage (also true), and that it was my exhaustively applied wax finish that made things shiny. To my surprise, the wax is actually there to protect the shiny rub-out job. Steve warns against rubbing-out the paint yourself unless you're experienced at it or your car's paint job is such that you are willing to practice on it — particularly if you intend to use a buffing wheel. (Steve says it's really best to go to a professional detailer and inspect the cars, preferably black ones, he has already rubbed-out. If he is not highly skilled, you'll see the telltale swirls, especially in bright sunlight.) Before rubbing-out is done, all badges are removed to insure an even result. Steve uses Meguiar's rubbing compound: "If the rub-out job is done properly and with the right product, it returns oils to the paint that help keep it alive. Some compounds I've seen actually remove these oils, and that will shorten the paint's life." Steve regards a car's paint as a living chemical skin that needs an occasional feeding of oils and removal of oxidation via rubbing-out, plus a permeable wax cover through which it can breath.

Waxing follows, and here Steve also avoids the latest miracle products, favoring old-fashioned carnuba waxes: "Our techniques are laborious, but they get the finest results. Products that clean and wax at the same time are easier to use, but they're taxing to the paint. Philosophically, I believe each step — washing, rubbing-out and rewaxing — should be performed as independent steps by products suited to each." Thus carnuba wax. Several are very good, among them Pro, Harley's and Meguiar. Whatever the wax, it should be used sparingly, and applied to the center of the body panel you begin with (so that as it spreads, there's little to overflow into the panel's surrounding seams). Working in cool shade, with a circular motion spread the wax — avoid rubbing — using the applicator that usually comes with the product. Progress from one panel to the next until you're back where you started (it should take ten-to-fifteen minutes to get around the car) and immediately check that the wax residue is ready to be wiped off by running your finger over that panel. The wax should have lost its greasiness, but not be dry. In fact, leaving the wax to dry completely allows it to draw back from the paint some of those precious oils. (Whatever you do, don't let it sit in the sun.)

Removing the excess wax should be done in the same panel sequence, using a circular buffing motion with a big, clean, fluffy towel. As usual, avoid exerting any significant pressure.

A chrome cleaner is used on external bright work, and then ArmorAll is applied with a cloth to external rubber moldings, bump strips, bumper guards and the like.

Cosmetic attention to the interior and trunk begins with cleaning almost everything with ArmorAll's special cleaning solution. This includes use on some darker colored leather dashboards and seats, and all vinyl surfaces. On light colored leathers, Steve recommends saddle soap.

Generally, it's best not to steam clean the carpets because most are more delicate than the household varieties and may mat from moisture. It's better to vacuum them vigorously and lightly spray on ArmorAll cleaner, which can then be wiped off with a towel. Once the interior is clean, Steve protects all vinyl surfaces with ArmorAll, which is diluted 50 percent with water to reduce its glossiness.

Leather preservation techniques are akin to those for paint because regular cleaning and feeding are the basic principles. Steve divides leathers into two types: the first is common to BMW, Ferrari and Rolls-Royce. For these, Connolly's Hide Food is Steve's choice, and he prefers to work it into the leather by hand. Most other leathers (notably those perforated for ventilation) profit from massaging in Lexol, which is a liquid applied with a towel. Finding Lexol may be a challenge though; Steve often has to hunt through livestock supply stores for it (Lexol is used on saddles). As ArmorAll has some sealant characteristics, Steve doesn't recommend its use on leather.

Last, the windows are washed, not with cleaner, but with towels, hot water and lots of rubbing. All this fuss is worth it because a car's paint, leather, vinyl, rubber and chrome can be kept in first-class condition a lot longer than you might expect. Indeed, I asked Steve how long a good paint job should last: "The paint of a Mercedes-Benz, which is of very high quality, can still look fine after thirty years with our practices and the leather can look good even longer."

And once you've used Steve Marchese's detailing techniques as Kim has described them, consider investing in a good car cover. Covers basically keep dust off the car and prevent sunlight from fading the paint and cracking the upholstery. They're no good at keeping the car dry; in fact if water condenses under them, the covers will actually harm the paint. So buy a polyester-cotton blend that allows the cover the "breathe." Covers cost about $100.

PART TWO

Rationalizations, Justifications and Explanations

Some people think any old heap over ten years old that still runs is a "classic." A '58 Studebaker Lark was a dumb car in 1958 and is still a turkey today. Just because a car is old or different looking doesn't mean it's a classic.

On the other hand, serious automobile collectors and historians have very rigid and precise rules about which cars deserve to be called classics. In their eyes, few of the cars in this book will ever rate classic status alongside such true (and costly) classics as an SJ Duesenberg or an SSK Mercedes.

So by calling the cars profiled here classics, we acknowledge that we're playing fast and loose with the purists' rules. Perhaps we should call these cars "popular classics" or "affordable classics." Our point is: while the cars in this book are neither rare nor expensive compared to true classic cars, in the opinion of *Road & Track*'s editors each of them has some special quality that gives it lasting appeal to the driving enthusiast. In this sense these cars are classics.

As you peruse the following profiles, bear in mind that for the most part they are just as they appeared in *Road & Track* at one time or another during the past decade. So while the descriptions and facts concerning the cars remain the same, of course, a few of the people and places mentioned in the profiles might have changed.

However, all the prices in the profiles including the "typical asking prices" and repair costs have been updated to reflect 1986 prices.

We primarily based typical asking prices on cars in good to excellent condition as advertised in the *Los Angeles Times*. If you live in another part of the country, particularly in the snowbelt, you may find a wider range of prices than we've given for a car. That's because California cars don't often have serious rust problems. For example, we list Porsche 914/4s as selling in the $2,500 to $5,500 range. But a rusty Porsche 914/4 in New England might sell for only $1,500 while another New England 914/4 in perfect, rust-free condition might sell for $6,500 because unrusted cars are relatively rare in that part of the country.

Under the heading "Typical Asking Prices," you'll also find prices for a professional engine rebuild for each of the profiled cars. Of all the predictable repairs (rust or collision damage is unpredictable), an engine overhaul will be the most costly. The figures given are for a "normal" rebuild; that is, for an engine that is partly destroyed (one with a rod thrown through the crankcase, or one with frozen pistons because of severe overheating) will be higher. The price ranges listed are for parts and labor, the latter figured at about $35.00 an hour.

The cost of an engine overhaul provides you with a rough guide to the general maintenance cost of the car. Obviously, if the repair costs are high for an engine overhaul, you can expect lesser repairs — replacing a water pump or overhauling a transmission — to be relatively expensive as well.

The full-length profiles generally follow the same format. Each begins with a brief history and description of the model. That's followed by a section describing potential problem areas common to the particular car. In some cases, we quote the findings from *Road & Track*'s own reader surveys that we've conducted throughout the years. In other cases, the authors of the profiles have turned to knowledgeable mechanics or members of car clubs for this important information. The final section of each profile is the "Owner Impressions" or "Driving Impressions." Here we relate one owner's experience with the profiled car and try to describe the car's performance and handling characteristics relative to more modern cars and to current driving conditions. The "Short Takes" are abbreviated versions of the longer profiles but without the owner or driving impression.

— Peter Bohr

ITALY

Alfa Romeo 1600, 1750 and 2000

Spider, Sprint and GTV 1964-1974

These Italian sports cars offer driving pleasure and good value for money

by Peter Bohr

1967 Alfa Romeo Duetto

In the minds of automobile enthusiasts Alfa Romeo is a name synonymous with great sports and racing cars. Nostalgic car enthusiasts might recall Tazio Nuvolari's finest race in 1935, when he drove his 3.8-liter P3 Alfa to beat the mighty German teams on their fiercely nationalistic, Hitler-crazed home ground in the German Grand Prix. Jumping two decades, one could remember when, in 1950, the Alfa Romeo Type 158 Alfettas took six out of six Grand Prix victories in an astounding display of absolute superiority.

But do most Americans know Alfa Romeo because of the competitive feats of Alfa *piloti* like Fangio, Farina, Nuvolari and Varzi? Probably not. Instead it took a movie star, Dustin Hoffman, and a movie, "The Graduate," to drive Alfa Romeo into the consciousness of thousands of movie-going Americans. Mr. Hoffman's sleek conveyance was a 1967 Alfa Romeo Duetto. The Duetto was a perfect choice for a movie about romance. Alfa's competition history is certainly imbued with romance, but one need only remember that Alfa Romeo is Italian and therefore "undeniably a product of a poetic and romantic race," as we once commented in a road test.

The Models

The Sprint GT coupe was first shown at the 1963 Frankfurt auto show. This 2+2 coupe was the work of master Italian stylist Giugiaro while he worked for *carrozzeria* Bertone. It's one of the great designer's greatest designs, and even today has wide appeal, perhaps more than the car that succeeded it, the Alfetta GT.

The 1,570-cc Sprint GT came to the U.S. market in late 1964, replacing another car that had worn its years well, the Giulietta-Giulia Sprint coupe. The chassis was new too, being the revised and improved Type 105. Not until the Duetto came along in 1966, though, could this chassis be had in an open Alfa. The open car, designed by Pininfarina, is still sold new, though in modified form with its originally rounded "boat-tail" trunk lopped off into a square one.

In 1967 the Sprint GT coupe got an extra 3 bhp (going to 109 bhp net) and was redesignated the GTV, for *Gran Turisimo Veloce*. *Veloce* means "fast" in Italian and had been used traditionally to indicate a hotter engine in Alfas. Aside from a few interior changes — redesigned seats and a fake wood dash — the only difference was the slightly more powerful engine, which was used from the beginning in the Duetto.

1972 Alfa Romeo 2000 GTV

1971 Alfa Romeo 1750 Spider

Alfa seemed to be caught off guard by the first U.S. safety and emission regulations and didn't import any 1968 models. But in 1969 the company returned to our market with a full line of "1750" models (the 1750 moniker recalling an illustrious prewar Alfa of the same name). The 1750 cars were powered by a new 1,779-cc version of the old Alfa 4-cylinder, twin-overhead-camshaft engine, a design that dated back to the 1950s and the Giulietta series. Perhaps the year's delay in meeting the new government standards indicated Alfa's determination to "do it right," whereas other European marques had 1968 models with less than satisfactory emission-control systems. With the 1750s, Alfa introduced a mechanical fuel-injection system that was used exclusively in the American versions and gave impressive results.

Thus the GTV became the 1750 GTV in 1969. The Duetto's name was also changed, to the 1750 Spider Veloce. Both models got new dashboards (with genuine wood trim this time in the GTV) and new instruments. Both models also received revised suspensions, enlarged brakes, alternators in place of generators and sealed cooling systems. And the GTV once more got a new type of front seats.

Though we're concentrating on the coupe and convertible here, it's worth mentioning that Alfa always offered a sedan version. The sedan in the 1750 series was called the Berlina (which means "sedan" in Italian) and shared everything including the engine and suspension with the sportier models. These sports sedans are excellent buys in the used-car market (they're currently selling for $1,500-$3,000) if you're not put off by their rather dowdy styling.

Alfa missed the 1970 model year too, but returned again in 1971 with the same 1750 series. The major change came to the Spider; 1971 was the year in which its tail was chopped. For 1972, however, all three models got a full 2-liter engine plus minor styling, interior and mechanical revisions. The 2-liter cars, called the "2000" series, remained essentially unchanged until 1975 when the GTV and Berlina were dropped.

The Alfa Charm

The people at *Road & Track* have always regarded Alfa Romeos highly, even when Alfa's current models haven't been the most up-to-date cars around. Whatever their state of development Alfas are true sports cars, honest cars designed to give drivers a large measure of enjoyment and passengers a reasonable level of comfort. In an Alfa you get an engine with either Weber carburetors or the Spica fuel-injection mentioned earlier; all the models covered here have 5-speed gearboxes and disc brakes on all four wheels. The engine is of all-aluminum construction with iron cylinder sleeves; sodium-cooled valves minimize the chance of burning a valve and a finned aluminum oil pan helps keep the oil cool. (It's also quite vulnerable to damage from bad roads or parking abutments.)

Alfa is not a member of the independent-rear-suspension camp; all the models we're discussing here have live rear axles. But the lack of irs doesn't mean Alfa handling is mediocre: the live axle is controlled by a unique and expensive linkage and proves that it's there for sound engineering reasons, not low cost. The GTV's and Spider's rear axle, however, has very limited space to move up and down and the ride is a bit stiff, though nothing like an old MG or some other British roadster.

When the 1,799-cc engine was introduced, net power output went up to about 115 bhp, the wheels were widened an inch and changed from 15-inches to 14-inches diameter and the suspension was revised with softer front springs, a higher front roll center and a rear anti-roll bar. These suspension changes accomplished a lot, reducing what we had considered excessive understeer, and the reader should bear in mind that the 1.6-liter cars are going to have this extreme degree of understeer. If one finds this bothersome, it can be reduced by the addition of a rear anti-roll bar from the 1750 series, and if the car has ATE(not Dunlop) brakes the wider 14-inch wheels can be installed too.

Checking Out A Used Alfa

To set the record straight, an Alfa Romeo is no Ford or Chevrolet to maintain; it was designed and built on the assumption that the owner cares enough to look after the car. Consider too that these are sports cars and are thus likely to have been driven hard by their previous owners.

The fragile little Giuliettas of the 1950s were hardly models of reliability, but Alfas of recent vintage are durable machines when maintained properly. A high-mileage Alfa shouldn't necessarily be avoided if it has had a loving owner. Here are some things to look for:

That beautiful engine is mostly aluminum, so it expands and contracts considerably as it warms and cools. Consequently, quarter-size drops of oil can be expected to drip from it occasionally, particularly if it has a lot of miles on it. Likewise, a bit of smoke from the tailpipe on acceleration is nothing unusual for an Alfa. Large puddles of oil, though, mean seals need replacing and a lot of blue smoke probably means bad rings or bad valve guides. "The key to keeping an Alfa in top shape is oil," says Blake Morris, owner of JAFCO, an Alfa Romeo repair shop in Costa Mesa, California. "It should be at least a 40-weight oil (20W / 40 or 20W / 50 is good) and should be changed every 2,000-3,000 miles along with the filter." Blake says that oil pressure at cruising speed after the car is warm should be at least 55 psi and that a quart of oil burned every 800 miles is an acceptable level of consumption.

1972 Alfa Romeo Spider Interior

There's only one lubrication point on 1750s and 2000s and three on the 1600s. A complete 12,000-mile service at a dealer, including replacement (if necessary) costs about $350 these days. Valve adjustment is to be checked every 12,000 miles, but as with other dohc engines they rarely need attention. When they do, it's a major project.

An Alfa with between 50,000 and 75,000 mi. may be due for a cylinder-head rebuild, which takes about six to eight hours' labor and will cost about $450 including parts. A compression check to determine the condition of the valves should be done with the throttle wide open. Pistons, bearings and rings of a well-maintained Alfa will comfortably survive 100,000 miles or more before an overhaul is needed. But when the time comes, a complete overhaul costs about $2,500.

With the 1750s and 2000s, if the engine is hard to start or puts out a lot of black smoke (not blue, which indicates oil burning), or if the fuel-pressure warning light doesn't go out right after the ignition is switched on, there may be fuel-injection difficulties. Despite some Alfa owners' preference for the carburetors of earlier models, the Alfa's fuel-injection is remarkably trouble-free if the fuel filters are changed frequently and if the fuel-injection system is properly set up and tuned by a knowledgeable Alfa mechanic. A peculiarity of the system, however, is the failure of an odd device called the thermostatic actuator (which determines the fuel mixture) and the cold-start mechanism. If an Alfa won't start at all, that's often the problem. Disconnecting a little wire on top of the fuel-injection unit is all that's necessary to get the engine going (ask an Alfa mechanic to show you the wire). Some Alfa owners have installed a switch under the dash that by-passes the system.

The gearbox is paradoxical: mainly unbreakable but notorious for failure of the second-gear synchronizer. You can live with a weak synchro, of course, but it takes some of the fun out of driving and sooner or later you'd want to have the gear-box overhauled to correct it. The clutch is a potential problem area too. It takes a fair amount of clutch-slipping to get an Alfa going smoothly, and if the seller shows any signs of being a hard driver pay particular attention to it.

Alfas tend to run very cool, so those who live in warm climates needn't worry about overheating on hot days. But the engine with its combination of aluminum and steel components is particularly susceptible to galvanic action so it's imperative that antifreeze/coolant always be used in the cooling system; check with the seller about this. Otherwise, the only unusual problem with the basic engine is the frequent head-gasket failures on the 2000 models. There is, however, a permanent fix for the malady.

Of the models being discussed here, only the 2000 GTVs (and a few Berlinas) were available with factory air conditioning. Quite a number of 2000 GTVs had an aftermarket A/C installed by the dealers, but the much rarer factory-installed units are far superior because of their neater integration. Any Alfa mechanic can immediately tell the difference between the two.

Differentials, electrics, brakes and suspension shouldn't pose any particular problems. Nor is body rust a special concern with Alfas, although they will rust around door sills, rocker panels and in wheelwells just as most other cars will when they're driven where salt is used on roads.

An Alfa is a good car for the home mechanic, aside from the fuel-injection system of the 1750s and 2000s. Most of the mechanical components are accessible and the engine compart-ment is relatively uncluttered. And genuine Alfa Romeo parts, though expensive, are of high quality and in good supply from the U.S. distributor. Your proximity to a local dealer, however, is something to consider carefully, as ordering parts from a distant distributor could cause delays.

Driving Impressions

It always brightens my day to see an older car that has escaped the ravages of time through the care of a conscientious owner. Carl and Julie Masters are such owners and have such a car, a pristine 1967 Alfa Romeo 1600 Duetto. Their car wouldn't win a concours-sanitation contest; the young couple drive it nearly every day. Even so, it looks almost showroom-fresh.

Unlike many older sports cars that are in exceptionally nice condition, the Masters' Duetto has never been restored; it has been kept in original, beautiful condition through care and

Brief Specifications

	1964 Sprint GT	1966 Duetto	1967 GTV	1971 1750 Spider	1972 2000 GTV
Curb Weight, lb.	2200	2196	2230	2315	2325
Wheelbase, in.	93.0	88.6	93.0	88.6	92.5
Track, f / r	51.5 / 50.0	51.5 / 50.0	51.5 / 50.0	52.2 / 50.2	52.1 / 50.1
Length	161.0	167.3	161.0	161.2	161.0
Width	62.0	64.2	62.0	64.2	62.2
Height	52.0	50.8	52.0	50.8	51.8
Fuel Capacity (gal)	12.2	12.2	14.0	12.0	14.0
Engine type	dohc inline 4	dohc inline 4	dohc inline 4	dohc inline 4	dohc inline 4
Bore x stroke, mm	78.0 x 82.0	78.0 x 82.0	78.0 x 82.0	80.0 x 88.5	84.0 x 88.5
Displacement, cc	1570	1570	1570	1779	1962
Compression ratio	9.0:1	9.1:1	9.0:1	9.0:1	9.0:1
Horsepower, bhp @ rpm	106 @ 6000	109 @ 6000	109 @ 6000	115 @ 5500	129 @ 5800
Torque, lb-ft @ rpm	95 @ 3000	100 @ 2800	100 @ 2800	110 @ 2900	132 @ 3500
Transmission	5-sp all-synchro	5-sp all-synchro	5-sp all-synchro	5-sp all-synchro	5-sp all-synchro
Final Drive Ratio	4.56:1	4.56:1	4.56:1	4.56:1	4.56:1

Performance Data From Contemporary Tests

	1964 Sprint GT	1966 Duetto	1967 GTV	1971 1750 Spider	1972 2000 GTV
0-60 mph, sec.	10.6	11.3	10.5	9.9	9.6
0-100 mph, sec.	31.8	33.0	35.5	31.7	NA
Standing 1 / 4 mile, sec.	18.5	18.5	17.6	17.5	17.6
Average mpg	25	23	23	24	24
Road test date	12-64	9-66	7-67	3-71	7-72

Typical Asking Prices

1964-1974 Sprint, GTV, Duetto, Spider — $3,000-$6,000

Typical engine-rebuild price — $2,000-$3,000

elbow grease. Even the charcoal-gray paint, though beginning to show its age, is original — and Italian paint isn't known for its longevity.

Carl and Julie bought their car (Carl maintains it and Julie drives it) when it was a year old. Since new it has gathered 33,000 miles on the odometer and has had one major mechanical difficulty: a bad second-gear synchro, that old bugaboo of Alfas, necessitated a transmission overhaul. The cylinder head hasn't been off and the valves have been adjusted once. Carl says the two Weber carburetors keep their tune and other maintenance is strictly routine.

The Masterses generously lent us their Duetto for an afternoon so that we could experience a good example of the breed. This duetto was comfortable, quiet and refined enough to almost pass for a new car. The cockpit is wonderfully roomy; no claustrophobic little 2-seater here. The seats are excellent with the right amount of padding and a wide range of adjustment. As most Alfa enthusiasts will remember, our road tests have criticized the Duetto and the coupe for their driver seating positions, which put the steering wheel well forward and the pedals well back and thus require the arms to be straight-out if the driver is to have any support for his or her legs. I find this relationship accommodating to my lanky frame, but then I happen to own an Alfa.

Comprehensive instrumentation has always been an Alfa forte, and in the Duetto the instruments are all handsome and readable. The top, which we lowered on the warm, sunny day of our test drive also earns kudos: unfasten the latches, fold neatly and quickly away behind the seats, and let the sun shine in.

If you can accept the odd driving position, then only in handling does the Duetto of this vintage seem dated. Pushed very hard, it understeers strongly and one must "twitch" the front end with the steering in a fast corner to get decent adhesion out of it — vivid evidence of why Alfa made the changes with the 1750s. The positive side of this understeer is that an inexperienced driver may be protected from mistakes by it, although there's such a thing as going off the road nose-first too.

The willing Alfa engine only begins to feel strong above 3,000 rpm. Getting off the line, the Duetto is no dragstrip wonder, but once the revs are up, the engine is strong for 1,570 cc. At speed (such "speed" as one can drive today) there's a delightful but subdued exhaust note and wind noise stays to a minimum. Even with the top down Carl and I could easily converse about the car's virtues and vices.

Another of the Duetto's certain virtues is the 5-speed gearbox. Fifth is actually an overdrive, which makes the Duetto an excellent and economical highway cruiser — about 28 mpg on the highway, Carl says. The disc brakes perform their appointed task well and will quickly haul the Duetto down from rapid speeds.

There's no denying that the Duetto is a mechanical manifestation of the Italian character — it has spirit. Carl and Julie insist that they'll keep their spirited Italian forever, but if they ever decide to sell it, I'm sure there will be no lack of buyers.
                                             — *Peter Bohr (November 1974)*

GREAT BRITAIN

Austin-HealeySprite/MG Midget

1958-1975 **by Thos L. Bryant**

The Austin-Healey Sprite, announced in May 1958, was destined to be as successful in its own way as the larger Austin-Healey 100 and 3000.

In the flush of success with the Big Healeys, Donald Healey decided to produce a smaller, more economical sporting car in the least expensive price range. As with the Big Healey, he based the Sprite on an existing sedan, the Austin A35, from which he took the 948-cc, pushrod-operated valve 4-cylinder engine. This unit was slightly tuned for the Sprite with twin SU carburetors, special valve springs, improved exhaust valves and modified crankshaft bearings.

A 6-inch single dry-plate clutch connected the engine to a 4-speed manual gearbox with synchromesh on second, third and fourth. The rear axle ratio was 4.22:1.

The rack-and-pinion steering system went from lock to lock in just 2.3 turns, giving the car very quick steering that took some getting used to initially. In our first road test of a Sprite (August 1958) we said, "...in fact, the steering is nearly perfect for the purpose, and light and accurate besides."

The front suspension was also taken from the Austin A35 and consisted of lower A-arms and coil springs with lever-type hydraulic damper arms providing the upper suspension link. The rigid rear axle was located by quarter-elliptic springs and lever-type shocks. The Sprite came with 7-inch diameter drum brakes and 13 x 3-1/2-inch steel wheels. Cornering characteristics were close to neutral with a small amount of understeer at moderate speeds. It was very difficult to get the rear end to break loose, and when it did it could be controlled quite easily.

The Sprite's body was uniquely odd in appearance—so much so, in fact, that after awhile it began to look rather attractive! This apparent contradiction struck many of us in those early Sprite days because most of the motoring journals of the time had unkind remarks for the shape and design of the car. Soon, the bulging headlights and smiling grille were characterized as giving the Sprite a frog-like appearance and it became known as the "frog-eye" or Bugeye, Sprite.

The body of the car was a pressed steel shell and the entire front end was hinged at the cowl to give easy access to the engine, steering and front suspension. The rest of the Sprite was fairly neat and clean with a simple, slightly sloping rear deck

Good handling and simplified design characterize these inexpensive sports cars

1961 Austin-Healey "Bugeye" Sprite

unmarred by a trunk lid. Entry to the trunk was from within the car, and although the seatbacks were hinged to move forward, access to the luggage space was limited.

The original Sprite was a classic roadster with removable soft top and side curtains. It was reasonably roomy inside with more pedal and leg room than the MGA, but getting inside to make use of that room could be rather challenging, especially for a driver more than 5 feet 10 inches tall. The top came down far enough to restrict vision to the sides somewhat and rainy weather often pointed up a few places where the fit was not absolutely water tight. But then this was a sports car in the traditional sense of the word and comfort was of secondary or perhaps tertiary importance.

The Sprite carved a new niche for itself in the sports-car world, offering superior and economical performance for a price comparable to the least expensive sedans of the day. Almost immediately, Sprites began to appear at sports-car races all over the world and soon dominated H production racing in the U.S. Who could ever forget those days of the late 1950s and early 1960s when a swarm of the little cars would take off sounding for all the world like a horde of angry bees chasing a hive-robbing bear! Not only did club racers turn to the Sprite; such big names as Stirling Moss, Walt Hangsen, Bruce McLaren, Briggs Cunningham and others competed in work cars or the Sebring Sprites of John Sprinzel.

Sprite Mark II

Three years after the introduction of the original Sprite and some 49,000 cars later, the Mark II version was unveiled in May 1961. Gone were the frog eyes, replaced by conventionally located headlights in fixed fenders, along with a wider grille and a hood that opened without lifting the entire front body just like most other cars. The rear was also restyled with a trunk lid that opened from outside and a 12-inch cut in the back of the cockpit for luggage or a small child.

There were also changes to the engine, including an increase in the compression ratio from 8.3 to 9.0:1, larger throats in the SU carburetors, larger intake valves and a change in the exhaust-valve timing. The result was more power (50 vs 48 bhp) without loss of torque. The gearbox was also revised; the close-ratio gears used on the Sebring Sprites in competition and available as an option for a year or so were now standard in the new car.

To the avid Bugeye Sprite fanatic, the Mark II was an abomination. To the rest of the motoring enthusiast world, however, the new car was a definite improvement: "Of course, the new model may be accused of some minor loss of personality, but no one can deny that the Sprite II is better looking" (R&T, August 1961). The Mark II was also a more convenient car to live with because of its outside-opening trunk and better use of space. Road & Track concluded that the Mark II, like the original Sprite, "offers more fun per dollar than anything we

1963 Austin-Healey Sprite 1100

1967 MG Midget

have driven for a long time."

Only a month after the announcement of the Sprite II, the same car was brought out under the MG banner as the Midget. The only differences were in the nameplates and a few minor trim details; this practice was to continue until the eventual demise of the Sprite name in 1970, when the Midget continued on by itself.

Sprite 1100

Four-and-a-half years after the introduction of the Sprite, a new 1100 model was shown at the London Motor Show in October 1962. The new Sprite (and Midget) had been upgraded with an increase in engine displacement from 948 to 1,098 cc, which raised the horsepower rating from 50 to 55 at 5,500 rpm. The clutch diameter was increased by 1 inch, front brakes were now disc rather than drum, and reshaped seats plus the addition of carpeting helped to make the Sprite more comfortable.

The additional engine displacement was the result of an increase in bore (2.54 vs 2.48 inches) and a new, longer-stroke crankshaft very similar to the one used in the MG 1100 sedans. The displacement increase made the Sprite more pleasant to drive because of the extra torque available (61 lb-ft at 2,500 rpm compared with 52.5 at 2,750 in the Mark II).

Although the new seats were certainly more comfortable and the noise level had been reduced by the carpeting, the Sprite was still characterized by many of its original features: no wind-up windows, separate key and starter (the latter a pull cable rather than button), no door locks or outside door handles and no glovebox. The only lockable portion of the entire car was the trunk.

In terms of performance, the Sprite 1100 was a much better car. Top speed improved by only a few miles per hour, but the change in the torque characteristics offered top-gear hill climbing and easier passing than in previous Sprites. This new-found performance could be used with increased confidence as a result of the change to front disc brakes. The former drum brakes were marginal when the car was being driven near the limit. Handling was unaffected by any of these changes, and the Sprite (and Midget) was still one of the most responsive cars on the road.

Perhaps more amazing than anything else was the fact that the new Sprite buyer was still getting all of this for less than $2,000! In the period from May 1958 to October 1962, the Sprite's list price had only gone from $1,795 to $1,985. And *Road & Track* was still saying that this car offered more fun per dollar than any other even after four-and-a-half years.

Sprite Mark III

March 1964 brought the introduction of the Mark III Sprite (Mark II Midget which was one number behind), and this new model reflected the need to bring the Sprite up-to-date with the modern sports car. Major improvements included wind-up windows, swiveling vent wings, updated instrument panel and further improvements in interior trim.

The rear suspension came in for revision with a change from the quarter-elliptic springs to semi-elliptics to reduce the tricky oversteer inherent in the original design. There was also a minor improvement in engine performance (stepped up to 59 bhp) through improved manifolding and the use of the MG 1100 cylinder head.

Sprite Mark IV / Midget Mark III

Once again the London Motor Show was the arena for the display of the new Sprite / Midget, this time in 1966. The car now became a thoroughly modern sports car with a proper convertible top that could be raised and lowered without dismantling. Another engine transplant had taken place and the Sprite / Midget now had a 1,275-cc powerplant similar to that used in the Mini Cooper S but detuned from 75 bhp to 65. This detuning allowed lower production costs because a normal forged crankshaft could be used in place of the more expensive nitrided steel crank of the S for example, while still maintaining the Sprite's reputation for reliability and long life. The net increase of 6 bhp over the Mark III Sprite (Mark II Midget) was enough to make a surprising improvement in performance as the new Sprite / Midget would accelerate to 60 mph in 14.7 seconds versus 18.3 seconds for the previous model.

1959 Austin-Healey Sprite interior

The crisp handling that had always been a characteristic of Sprites remained, and there was still some roll oversteer built into the rear suspension that made the car great fun to drive sideways. The ride was a bit jouncy over uneven surfaces, but it was truly sporting in nature and aficionados of the breed didn't mind it at all and in fact felt (and still feel!) that it was necessary or you might as well have been driving a large sedan.

The Sprite / Midget cars remained little changed from this setup until 1975. Of course, the Sprite version was discontinued in 1970. The Midget continued without any drastic changes except for the addition of more and more emission controls and other government-required items such as the over-large bumpers, until the 1975 model which received the 1,493-cc Triumph Spitfire engine with slightly different exhaust manifolding. Emission controls had become so stringent that despite the increased displacement the engine was only capable of putting out 55.5 bhp at 5,000 rpm.

Car Selection Tips

As with most British sports cars of the time, the early Sprite / Midget is a remarkably sturdy and simple car. The engine and transmission having come from a sedan of some years' standing, they were time-tested and of proven reliability. The twin SU carburetors have a tendency to be touchy in adjustment so many times a car that does not seem to be working properly may just need a delicate hand applied to the carburetors. Also, the linkage runs right into the carburetor throat, and the opening can become worn, allowing air to seep in and upset the mixture. The use of some rubber grommets can cure this malady. One of the few weak spots in the engine is the center main bearing on the crankshaft. If it's at all suspect, replace it.

The early Sprite / Midgets have a non-synchromesh first gear. While the gearbox is sturdy, a heavy-handed driver can wreak damage on the unit, especially first, and it may be necessary to consider rebuilding it. On the other hand, we have been told by Sprite owners that they have put considerably more than 100,000 miles on their cars without the gearboxes showing signs of wear.

The potential buyer may be fortunate and find a car that has a number of holes drilled in the rocker panels and the bottom edge of the hood (Bugeye models). These are to permit water to drain out and prevent rusting. In any case, keep an eye out for rust.

Prices for used models vary from area to area of the country, but the Bugeye is rapidly approaching serious collector-car status, and the prices are beginning to reflect this.

The Sprite / Midget series of cars is perhaps one of the most logical ones for inclusion in our Used Car Classic series of reports. They are simple, relatively easy to maintain and, just as when they were new, return more driving fun per dollar than just about any sports car we can think of. If you are the proper size to fit inside one, you couldn't do much better.

Driving Impressions

Once again we find ourselves indebted to Ken Schwartz of the Long Beach (California) MG Club for leading us to a Used Car Classic owner who was willing to have us photograph and drive his car. Eddie Martinez runs a speedometer repair shop in Long Beach, owns two Bugeye Sprites and writes music and performs in musical productions. He is one of those rare persons who seems to enjoy life just a little more than the rest of us, and his Sprites provide him with a lot of enjoyment — and frustration, he adds.

Eddie has been a Sprite owner for twelve years, and both of his Bugeyes are 1959 vintage; both are painted bright yellow and both have received his personal attention in interior improvements. These include redoing the dash, adding a center console and installing a vinyl-covered plywood bulkhead between the seats and the trunk. Eddie claims this last item has cut down on the noise level considerably, and he is justifiably proud of his work.

To the accompanying snide comments and laughter of Eddie, I gingerly eased my portly 6-foot-2-inch bulk into his roadster. His second car had the hardtop on it and I wasn't even about to try getting into that one! Gad, but these are tiny little devils. I soon found that I was indeed in (no need for a seatbelt here as it would take more than a collision to pry me out) and that I could operate the pedals. I could not, however, put my left foot anyplace once I had activated the clutch and let it up, so I drove along holding it in the air just above the pedal. The controls fell readily to hand — there was no place else for them to fall — and with a turn of the key and a pull on the starter we were off.

Eddie mentioned to me as we were motoring along that I looked sort of funny in the car — I suppose he meant that I bore a strange resemblance to a trained circus bear driving a kiddy car — but I was undaunted, dividing my time between bending down to look through the windshield and craning upward to look over it. It was one of those magnificent California days after a rainstorm, with a freshness to the air we rarely enjoy. The wind was in my face and the exhaust was singing with a healthy note. "This is what it's all about," I told myself as my left leg began to cramp up from being suspended in air for half a mile.

The ride was sheer sports car delight — jouncy and stiff, giving the driver and passenger intimate knowledge of each and every surface irregularity along the way. At the same time, however, there is a feeling of maneuverability and control so that the bumps fade away, replaced by a fiendish desire to cut and slice through and around all those behemoths blocking the

Brief Specifications

	1958 Austin-Healey Sprite	1961 Austin-Healey Sprite II	1963 Austin-Healey Sprite 1100	1967 MG Midget III
Curb Weight, lb.	1460	1540	1560	1560
Wheelbase, in.	80.0	80.0	80.0	80.0
Track, f / r	45.4 / 44.8	45.8 / 44.8	47.2 / 45.0	46.3 / 44.8
Length	137.0	136.0	138.0	137.4
Width	54.0	54.0	54.0	56.5
Height	48.0	48.8	47.8	48.6
Fuel Capacity (gal)	6.0	7.2	7.2	7.5
Engine type	pushrod inline 4	pushrod inline 4	pushrod inline 4	pushrod inline 4
Bore x stroke, mm	63.0 x 76.2	63.0 x 76.2	64.5 x 83.8	70.6 x 81.3
Displacement, cc	948	948	1098	1275
Compression ratio	8.3:1	9.0:1	8.9:1	8.8:1
Bhp @ rpm, SAE gross	48 @ 5000	50 @ 5500	55 @ 5500	65 @ 6000
Torque @ rpm	52 @ 3300	52.5 @ 2750	61 @ 2500	72 @ 3000
Gearbox	4-speed, non-synch 1st gear	4-speed non-synch 1st gear	4-speed non-synch 1st gear	4-speed non-synch 1st gear
Final drive ratio	4.22:1	4.22:1	4.22:1	4.22:1

Performance Data From Contemporary Tests

0-60 mph, sec.	20.8	19.6	18.3	14.7
0-80 mph, sec.	35.5*	49.0	42.5	31.0
Standing 1 / 4 mile, sec.	21.8	21.5	20.9	19.9
Average mpg	34.0	34.0	33.0	24.0
Road test date	8-58	8-61	8-63	9-67

*0-70 mph

Typical Asking Prices

1958-1961 Austin-Healey Bugeye Sprite	$2,000-$4,500
1961-1975 Austin-Healey Sprite / MG Midget	$1,500-$3,000
Typical engine-rebuild price	$1,200-$1,800

way. The 948-cc inline 4-cylinder engine revs freely up to about
4,000 rpm and then begins to hint at a bit of strain. Eddie said
that the crankshaft in his car was beginning to make trouble, so
we didn't run the engine up to the 6,000-rpm limit. The handling is close to neutral and getting the tail to hang out takes a
definite effort. Once you do, it's very easily controlled — in fact,
you really have to work at it to get in over your head driving a
Sprite, which is why they have always been so outstanding for
the young sports-car enthusiast learning the ropes.

The Bugeye was once considered an unappealing design,
but I've never agreed with that — it's strange enough to have a
beauty all its own. The smiling front end, which teenage girls
tend to label "cute," is actually a grin with a touch of leer in it.
And that's precisely what driving the Sprite is like. It's not fast,
not terribly comfortable, not very refined. So why are all those
Sprite / Midget owners grinning? — *Thos L. Bryant (May 1976)*

Owner Impressions

Mike Griswold was getting married so I bought the Bugeye
Sprite from him for $400. Then Bill Holley and I nursed the car
from the wedding in Salt Lake City back to Madison, Wisconsin,
sleeping under the stars and occasionally in the rain, eating
cheap greaseburgers and only making it home because buried
behind a pile of recap carcasses at the Goodyear store in Cody,
Wyoming, was one dusty 5.20-13, which they sold to me for
cost.

Privation — it was a fitting introduction to my Sprite. That
car was an adventure from the first time Holley hit a pot hole in
Utah and we realized the right front shock was broken. That car
taught me to be a very good diagnostic mechanic.

Yet, I've never again gotten as much pure automotive joy as
I did from the Blue Bugeye. It was just me, my swimming trunks
and this car with the top and side curtains I could remove and
stow behind the seats in under 30 seconds. The early runs in
the cool, damp Wisconsin mornings with the wind knotting my
hair and fighting to get inside my nylon ski jacket are still very
alive in memory. It was a summer of cut-off Levis, cut-off sleev-
ed sweat shirts, white tennis shoes (no socks) and driving this
little British roller skate to Elkhart Lake, Meadowdale or the
USAC races at Milwaukee. The little bugger even crapped out
one night so I could forsake it for a blind date and meet the lady
who is now my wife.

Every reaction of that roadster was crisp and immediate —
a sudden sneeze could prompt a lane change. Best of all, the car
was joyfully simple, which is why they ruined it when they added roll-up windows and a fold-down top. Complication was the
very antithesis of the Sprite. Why must we reject simplicity and
call its complicated replacement "sophisticated"? The British, of
all people, should know better. I still look at Bugeyes lovingly
and occasionally think of buying another, this time in British
Racing Green, with wire wheels and a Nardi steering wheel.

— *John Lamm (May 1976)*

GREAT BRITAIN

Austin-Healeys: 100-4, 100-6, 3000

by Thos L. Bryant

1953-1967

Marvelous cars that changed the sports-car world

1960 Austin-Healey 3000

One could write reams about the history, charm and charisma of the Austin-Healey cars and their impact on the motoring enthusiast world. The Big Healeys (to distinguish them from the Sprite) were produced for some fifteen years and carved out a niche for themselves as the best-selling medium-size sports cars of their day.

The Healey was something of a natural progression for the American sports-car driver of the 1950s, who had started with an MG TC or TD and wanted to move up to a more powerful car. I remember this was the case with one of my brothers who owned a bright red, 1952 MG TD, which he rather generously shared with me. Eventually the red TD gave way to a jet black Austin-Healey 100-4, which seemed to our youthful eyes ever so much more rakish and befitting our dashing self-images.

The point is, the Austin-Healey was an important factor in the development of the sports-car movement in America, and it's a car that still has a surprising number of devotees years after its demise. *Road & Track* Contributing Editor Cyril Posthumus wrote about the Big Healeys in April 1972. "Incredibly rough and solid, yet handsome and amazingly cheap. In short, it was a lovable bastard." Posthumus was referring to the fact that the original Healeys had humble origins, using the Austin A90 4-cylinder engine mated to a 4-speed gearbox designed for a utility vehicle that had such a low first gear it was blocked off in the earliest cars.

The Austin-Healey 100 made its debut at the London Automobile Show in 1952 and was an immediate hit. Donald Healey and his son, Geoffrey, designed the car to be a lightweight, well-shaped automobile, using as many stock Austin components as possible to keep the cost down. The original A90 Austin engine was a 2,660-cc pushrod-operated-valve affair, which produced 90 bhp at 4,000 rpm. Coupled with the A90 4-speed gearbox, which had been slightly modified so that it could have a floor-mounted shift lever rather than one on the column, the combination gave the Healey an excellent power-to-weight relationship. The final drive ratio was 4.10:1, which further aided the acceleration but did little for high-speed cruising. Thus, a Laycock de Normanville overdrive unit was fitted.

The chassis was a relatively simple one with two main 3-inch square box-section frame rails with crossmembers that carried steel floor pressings. The front suspension consisted of coil springs and A-arms with lever-type shock absorbers. The rear suspension consisted of a rigid live axle suspended and located by leaf springs and lever shocks.

The 100-4 went into production at Longbridge in May 1953 and continued little changed until June 1955. In August of that year, improvements were made to the brakes and front springs, and the 4-speed BMC C-type gearbox was installed. Almost 15,000 100-4s were built between the start up and November 1956, including the relatively rare 100M (for LeMans) and very rare 100S (for Sebring) competition models.

The Sixes

In the late summer of 1956, the Austin-Healey 100-6 was born with the BMC C-series 2,639-cc engine. This new powerplant produced 102 bhp at 4,600 rpm, but this improvement in horsepower was pretty well eaten up by the increased weight of the new Healey. The cockpit had been enlarged at the expense of the trunk and two very small seats had been placed behind the front seats. There were minor revisions to the body, the wheelbase was slightly longer and the original fold-down windshield was replaced with a fixed one. The gearbox remained unchanged from the late 100-4s.

In 1957, modifications were made to the 6-cylinder engine in the form of a new 6-port head, aluminum alloy intake manifold, modified distributor and twin 1.75-in. SU HD6 carburetors. These changes brought the compression ratio up to 8.5:1 and the horsepower rose to 117 at 5000 rpm, giving the 100-6 a slightly quicker elapsed time for the quarter-mile run (18.1 vs 18.8 sec) and improved the top speed in overdrive from 103 to 111 mph.

While the bulk of 100-6 Healeys were of the new 4-seat configuration, the demand for a 2-seater was so strong that in June 1958 the factory began turning out 100-6s with only two seats. Again, almost 15,000 100-6 cars were produced, with more than

10,000 of them being 4-seaters. Production of the 100-6 ended in March 1959, and three months later the first of the 3000s emerged from the factory, which had by now been moved to Abingdon.

The Healey 3000

Some 42,000 Austin-Healey 3000s were built during the period from June 1959 to December 1967, when the famed marque came to an end. The 6-cylinder, C-series engine was bored and stroked to 2,912 cc, compression was raised to 9.0:1 and power went up to 124 bhp at 4,600 rpm. The 3000 also featured a larger diameter clutch, stronger cluster gears and the addition of Girling disc brakes. In appearance, the early 3000 was little changed from the 100-6, except for the flash on the grill and the 3000 insignia.

The 3000 Mark II was introduced in May 1961 and had three SU carburetors, a new camshaft and stronger valve springs, bringing the bhp figure up to 132 at 4,750 rpm. The new triple-carb arrangement provided more power, mostly in the top end, and slightly better fuel economy when properly tuned, and those last three words are important. Difficulties in maintaining the proper state of tune were so widespread that the 3-carburetor setup lasted less than a year, and in March 1962 a return was made to twin carburetors.

Several changes were made to the body. These included a fully convertible top (as opposed to a roadster with removable top), a wrap-around windshield, wind-up side windows in place of curtains and other refinements that moved the Healey away from its traditional sporty image and toward a more comfortable touring-car position. Performance did not deteriorate with the loss of the third carburetor and, in fact, the convertible became the fastest production Healey ever with a top speed of 117 mph and a quarter-mile time of 17.1 seconds.

Over the next five years, until the end of production in 1967, the Big Healeys were marked by modifications designed to make them well-fitted, pleasant GT cars. The horsepower climbed to 150 at 5,250 rpm, servo assist was added to the brake system and the interior was groomed with a wood veneer facia and lockable glovebox. The Austin-Healey was still marked by an abundance of smooth power and torque, along with a heavy feel to the handling that inspired confidence in the car's durability. The styling was timeless, one of the cleanest and best-looking sports cars ever. But the U.S. federal safety regulations were announced for January 1, 1968, and the factory decided that too many modifications would have to be made to meet them. After fifteen years and more than 70,000 cars, Austin-Healey became a marque of the past.

Buying a Used Healey

To many of us, buying a new sports or GT car may be financially difficult (if not impossible) or we may simply be caught up in a euphoria of nostalgia that tells us they just don't build them like they used to. Whatever the reason, great joy and exhilara-

1954 Austin-Healey 100-4

1963 Austin-Healey 3000

tion can result from owning a car such as the Austin-Healey. It's also prudent to point out that equally great frustration and despair can arise if the buyer makes an unfortunate choice.

For this portion of the report, we solicited the advice of David Ramstad of Everett, Washington, a Healey owner and active member of the Austin-Healey Club, Pacific Centre. Dave writes:

Thinking about adding an Austin-Healey to your stable? But hesitating because well-meaning-though-ignorant friends have done their best to divert you from the heartbreak of cranky old English sports cars? Did they hit you with dire warnings about those devilishly complicated SU carburetors or could it have been hideous word pictures of wire wheels flying off worn splines at speed? While some British sports cars may have earned such reputations (I love them all, regardless), I don't mind shouting that the Austin-Healey is not among them!

Now, let's go into the pleasant task of making a wise purchase. All the standard guidelines for choosing any used car apply and will not be dealt with at length here. Our main concern is things peculiar to the Austin-Healey.

Mechanicals

The powerplant, be it A90 4-cylinder or C-series 6, is a rugged, low-stressed, heavy cast-iron unit producing a considerable amount of torque at low speeds. These engines are noted for their reliability and long lives, quite lacking in major trauma. Unlike the highly tuned engines found in Alfas and Porsches, the Healey's engine almost never breaks, but simply increases its clearances with a corresponding increase in oil consumption over a comparatively long period of time. The engine is very easy to live with because of its ample power and infrequent mechanical needs and, happily, pollution control devices are absent because all Healeys were produced prior to 1968.

The prospective buyer should perform a compression check and if possible a full leak-down test to see if copious amounts of oil are coming from the lower rear of the engine. If so, this may indicate either a failure in the rear plate gasket or a crack in the rear main bearing area, among other less likely possibilities. If you are not planning to tear down the engine, you should avoid a car with this problem. The average, reasonably well-cared-for engine usually requires little more than a careful valve grind, piston-ring replacement and complete tune-up to put it back in the pink. With good lubrication practices, the lower ends of these engines seem to last forever.

The BMC C-type 4-speed gearbox fitted to all Big Healeys from August 1955 on can be a problem if found in a car once owned by an insensitive (read brutal) gear changer. First and second gears normally produce a distinct but not excessive whine, but the mauled gearbox will make obviously expensive noises (most often in first and reverse) and will usually exhibit slow or nonexistent synchromesh action. Because of the Healey's ample torque, synchromesh was never felt to be necessary in bottom gear. The Laycock de Normanville overdrive unit seldom suffers failure in its internals. Poor or no overdrive function is often cured by careful troubleshooting in the unit's electrical control system or by adjustments to the hydraulics. If questions remain after a test drive, consult local Healey enthusiasts, British car repair shops or the nearest Leyland dealer, in that order.

The Big Healey's rear axle is very strong and trouble free, seldom needing more than a seal replacement to cure a leak.

Body and Chassis

Enemy number one to the A-H semi-unit, aluminum and steel construction is rust. The buyer should carefully examine the lower 12 inches all around the car to determine the extent of deterioration. Lower fender to chassis joints (front and rear), rear fender lower cavity, lower door area and sills and lower flange of the trunk lid are the most common areas for rust. Cars in the north central and eastern U.S. and eastern Canada, where salt is used on winter roads, have usually suffered the most. Many Healeys show some minor, nonstructural rust, which can be easily repaired, but those cars with major rust in the inner body sills, outrigger beams and floor sections are to be avoided.

I should stress the Big Healey can be kept free of rust with some precautions. The car has few totally closed areas, and if water drains in doors, sills and convertible top channels (1963-67 cars) are kept open, and if accumulations of road dirt and salt are frequently flushed out of wheel wells and lower body areas, the Healey can be preserved intact for many years. Speaking of rust problems, a fast-moving item in the Healey world is the replacement fuel tank. The tank is in the trunk cavity and will occasionally have deteriorated to the point of seepage. Fortunately, replacements are available.

The substantial box-section chassis appears to be indestructible. This is not an illusion — terribly bent Healeys have been reconstructed because of the strength of the frame. However, carefully examine the forward and aft crossmembers. Lack of care when jacking up the car at these points (Healeys are never raised by their bumpers!) has led to serious bending or holes punched through the welded seam by a small but lethal jack pad. Using jacks with wide flat pads or a block of wood will prevent damage.

Healey front suspension and steering may exhibit considerable looseness. The cure here is to overhaul and rebush the lower A-arm pivot points and swivel pins, replace the tie-rod ends and adjust or overhaul the steering box. You should recognize that the Healey's cam-and-peg steering lacks the taut feel of rack-and-pinion, and Healeys always display a certain amount of play in the steering wheel.

Rear leaf springs occasionally turn up with broken leaves, in which case the car's attitude will take on a marked list. The four Armstrong lever-type shock absorbers will need to be replaced if leaking badly. Americans haven't seen a car in years that requires refilling the shocks; often a neglected Healey may

1965 Austin-Healey 3000 interior

simply be in need of shock fluid to restore its proper ride and handling. The price of replacement lever shocks has risen to the point where the cost of converting to tube-type shocks is justified. This requires the addition of mounting brackets to the chassis, and these are available along with the proper shocks from major Koni suppliers.

The Achilles heel of most wire-wheel-equipped sports cars is the splined hub on which the rear wheels are mounted and, of course, the wire wheels themselves. If you test drive a car that exhibits a momentary lag followed by a clunk from the rear when you engage the clutch, you face a large cash outlay to replace or remachine the splined rear hubs. There has been a love-hate relationship with wire wheels forever; their periodic maintenance is costly, and this situation is not helped by the fact that the noble profession of wheelwright is disappearing. Many owners do convert to stamped steel discs or cast alloy wheels. Few owners of traditional British sports cars can tolerate the accompanying character alteration, however. Talk around before committing your wobbly rims to the local wheel wizard because quality varies considerably.

Parts and Prices

What's the story concerning parts? Initially, as established dealer spares inventories shifted away from the Healey when it was discontinued, the situation looked quite bleak. Fortunately, circumstances began to turn around just a few years ago, and today there is no need to fear any serious shortage of general spare parts. With the Big Healey's emergence as a collectible car there has been a rise in small, specialized businesses in North America and Great Britain dealing in used, new-old stock or newly manufactured copies of obsolete parts. Simply combing the "Market Place" section of *Road & Track* will yield several firms offering extensive lists of spares. You must remember though, that Healeys are not Beetles or Impalas so you may have to do a certain amount of legwork. Considering the car has been out of production for years and compared to other sporting cars of recent decades, parts are surprisingly reasonable.

Conclusion

Undaunted by those who consider seekers of old British sports cars completely mad and equipped with the basic data necessary to distinguish a good prospect from a dog, the search for that fine old Austin-Healey can begin. At this point, a mighty plug for Healey clubs is in order. Far from being simply mutual admiration societies, these groups of true believers diligently pursue sources of spare parts, offer discounts to their members on various Healey-related merchandise and publish priceless technical and historical information. And that only accounts for half of their efforts. The number of club tours, regional meets and other happenings increases by the year.

Driving Impressions: Three Austin-Healeys

One of the pleasures of authoring a Used Car Classic is the opportunity to drive a good example of the car being covered. In this case, I had the fun of driving three Austin-Healeys at Orange County International Raceway one afternoon, thanks to the efforts of Don Mollett, President of the Austin-Healey Association of Southern California. Don brought his 1960 3000, which he bought in 1971 for a mere $300. It was in sad shape then, but Don has restored the car from the ground up. It is now a very good-looking car and is in good mechanical condition with the exception of the synchromesh.

In addition, two other members of the club brought their cars: a 1956 100-4 owned by Don Rould of Buena Park, California, and a 1967 3000 Mark III owned by Jim Whitehead of Fullerton, California. Rould is the second owner of his 100; he purchased it in 1959 and has kept it in excellent shape ever since. Whitehead bought his 3000 in 1972 and repainted and reupholstered the car, making it like new. All three owners were kind (and courageous) enough to allow me to drive their cars, and they all managed to hide their fears rather well.

I started out with Rould's black 1956 100, which brought back a flood of memories of my brother's Healey. The clutch is mechanical rather than hydraulic, requiring a deft touch. Once in motion, the gear change to second will produce a clunk if you're not careful, but this problem soon recedes as you drive along with the top down, the wind in your face (literally if you are my size and protrude above the windshield) and that great exhaust note ringing in your ears. The tailpipe exits the left side of the car, just behind the door and ahead of the rear wheel, so

Brief Specifications

	1954 100-4	1957 100-6	1959 3000	1963 MK II	1965 MK III
Curb Weight, lb.	2150	2480	2520	2530	2650
Wheelbase, in.	90.0	92.0	92.0	92.0	92.0
Track, f / r	48.8 / 50.0	48.8 / 50.0	48.8 / 50.0	48.8 / 50 / 0	48.8 / 50.0
Length	151.5	158.0	158.0	158.0	158.0
Width	60.0	60.5	60.5	60.5	60.5
Height	49.0	49.0	49.0	50.0	50.0
Fuel Capacity (gal)	14.4	14.4	14.4	14.4	14.4
Engine type	pushrod inline 4	pushrod inline 6	pushrod inline 6	pushrod inline 6	pushrod inline 6
Bore x stroke, in.	3.44 x 4.38	3.12 x 3.50	3.28 x 3.50	3.28 x 3.50	3.28 x 3.50
Displacement, cc	2660	2639	2912	2912	2912

Performance Data From Contemporary Tests

	1954 100-4	1957 100-6	1959 3000	1963 MK II	1965 MK III
0-60 mph, sec.	11.7	12.2	9.8	11.2	9.8
Standing 1 / 4 mile, sec.	17.9	18.2	17.1	17.6	17.4
Average mpg	23.5	20.0	20.0	18.5	18.5
Road test date	7-54	1-57	1-59	11-62	2-65

Typical Asking Prices

1956-1967 100-4, 100-6, 3000, 3000 MK II, 3000 MK III	$5,500-$11,000
Typical engine-rebuild price (all models)	$2,000-$3,000

you can listen to the exhaust note at all times!

I had remembered my youthful days at the wheel of the Healey as being filled with excitement at the relative power and performance of the 4-cylinder engine. I was happy to note my memory had not glamourized the effect and the power is really there. The brakes are not as efficient as we have come to expect with modern cars, but to hell with the brakes and press on regardless!

I rejoined the group and drove Mollett's 3000 next. The 6-cylinder engine has a more throaty rumble than the 4-cylinder engine in the 100, and Mollett's car has that peculiar Healey exhaust whine. Trying to keep in mind the marginal synchros, I sped off down the course, enjoying the power of the 6 and especially the low-end torque that allows it to pull smoothly from about 2,000 rpm up. The brakes felt somewhat better, and the handling was absolutely classic in the sports-car tradition, with slight understeer that changes to oversteer with heavy throttle application in a corner. The rigid rear axle produces some jumping on uneven surfaces and the ride is firm in the manner of sports cars of that day. None of these comments should detract from the fact that the car handles quite well, and

WEST GERMANY

BMW 1600 and 2002

1967-1976

From the very beginning, it was obvious that the cars of the BMW 1600/2002 series are exceptional sport sedans. In the first road test of the 1600 (May 1967), we talked about the car's "excellent handling and stability," and concluded, "At the risk of becoming tiresome, let us say just once more that the BMW 1600 is a great automobile at the price" (at the time, just a little more than $2,600 on the West Coast).

The 1600 was a pacesetter car for BMW, reviving the firm's flagging financial position and introducing significant numbers of Americans to the joys of the marque. The single-overhead-cam, 4-cylinder engine displaces 1,573 cc and is rated at 96 bhp at 5,800 rpm, with 91 lb-ft of torque at 3,000. Fuel delivery is by a single Solex downdraft carburetor. Our original road test described it as "one of the smoothest 4-cylinder engines we've encountered and there is just enough roar on acceleration to make it sound meaningful. It winds smoothly right through the rev range and is still pulling eagerly at the 6,000-rpm redline." We were also impressed with the appearance of the engine, appreciating its aluminum cam cover, clean castings of the head

They're great fun and good investments

by Thos L. Bryant

1968 BMW 2002

the ride is certainly pleasant enough.

Whitehead's 3000 Mark III is representative of the last year of the Big Healey. It has the comparatively luxurious features, such as the roll-up windows and walnut veneer facia of a modern sports or GT car and really does not seem dated much. There is plenty of power, but it seems to be slightly flatter than the earlier 3000. On the other hand, the servo-assisted disc brakes make themselves evident immediately and give the driver the secure feeling that he can use the power and still avoid unpleasantness. Another nice feature of the later Healey is that you don't get the constant flow of warm air on your feet that is noticeable with the earlier models. All in all, the Mark III compares quite favorably with most of the present sports and GT cars still on the market in looks, comfort and performance.

Driving those Austin-Healeys brought back a lot of memories and helped to bring into focus the meaning of being a car enthusiast — a small, open car with room for two persons, ample power and a feeling of freedom. These are cars for escaping everyday living and entering the fictional world of wine, women and song and a general state of excitement... if only for a few hours on a sunny afternoon. — *Thos L. Bryant (June 1976)*

---

and block and the obvious care taken in installation.

Just a year later (May 1968), we published a road test of the 2002, which was essentially the same car but with a 2-liter (1990-cc) engine. The 2002 was meant as a replacement for the 1600 TI — the dual carburetor, highly tuned version that boasted 118 bhp at 6,200 rpm. It seemed clear that BMW foresaw that the TI model was going to have difficulty conforming to the coming U.S. emission standards, but that the 2-liter engine from the 2000 TI sedan would fill the bill. Because the engine's exterior dimensions were virtually the same as those of the 1600 engine, there were no installation problems.

The 2002 was somewhat disappointing to our road testers of the day, who found it "...noisier and not much quicker than the 1600... usual BMW traits of quality, handling, ride... modern sports car performance for four passengers at a reasonable price." The 2002's performance was obviously affected by the air injection and carburetor / distributor changes needed to meet the new emission standards. Despite the larger engine, 0-60 mph acceleration was 11.3 seconds, compared to 11.6 seconds for the previous year's 1600. We did point out, however, that the 1600 with similar emission controls probably would not be that quick. Nevertheless, the initial 2002 did not gain the editors' nod over the 1600, and the road test report ended: "Our conclusion, then, is that the 1600 remains the best value in the BMW line." This judgment reflected the roughly $300 difference in price between the two at the time.

We didn't road test either model in 1970 (unbeknownst to us at the time, 1970 was the last year that the 1600 was sold in the U.S.), but in 1971 there was much to report. In our August issue we named the BMW 2002 the "best sedan in the world" in the $2,200-$4,000 price range. The description of the car that appeared in that article is worth repeating: "The BMW 2002 is not just a sedan for transportation but a car for the enthusiast who needs space for four people. A family sports car, you might say. And while the 2002 is not big on carrying capacity, it will carry a family if need be and when it's not busy with such mundane chores, it provides the driver with great motoring. Its 2-liter engine is torquey and smooth, if not quiet, its gearbox is a delight to operate, its suspension supple, yet competent, and its brakes reassuring. For a long time we've said that BMW has the best set of mechanicals in the world for a medium-price sports car, sitting right here in this upright sedan."

By October of that year, BMW had introduced the 2002tii version into the U.S. and that called for an examination. The tii was the high-performance 2002, with Kugelfischer mechanical fuel-injection instead of the single carburetor. The compression ratio was down to 9.0:1 compared to the 10.0:1 of the earlier 2002 but the tii did offer impressive horsepower and torque gains over the carbureted version: 140 bhp at 5,800 versus 113 at 5,800, and 145 lb-ft torque at 4,500 compared to 116 at 3,000. It was obvious, however, that the fuel-injected engine had to be wound up rather high to get the most out of its capabilities.

The fuel delivery system was not the only change, as the tii also was fitted with different gearbox ratios for the standard 4-speed as well as having a 5-speed transmission available as an option. The 4-speed's ratios were slightly taller than those of the normal 2002, as was the final drive (3.45:1 versus 3.64), making the tii a car more readily suited to high-speed cruising. The 5-speed model came with a 4.11:1 final drive.

The other differences also played a part in giving the tii a more sporting character: larger brakes, 1.4-inch greater track width with wider wheels (5.0 inch instead of 4-1/2 in.), Michelin XAS radial tires with an H speed rating in place of the S-rated tires, and slightly beefier chassis components.

In our performance testing of the fuel-injected 2002, we found that it was not significantly quicker to 60 mph or through the quarter mile than the normal model. The 0-60 time for the tii was 9.8 seconds and the quarter-mile was covered in 17.3 seconds at 78.5 mph — these times were 0.6 and 0.3 seconds quicker, respectively than for the carbureted 2002 of the day. The road testers reported that the tii used for that acceleration testing was not as thoroughly broken in as they would have liked, and mentioned too that there was "particular difficulty getting the 2002tii 'off the line' smoothly (BMW rear suspension always lets the wheels patter badly anyway) and when the wheels finally settled down the engine bogged."

The tii's handling garnered its share of praise in that road test. We gave high marks for the car's responsive engine, nice gearbox and good controls: "Then comes handling, and for a

1975 BMW 2002

1975 BMW 2002

rather tall sedan the 2002tii is quite good. Its steering seems somewhat lighter than previous 2002s we've driven, despite the new car's greater weight; it's still not the lightest thing going but is very precise and quite quick enough. The tii comes with anti-roll bars front and rear, which keep body roll down to a moderate level, and the wider track, wider wheels and slightly stiffer tires all conspire to make the tii significantly better-handling than a 2002."

Our next encounter with the 2002 occurred in May 1972, when we compared the tii version with the Alfa Romeo 1750 Berlina and the newly introduced Mazda RX-2. The test was designed to discover if the new Japanese sedan could compete with two of Europe's most successful sport sedans (we concluded it could). We were dismayed that price increases had shoved the small BMW sedan from $2,500 when introduced as the 1600 in 1967 to $3,803 for the 2002 and $4,360 for the tii version. Nonetheless, the BMW won the comparison test.

The 1972 emission regulations were tough on cars. The 1972 2002's compression ratio had fallen to 8.3:1 and the air pump for emission control was engendering backfiring on deceleration, exhaust back pressure and extreme underhood temperatures.

To help correct these problems, BMW adapted its trispherical turbulence-inducing combustion chamber, used in the 6-cylinder BMW engines, to the 2002's engine. "The chamber apparently gives good emission characteristics, power output and fuel economy," we noted in the January 1973 issue. "Our test car ran with practically no symptoms of lean carburetion and went as well as the 2002 we tested for our June 1968 issue."

In June 1974, the 2002tii was again in a comparison test — "Sports Cars Versus Sports Sedans" — as it went up against the Jensen-Healey. The report noted that the 2002, in carburetor and fuel injection models, received a face-lift that year, with a redesigned grille and new, larger taillights. Perhaps the most significant alterations to the 1974 2002, however, were the big ugly bumpers required by U.S. government standards. Although they were made of aluminum, they still added 9.5 inches to the car's overall length and more than 100 pounds — and BMW purists, of course, thought them unsightly, to say the least.

In its confrontation with the Jensen-Healey, the 2002tii got the nod in 0-60 mph acceleration (9.5 seconds compared to 9.7) but the British sports car won the quarter-mile with a time of 17.4 seconds at 81.0. On the winding road portion of the test, the Jensen-Healey "does have the greater capabilities," we concluded, although "the BMW is still highly satisfying and sporty to drive...."

It's interesting to me that perhaps the best summary of the 2002 came in the form of a eulogy when we presented the initial road test of its successor, the 320i, in the December 1976 *Road & Track*: "Despite a base price that had risen to more than

$6,500, the 2002 was a brisk seller even in its final days. It was out of date in some important areas, particularly ventilation, but its reputation for reliability combined with ride, sporty performance and handling were hard to beat. It was the ideal car for the practical enthusiast who refused to give up the joy of driving simply because his automotive requirements dictated room for more than two people and generous trunk."

Buying a Used BMW 1600 / 2002

One of our earliest Owner Survey reports featured the 1600 and 2002 (October 1969), and we received nearly 1,000 responses to our Used Car Classic Questionnaire (September 1979) from BMW owners, so we have a considerable amount of background information on choosing one of these cars.

First, from the Owner Survey report, there were two problem areas mentioned by more than 10 percent of the owners: clutch-throwout-bearing and emission-control-system ills. The clutch troubles were cited by 13 percent and usually required one or more replacements. The emission control complaints were mentioned by 17 percent of the 1968-69 model owners (the 1967 1600s had none) and generally dealt with poor driveability rather than actual failures, although the air pump's antibackfire "gulp" valve did fail on some cars.

Other problems listed in our Owner Survey included easily broken interior fittings — specifically window-winders — mentioned by 10 percent, while 8 percent reported failed door latches, and 7 percent listed problems with three items: speedometers, wiper motors and gearboxes (usually synchronizers). Problems with mufflers and the exhaust system were mentioned for every year from 1967 through 1975. In our 1979 questionnaire, overheating and radiator troubles were commented on by owners of 1600s and 2002s for each model year except 1973 and 1975-76.

Other problems that surfaced in our review of the Used Car Classic Questionnaires included front-end shimmy related to tie rods (1967 through 1971), gearbox output shaft and flange wear (1969, 1972 through 1975, with 1973 models seeming to suffer the most in this area) and cylinder-head leaks resulting from overheating and warpage of the aluminum head (1970 through 1972 models). Carburetion problems surfaced most commonly on 1971 through 1973 models, and again on 1975-76 2002s, probably reflecting driveability complaints related to emission standards.

In pointing out things to look for when buying a used 1600 or 2002, many owners cited rust around the front turn-signal housings, wheel wells, rocker panels, the rear shock towers and along the bottoms of the doors. Owners of early 1600s found the 6-volt electrical system a trial, and almost everyone was resigned to the gearbox synchros going bad, especially in first and second.

It may seem that I've listed more problem areas for BMWs than are common in other Used Car Classic articles, but I suspect we simply have more input from more owners than ever before. Most BMW drivers wrote glowing comments about the joys of their 1600 or 2002. The 1600 / 2002 has begun to assume cult-car status, as many BMW fans find the newer models are not perhaps as sporting, and because many enthusiasts have simply been priced out of the market for new BMWs. As one New York owner wrote on his questionnaire, "Please don't buy these cars! I need a lifetime supply and can't afford the new BMW junk." Or, in the words of an Orlando, Florida, owner: "Being an avid car enthusiast, I have owned and driven many diverse specimens and still consider the 2002 to be the greatest all-around car *ever*, and worthy of any necessary expense."

That brings up a final point about buying a used BMW 1600 or 2002. The price of parts is high and getting higher the longer the cars are out of production. Also, BMW specialists often charge relatively high labor prices for their expertise.

Driving Impressions

David Anderson is a Los Angeles attorney who is a BMW *aficionado* of the first order. He drives a 1972 2002tii that he bought new and on which he has rolled up 128,000 miles. He also owned a 1968 1600 that he bought used in 1969 and kept for ten years — clearly not a man given to changing cars willy-nilly. His 2002tii is what I think a Used Car Classic example should be: clean, well cared for, mechanically excellent and, most importantly, used daily for driving pleasure.

Anderson admits to driving his BMW quite hard: it's his belief that's what these cars are designed for, and it's the best way to enjoy them. His engine developed worn rocker shafts at 87,000 miles, so David had it rebuilt, blueprinted and balanced by Hyde Park BMW in Los Angeles just over 40,000 miles ago. Along with Koni shocks and adjustable anti-roll bars, at 105,000 miles he invested in a new set of springs and was impressed with how they restored the car's supple ride and good handling characteristics. He has also been running different distributor advance springs (either BMW 1600 or Corvette distributor springs, he says) and finds this modification improves performance and fuel economy. He also replaced the radiator core with an American-made one to give greater cooling capacity and prevent chronic overheating for which 1600s and 2002s are famous. He has also put in a Recaro seat at the driver's position, and runs Phoenix Stahlflex 205 / 60-13 tires on 6.0-inch alloy rims. Anderson feels the wider wheels and tires give his car extra bite in cornering and braking, and after driving the car I heartily agree. David also tipped me off that there is an aluminum disc in the front shock towers of 1974 through 1976 2002s to raise the front end in compliance with U.S. bumper height rules. Removing those discs, Anderson says, results in better handling.

Anderson's 2002tii is an exciting car to drive. It has the taut feel of a well-made, well-maintained car, and the engine and chassis are both first-class in response. The engine revs freely right up to (and through) the 6,500-rpm redline without missing a beat. The acceleration is not blindingly quick but the 2002tii is no slouch getting up to speed. David's car, like many 1600s and 2002s, suffers from bad gearbox synchros, especially noticeable in making the first / second shift. But, as he says, there's really no known cure for this that will last any length of time. You can redo the gears, but it doesn't take very long for them to go bad again, so you simply learn to live with this condition. Other than the synchros, however, the gearbox is a delight to use and has a strong, positive feel.

The handling is stimulating and made me want to press on with more and more daring. The 2002tii is a car that feels comfortable right from the start, and I didn't have any sensation of needing time to get used to any idiosyncrasies beyond the characteristic oversteer when the car nears its limits. David's wheel / tire combination seems a perfect choice to me, as driving at speed down a winding lane with a touch of water and sand here and there was a lark, with the speed limited only by body roll (not inordinate) and common sense.

David Anderson's philosophy about his 2002tii is that it's a car built to offer maximum driving pleasure. He believes that it's a car that requires the finest maintenance and he's quite fastidious about it. He admits that it isn't an inexpensive car to keep in tip-top shape, but it gives him so much driving fun that it's worth it. Also he can't think of a new car that offers near the pleasure he derives from his 2002tii. That's understandable — it is an exceptional automobile.   — *Thos L. Bryant (March 1981)*

Brief Specifications

	1967 1600	1968 2002	1971 2002tii	1974 2002tii
Curb Weight, lb.	2050	2210	2310	2410
Wheelbase, in.	98.4	98.4	98.4	98.4
Track, f / r	52.4 / 52.4	52.4 / 52.4	53.8 / 53.8	53.8 / 53.8
Length	164.5	166.5	166.5	176.0
Width	62.6	62.6	62.6	62.6
Height	54.0	54.0	55.5	55.5
Engine type	sohc inline 4	sohc inline 4	sohc inline 4	sohc inline 4
Bore x stroke, in.	3.30 x 2.79	3.50 x 3.15	3.50 x 3.15	3.50 x 3.15
Displacement, cc	1573	1990	1990	1990
Horsepower, bhp @ rpm	96 @ 5800	113 @ 5800	140 @ 5800	125 @ 4000
Torque, lb-ft @ rpm	91 @ 3000	116 @ 3000	145 @ 4500	127 @ 4000

Performance Data From Contemporary Tests

0-60 mph, sec.	11.6	11.3	9.8	9.5
Standing 1 / 4 mile, sec.	18.2	17.9	17.3	17.7
Average mpg	25.0	22-27	22.7	23.5
Road test date	5-67	5-68	10-71	6-74

Typical Asking Prices

1967-1976 1600, 2002, 2002tii	$2,000-$6,500
Typical engine-rebuild price (all models)	$2,000-$2,500

WEST GERMANY

BMW 6-Cylinder Sedans

1969-1976

1971 BMW Bavaria

*A bargain-hunter's
guide to the 2500, 2800,
3.0 and Bavaria*

by Peter Bohr

1971 BMW Bavaria

During the past decade as the BMW marque made its rapid ascent from relative obscurity to status symbol, the Bavaria and its various permutations, including the 2500, 2800, 3.0S and 3.0Si, seem to have fallen between the cracks of the used-car market. As a cult develops around the 2002, as automotive connoisseurs acknowledge the 2800/3.0CS coupes to be up-and-coming classics, and as preppy girls beg their daddies to buy them 320is, prices for these models remain strong. But the poor Bavaria, etc., languish at bargain-basement prices, which is wonderful news for driving enthusiasts with limited budgets.

Evolution of the Sixes

While it's true that the 1600/2002 established BMW in America, the early 6-cylinder sedans were an important benchmark in BMW's history as well. These cars showed the world that the pipsqueak car company on Mercedes' home ground was determined to become a grand marque too.

A pipsqueak car company? That might come as a shock to Americans who speak of BMW in the same breath as Rolex, Tiffany, Polo and other labels imbued with great cachet. But just twenty-five years ago, BMW was so weak and vulnerable that American Motors flirted with the notion of buying it out.

However, in 1961 BMW staved off financial ruin and remained independent by unveiling a sensible but technically advanced family car, something altogether different from the ungainly V-8 sedans (the "Baroque Angels") and the comical Isetta (the "Bubblecars") that BMW had built during the 1950s. The new car, called the 1500, was not only the marketing success that BMW so desperately needed, but also the direct forerunner of all the models that came later and filled the company's coffers with cash.

One of these was a smaller, lighter version of the 1500, the 1600 introduced in 1966. Of course, we all know the story: American enthusiasts fell in love with this sports car disguised as a boxy sedan. When Max Hoffman, the U.S. BMW importer, talked the factory into putting a larger 2.0-liter engine in the 1600 body, the enthusiasts' passion for BMW intensified.

By the late 1960s, BMW was financially sound. But in America, at least, the virtues of BMW cars were still primarily known only to enthusiasts. If you asked the average American of the time about a BMW, he was likely to think it was made by the "British Motor Works" or some such thing.

Not content to rest in its cozy but narrow marketing niche

as a producer of little sports sedans, the company expanded its line in 1968 with a group of new luxury models, two 6-cylinder sedans and a fancy 6-cylinder coupe. This was a gutsy move, for BMW was now trying to encroach on Mercedes territory as a maker of pricey, high-quality, high-performance sedans.

The two 4-door cars, called the 2500 and 2800, are nearly identical except for engine displacement and trim. They both have many of the styling cues that had come to be BMW trademarks since the 1500: a low beltline, a tall greenhouse, a relatively flat hood and trunk, a continuous fenderline and the completely distinctive grille.

Perhaps the most brilliant features of the 2500 and 2800 are their 6-cylinder engines, with displacement of 2,494 cc and 2,788 cc, respectively. It was another of Alex von Falkenhausen's masterpieces. Von Falkenhausen directed BMW's racing activities before World War II and had designed the 4-cylinder engine and its variations for the 1500, 1600 and 2002. Like the 4-cylinder engines, the 6-cylinder had a cast-iron block and an aluminum cylinder head with an overhead cam. But it had another feature as well, a trispherical turbulence-inducing combustion chamber, with the delightfully difficult-to-pronounce German name of *Dreikugelwirbelwannenbrennraum*.

The idea of the new chamber was efficiency. It allowed more complete burning of the air / fuel mixture with a minimum of residual hydrocarbons, and in the late 1960s, as U.S. emissions regulations came into effect, that was a major concern. Von Falkenhausen's engine was clean enough that it didn't require an air pump in the U.S.

Road & Track's road testers called the engine a "jewel... with a sporting exhaust note... and practically no underhood noise." We added, "at low speeds it belies its modest displacement with surprisingly generous torque and flexibility." We went on to proclaim the engine the best inline 6-cylinder unit in the world.

The buyer of a 2500 or 2800 had the choice of a 4-speed manual transmission or a ZF 3-speed automatic. *Road & Track*'s road testers had praise for the crisp 4-speed, but as for the automatic, the testers minced no words: "the worst we've encountered in any car." Oh, dear.

Well, at least the other important components are up to the standards of the marvelous engine. The suspension is independent at all four corners with MacPherson struts up front and semi-trailing arms in the rear, an arrangement very similar to the 1500, 1600 and 2002. It gives an excellent ride over rough surfaces, with generally neutral handling. The 2800 also came with a limited-slip differential and a novel Boge Nivomat automatic load-leveling device as standard equipment.

Both sedans have 4-wheel ATE disc brakes. Oddly enough, the more sporting 2800CS coupe has discs only in front with drum brakes in the rear. So, in this respect, the 2500 / 2800 sedans are more advanced.

The simple instrument panel, which contains very legible round dials with black-and-white facings, is exactly as an instrument panel should be: no digital displays or video-game gizmos here, thank goodness.

In fact, the whole interior is utterly functional. There's room enough to carry five people quite comfortably, and ingress and egress are very easy. The trunk is huge, and with all the glass, outward vision is outstanding. Yet, there's simple elegance inside, with high quality fittings and materials, including the leather upholstery that came as standard equipment on the 2800.

All the 6-cylinder cars first appeared in this country as 1969 models. The 2500 listed for $5,367, while the 2800 went for $6,369. Five or six grand isn't much today, but back then it was not an inconsiderable sum — a 1969 2002 was only $3,053. When you consider that upstart BMW was competing against well-established Mercedes-Benz for big-buck import car buyers, in retrospect it's not surprising that sales of the 2500 and 2800 were less than robust.

But Max Hoffman came up with a clever marketing plan. He suggested that the two models be combined into one called the Bavaria. The car appeared in 1971 and was actually a 2800 minus the leather upholstery and Nivomat rear suspension. A few items that had been standard on the 2800, such as the heated rear window and the handsome tool kit attached to the underside of the trunk lid, were made optional.

However, the Bavaria's most important feature was a lower price tag. At less than $5,000 — $4,987 east coast point of entry (POE) — the car suddenly became a bargain. The name, too, was clever strategy because it reinforced the Bavaria's Teutonic origin.

It worked splendidly and sales firmed up. In 1972 BMW increased engine displacement to an even 3.0 liters and decreased compression so the car could use regular gasoline. But the Bavaria name remained. That year BMW also switched from the miserable ZF automatic to a more acceptable Borg-Warner unit.

Then in 1973, BMW resurrected the idea of having two 6-cylinder 4-door models, and added the 3.0S, a car identical to the Bavaria but with every conceivable option, from leather and air conditioning to power-assisted steering and stereo.

The same two models were offered in 1974, but by that time the Bavaria's base price had nearly doubled to $10,000 — in just three years. The 1974 cars also received simple but not very well integrated 5-mph bumpers.

In the following year, the Bavaria nameplate was dropped. But it lived on through 1976 in the form of the 3.0Si, which was the old loaded-up Bavaria with the addition of Bosch electronic fuel injection instead of the previous twin carburetors. In fact, the 3.0Si and the new 530i shared the same engine. When emissions standards tightened in 1975, BMW chose to use thermal reactors, unlike most manufacturers who went with catalytic converters. Thus, these Bimmers are some of the few 1975 and 1976 cars that can use leaded gas.

1971 BMW Bavaria interior

So which model of the series should you select? Among BMW aficionados, there doesn't seem to be much consensus. The 2800 and the 3.0S/Si have fancier interiors with lovely leather upholstery, but the 3.0Si also has the ugly "rubber baby-buggy" bumpers. And the 3.0Si's thermal reactors have proven troublesome. On the other hand, the 3.0Si's fuel injection gives better performance than the earlier carbureted cars. Fuel economy steadily declined over the years as emission standards stiffened. However, the post-1971 models can get by on cheaper, regular gas. There are plenty of tradeoffs, to be sure, but as in most used-car purchases, what counts is finding a car that's had a life of tender loving care.

Problems, Problems — and Solutions

When the BMW engineers designed their cars in the 1960s and 1970s, apparently they had in mind cool breezes wafting through Bavarian forests, not the sizzling summertime temperatures of the U.S. Both the 2002 series and the early 6-cylinder cars are notorious for bursting radiator hoses and boiling coolant. Not only is such overheating annoying — who needs Old Faithful under the hood when you're creeping through rush-hour traffic? — but the aluminum heads of a BMW are extremely susceptible to warpage, and that means blown head gaskets and other expensive maladies.

Because overheating is so pervasive among these BMWs, owners have come up with a roster of cures. First is modification of the radiator. There are two ways to accomplish this. You can have the radiator recored with a thicker core, but there's a hitch: With less than an inch of clearance between the fan and the stock radiator, a thicker core, a worn engine mount, a quick stop and — bingo! — the fan grinds itself up in the radiator.

Another, safer solution is to recore the old radiator entirely with a so-called "optimum core" unit. Eskimo makes one for these 6-cylinder BMWs that costs about $200. The radiator isn't any thicker, but it does contain more tubes per square inch, which effectively increases the cooling area.

Roger Moon, chairman of the board of the BMW Automobile Club of America, suggests removing the regular engine-driven fan and replacing it with two electric "pancake" fans. Both of them can be mounted behind the radiator, one in the upper left corner and one in the lower right. This modification will also cost around $200.

Locking up the temperature-controlled fan clutch is yet another trick that might help; the fan then spins continuously. Of course, it's important to remember that we're discussing 10- and 15-year-old cars with cooling systems that may be filled with rust and built-up crud. So regular radiator flushing and the use of a 50/50 mixture of coolant and water are important maintenance procedures with these BMWs.

Cracked cylinder heads are also heat-related problems. Though many early 6-cylinder BMWs developed cracked heads sooner or later, the 3.0Sis are especially plagued because of the enormous heat generated by the twin thermal reactors (at night you can see them glowing red-hot). The primary symptom is a cloud of steam from the exhaust pipe and rough running at start up. Substituting a 1980 or later cylinder head with revised water jackets is the cure.

The stainless-steel reactors are troublesome too, and expensive to replace — about $1,200 for the pair. Baffles inside the reactors break and block the flow of exhaust gases. Heat shields around the reactors frequently crack and cause vibrations.

In an *Road & Track* Owner Survey of the early 6-cylinder cars, published in the July 1973 issue, we discovered that water pumps fail on a regular basis at about 40,000 miles. Fortunately at about $40, they're not too expensive. We also found considerable dissatisfaction with the performance of the air conditioners: "It's paradoxical that even such expensive cars don't have air conditioners that can match a Chevrolet's."

Ranking right up there on the gripe list with the cooling system is carburetion. The carbureted 6-cylinder cars use twin Solex/Zenith carbs, which are difficult to maintain. And even when set up properly, they're cursed for their stumbling and hesitation upon acceleration, particularly when the engine is cold, and for surging and flat spots at moderate speeds. Many owners of 6-cylinder BMWs have switched to Weber carbs, and they're glad they did. This kind of modification poses sticky questions for owners who live in states with stringent emission-control-device inspections (like California) where nonoriginal equipment is grounds for a failure. However, several companies are marketing "smog-legal" Weber conversion kits. JAM Engineering in Monterey, California expects to have its Weber kit for 6-cylinder BMWs certified by California state officials by the time this book appears. JAM's kit uses the stock air cleaners and costs $640.

Okay, we admit that these early 6-cylinder sedans aren't troublefree. Nor are they cheap to repair. Joe Schneider (Schneider Motors in Orange, California) gives some typical prices for jobs performed in his shop (all include parts and labor): engine overhaul with new pistons, $3,000; cylinder head rebuild, $1,800; brake master cylinder rebuild, $85; new clutch, $350; overhaul of manual gearbox (if the gears aren't completely shot), $400.

But once the chronic cooling and carburetion problems are cured, the 6-cylinder sedans are rugged machines. And rust doesn't appear to be a terrible problem either. Unlike their little brothers, the 2002s, and especially unlike the 2800/3.0CS coupes with their Karmann-built bodies ("Karmann invented rust and then licensed the process to the Italians," says Roger Moon), the 6-cylinder sedans are slow to corrode. When rust appears, it's likely to start in the doors at the lower back corners.

Driving Impressions

Sometimes a drive down memory lane seems filled with

1974 BMW 3.0S

potholes. You've probably had the disconcerting experience of running into former lovers or close friends and wondering, "What the devil did I ever see in them?" And you've undoubtedly had the same thing happen with cars; you fondly remember a certain car, but when you drive one again after many years, it feels disappointingly old.

One of my treasured motoring memories is the year I shared with a 1969 BMW 2500. Together we conquered the mountain roads of the Sierra Nevadas on the way to favorite ski slopes. We challenged the twists and turns of Route 1 along the California coast. And we pretended we were on a German *autobahn* and cruised down the empty, endlessly straight miles of Interstate 5 at 90 mph for hours.

The car was such a chameleon. When we were alone, it was a sports car. I came to love the sparkling power of the 6-cylinder engine, to revel in the feel of the communicative steering and to delight in the bite of the disc brakes as I used them to duck the car in and out of the corners.

But when we had company, the 2500 was a luxury sedan. The engine was quiet and silky smooth. The cabin was civilized with the amenities of reclining seats, a decent stereo and air conditioning. The suspension soaked up the bumps in the road, and the trunk easily carried our guests' belongings.

So with such good memories, memories that had stayed with me through ten years and drives in hundreds of different cars, I stepped into Dale Cassel's 1971 Bavaria with some trepidation. It was *deja vu* all right. The big steering wheel, the upright seats and the expanse of glass were there, just as I had remembered. So too was the wonderful engine. Oh sure, there was a trace of wear in the second-gear synchro; there was the old stumble on acceleration when the engine was cold (Dale still uses the original carbs in the car); and there was more wind and road noise than any modern BMW would have.

But you know what? Dale's dusty blue (the factory called it "Riviera") Bavaria didn't seem very dated. The precision, tightness and tossibility for which BMWs have become famous were quite evident in the car, even with 159,000 miles on it.

Dale co-owns a shop that's been repairing BMWs for more than two decades (Adams Service Inc. in Riverside, California). He bought the car several years ago from one of his longtime employees, Cy Franke. Both Dale and Cy are the kind of knowledgeable and dedicated mechanics in whose care every BMW should fall. Though the car is not a pampered pet — Dale uses it as an everyday car — Dale and Cy have adhered to a rigorous maintenance schedule. They change the oil every 3,000 miles, perform a major service every 8,000-10,000 miles and change all the cooling system hoses every two years. In return, the Bavaria has given them all those miles with little more than a chattering clutch, a couple of busted water pumps and the inevitable cracked cylinder head (at 112,000 miles).

After driving Dale's car, and considering that 2002s are sell-

Brief Specifications

	1969 2500	1971 Bavaria	1975 3.0Si
Curb Weight, lb.	3005	3170	3420
Wheelbase, in.	106.0	106.0	106.0
Track, f / r	56.9 / 57.6	56.9 / 57.6	58.3 / 57.9
Length	185.0	185.0	195.0
Width	68.9	68.9	68.9
Height	56.1	56.1	57.1
Engine type	sohc inline 6	sohc inline 6	sohc inline 6
Bore x stroke, mm	86.0 x 71.6	86.0 x 80.0	89.0 x 80.0
Displacement, cc	2494	2788	2985
Horsepower, bhp @ rpm	170 @ 6000	192 @ 6000	176 @ 5500
Torque, lb-ft @ rpm	176 @ 3700	200 @ 3700	185 @ 4500
Transmission	4-sp M / 3-sp A	4-sp M / 3-sp A	4-sp M / 3-sp A
Suspension, f / r	ind / ind	ind / ind	ind / ind
Brakes, f / r	disc / disc	disc / disc	disc / disc
Steering type	Worm and roller	worm and roller	worm and roller

Performance Data From Contemporary Tests

0-60 mph, sec.	10.0	9.3	NA
Standing 1 / 4 mile, sec.	17.3	16.8	NA
Average mpg	20.9	18.0	NA
Road test date	6-69	8-71	NA

Typical Asking Prices

1969-1971 2500, 2800	$2,000-$4,000
1971-1974 Bavaria	$2,500-$5,000
1973-1976 3.0S, 3.0Si	$3,000-$6,000
Typical engine-rebuild price (all models)	$3,000-$4,000

ing for the same prices as Bavarias, the big 4-door sedans seem an incredible bargain. Fuel economy might not be as good; Dale says his car gets only 16-18 mpg around town. Otherwise the Bavaria feels like a slightly larger but vastly refined 2002.

Maybe some memories stand the test of time after all.

— *Peter Bohr (March 1985)*

U.S.A.

Chevrolet Corvette Sting Ray

1963-1967

by Ron Wakefield   *Fast, reliable sports cars*

1963 Chevrolet Corvette Sting Ray

During its three decades of production, the Corvette's place among its international competitors has waxed and waned. It got off to a rather halfhearted start in 1953 as a 2-seater with Chevrolet sedan suspension components, a 6-cylinder engine and automatic transmission—only an automatic transmission.

Things got better in succeeding years. The 1963 Corvette was an almost all-new car. Gone was the now outdated (in such a high-powered car) rigid rear axle, replaced by new independent rear suspension; the front suspension became 1963 Chevrolet instead of 1953; and the new body and frame were both smaller and lighter. The 1963 car represented real progress over any previous Corvette.

To the serious shopper for used sports cars, this middle category of Corvettes—1963 through 1967—offers great appeal. Two *Road & Track* editors owned Corvettes of this series, one a 1963 and the other a 1964, and both look back on their cars with fondness. Of course those "middle period" Corvettes weren't perfect, but they were handsome and comfortable, had plenteous V-8 power and offered a long list of options that allowed buyers to tailor the car to their own tastes. And they were fun to drive.

The Corvette was General Motors' move to capitalize on the still small but burgeoning sports-car market in the U.S. In 1952 just slightly more than 11,000 new sports cars were registered in this country, the majority of them MG TDs. In Detroit, where new-car sales had gone past the 4-million-yearly mark, 11,000 anythings weren't very significant. But Harley Earl, head of GM Styling, liked sports cars and was "secretly" at work with a few members of his styling staff on a 2-seater he figured GM could sell in sufficient quantities to make a profit on it. With a series of well-timed moves, Earl got the approval and support of first one, then another top GM executive and the initial Corvette was previewed at the 1953 Motorama, a road show GM then took around America each year. The rest, as they say, is history.

Of the new 1963 Corvette, a special supplement to Chevrolet's *Corvette News* said, "In the last few years Corvette demand has exceeded supply; so from the standpoint of popularity an entirely new vehicle was not necessary. Nevertheless, we felt that the original design no longer represented our best engineering, so plans for a change were initiated in 1959."

The new Corvette was offered in both roadster and coupe versions, and it appeared larger than its predecessor despite its smaller dimensions. But more important than the new styling were the changes beneath the new shape. The independent rear suspension, for instance, was straightforward and effective: there were simple lower links, tubular shock absorbers and, surprisingly, a single transverse leaf spring mounted at its center to the differential housing. The axle halfshafts themselves did the work of top lateral links, and trailing arms took braking and acceleration loadings. Front suspension was also much improved. The Elliott kingpin system, actually dating back to the 1949 Chevrolet, was replaced by a spherical balljoint design, basically the same one that had been used on Chevrolet's passenger cars since 1955. There was a new, more precise steering system that permitted a change in overall ratio from 19.6:1 to 17.0:1 by simple relocation of the tie-rod ball studs on each steering arm. For the first time, power steering was a Corvette option. What had been an optional wheel width (5-1/2 inch) became standard. There were also changes in seating position, pedal location, heating and ventilation — you name it. Our sister publication at the time, *Car Life*, gave the car its Award for Engineering Excellence that year, and our own summation was that "in its nice, shiny new concept it ought to be nearly unbeatable."

The 1963 Sting Ray, then, was something of an engineering *tour de force*, especially for the cost-conscious domestic car industry. And if the 1963 wasn't quite perfect — it still had drum brakes, there were unpleasant body resonances and the shift linkage buzzed — it was to be refined steadily over the next four years under the able guidance of Zora Arkus-Duntov, acquiring better engineering and shedding styling excesses.

The 1964 version benefited from very small refinements. The fake grilles in the hood were the first excrescences to go, although the indentations for them remained. The divided rear window in the coupe was replaced by a single, full-width rear window. (Ironically, the split rear window, which was the least-liked styling feature of the first Sting Ray and made rearward vision a problem, now makes the 1963 model very desirable among Corvette enthusiasts.) There was better sound dampening, the chronically noisy shift lever was tamed somewhat and the ride was made less harsh with variable-rate springs.

For 1965 there was a great leap forward: four-wheel disc brakes were made standard. Also, a 396-cubic-inch V-8 joined the 327 that had been standard Corvette fare since 1962. The 396, offered only that one year, developed 425 horsepower (gross) at 6,400 rpm, more power than had ever been available in a Corvette, and added about 200 pounds. In this year the hood indentations were smoothed out (although 396-engine cars had a "power dome") and fake body-side vents became real.

The next two years were basically ones of refinement, but some dramatic engine changes are worthy of note. It was the brute-performance era. Great throbbing gobs of horsepower and torque, that's what it was all about in those halcyon pre-energy-crisis pre-emissions-crunch days. The 396 grew to 427 cubic inches — a full 7 liters — and plain old cubic inches replaced fuel injection as the route to power. In 1965 the injection 327 engine had been a $538 option. The new 427, which generated 425 bhp at 6,400 rpm vs 375 at 6,200, cost only $313 additional.

The 1967 Corvette was originally scheduled to get a new body style, but as final decision time approached, it was obvious the new design still carried some flaws that couldn't be worked out in time so the original Sting Ray design was retained for one more year with minor cosmetic changes. This was the year the body finally looked as it should have all along — most of the identification badges were gone, the wheels were now handsome ventilated discs without fake knockoff hubs and there wasn't a false scoop or vent left. Two 427 engines with three 2-barrel carburetors were added to the option list, one with hydraulic lifters and one with mechanical. The mechanical-lifter version was conservatively rated (unusual in those days) at 435 bhp at 5,800 rpm. There was also a special-order 427 with aluminum heads: the legendary L88 option, first offered in the spring of 1967. According to Karl Ludvigsen in his book *Corvette, America's Star Spangled Sports Car, The Complete History,* "There was no hedging on the output of this engine; Chevy didn't say anything about it at all." However, Ludvigsen goes on, reliable reports said 560 hp at 6,400 rpm on 103-octane fuel. The L88 engine could be ordered only with all the competition options — plus one option called C48: deletion of the otherwise standard heater and defroster, "to cut down on weight and discourage the car's use on the street," according to *Corvette News.* We have no figures on the production of L88-equipped Corvettes, but then you don't really want 560 bhp. Do you?

The market for used Corvettes is in a curious state. There are relatively few Corvettes still in good, unaltered (not customized) condition. A high percentage of Corvettes seem to have been stolen at one time or another. Many are gone for good, after being stripped for parts or what have you. Take away the Corvettes that have been customized or turned into race cars of various types and perhaps only 20 percent of pre-1968 Corvettes are still available in basically good, stock condition. It's those clean, stock Corvettes so sought after by collectors that fetch prices of $15,000 and more.

Checking Out a Used Sting Ray

These second-generation Corvettes were the answer to a street racer's dream, so look for obvious signs such as dump tubes (exhaust cutouts) or welded patches on the head pipes that might indicate dump tubes were once installed. Check the U-joints for looseness. There are six of them, one on each end of the driveshaft and one on each end of the two rear axle halfshafts. They take a beating from all that Corvette torque, especially if the car has gone through life at the hands of a competitive driver. Likewise, the Positraction (limited-slip) differential that is most Corvettes can suffer from frequent hard driving. To check it, drive around a very tight turn, applying and releasing power gently. If the Positraction chatters or pops it needs attention. Make sure the noise-suppressing metal shields around the distributor, coil and plug wires have survived: without them the radio is worthless. And of course check for clutch slippage. The easiest method is to hold the brakes on firmly and rev the engine while slowly releasing the clutch with the transmission in second gear. If the engine doesn't quickly stall, the clutch is slipping. Watch the exhaust for blue smoke too; Chevrolet V-8s aren't especially easy on oil.

Cosmetically and aesthetically there are some items to note. Flared fenders, three taillights, mag wheels and the like detract from the car's value, so don't pay top money for a car that's modified. On the other hand, don't be scared off by hairline cracks in the paint, but if they go into the fiberglass look underneath for patching that would indicate an accident. And don't be bothered much by rattles and squeaks. They are standard, especially in the convertible, and a little patient work can eliminate a lot of them.

With all the engine options that were available over the five years this series was built, it's no surprise that the character of a 1963-67 Corvette can range from quiet, docile GT car to rip-snortin' sports car or near-dragster. Even the mildest 327 — rated at 250 bhp by the old SAE gross system but probably something like 180 bhp by today's more conservative method — has a lot of performance by today's standards, though, and with the 4-speed gearbox can do 0-60 in about 8 seconds or cover 18 miles per gallon depending on how it is driven. The Powerglide automatic transmission, though it's only a 2-speed, did pretty well in the Corvette with the ample power and light weight, and it's worth noting that from 1963 on the Corvette's factory air conditioning was better than that of some of the most expensive European sports cars of the 1970s. The 4-speed manual gearbox is a delight to use, especially in the later models where its

1963 Chevrolet Corvette Sting Ray

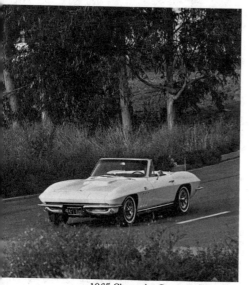

1965 Chevrolet Corvette Sting Ray

characteristic "buzz" was reduced or (in 1967) completely eliminated. You won't find many 3-speeds, but if you do, expect to get a bargain price. Though the 3-speed is perfectly adequate, it's not in demand.

Driving Impressions

The 1965 fuel-injection Corvette was the technical high-water mark for the whole Sting Ray series. Until that model year, Corvettes still had drum brakes and one had to pay more than $600 extra to get a fancy set of drums and real stopping power. On the other hand, 1965 was the last year for fuel-injection: from 1966 on, Chevrolet got Corvette power by adding cubic inches. So in the 1965 there was a fortuitous coming-together of technologies, and for one year America produced a sports car with fuel-injection, all-independent suspension and all-disc brakes.

It now seems strange to think that a leading manufacturer had airflow-controlled, continuous-flow fuel-injection and dropped it. The Rochester system was just that, and though it was quite different in detail and designed for a lot of power rather than low emissions, it answers the same basic description as the system later used on Volvos and Porsches, for instance, to meet current emission regulations. How times change.

Paul and Mary Jacobson of Mission Viejo, California, loaned us their bright blue 1965 FI Corvette for this test. It is a prize: they bought it new and had driven it only 38,363 miles when Mary brought it to us. It looked better than new, thanks to some nice chroming Paul has had done under the hood, and performs like the thoroughbred we all know the fuel-injected Corvette to be.

Look at those specifications: a bit over 5 liters (the good old 327)... 11.0:1 compression ratio!... 375 bhp @ 6,200 rpm. Okay, gross horsepower they were. But these days 300 bhp net, which is about what this engine developed, is staggering.

Driving the fuel-injected Corvette reminded us that fuel injection meant something altogether different in 1965 from what it does today. From our recent experience with fuel-injected engines we might have assumed the FI Corvette would be remarkably docile, idle at a low speed and pull strongly from 1,000 rpm in fourth. Not so. This is a pushrod, not an overhead-cam, engine and that means lots of valve overlap to get high output. No doubt this engine was more tractable than its 365-bhp carbureted counterpart, but the fuel-injected Corvette has the character of a semiracing engine by contemporary standards. The Jacobson car idles at 1,300 rpm and not all that smoothly. And if we cracked open the throttle sharply at, say, 1,500 rpm in any gear the engine was likely to bog down a bit. It felt like a classic case of over-carburetion — something we haven't experienced in a long time.

But once the revs begin to build up, hang on! By the time the big tach needle reaches 3,000 rpm, things are beginning to happen so fast it's dizzying. The fuel-injection cars always had the close-ratio-4-speed gearbox; this car had the numerically high 4.11:1 final drive ratio, which makes the most of the close ratios. Even with the 4.11 it takes a good bit of clutch slipping to get the car off the line and it's a nice long climb to the redline at 54 mph. But after that the driver works hard just to keep up with the engine, so fast does the redline come up in second and third, and it takes very little time to redline the engine in fourth gear either for that matter. The pull begins to fall off above 5,500 rpm, but it is a brilliant show up to that point.

Extracting all this performance — 0-60 in 6.3 seconds, 0-100 in a flat 15 — is great fun. The Corvette gearbox and shift linkage are in a class by themselves: a strong, unbeatable set of gears and synchronizers and a crisp, light, short-throw lever to control them. There was a tendency in the early cars for the linkage to develop a "buzz" as the miles piled up, but we found none of this in the Jacobson car.

Fuel economy? Well, that's another matter. Tests of the fuel-injected Corvette indicate about 13.5 mpg in daily use. The Jacobsons have done 17 mpg on a trip, which is probably about tops. No, it was not designed for economy. We really weren't even thinking much about fuel economy in those days. Quietness isn't one of the car's virtues either. These Corvettes had two big reverse-flow mufflers in their dual exhaust system, which suppressed any outright display of exhaust note in the old sports-car tradition but didn't keep a tinny sort of power sound from coming through. This, the mechanical tappets and the 4.11 gearing conspire to make the Corvette plenty noisy — by 30 mph it has already reached the 70-dB mark inside. At highway speed the engine sounds as if it's really working and the usual wind leaks around poorly matching windows and hardtop weatherseals contribute their part to the general cacophony. If you wanted a GT car, you bought a 250-bhp Corvette with the 3.36:1 or 3.08:1 axle.

1964 Corvette interior

The Jacobson car has neither power steering nor power brakes. From 1963 on it has been possible to alter the Corvette's nonpower steering ratio from 3.4 turns lock-to-lock to 2.9 just by changing from one attachment point of the steering arms to the tie-rod balljoints, and naturally this had been done on the test car. Even at that the steering isn't unduly heavy, and it feels precise as well as being plenty quick. But the bias tires used in the early 1960s — or even the newer bias-belted Uniroyals Paul had put on the car just before turning it over to us — follow every groove or ridge in the road and remind us how much better radials are. It took the Corvette people a long time to get around to radials.

We weren't able to test the Corvette for cornering power but would estimate it to be capable of about 0.7g on the 100-ft skidpad, about the level of a small sedan on radial tires in 1975. Tires are the big difference, of course, because the suspension can hardly be faulted in the matter of cornering. It can be faulted on ride, though; at low speeds the car jiggles constantly, and yet going over those gentle freeway undulations it has the feeling of being underdamped as the front end floats up and down. Despite the all-independent suspension and how advanced it was in 1963 or 1965, the Corvette's combination of ride and handling isn't impressive by todays standards even if you allow for the skinny tires.

The driver sits low in the Corvette cockpit, bolt upright in seats with fixed backrests; the angle of the entire seat assemblies can be varied with the seat mounting bolts but the range is small. The Jacobson car has the optional telescopic steering column, which helps get the wheel a bit farther from the driver than the standard, very close position for the large wheel. Another option on the car we drove was the teak steering-wheel rim, a $48 item for which the owner had to wait an additional fifteen weeks after ordering the Corvette. We'd never seen one before, so these must indeed be rare. But what an improvement over the standard fake-wood rim.

By 1965 flat dial faces had replaced the original Sting Ray plastic cones, thankfully, and the result was an aesthetically pleasing and highly legible set of instruments — huge speedo and tach, four small gauges, a trip odometer (extremely rare in American cars) and a large clock in the center of the double-cowl-effect dash. Heater controls (and air conditioning if ordered) consist of pull-and-twist knobs just under the clock and are odd but simple — and effective: no imported car of the time and few today can match this Corvette's powerful heater and capable air conditioning. Another wonderful Americanism in this cockpit are the lightning-fast electric window lifts, which cost just $59 when the car was built.

The convertible top of this Corvette was another standard setter for other open sports cars to follow. It never quite fit as installed at the factory but there were adjustments here and there and a patient owner could eventually get it snug everywhere. Snug or not, it was marvelously easy to put up and down, folding neatly into the compartment behind the seats after the cover panel was released by a single lever and going into place just as handily with two latches at the windshield header and two pins dropping into holes in the cover panel. The removeable hardtop is another matter, requiring a lot of bolting and unbolting to install or remove, and one assumes the body designers saw it as an all-winter proposition.

What a pleasure it was to try this 10-year-old injection Corvette! Jacobson has not only kept it looking good and in top mechanical condition, but he regularly tends to the rattles that so quickly develop in Corvettes and hence it was tight and solid feeling. All that muscle was never practical, given the restrictions on American driving that were almost as intimidating then as they are now, but at least there were Nevada and Montana without speed limits when this machine was built. With a numerically lower final drive ratio, this would have been a Nevada roadburner; in the form we drove, its character is more dragster-like and there was a 4.56:1 final drive to make it even more so.

Brief Specifications

	1963-1967 Corvette
Curb Weight, lb.	3050
Wheelbase, in.	98.0
Track, f / r	56.8 / 57.6
Length	175.1
Width	69.6
Height	48.1
Fuel Capacity (gal)	18.5
Engine type	pushrod V-8
Bore x stroke, in.	(327) 4.00 x 3.25
	(396) 4.09 x 3.76
	(427) 4.25 x 3.76
Transmission types:	3-speed manual, 4-speed manual (wide or close ratios), 2-speed automatic
Front suspension:	Unequal-length A-arms, coil springs, tube shocks, anti-roll bar
Rear suspension:	lower lateral links, halfshafts as upper links, trailing arms, transverse leaf spring, tube shocks; anti-roll bar with 396 or 427
Brakes:	1963-64, all-drums; 1965-67, all-disc, vented rotors
Tires and wheels:	various sizes bias-ply tires on steel or aluminum 15 x 5-1 / 2 or 15 x 6 wheels

Performance Data From Contemporary Tests

	1963 327 FI	1964 327 auto	1965 396	1966 427	1967 327
0-60 mph, sec.	5.9	8.0	5.7	5.7	7.8
0-100 mph, sec.	16.5	20.2	13.4	13.4	23.1
Standing 1 / 4 mile, sec.	14.9	15.2	14.1	14.0	16.0
Average mpg	12.5	14.0	10.5	12.0	16.0
Road test date	10-62	3-64	8-65	8-66	2-67

Corvette Engine Options

(cubic inches / gross bhp)

1963	1964	1965	1966	1967
327 / 250	327 / 250	327 / 250	327 / 300	327 / 300
327 / 300	327 / 300	327 / 300	327 / 350	327 / 350
327 / 340	327 / 350	327 / 350	427 / 390	427 / 390
327 / 360*	327 / 365	327 / 365	427 / 425	427 / 400
	327 / 375*	327 / 375*		427 / 435
		396 / 425		

*Fuel-injected

Typical Asking Prices

1963-1967 Corvette Sting Ray	$9,000-$21,000
Typical engine-rebuild price (all models)	$1,800-$2,500

Come to think of it, aside from the sound basic design, this variety of options was one of the Corvette's main attractions in those days. In any form it was a true sports car, able to hold its head up among the world's best, but its personality could be varied by large or small increments with the selection of well-conceived engine, transmission and suspension options.

— *Ron Wakefield (February 1975)*

U.S.A.

Chevrolet Corvette

1968-1977

The most daunting thing about buying an older Corvette isn't the prospect of gasoline bills the size of your monthly mortgage payments. The toughest part is just trying to figure out the Corvette market.

Corvette is the great American sports car. And it always has been a great American tradition to offer the domestic-car buyer a vast array of options. In 1969, for example, General Motors gave the Corvette customer a choice of no less than eight engine variations, five transmissions and all manner of luxury features, from the significant (air conditioning) to the trivial (front fender louver trim). Let's not forget that the car also came in two different configurations, a coupe with a pair of removable "T-top" roof panels or a full convertible with an optional removable hardtop.

There were often important year-to-year changes in the base cars as well. Selecting an older Corvette of the right configuration, of the right year, with the right options will make a big difference not only in what you'll have to pay for the car, but also in your subsequent enjoyment of it.

And that's not all you'll have to consider when you go Corvette shopping. Corvettes have long been a favorite car for amateur customizers and hot-rodders, so finding a car in the right condition can also be a challenge. Moreover, the older Corvette market is an active and lucrative one, which means it has more than its share of disreputable, fast-buck repair shops and dealers.

An unknowledgeable used-Corvette buyer is a plump chicken ready for plucking. But—fanfare,please—never fear, for R&T is here. With this Used Car Classic, we'll try to guide you safely past the perils of selecting a good 1968-1977 Corvette.

We didn't choose this time span arbitrarily. Nineteen sixty-eight is a logical point to begin our discussion because that year marked the debut of the model inspired by the Majo Shark

Yankee Doodle dandies

by Peter Bohr

1970 Corvette convertible

show car of 1965. As for our cut-off year of 1977, the 1978 Corvette, while not all-new, was the most changed since the 1968 car.

In fact, fans of the marque like to divide this 10-year span of Corvettes into two groups, the 1968 to 1972 cars, and the 1973 to 1977 cars. The earlier group is just now gaining collectible-car status and prices for these cars are on the rise. Included in this group are Corvettes with monster engines that make terrific weekend toys. The later group consists of newer, more refined cars that are well-suited for everyday driving.

The 1968 through 1972 Corvettes

When R&T's editors got their first good look at the new Corvette body in 1968, they were decidedly underwhelmed. Had they known then that the basic design would linger on through 1982, they probably would have been appalled. Our editors kept expecting GM to bring out a mid-engine Vette like the one on display at the 1970 New York Automobile Show. Alas, it never happened.

R&T described the 1968 Mako-style car as having a "Vintage Show Car look" and a "gross avoirdupois." We said the new model was a move away from "Sports Car and toward Image and Gadget Car." There were plenty of gizmos: pop-up headlights, a fiber-optic lightbulb monitoring system, and a vacuum-operated lid that hid the windshield wipers. "Here is a car," we declared, "that can take people on a trip without even going anywhere."

What galled the editors was that the new car was longer, heavier and less spacious inside than its predecessor, the now-classic Sting Ray, even though it still used the Sting Ray's chassis. Despite these annoyances, R&T acknowledged the Corvette's two indisputable virtues: value for the money and power. At a base price of just over $4500, we thought it was one of the world's best values in a sporting automobile. As for power, back in those twilight years of the Mako-style car, it had plenty. Like the chassis, the engine lineup was a direct carryover from the old Sting Ray. The base small-block engine displaced 327 cu in. and came in two horsepower versions. General Motors also offered several variants of the big-block 427-cu.-in. engine, including the 435-bhp L88. For 1969, the 327 was replaced by the 350-cu.-in. engine, and for 1970 the 427 was replaced by the 454.

1974 Corvette coupe

This is a good place to digress for a primer on Corvette nomenclature. The Sting Ray moniker was dropped in 1968 and the Mako-style car was called simply the Corvette. But in 1969, the old name was revived as one word, Stingray, and was retained until 1977 when the car became simply the Corvette once again. Stingray doesn't distinguish any particular Corvette from another, so you'll often hear Corvette owners refer to their cars according to engine displacement, i.e., a "327 car" or a "427," or a "small-block" or "big-block" car.

But Corvette connoisseurs who really know their stuff call a car by GM's engine option order designation. Thus the designation L88, for example, meant the 427-cu.-in., 435-bhp engine available as an option during 1968 and 1969.

There are two other points to keep in mind regarding Corvette engines. First, for 1971, General Motors decreased compression ratios and hardened valve seats to allow Corvette engines to run happily on lower-octane, unleaded fuel.

Second, for 1972, in a bow to anti-muscle car sentiment from the Naderites, GM decided to switch from gross horsepower ratings to more conservative SAE net ratings. So GM's horsepower ratings for 1971 and earlier Corvette engines aren't directly comparable with 1972 and later engines.

During 1968, 1969 and 1970, R&T tested Corvettes with several different engines and transmissions. Here are some comments gleaned from these tests:

A 1968 L71 427-cu-in. engine with manual transmission: "It had a marked tendency to overheat both itself and the passengers. Its galloping idle was enough to wake the dead. Everything has been sacrificed to one cause—blinding acceleration."

A 1968 L79 327-cu-in. engine with 4-speed manual: "At idle it isn't exactly smooth and quiet, but it does run pretty quietly and tractably at anything above 1200 rpm. The Muncie 4-speed gearbox is a beauty."

A 1969 standard L48 350-cu.-in. engine with 3-speed Turbo Hydra-matic: "This Corvette scores high on power, response, smoothness and on its automatic transmission."

A 1970 LS5 454-cu-in. engine with 3-speed Turbo Hydra-matic: "By far the most tractable big-engine Corvette we've tried. The Turbo Hydra-matic is still our favorite automatic— marvelously smooth and perfectly suited to the characteristics of a large-displacement engine. Performance of our test car was hampered by great weight. The weight, engine size and automatic all conspire to produce 9-mpg fuel guzzling."

A special mention must go to the Corvette with the LT1 engine, an option in 1970, 1971 and 1972. Though not as rare as the big-block L88, the small-block, 350-cu-in. LT1 is a high-revving, high-horsepower unit with mechanical lifters (all other Corvette small-block engines from 1968 on have hydraulic lifters) and is highly regarded by collectors. It's not difficult to spot an LT1 Vette; it has a hood with a bulge like a big-block 454 and painted pinstripes with decals that say LT1.

So, which car to buy? If you're after that weekend fun car— a car in which to go out and raise hell—then consider a big-block car. But understand it will probably overheat a lot and can be a handful to drive around town. The standard small-block is more sedate (relatively speaking, of course), but a high-performance small-block, especially the LT1, will certainly stimulate your senses.

Some Corvette fans like the 1970 and earlier cars because of their higher compression ratios; but keep in mind that they were not designed to run on today's fuels (more on that later). Of course, macho types will want a manual tranny, though the automatic works very well. And in this 1968-1972 group, whether a car is a coupe or convertible won't affect price, although a convertible of this vintage with air conditioning is a rare find.

The 1973 Through 1977 Corvettes

This was the era of the softened Corvette. The most obvious change on the 1973 Vette is the plastic body-color nose that covers a 5-mph-impact bumper in place of the pretty, but delicate, chrome bumpers of previous years. During that year only, the aggressive spoilered tail with its chrome quarter bumpers remained.

However, in 1974, the chrome rear bumpers also gave way to plastic, body-color 5-mph bumpers. For 1974 only, the rear bumper was a clean shape with a split running down the center. But from 1975 on, the split disappeared and rather ugly black overriders were added front and rear. Nevertheless, Chevrolet integrated the government-required bumpers into the Corvette body much more gracefully than did most European automakers at the time who simply tacked on ugly protuberances.

Partially because of the bumpers, Corvettes got heavier and slower during this period. They also became more civilized. For 1973, there were new cushioned body mounts, which, combined with thicker insulation under the carpets and sprayed-on sound deadener, lowered road-transmitted noise.

The Corvette gradually evolved into a long-legged, comfortable highway cruiser and away from a hairy-stoplight drag racer. That impressive option list of previous years shrank, and by 1975 optional engine choices were down to one. The last big-block, the 454, fell off the option list in 1975. The standard engine during the 1973-1977 period was the L48 350 V-8.

But what many casual Corvette owners and fans don't realize is that the remaining optional engine, the L82 350, is a real honey. It was available in 1973 as a replacement for the LT1. It doesn't have the LT1's mechanical lifters, but like that engine it has heavy-duty components including a 4-bolt block, forged aluminum pistons and a forged steel crank. By contrast, the L48 has a 2-bolt block and cast pistons and crankshaft. Though the stock L82 has modest rev limits, with a few changes in the top end the engine is capable of handling 7000 rpm without self-destructing.

The L82 is a sleeper because, unlike the big-block cars and the LT1 with their bulging hoods and identification badges and decals, the L82 Vette is virtually indistinguishable from the standard L48 350; undoubtedly many L82 owners who've bought their car second-hand aren't aware of the special engine they possess. Only when you open the hood and see the aluminum valve covers do you have a indication that the car has the L82 engine. Even then you can't really be sure; the valve covers on the L48 were painted to match the rest of the engine and many L48 owners have swapped their covers for the prettier L82's.

R&T tested a 1973 L82 in the June 1973 issue. (If you look in your back issues, be aware that we entitled the test "Corvette LT-1 Coupe," which was a big boo-boo because the LT1 was dropped in 1972.) We nitpicked at the usual things—the car's weight and size—but we liked the engine and called the car "one of the best Corvettes we've ever driven."

One other important event in Corvette history occurred in the 1973-1977 period. Nineteen seventy-five was the last year for the full convertible. In 1968 twice as many soft-tops were produced as coupes; by 1975, only 4629 convertibles were made out of a total of 33,836 Corvettes. Because it was the final year and there were so few of them, the 1975 convertible is one of the few 1973-1977 cars that's a real collectible.

If your're in the market for a Vette of this time period, look for one with an L82 engine and a full complement of luxury items—leather seats, electric windows and especially air conditioning. These options will increase the value of the car.

The Quest

To aid in your quest for a used 1968-1977 Vette, we've consulted three highly regarded experts in Corvette circles. Sonja Keith, aka The Corvette Lady, in Costa Mesa, California, has been an independent dealer selling Corvettes exclusively for 12 years. Scott Jones, co-owner of Moroso Corvettes, also in Costa Mesa, is a wizard when it comes to rebuilding or modifying high-performance GM engines. Rick Brown, owner of Corvette Body and Service Center in San Francisco, has been repairing and restoring Corvette bodies and mechanicals in his shop since 1969.

1970 Corvette interior

This trio suggests the one key point to bear in mind when searching for any used Corvette is originality. Corvette lovers have a fetish about it, but unfortunately many owners have subjected their cars to all manner of indignities, from hideous custom paint jobs to absurdly wide fender flares. Sonja won't even consider adding such cars to her inventory.

It's usually a cinch to swap engines in a Vette (or parts of engines like the L82 valve covers), so when examining a car, your first task is to check that engine and vehicle ID numbers match. There's a Vehicle Identification Number (VIN) stamped onto the windshield pillar on the driver's side. Match that number to the one stamped on the engine block on a pad just forward of the passenger-side head.

Once you've established a Corvette's basic authenticity, inspect the body. Of course, it's fiberglass, and relative to steel-bodied cars, fiberglass presents some unusual bugaboos. Rick Brown compares a Vette's body to the shell of an egg; both will take a lot of abuse, but once they break, they break bad. Furthermore, says Rick, anyone who's repaired a surfboard thinks he can buy an aftermarket fiberglass front end and repair his bashed-up Vette all by himself. There are problems with this. First, though some aftermarket body panels or units are of good quality, they're not factory-made so they reduce the value of the car. Second, the fellow may forget all about the bent frame or damaged suspension. Rick recommends that the prospective Corvette buyer measure a prospective purchase from the center of the front-wheel spindle to the center of the rear-wheel spindle; it should read 98.0 on *both* sides of the car. If one side is shorter, watch out!

You can also spot aftermarket body panels by checking the finish of the fiberglass. Look inside the engine compartment. GM's fiberglass is nearly smooth while aftermarket fiberglass will have a definite texture. GM's bodies are made of panels joined together with bonding strips; aftermarket front ends are usually 1-piece units with no bonding strips on the inside corners.

The engine bays of all Corvettes were black when they left the factory, so changing paint colors is not the chore it is on most cars. But, of course, a car with its original paint, or with its original paint color if resprayed, is more valuable. A bad paint job that shows cracking or crazing will be expensive to redo because the old paint will have to be stripped. And stripping paint off fiberglass without damaging it requires some skill.

Please don't assume that a Corvette is immune to the ravages of rust—the body is, but the steel chassis frame and windshield frame aren't. Sonja says she's seen Vettes from the midwest that have holes clear through their chassis frames.

Replacement interior fittings in the original materials, from seat covers to carpets, are all readily available at reasonable prices. But once again, because of the importance Corvette folks place on originality, be sure the materials are identical to the original.

One of the great advantages of the good 'ole American Vette over foreign sports cars is the cost of maintaining the drivetrain. Either Scott or Rick will provide a first-class engine rebuild, including a cylinder bore, new camshafts and new pistons for about $2500. Rebuilding a 6-cylinder Porsche will cost about double that, and a rebuild on an 8-cylinder Ferrari could set you back three or four times the Vette's rebuild price.

But repair costs for other Corvette components aren't especially inexpensive. The 4-wheel disc brakes will usually cause a Vette owner more headaches than any other component. Each brake caliper has four aluminum pistons running in machined bores. If the fluid isn't changed frequently, water absorbed into the system (brake fluid is hygroscopic) will corrode the bores and fluid will leak out and/or the brake system will fill with air. A spongy pedal or seepage on the back sides of the tires indicates that something is amiss. However, stainless-steel-sleeved calipers will cure the problem, but replacing all the calipers and performing a complete brake job will cost between $600 and $1200, according to Rick.

Rick gives other common repairs and prices: If you hear clunking in the front end or feel the car wander, the car may need a complete front-end rebuild. Replacement of springs, shocks, ball joints and idler arms will cost about $700. If the power assist steering unit leaks, you may need to replace the valve and ram assembly, which can run $500. If you hear a violent chatter from the rear at low speed after the car has warmed up, you may need to replace the Positraction limited-slip differential unit for about $500.

Finally, there's the problem of running the 1968-1970 Corvette engines on today's fuel. Believe it or not, Scott says some of the lower-compression engines give more trouble on low-octane fuel than some higher-compression, higher-performance engines. That's because the engines with the higher 11.0:1 ratios have a longer-duration cam, meaning the valves open earlier and close later, which gives less time for pressure to build up in the cylinder. If your 1968-1970 Corvette engine pings badly, be it one with a 10.0:1 or 11.0:1 ratio, Scott's remedy of first choice is to recurve the distributor. If that doesn't work, change the camshaft to one with a newer, updated profile, which will cost about $500.

Of course, neither of these changes will do anything to compensate for the lack of lead in gas, but Scott says he's seen very little damage from unleaded fuels in the 1968-1970 Corvette engines. That could change, however, as the lead content in gasoline decreases even more.

Scott suggests a neat modification to solve both the pinging and lead problems on big-block engines, all without any loss of performance: If you have an early big-block car, switch the cylinder heads to a 1971 or later open-chamber design from a 454 engine. The better breathing of the design will compensate for the lower compression. And it's not an expensive modification either; Scott says a pair of the later heads costs only about $125.

Though you can also change to 1971 or later heads on an earlier small-block engine and solve the pinging and lead problems, you will lose performance. Unfortunately, Scott says the small-block engines don't respond as well to the later open-chamber heads.

Driving Impressions

I was raised not to like Corvettes, and it's all *Road & Track's* fault. When I was just a tyke—well, a freshman-in-college-age-tyke—and quite inexperienced in things automotive, I read a comparison test in R&T that profoundly influenced my view toward Vettes. The magazine was my automobile bible and when it described the Corvette as plastic, flashy and lacking in finesse, I took the comments to heart. Even more damning, the article said that "The personality we associate with the Stingray is the Animal, one who prefers to attain the goal with brute strength and bared chest rather than art and fast footwork."

The Rambo-type may be in fashion today, but in 1969 when that article appeared, I certainly didn't think of myself as "Animal." I much preferred to identify with R&T's description of the person who would own a Jaguar E-Type, another car in that comparison test. Class and charm were some of the words used. "The personality would be one that swings. But with dignity," said R&T. That's me, I thought.

Later, in the mid-Seventies when I joined R&T's staff, I had many opportunities to drive new Corvettes. Of course, by then they were pretty tame machines. And because the quality of a car—its finish and the precision of its construction—has always been important to me, the Corvette just didn't flip my switch.

Now, a decade later, I think I was wrong to have been so narrow-minded about all Corvettes. My new opiinion came about because I recently drove Ed Campbell's small-block LT1, an impeccably maintained, completely original (down to the paint and even the hose clamps) 1971 coupe. I haven't driven anything so exciting since I drove some outrageously priced piece of European exotica or other that was hanging about R&T's parking lot.

As soon as I fired up the engine, my animal instincts began to take charge. At idle, the lopiing, burbling LT1 sounded for all the world just like a big Bertram sportfishing boat ready to go out and chase marlin. And when we were in the street and I opened her up to 5000 rpm or so, all hell broke loose. My neck literally jerked back as I flicked through the gears.

Brief Specifications

	1968 Coupe	1969 Coupe	1969 Conv.	1970 Coupe	1973 Coupe	1977 Coupe
Curb Weight, lb.	3260	3505	3262	3740	3520	3540
Wheelbase, in.	98.0	98.0	98.0	98.0	98.0	98.0
Track, f/r	58.3/59.0	58.7/59.4	58.7/59.4	58.7/59.4	58.7/59.5	58.7/59.5
Length	182.1	182.5	182.5	182.5	184.7	185.2
Width	69.2	69.0	69.0	69.0	69.0	69.0
Height	47.8	47.8	47.9	47.4	47.7	48.0
Engine type	pushrod V-8	pushrod V-8	pushrod V-8	pushrod V-8	pushrod V-8	pushrod V-8
Bore x stroke, in.	4.00 x 3.25	4.00 x 3.48	4.25 x 3.76	4.25 x 4.00	4.00 x 3.48	4.00 x 3.48
Displacement, cu in	327	350	427	454	350	350
Horsepower, bhp @ rpm	350 @ 5800	300 @ 4800	435 @ 5800	390 @ 4800	250 @ 5200	210 @ 5200
Torque, lb-ft @ rpm	360 @ 3600	360 @ 3200	460 @ 4000	500 @ 3400	285 @ 4000	255 @ 3600
Gearbox	4-speed manual	3-speed auto	4-speed manual	3-speed auto	4-speed manual	4-speed manual
Suspension, f/r	ind/ind	ind/ind	ind/ind	ind/ind	ind/ind	ind/ind
Brakes, f/r	disc/disc	disc/disc	disc/disc	disc/disc	disc/disc	disc/disc
Steering type	recir. ball	recir. ball	recir. ball	recir. ball	recir. ball	recir. ball

Performance Data From Contemporary Tests

	1968 Coupe	1969 Coupe	1969 Conv.	1970 Coupe	1973 Coupe	1977 Coupe
0-60 mph, sec.	7.7	8.4	6.1	7.0	7.2	6.8
Standing ¼ mile, sec.	15.6	16.0	14.3	15.0	15.5	15.5
Average mpg	13.0	14.3	10.0	9.0	14.5	15.0
Road test date	1-68	6-69	3-69	9-70	6-73	6-77

Typical Asking Prices

1968-1972	$7,000-$13,000
1968-1972 big-blocks, LT1	$8,500-$15,000
1973-1977	$6,000-$11,000
1974-1975 convertible	$10,000-$15,000

These are typical prices for cars in good to excellent condition. Prices may vary considerably if the car is an extremely rare model (an L88, for instance), has an unusual option package (a 1972 LT1 convertible with air conditioning, for example) or is in absolutely original mint condition.

Typical engine-rebuild price (all models)	$1,800-$2,500

And how sweet it is, that Muncie close-ratio gearbox. And what competent 4-wheel disc brakes. And what quick steering, rather like an old Austin-Healey Bugeye when, if you sneezed, you'd find yourself in another lane.

Despite its blistering performance when you lay your foot into the throttle, Ed's LT1 is as docile as a car can be if you need to cruise unobtrusively past a highway patrol car. With so much torque available, just put the gear lever in 3rd, or even 4th, and you can poke around town without any fuss and not much noise. The clutch, too, is much lighter than I had expected.

Naturally, the car's chassis shows its age. Cornering power is quite high and response is near neutral. But the ride is firm on good surfaces and is downright jarring on poor ones. And Ed's car is just like it came from the factory, which means you wouldn't want to match its fit and finish against an inexpensive modern Japanese car.

But, oh piffle—the car's a blast. It has been said that driving a Ferrari or a Lamborghini at the 55-mph speed limit is like asking the Mormon Tabernacle Choir to hum. But unlike the European grand touring cars, the LT1 Vette wasn't designed to be driven mile after mile at 130 mph. With this Corvette, all the fun lies in its acceleration capabilities in the lower speed ranges— it's an ideal adult toy well suited to modern-day driving conditions.

"I take the car for a drive when I'm depressed," says Ed. "And if I'm really depressed, I take off the roof panels. I always perk up." I understand, Ed, I understand.

—Peter Bohr (April 1986)

JAPAN

Datsun Sports Roadsters 1962-1971

It's very tempting to start this report with some line or other from the musical *My Fair Lady* because the Datsun Sports roadster was called "the Fair Lady" in Japan, but I'll refrain from that.

The Datsun Sports series began with the SPL-310 (1500), which was introduced in the U.S. in 1962. The 1500 was not a major sales success but it did open the way for the 1600 and 2000 versions, of which close to 40,000 were sold in this country.

In our first road test of the SPL-310 (January 1964), we offered some comments on the styling of the car: "The appearance... is not displeasing, even though most of the design features are reminiscent of other, more familiar marques. There are the half-buried headlights of the MGB, the vertical rear fender line of the Fiat 1200, the stacked, round taillight decor of

All the attributes of classic European sports cars but from the other side of the world

by Thos L. Bryant

the 1955-56 Buick, the grille shape of the Lancia Flavia, the roll-up windows and top of the Triumph Sports Six, and so on. The list of sources could go on, but let it suffice to say that these various bits have been blended into a design that hangs together well even though they do not add up to an appearance that is striking or different."

The SPL-310 is powered by an overhead-valve, 4-cylinder engine of 1488-cc displacement, which develops 85 bhp at 5,600 rpm (torque is 92 lb-ft at 4,400 rpm). Twin side-draft Hitachi (SU licensed) carburetors provide the fuel mixture. The SPL-310 does not offer startling performance by any means, but it was competitive with its contemporaries, managing 0-60 mph in 15.5 seconds, getting almost 29 mpg of fuel in our test. It also gave the buyer an impressive amount of standard equipment for his $2,465 (radio, tonneau cover, cigar lighter, white sidewall tires, outside mirror, back-up lights and seat belts all included).

In 1965, Nissan introduced the 1600 Sports, which was little changed from the SPL-310 except for increased engine displacement and some exterior trim alterations: a horizontal-bar grille in place of the eggcrate, repositioning of the chrome side strip, 1600 badges rather than 1500, a key-turn lock for the trunk instead of the large handle and 14-inch wheels versus the previous 13s. The displacement increase from 1,488 to 1,595 was accomplished by increasing the bore from 3.15 to 3.43 inches while shortening the stroke from 2.91 to 2.63 inches. The result was an increase in horsepower to 96 at 6,000 rpm, while torque improved to 103 lb-ft at 4,000 rpm.

The 1600 Sports was given a new, all-synchromesh 4-speed gearbox, which we praised in our May 1967 road test of the car: "This gearbox is superior in every respect and is as good as any 4-speed manual we've ever driven. In our test car, which had more than 5,000 miles on the odometer, the gearbox was quiet, the linkage crisp and light, and the synchromesh faultless."

Another improvement over the earlier roadster was the conversion to disc brakes up front from the previous all-drum arrangement. The significant interior changes included a fold-down top instead of the take-off-and-store-in-the-trunk one of the SPL-310, a padded shelf behind the front bucket seats to replace the cross-facing occasional seat, a console over the driveshaft tunnel with a locking map box and a cleaned-up instrument panel.

The 1600 Sports follows classic sports-car design. The steel body sits on pressed-steel box rails with cross-member, and the suspension is independent in front with A-arms, coil springs, tube shocks and anti-roll bar, while the rear suspension consists of a live axle with semi-elliptic leaf springs and tube shocks. The suspension travel is quite limited, and the ride can fairly be described as harsh. The 1600 Sports driver is constantly informed of the nature of the surface over which he or she is driving.

The 1600 engine moved the Datsun up a notch in perfor-

64 Datsun SPL-310

mance compared to the 1500, with the 0-60 mph time dropping to 13.3 seconds, while the quarter-mile run was accomplished in 19.9 seconds at 70 mph (20.2 at 66 for the 1500). Fuel consumption suffered slightly with the more powerful engine, as our road-test car consumed 21-26 mpg in normal driving.

Despite the jouncy ride and vintage handling, our road test concluded, "...the Datsun 1600 Sports offers more for the money ($2,621) than any other sports car in the low-priced field."

Advent of the 2000

Six months after our 1600 Sports road test, we reported on the 2000 Sports. The two primary differences were the larger engine and a 5-speed all-synchromesh transmission. The new 1,982-cc engine was basically the same 4-cylinder, 5-main-bearing design as the 1600, but with a single overhead camshaft instead of the pushrods and rocker arms of its smaller brother. The growth in displacement was achieved by increasing the stroke from 2.63 to 3.27 inches while leaving the bore at 3.43 inches. The bottom end of the engine came in for strengthening to handle the greater output, and a more rugged crankshaft was also fitted. The 2-liter engine produces 135 bhp at 6,000 rpm and 145 lb-ft of torque at 4,000 rpm with larger carburetors. All this brought about a 40 percent increase in power, and the weight penalty was only about 15 pounds, yet Datsun didn't feel the need to change the chassis, spring rates or brakes.

Along with the new 5-speed gearbox, there was a change in the final drive ratio from 3.89:1 on the 1600 to 3.70:1 with the 2000, and the wheels grew a half-inch in width to 4.5. The fifth speed in the transmission was an overdrive ratio of 0.85:1, which made for an excellent cruising gear that allowed the 2000 Sports to lope along at 3,200 rpm at 70 mph.

There was a limited-production version of the 2000 Sports with a 150-bhp engine designed primarily for competition purposes. The additional power came via a different camshaft and Solex carburetors, and while the greater output was significant, it was also rather unpleasant to drive around town as this setup delivered the power way up on the cam.

Our test of the normal 2000 showed that it would accelerate to 60 mph in 10.2 seconds and cover the standing-start quarter mile in 17.3 seconds, while the 150-bhp model turned in a quarter-mile time of 16.8 seconds compared to 19.9 for the 1600.

The only significant differences between the 2000 and 1600 Sports were the engine, gearbox, grille and badges. The 2000 used the same suspension, brakes, steering, chassis and body as the 1600, and the 2-liter car also carried on the tradition of offering the buyer many features that cost extra on other sports cars of the day, at a basic list price of $2,950 at the time of the car's introduction in late 1967.

What to Look For in Buying a Datsun Sports

Of the three models covered, the early SPL-310 (1500) is the least common. It was introduced late in 1962 and continued to be offered for sale in the U.S. into mid-1966. Over that time span only 3,148 cars were sold in this country. The Datsun 1600 Sports went on the American market in the last half of 1965 and continued to be sold until the end of 1970, with total sales of just over 23,600 cars. The 2000 Sports came to the U.S. in late 1967, and the last few copies were sold in early 1971; total sales were 15,718.

One of the virtues of the 1600 and the 2000 is that very few changes were made in the cars from year to year aside from the U.S. government-required safety and emissions features. Naturally, there will be those collectors who will consider only a pre-1968 version without emission controls. But for those potential buyers who are not too choosy about that, the lack of annual change for change's sake could make shopping easier.

For guidance in selecting a 1600 or 2000 Sports, we turned to Ron Johnson who works in the Datsun Competition Services department of Nissan Motors in Carson, California; Ron's expertise is overshadowed only by his enthusiasm. He pointed out two key factors that account for the lack of recognition received by these cars: First, they were initially imported into the U.S. at a time when the Japanese auto industry in this country was in its infancy and, second, the overwhelming popularity and success of the Datsun 240Z (introduced in 1970) completely stole the limelight. The upshot of this is that many, if not most, of the roadsters available today have been pretty well thrashed by owners who did not consider them valuable. Also, according to Johnson, many 1600s and 2000s have fallen victim to incompetent and uncaring mechanics. The good side to this state of affairs is that the buyer today should, with diligence, be able to find a roadster at a cheap price.

Johnson says the more costly items to look for include rust around the front door pillar's leading edge and the rear side-quarter panels, and problems with the synchromesh, clutch assembly or rear engine seals. Repair or replacement of these last items requires removing the engine, *a la* MGB. Otherwise, the 1600 and 2000 engines and gearboxes are noted for durability, much the same as comparable British sports cars of the 1960s.

Driving Impressions

Ron Johnson's wife, Robin, owns a 1967 Datsun 1600 Sports and was generous enough to loan it to me for 24 hours. Ron has spent a considerable amount of time making this 1600 an exceptionally pleasant car. Robin bought the car in 1974 for $750 and, according to Ron, "As very few things worked, it was surprising we got it home." However, today Robin's 1600 is stunning. The Johnsons had the interior redone and got a new paint job, while a new engine and the 5-speed transmission from a 2000 roadster gave their car a new lease on life. Other extras added include Koni shock absorbers, Metzeler 185 / 70-14 radial tires, Marchal headlights, AM / FM stereo radio and air horns.

Driving the Datsun Roadster was, in many ways, an exercise in nostalgia. It is so very vintage in handling, steering and braking that I found myself looking around frequently to be sure

1969 Datsun 2000 Sports

that the car had not been magically transformed into a Triumph TR3! And lest Datsun fans jump to an irate and erroneous conclusion, this is no criticism of the car. It provides classic sports-car motoring at its very best: the top down, the engine making appropriate noises, the handling so predictable and the gearbox working just the way it should. For those who missed the 1950s and early 1960s of British sports cars with rigid rear axles and stiff suspension, the 1600 and 2000 Sports will provide an excellent means of filling the gap in your education.

There is ample space for the tall driver, especially when the top is down and, frankly, that's the only way to get full benefit from these cars. Open-air motoring is still better than any other manner of driving and should be taken advantage of at every opportunity. The controls fall readily to hand and foot, there's a dead pedal and the seats are reasonably comfortable for all but the broadest of beam.

Robin's 1600 is painted a yellow so bright it fairly hurts your eyes on a sunny day and perhaps that accounts for the unexpected amount of attention I got from the other motorists while driving her car. On the other hand, perhaps it was the look of obvious pleasure on my face, or even the dashing figure I cut while having a grand time at the wheel of the car. For those like myself who have never tried a Datsun Sports roadster, you've been missing something very worthwhile.

— Thos L. Bryant (January 1978)

Brief Specifications

	1964 SPL-310	1967 1600 Sports	1967 2000 Sports
Curb Weight, lb.	2030	2085	2110
Wheelbase, in.	89.9	89.8	89.8
Track, f / r	47.8 / 47.1	50.0 / 47.1	50.2 / 47.1
Length	155.6	155.6	155.6
Width	58.9	58.9	58.9
Height	50.2	51.4	51.6
Fuel Capacity (gal)	11.4	11.4	11.4
Engine type	pushrod inline 4	pushrod inline 4	pushrod inline 4
Bore x stroke, in.	3.15 x 2.91	3.43 x 2.63	3.43 x 3.27
Displacement, cc	1488	1595	1982
Horsepower (gross)	85	96	135

Performance Data From Contemporary Tests

0-60 mph, sec.	15.5	13.3	10.2
Standing 1 / 4 mile, sec.	20.2	19.9	17.3
Average mpg	28.5	23.5	23.0
Road test date	1-64	5-67	11-67

Typical Asking Prices

1962-1971 SPL-310, 1600, 2000 Sports	$1,500-$2.500
Typical engine-rebuild price (all models)	$1,500-$2,500

JAPAN

Datsun 240Z *1970-1973*

One of the most significant sports cars of the 1970s

by Thos L. Bryant

1970 Datsun 240Z

Remember when the Datsun 240Z made its debut? All the sports-car world was electrified by this fastback coupe whose styling called to mind the Jaguar E-type coupe and a touch of the Toyota 2000 GT. And the $3,500 price was a rare bargain considering the 240Z's single-overhead-cam, 6-cylinder engine, independent rear suspension, 122-mph top speed and 0-60 mph time of 8.7 seconds. Our initial road-test report on the Datsun (April 1970) forecast a great future for the car: "...at this price, it is a super-bargain, with a combination of styling, performance and handling far ahead of anything else under $4,000.... We expect to see the Datsun establish a market of its own, one which will force other makers to come up with entirely new models to gain a share in it. The Japanese industry is no longer borrowing anything from other nations. In fact, a great struggle may be ahead just to prevent a complete reversal of that cliche."

However, all was not perfection with the original 240Z. We discovered during our testing that high-speed stability was poor, the synchros in the gearbox could easily be beaten in quick shifting, and the ride characteristics definitely pointed out the shortcomings of the stock shock absorbers. We also noted that braking ability in the rain suffered badly from the effects of spray, although dry braking was most impressive. But all in all our summary of the 240Z was highly favorable.

Our next association with the Datsun came in a July 1971 comparison test entitled "The $3,500 GT," which pitted the 240Z against the Fiat 124 Sports Coupe, Opel GT, MGB GT and Triumph GT6. In that matchup we noted, "The Datsun 240Z set U.S. motoring on its ear when it appeared in early 1970. It seemed too good to be true: a really fast, good-handling and good-looking coupe with great refinement and extensive standard equipment — all at what seemed an incredibly low price." The Datsun garnered the most points in that comparison and we concluded that the "240Z lives up to its promising specification. Its generous-size engine delivers the smoothest, quietest and dramatically the most powerful performance in the group; it is an engine that pulls strongly from low speeds, runs silently at high cruising speeds and continues to be impressive right up to its 6,500-rpm yellow line on the tachometer, thanks to improvements in the crankshaft since our earlier road test." We mentioned that the Z-car still suffered from high-speed instability, and that it proved the least frugal with fuel, returning 21.0 mpg during the comparison test. "In sum," we noted, "the Datsun 240Z's plusses are its striking looks, its effortless, strong performance, its good brakes and low-speed handling, and its comfort and equipment." We suggested that if you could buy one for the list price rather than the inflated prices Datsun dealers were asking, you would be getting not only the best car in the group, but also the best buy.

1971 Datsun 240Z

The next month (August 1971), the 240Z was named one of the "Ten Best Cars in the World" in our first-ever listing, and was additionally selected the best Sports / GT $3,000-$4,500 category winner in the accompanying list of "The Best Car in Each of Ten Categories." The justification for these honors was, "The Datsun 240Z is such a remarkable car relative to its price that it has become nearly mythical. Yes, it really is a handsome, exciting 2-seater GT coupe with a single-overhead-cam, 6-cylinder engine of 150 horsepower, a nice 4-speed gearbox, independent suspension all around, good finish, good brakes, an impressive list of standard equipment and a list price of under $3,600. We are aware it is not a perfect car. All things considered, with its fine combination of performance, comfort and sportiness it must be considered one of the most significant automobiles in the history of sports motoring."

In that same issue of *Road & Track*, we published a road test of the newly available 240Z with 3-speed automatic transmission and found that it blended quite nicely with "the super-smooth 240Z engine." We characterized the upshifts as silky and applauded the provision for part-throttle downshifts, while criticizing the whirring noises during acceleration from rest and the occasional slippage in second / third shifts. The automatic gearbox did take its toll in performance and fuel efficiency. The 0-60 mph time rose from 8.7 seconds to 10.4 with the automatic, the quarter-mile now took 17.6 seconds at 82.0 mph versus 17.1 sec at 84.5, and the mpg figure slipped from

21.1 mpg for the 4-speed to 19.0 for the automatic. All in all, however, the automatic made a reasonably good impression: "...for those who like the unique combination of sportiness, style, compactness and performance the Z offers but don't like to shift, we can only say Go Ahead."

Our final report on the 240Z came in the *Road & Track Guide to Sports & GT Cars for 1973*. The following year the engine displacement would grow to 2.6 liters, emission standards would become considerably more stringent and safety laws (primarily affecting the bumpers) would invoke noticeable changes to the Z's silhouette as it became the 260Z. There were two distinctive alterations to the 1973 version of the 240Z: The price had climbed to near $5,000, and the engine had begun to lose its performance edge because of emission controls. The horsepower rating was down to 129 at 6,000 from 150 at the same revs, while torque had fallen from 148 at 4,400 to 127. "Very strong performance used to be a 240Z strong suit," we reported, "but Datsun has not been able to maintain it and meet 1973 emission regulations: Our 1973 test car took 1.4 seconds longer to reach 60 mph and 0.6 seconds longer to cover the quarter-mile from a standing start. Fuel economy has suffered too, and the driveability of our test car (which already had modifications supposed to cure early 1973 driveability faults) was wholly unacceptable. That nice [manual] choke was handy because the Z needed it nearly all the time!" Our conclusion was that perhaps it was time for a face-lift and some mechanical improvements to the Z-car now that its price had risen so that it was no longer the super bargain it had been.

Buying a Used 240Z

We received several hundred completed Used Car Classic Questionnaires from our readers concerning the Datsun sports coupe, and there was near unanimity among them that the Z is a rewarding car to drive and own with its fundamentally strong and reliable engine. In general terms, there was consensus that 1973 models were somewhat less desirable than 1970-72 Z-cars because of the emission-control related problems already mentioned. Several owners had altered their 1973s by fitting the carburetion system from earlier Zs; while this does solve the driveability problem, it's not legal.

Quite a number of Z-car owners took the trouble to write letters filled with good advice for a novice wanting to buy a used 240Z, and perhaps the most complete such letter came from William Hampton of Ann Arbor, Michigan, who described himself as the former editor of a newsletter for a now-defunct Z-car owners group. Along with virtually every owner who sent in the completed questionnaire, Hampton stressed the rust problem: "Every 240Z will develop body rust around the rear fender wheel wells. Eventually it will also develop along the tops of the front fenders and the bottom edges of the doors," says Hampton. Other Z-car owners suggested looking for rusted areas along the rocker panels, the boxed frame sections on each

1970 Datsun 240Z

side of the engine compartment and the shock towers. Fiberglass replacement pieces for fenders and panels are readily available and have been installed by many owners whose cars have rusted badly.

Overheating problems are fairly common as the radiator evidently lacked sufficient capacity for American summers, especially in cars that have air conditioning. Various fixes have been tried, Hampton writes, including louvers and belly pans, but the best solution "is to remove the stock radiator and have its core replaced with one having greater capacity." Hampton and others also mentioned installing a thermostatically controlled electric fan.

Another reader who offered copious notes on things to look for with Z-cars was Harold Kunsch of Santa Ana, California: "Look for the U-joints in the rear end to go at about 75,000-100,000 miles. Most older Zs have a characteristic rear-end whine at about 60-65 mph at about 3,000-3,500 rpm, and the differential will tend to snap and clunk. When the U-joints are beginning to go, the snap and clunk will get louder and a slight vibration may be noticed." Other items that have a tendency to fail as mileage increases are the mechanical fuel

1970 Datsun 240Z interior

Brief Specifications

	1970-1973 240Z
Curb Weight, lb.	2355*
Wheelbase, in.	90.7
Track, f / r	53.5 / 53.0
Length	162.8
Width	64.1
Height	50.6
Engine type	sohc inline 6
Bore x stroke, in.	3.27 x 2.90
Displacement, cc	2393
Horsepower, bhp @ rpm	150 @ 6000**
Torque, lb-ft @ rpm	148 @ 4400***

*The curb weight for the 1971 Z with automatic grew to 2,405, and the 1973 4-speed weighed 2,450.

**In 1973, horsepower dropped to 129 @ 6,000.

***Torque fell to 127 @ 4,400 in 1973.

Performance Data From Contemporary Tests

	1970 4-speed	1971 Automatic	1973 4-speed
0-60 mph, sec.	8.7	10.4	10.1
Standing 1 / 4 mile, sec.	17.1	17.6	17.7
Average mpg	21	19	19
Road test date	4-70	8-71	'73 S&GT*

*1973 R&T Guide to Sports & GT Cars

Typical Asking Prices

1970-1973 240Z	$2,500-$4,500
Typical engine-rebuild price	$1,400-$2,000

pump and the water pump. Also, the front disc brakes tend to need fairly constant attention, especially on cars in the states where salt is used on winter roads, resulting in damage to the calipers.

There are a number of small items that are susceptible to breakage on 240Zs, including choke cables, window cranks and instruments. These relatively minor items can be annoying but shouldn't stop the prospective buyer from selecting an otherwise good car because the availability of replacement parts through Datsun dealers as well as the many aftermarket companies is one feature that makes the 240Z such a desirable Used Car Classic. Reader Jim Gozdzialski of Florissant, Missouri, put it this way: "With the availability of so many new and used repair parts and the relatively inexpensive price of a Z as compared to the ZX, it makes [the 240Z] a great car to tinker with if you're the least bit handy." Robert Snipes of Reston, Virginia may have summed it up best: "Fast, excellent handling; a terrific buy used — even at its original price. Mine's not for sale!"

Driving Impressions

Dean Davison bought his first 240Z in 1972: "I fell in love with the car when it first appeared in 1970 and finally was able to buy one two years later." Dean drove that car for about 130,000 miles and eventually parted with it, but in the meantime acquired a 1972 Z, which is primarily driven by his wife, Judy. They were gracious enough to lend me the car for refreshing my memory of what it's like to drive an original 240Z.

We have often mentioned in *Road & Track* the changes that have taken place with the Datsun Z-car over the years — how it has become much more a GT car, perhaps even a personal luxury car, and less a sports car. Driving the Davison car quickly brought back the initial excitement everyone in the enthusiast-car world felt when the 240Z was introduced. Even all these years later, the performance is exhilarating as the 2.4-liter six dredges up gobs of torque to send the car briskly on its way. The response is immediate and continues to build smoothly right on up to about 6,000 rpm.

The 4-speed gearbox does its part by providing crisp and precise shifting, even as the synchros begin to wear with the years and miles. The suspension has a taut feeling that's lacking in the newest Z-cars, although there is a considerable amount of body roll when cornering. The sensation, altogether, is one of a sports car that's anxious to get on with the business at hand, i.e., hurrying on down the twisty road.

Dean tells me that he and Judy love driving the Z, and that the reliability of his original car and this one, which they've had for five years, has been quite good. Their 240Z, like many others, is used daily and maintained with normal care — it's not a show car, but a car that fulfills its design purpose: exciting driving pleasure for two people. — *Thos L. Bryant (October 1981)*

JAPAN

Datsun 510

1968-1973

The poor man's BMW   by Thos L. Bryant

1968 Datsun 510

Datsun started to make its presence felt in the U.S. car market in the mid-1960s, particularly in the Southern California area where imported cars have always been strong sellers. But it was the introduction of the 510 sedan in 1968 that spread the Datsun name far and wide — it also coincided, of course, with steady growth in the dealer network.

The Datsun 510 is a handsome, cleanly styled car with a bit of Ford Cortina influence about its lines and a little of the heretofore traditional Japanese styling, i.e. narrow, too-tall boxes with a heavy appearance. The 510 was initially available in 4-door sedan and wagon configurations, with the 2-door sedan following a few months later. Throughout the 510's 6-year life span, changes were few and generally confined to trim, bumpers and interior upgrades.

Road & Track's first road test of the 510 appeared in the March 1968 issue. In comparing the new car to the previous 410, we noted that "the new Datsun is as near to an all-new car as you're likely to see these days. Its unit body chassis is entirely new, slightly larger and considerably roomier; its engine is also entirely new; and its suspension is not only entirely new but also representative of the best current practice."

The 510 sits on a wheelbase of 95.3 inches and measures 162.2 inches overall. Light weight (2130-lb. curb weight) was one of its strong suits in terms of performance, but also provided a shortcoming *vis-a-vis* long-term durability of body panels.

The 510 was something of a pioneer among low-price Japanese cars because of its relatively sophisticated suspension design. MacPherson struts (a compliance strut was used for longitudinal location instead of the anti-roll bar) took care of the front end. The independent rear suspension, normally associated with much more expensive cars, used semitrailing arms pivoted from a rubber-mounted subframe for noise isolation. The 510 station wagon used a live axle with leaf springs to prevent camber changes with heavier loads.

The 510 was equipped with front-disc/rear-drum brakes similar to those used on the 410 SSS model. The steering was by recirculating ball with 3.0 turns, lock-to-lock.

The new engine for the 510 displaced 1595 cc and was less oversquare than the previous 1.6-liter as the longer stroke was deemed advantageous for controlling emissions. Datsun adopted a 5-main-bearing crankshaft, and used a roller chain to drive the overhead camshaft, which in turn activated the inline valves by rocker arms.

"Power and torque curves show that Nissan engineers chose, for the U.S. version at least, to take advantage of the new design in refinement rather than in peak power," we said in our road test. "The latter quantity remains at 96 bhp but is developed at 5,600 rpm rather than the 6,000 of the 410 SSS. Peak torque is down from 103 lb-ft at 400 rpm to 100 lb-ft at 3,600." The compression ratio was 8.5:1, which permitted the use of regular-grade fuel, although we later discovered in a long-term test of a 2-door 510 that from about 4,000 miles on, we had to use premium to avoid knocking and pinging.

Datsun made a twin-carburetor version of the 510 that developed 109 bhp at 6,000 rpm, but it was never imported into the U.S. Because of emission regulations, the twin SUs and manifold could be ordered through the Datsun Competition Department for racing purposes only.

The clutch and the fully synchronized 4-speed manual gearbox were carried over from the 410. Manual-shift cars were fitted with a 3.70:1 final drive ratio while automatics had a 3.90. With the introduction of the 2-door sedan, the 3.70 ratio was discontinued and 3.90 became standard with both gearboxes.

Inside, the 510 came with individual front seats that initially had no provision for back angle adjustment, and a rear bench. The 4-door models had carpeting while the first series of 2-doors made do with rubber mats, but that too was changed fairly quickly. The front seats were rated as reasonably comfortable in our 1968 road test and overall driver comfort was deemed excellent for people less than 6-feet tall, while larger folks could get by fairly well. The interior design and trim were clean and uncluttered, and as the years went by there was a general upgrading of comfort features and materials.

The postwar period of Japanese automaking had been characterized by stodgy and old-fashioned cars. But the 510, with its use of a sohc rather than pushrod engine, front disc brakes instead of drums and irs, was a major breakthrough for a Japanese manufacturer. Overall, the Datsun 510 can be classified as Nissan's first real effort to build an up-to-date car. In many ways, the 510 could also be considered an overbuilt car because it used components that were much stronger than necessary. For example, the stock crankshaft and valve train were used in the racing cars, and the U-joints, connecting rods and main bearings were the same ones later used in the 240Z with its greater power output. According to Datsun expert Ron Johnson, competition specialist with Nissan Motor Corp., the 240Z's 6-cylinder engine can be considered an extension of the 510's 4-cylinder engine.

We had noted in our initial and subsequent road tests of the 510 that its handling was limited by its stock bias-ply 5.60-13 tires and 4.0-in rims. It didn't take long for many owners to discover that radial tires on wider rims made a considerable difference in cornering power. Tires as large as 185/70-13 on 5.5- or 6.0-inch rims could be fitted to the 510 without fender interference as long as the wheels had zero offset. Many 510 owners discovered that Corvair 5.5-in. rims would fit perfectly, and they were readily available.

In addition to wheels and tires, 510s also benefitted from suspension tuning, including shorter, stiffer springs, larger front anti-roll bar, and Koni shocks. Indeed, in the hands of many owners, 510s became high performance sports sedans. The 510 could be purchased new for less than $2500, while another $1,000-$2,000 would convert it into a street racer that would blow the doors off some considerably more expensive European sedans.

Selecting a Used 510

We had an enormous number of responses to our Used Car Classic questionnaire from Datsun 510 owners all across North America — and a couple from Europe. We also received an unusual number of replies from people who owned several 510s and from family groups that owned two, three or four of them. In perusing the questionnaires and in talking with experts such as Ron Johnson of Datsun, I found that the 510 doesn't have very many weak points that are common to the series.

Let's start with rust. West Coast cars will show very little; Midwest and East Coast cars will show a lot. The general feeling is that the 510's body panels were lightweight and prone to rust in snowbelt states because of inadequate rustproofing. In fact, several owners in the Northeast commented that the 510s have become scarce there because of the rust problem. In examining a car for purchase, check for rust in the usual places: rocker panels, door bottoms, above and below the bumpers and around the wheel wells front and rear. The rear part of the front fender where it joins the body is another spot that is given to rusting.

Quite a number of owners reported head gasket troubles, and a prospective buyer should check for the first sign of seepage of oil and water around the head. This problem is not all that unusual in mating an alloy head to an iron block in cars of this vintage. The bright side is that the bottom (and expensive) end of the 510's engine is virtually bulletproof. Various people reported replacing piston rings or doing valve work and checking the crank and cylinders at the same time. Nearly all of them found tolerances very close to manufacturer's specs even after 100,000-plus miles.

The gearbox turns out to be just about as sturdy as the engine, although the second-gear synchros tend to wear out before any of the others. Some owners also felt that the stock clutch was not particularly beefy, and many replaced theirs with heavier duty ones from the Competition Department or the Datsun Sports roadster. Others, however, reported 70,000 miles or more without any clutch problems. If you are looking at a used 510, a poor clutch may be an indication of the type of driver who now owns the car. Nonetheless, it's not a terribly expensive or complex job to replace it.

Although the U-joints are the same ones later used in the 240Z, a number of owners did have to replace them at various times, along with the halfshaft seals in the irs. The front suspension was rated quite highly by most owners for durability and proved trouble-free as long as the car was not abused. Those who mentioned alignment problems generally were those who added larger wheels and tires and, as a result, drove their cars quite hard. The 510's interior appointments held up reasonably well with routine maintenance. The vinyl upholstery and carpeting were not of the very best quality and consequently wore thin after a few years.

All in all, the Datsun 510 seems to have held up through the years as well as or better than many of the cars we've covered in this series.

Owner Impressions

Chris Towner is an auto body mechanic who lives in Orleans, Massachusetts. He has owned his 1972 2-door 510 since new. In fact, there are three 510s in his family. His father has a 1971 4-door in California, and the family keeps a 1972 4-door at their summer home at Cape Cod. Chris says when he bought his car his decision was based on various elements: He wanted a new car and the 510 was affordable ($2,175); his father was having good luck with his 510; and the car had enormous potential. "It was a poor man's BMW," Towner says, "with enough reasonably priced aftermarket equipment to convert that family sedan into a full-bore racer. The basic handling was poor by enthusiast standards, but simply adding good radial tires, wider rims, stiffer anti-roll bars, lowering the springs, etc.,

Race-prepared Datsun 510

Brief Specifications

	1968-1973 510
Curb Weight, lb.	2130
Wheelbase, in.	95.3
Track, f / r	50.4 / 50.4
Length	162.2
Width	61.4
Height	55.1
Engine type	sohc inline 4
Bore x stroke, in.	3.27 x 2.90
Displacement, cc	1595
Horsepower (SAE net) @ rpm	96 @ 5600
Torque (SAE net), lb-ft @ rpm	100 @ 3600

Performance Data From Contemporary Tests

	1968 4-speed	1970 Automatic	1971 4-speed
0-60 mph, sec.	13.5	15.1	13.9
Standing 1 / 4 mile, sec.	19.7	22.3	19.6
Average mpg	23-27	22-24	24-26
Road test date	3-68	12-70	1-71

Typical Asking Prices

1968-1973	$600-$3,000
Typical engine-rebuild price	$1,000-$1,500

made all the difference in the world."

Chris finds 510s in the Northeast extremely prone to rust. He also notes that the thin sheet metal is very hard to work with because it stretches easily. When driving his 510 in slaloms, Chris found the battery caps leaked acid onto the radiator hoses, fan belts and fuel pump, which he had replaced (under warranty). He switched to aircraft-style battery caps to solve the problem. Chris says that the rubber weather stripping around the windows and doors rots away in just a few years. The head gasket leaks most often at the right rear near a water jacket; he had his gasket replaced at 12,000 miles and hasn't had a problem with it since. One item that seems to go quickly, however, is the exhaust system. Along with a number of other owners, Towner thinks the problem may be a result of the muffler being exposed to debris kicked up by the left rear wheel.

Towner equipped his 510 with most of the suspension pieces designed to improve the car's handling characteristics, as well as adding a spoiler, VDO gauges and other aftermarket products. He still finds the car will average 32 mpg on a long trip. And as for the question about buying another one: "Would you buy a practical, good looking family sedan that runs on regular fuel, all for $2,475 out the door? You must be kidding! There is still nothing from Japan that comes close to what the 510 was (and is) in my opinion." — *Thos L. Bryant (August 1983)*

ITALY

Ferrari 330GT 2+2 and 250GTE 2+2

Bargain-priced exotica

1961-1967

by Peter Bohr

Imagine you're cleaning your attic one day and you come across a tarnished Aladdin's lamp. You rub it a bit and out pops a genie. It seems your Aladdin's lamp is a discount model, because instead of the customary three wishes, the genie simply offers you a car. "You can have a Mazda or a Ferrari," he says. "Which will it be?"

What a strange choice, you think. But not wanting to look a gift genie in the mouth, naturally you choose the Ferrari. After all, you have a passion for automobiles and it's every enthusiast's dream to own a Ferrari. Mazdas, especially RX-7s, are desirable cars. They're entertaining to drive and easy to maintain. But, my goodness, a Ferrari is a Ferrari. There are those who believe that when Enzo Ferrari passes from this earth, he will be granted sainthood for delivering automobile lovers from the throes of mundane transportation.

Actually this little fairy tale isn't so fanciful. Anyone who has about $15,000 and wants to buy a sports / GT car has the very real choice of a Mazda or a Ferrari. A 1985 top-of-the-line RX-7 GSL-SE costs over $15,000. According to Gerald Roush, publisher of the *Ferrari Market Letter*, that's also the going rate for a clean Ferrari 250GTE 2+2 or 330GT 2+2 from the early and mid-1960s.

Understand we're talking about *real* Ferraris, not the "fancy Fiats of the gold-chain set," as some purists derisively (and probably unfairly) call the contemporary 8-cylinder 308s and Mondials. The 250 and 330 2+2s do have honest-to-God V-12 engines. Enzo Ferrari, being Italian, never forgets about the importance of style, so over the years he's engaged the greatest designers to put beautiful bodies on his cars. And, of course, he's well aware of the importance of a good chassis. But as anyone worth a year's subscription to *Road & Track* knows, the engine is the heart and soul of a Ferrari, especially the Colombo-designed V-12 engine. And unlike the 308 and Mondial, the 250 and 330 2+2s, have that V-12 engine.

So despite $15,000 being two, three and even four times the price of most of the cars we've covered during the last decade in our Used Car Classic series, for a Ferrari it's a paltry sum. That's why we couldn't resist reporting on the 250GTE 2+2 and the 330GT 2+2.

1966 Ferrari 330GT 2 + 2

1961 Ferrari 250GTE 2 + 2

1961 Ferrari 250GTE 2 + 2

Evolution of the 2+2s

"Undervalued." "Underrated." "Overlooked." These were the adjectives we heard time and time again to describe these 2+2s. And if you know their backgrounds, you'll understand why.

Enzo Ferrari's passion is, and always has been, racing. It's fair to say he never aspired to become the Italian equivalent of GM mogul Alfred P. Sloan. No, his street cars were primarily cash cows used to finance his racing pursuits, at least in the early days. His company's efforts went into race cars, which, with as few modifications as necessary, made them civilized enough to be sold to hairy-chested, wealthy folk who could use them as street cars. In the decade or so after World War II, it was feasible to drive a 166MM Barchetta, for example, to the track, win a race and then drive it home again.

But with the dawning of the 1970s, the rules of international automobile racing, not to mention onerous government regulations, severely restricted the dual-purpose car. As years passed, Ferrari's race cars and street cars have come to bear less resemblance to one another. But between the innocent times of the early 1950s and the burdensome years of the 1970s, the dual-purpose Ferrari reached its peak with variations of the 250GT, the 250GT Berlinetta Tour de France, the 250GT short-wheelbase Berlinetta, the 250GT Spyder California, and the legendary 250GTO. With them, Ferrari dominated rallies, hillclimbs and endurance racing. To many Ferrari lovers, these models have come to represent the grandest and most charismatic examples of the marque. And their current values, $85,000 and up, reflect their esteemed status.

All of these 250GTs have much in common. Their bodies were styled by Pininfarina and built by Scaglietti, with the exception of the GTO, which was built by the latter firm but designed in-house by Ferrari. They all used strong, ladder-type frames constructed of welded, tubular steel. They all have wheelbases of 94.4 inches, except for the long-wheelbase cars (or LWBs in Ferrari lingo), which are longer by some 8 inches. Their rear suspensions consist of a live axle with semi-elliptic springs, located by parallel trailing arms. The Tour de France and California Spyder have drum brakes, but the SWB cars and the GTO use discs. However, all 250GTs came with gorgeous knockoff Borrani wire wheels. And all the 250GTs came with the same basic engine, though there were a number of compression, carburetion and horsepower variations. The basic design of the engine, a single-overhead cam V-12 with a 60-degree angle between the cylinder banks, was laid out in 1946 by then-Ferrari chief engineer, Gioacchino Colombo.

All these 250GTs had something else in common too: They were strictly 2-seaters as befitted race-cum-street cars. If you wanted four seats, you bought two Ferraris. But Aston Martin with its lovely DB4 proved it was possible to provide four seats in a high-performance car. So Ferrari and Pininfarina went to work on a 4-place 250GT, using the components of the various

250GT models. Their efforts resulted in the 250GTE 2+2 prototype of 1960 (the E stands for the so-called E-series versions of the Colombo V-12 engine).

Under the sheet metal, the 250GTE 2+2 and other famed 250GTs such as the Tour de France are basically the same. Even the sheet metal of the GTE and the other 250GTs was styled by the same designer. True, the GTE was not a dual-purpose car, but a heavier grand touring car. Still *Road & Track* reported in 1962 a top speed of nearly 150 mph and a 0-60 mph time of 8.0 seconds for a 250GTE. Yet a Tour de France costs five or six times more than a GTE today. The 2+2s are God's gift to us poor (relatively speaking, of course) but honest Ferrari lovers.

1963 Ferrari 250GTE 2+2

After making the rounds of the European auto shows in 1960, the 250GTE was well into production the following year. The bodies were built by Pininfarina while the rest of the car was made in Ferrari's factory. Between 1961 and 1963, the 250GTE remained essentially unchanged. There were minor improvements during those years, but the major change didn't come until the end of 1963. It's hard to imagine in these days of anemic econo-boxes, but the GTE's trusty 2,953-cc., 240-bhp engine was beginning to seem a tad tame. Thus Ferrari decided to equip the 2+2 with the engine from the very limited production model, the Superamerica 400. It was basically the same Colombo-designed V-12, but it had a displacement of 3,967 cc and produced 300 bhp. The idea was actually more ambitious than just a larger engine; there was to be a new 2+2 car to carry the engine as well. But the new car wasn't ready, and as an interim measure, about 50 250GTEs received the 4.0-liter engine. The amalgam was christened the 330 America.

The new body finally came along a few months later, in 1964. This new 330GT 2+2 (not to be confused with the 330GTC, a later two-passenger car) was not dissimilar from the 250GTE, but the pundits were astonished to see that Pininfarina had taken the old car's perfectly nice front end and had added a baroque cluster of twin headlamps on each side in place of the 250GTE's single lamps. Other styling changes, including eliminating the tailfins, were pleasing, however.

Functional changes included a longer wheelbase that allowed more trunk and rear-seat room. The driveline was also strengthened to handle the added horsepower, and the front and rear brake systems were separated to avoid the possibility of a total brake failure.

The 330GT 2+2 sold well enough, but Ferrari and Pininfarina seemed to realize they had goofed with the four headlights. In the summer of 1965, the 330GT returned to single lamps and became the Series II 330GT. At the same time, Campagnolo alloy wheels replaced the Borrani wires as standard equipment. Moreover, the Series II cars received a 5-speed gearbox instead of the 4-speed unit with electric overdrive as used on previous 2+2s. (Some 125 4-headlight Series I 330GTs also had 5-speeds instead of overdrives. Model changes at Ferrari are always confusing, which makes keeping track of them like keeping track of Italian governments.) In addition, the Series II 330GTs were the first of the 2+2s to come with power-assisted steering and air conditioning as factory options.

By the time the last 330GT 2+2s left the Maranello factory around the end of 1967, the scorecard read as follows: 950 250GTEs, 50 330 Americas, 500 Series I 330GTs with overdrives, 125 Series I 330GTs with 5-speeds and 455 Series II 330GTs. Today these cars may not be the most coveted Ferraris, but with a production total of more than 2,000, they were a huge success for a small specialty maker such as Ferrari. And remember, at the time Ferrari salesmen didn't try to convince their customers to buy 2+2s instead of the racier two-passenger models. In fact, there was only about $1,000 difference between a SWB Berlinetta and a 250GTE 2+2, the latter selling for just over $12,000 when new. No, people really preferred the practicality of the 2+2s.

Buying a 2+2

The older Ferraris are a paradox. They can be as trouble-free as the new Mazda. But they can also be so horrendously expensive to maintain that you'd think they were weapons systems ordered by the Pentagon. You see, if one of these cars is well cared for, it won't break easily. But if neglected, repairs come dear, which, of course, is why the more cautious among us buy new RX-7s instead of old Ferraris.

These Ferrari 2+2s are really endurance race cars disguised as grand touring cars. And Enzo didn't win so much glory over the years with temperamental, unreliable race cars. In their last years as publishers of *Road & Track*, John and Elaine Bond owned one of the 2+2 hybrids, a 330 America. They'd often return home from lengthy business trips and find that of their several cars, only the Ferrari would start — and their stable usually included at least one highly regarded German car.

In the November 1971 issue, we published a Ferrari Owner Survey that confirmed the Bonds' experience. Many of the cars in the survey were 250 and 330 2+2s, and most of the respondents had a difficult time coming up with complaints. A few mentioned cooling and electrical system problems. Claude Gray, manager of European Automotive in Riverside, California, and an experienced Ferrari mechanic, says that overheating can often be traced to bad head gaskets in these old 2+2s. If all's well there and the car still runs too warm, especially in stop-and-go traffic (Enzo's engineers were thinking more of LeMans than rush-hour driving on the Long Island Expressway when they designed the cooling system), Gray suggests replacing the old-fashioned metal fan with a modern plastic one, or even adding an auxiliary electric fan.

As for electric maladies, Gray and another Ferrari expert, Lyle Tanner, agree that ham-fisted mechanics are often the real problem. It seems that back in the days of the 250 and 330 2+2s, Ferrari electrical systems were arcane, with wiring and placement of switches varying from car to car. Over the years mechanics often confused things even more with their fiddlings. Tanner owns Lyle Tanner Enterprises in Carson, California, one of the major suppliers of Ferrari parts in the country. Tanner recalls a nice 330GT with a seemingly minor electrical problem. Upon inspection, he was horrified to discover some dumb cluck had taken all the connections from the back of the fusebox and had welded them into a giant glob.

And therein lies the rub with 250 and 330 2+2s. These are now old cars — 20- to 25-year-old cars. They've not only been subjected to the normal ravages of age, but often to inept owners and mechanics as well. One respondent in the 1971 survey listed the "improvements" he had made to his 250GT: an American alternator and regulator, a custom exhaust system and a Ford differential. This is what you have to watch out for in your search for an older Ferrari.

More than the owners of 250 Berlinettas or Spyders, 2+2 owners are likely to be low-budget folks who try to avoid high-budget Ferrari parts and service. Every one of the Ferrari experts we contacted eventually uttered the same words: A $15,000 250GTE or 330GT 2+2 costs just as much to fix as a $100,000 250GT SWB Berlinetta. Tanner gives a sampling of repair prices (are you sitting down?): normal engine overhaul, parts and labor, $6,000-$8,000; brake system overhaul, parts only, $700-$800; front wheel bearing, part only, $90; complete exhaust system, parts only, $700; overhaul of electric overdrive unit, parts and labor, $1,300; transmission overhaul, parts and labor, $2,000. Worn valve guides are often a source of excessive oil burning on V-12 Ferrari engines, and a cylinder-head rebuild is $2,000. Rear ends tend to wear on these older Ferraris; parts and labor for a rebuild are $2,000.

1962 Ferrari 250GTE interior

And there's not much you can do to avoid paying these prices if you want the jobs done right. Though some body parts — door handles and the like — were shared with lowly Alfas and Fiats, there's little else that's interchangeable with other cars. Even the British-made Laycock de Normanville overdrive, though very similar to those used on Jaguars, has input and output shafts peculiar to Ferrari. The good news is that aside from certain body and trim pieces, parts for 2+2s are readily available if you can pay the price.

Because these Ferraris represent an unparalleled opportunity for personal bankruptcy, we can't emphasize enough the need for a complete inspection by a knowledgeable Ferrari mechanic before you buy. He should remove all the inspection plates, of which there are many on old Ferraris, and in general, go over just about every inch of the car.

In our Used Car Classic articles we usually give the same advice, which is to worry less about the mechanicals because you can always rebuild an engine or rear end, but rust or body cancer is often forever. This axiom doesn't always hold true with Ferraris because of the parts costs. Certainly you want to avoid a

Ferrari that's nothing but iron oxide, but a little rust on the rocker panels, leading edges of the doors or under the windshield wipers (all common spots for rust on 2+2s) is preferable to a blown engine.

In sum, when a V-12 Ferrari is good, it's very good. But unlike Mae West, when it's bad, it's very bad indeed.

2+2 Price Appreciation Potential

Ferraris aren't just cars. They're not even just cars for automotive connoisseurs. They've become investments. Around 1976, when the country entered into an inflation binge, Ferraris joined that group of highly desirable items such as California real estate and Persian rugs known as inflation hedges. In 1971, a Tour de France would be advertised in *Road & Track*'s "Market Place" for $5,000 or $6,000. For people who simply love cars and don't give a hoot about hedges, this idea of buying Ferraris for their investment value is, as William Bendix used to say, "a revoltin' development." Now you can't become involved in Ferraris without thinking about investment potential.

In the last five or six years, the 2+2s have doubled and tripled in value. But can we expect them to skyrocket in value like other 250GTs? According to Gerald Roush, the answer is no. First, he doesn't foresee any Ferrari, 2+2 or otherwise, increasing at the rate they did during the 1976-80 period. Second, there's rarity: the 2+2s are far more numerous than their two-passenger counterparts. Third, when it comes to collectible cars, people always prefer the racier-looking models.

Instead, Roush thinks the 250 and 330 2+2s will appreciate at 5 or maybe 10 percent a year or, in other words, a little more than inflation. There is, however, one event that could cause a more rapid rise in Ferrari prices — Enzo's death. He is in his late eighties and the theory goes that when he dies it will remind people that he made these wonderful cars and then everybody will suddenly want one. People have invested in things for sillier reasons.

Among the 2+2s, the pecking order according to Roush begins with the America. It's the most rare, and its body is lighter than the 330 yet it has the bigger engine. The second most desirable model would be a Series II 330. Third, a 250GTE. And finally, the 4-headlight 330. But the price differences among them are actually very slight.

Driving Impressions

You might have thought Terry Baldwin just another hopeless dreamer, or you might have thought him a gutsy, grab-all-the-gusto-you-can kind of guy — arguments could have been made either way. When Terry bought his 1965 330GT 2+2, he followed absolutely none of the golden advice I have just carefully expounded. He didn't have an expert Ferrari mechanic inspect the car before he bought it. He didn't buy the car because it seemed mechanically sound. In fact, the cosmetics were okay and the mechanicals were awful. The engine more or less ran on 10 cylinders, but it didn't matter much because the gearbox was frozen like arctic tundra in January. As if this wasn't bad enough, Terry bought the car intending to rebuild the engine and transmission himself. It didn't daunt him in the least that his hands had never entered the innards of *any* engine before, let alone the sanctum sanctorum of a Ferrari V-12.

We all know about those poor souls who optomistically embark down the primrose path of a do-it-yourself automobile restoration with their basket-case sports cars only to end up in the ditch of disinterest and frustration. I've done it myself. I bought a car, tore it apart, invested in new parts, lost interest and then sold the whole mess for much less than I had in it. But Terry Baldwin proved the exception, the kind of exception that inspires dreamers to buy basket cases. He now has a handsome, smooth-running 330GT 2+2 for an investment of about half what it's worth on today's market — not including his own labor or Blake's.

You see, Terry had divine intervention in the form of Blake Morris — a renowned Italian-car mechanic, proprietor of a shop called JAFCO in Costa Mesa, California, owner of a 250GTE 2+2, and a guy with a big heart. But Terry only met Blake after Terry had managed to remove the transmission of the 330 and had it placed in the corner of his cramped garage. Blake was so impressed by this feat (a 2+2's tranny weighs about 200 pounds and must be removed through the car's interior) that he invited Terry to bring the engine and transmission to his shop where he could rebuild them in a proper environment and benefit from Blake's advice.

After a year and a half of weekend and spare-time work, Terry had his 330 running. They encountered no major problems except for discovering one example after another of previous, shoddy repair jobs. For instance, someone had installed two pistons that were of a completely different type from the other ten.

But getting behind the wheel and firing up that magnificent creation of Signore Colombo's for the first time was a triple thrill for Terry. Not only had he rebuilt the engine and transmission himself, not only was it his very own Ferrari, but it was his first time ever to even drive a Ferrari! Blake had offered him the keys to his 250GTE, but Terry demurred, preferring to remain a virgin Ferrari driver until his own car was ready.

So what's it like to drive Terry's car? To somebody used to modern Hondas or Mazdas, or, like Terry and me, to old Porsches and Alfas, the Ferrari gives the impression of being, well, ponderous. At low speeds the steering is heavy, and the vintage suspension amplifies the tar strips and chuckholes. But once up to 60 mph or so, the car's breeding suddenly becomes apparent. The ride smooths, the steering lightens, and the car feels almost nimble. The 250 and 330 2+2s are basically understeerers, but if you tweak the steering wheel at the right moment, break the rear wheels loose and use the throttle for control, you can corner the old gals surprisingly well. Out of respect for Terry, on my drive I kept to speeds around the legal limit, but I'm told by owners of 2+2s that the cars come into stride around 100 mph.

The rest of the car may be at its best at higher speeds, but the powerful V-12 is surprisingly flexible at any speed, and in this respect the 330GT is easy to drive. But that doesn't mean any Cadillac driver will feel right at home in the Ferrari. As Blake says, "These old Ferraris demand that you do things in a precise way, especially when it comes to shifting. But once you master the rhythm, the cars are capable of tremendous performance."

In a 1962 road test of a 250GTE, *Road & Track* called its door "the portal to a driver's paradise." The well-formed, pleated leather bucket seats, the proper 3-spoke steering wheel, and the big, easy-to-read instruments are indeed a delight, and few modern cars offer better interior fittings. Of course, by current standards, ventilation is inadequate, interior space isn't outstanding (a modern car this size would probably offer more rear-seat room) and there are no head restraints on the seats.

Brief Specifications

	1962 250GTE 2+2	1965 330GT 2+2
Curb Weight, lb.	3100	3040
Wheelbase, in.	102.3	104.2
Track, f/r	53.3 / 54.9	55.2 / 54.7
Length	185.0	190.5
Width	67.3	55.5
Height	52.8	53.5
Engine type	sohc V-12	sohc V-12
Bore x stroke, in.	2.87 x 2.32	3.03 x 2.79
Displacement, cc	2953	3967
Horsepower, bhp @ rpm	240 @ 7000	300 @ 6600
Torque, lb-ft @ rpm	181 @ 5000	240 @ 5000
Transmission	4-speed + OD	4-speed + OD
Suspension	ind coil / live leaf	ind coil / live leaf
Brakes, f/r	disc / disc	disc / disc
Steering type	worm and peg	worm and peg

Performance Data From Contemporary Tests

0-60 mph, sec.	8.0	NA
Standing 1/4 mile, sec.	16.3	NA
Average mpg	14.5	NA
Road test date	8-62	NA

Typical Asking Prices*

1961-1963 250GTE 2+2	$8,500-$24,500
1964-1967 330GT 2+2	$10,000-$25,000
Typical engine-rebuild price (both models)	$6,000-$8,000

*Prices were compiled by Gerald Roush, publisher of Ferrari Market Letter.

But, the 330's simple, elegant interior is a wonderful contrast to the crushed-velour, video-game instrument panels, electronic voices and gimmicks of so many cars today.

Terry couldn't be more pleased with his car, which is not only his toy but also his everyday transport. After six months and 10,000 miles on the road, the car has never failed him (except for a frozen front-wheel bearing). As a bonus, Terry has found the Ferrari to be a perfect prop in his career as an assistant film director. In Tinseltown, where image is everything, Ferrari drivers have cachet. And you can bet that the owner of the 308 parked in the studio lot next to Terry's 330 hasn't rebuilt his car's engine with his own hands.

— *Peter Bohr (November 1984)*

ITALY

Fiat 850 Spider
1967-1973

by Thos L. Bryant

Lovely to look at, fun to drive, but be prepared to maintain it

1968 Fiat 850 Spider

Our initial exposure to the Fiat 850 Spider was provided by Henry N. Manney III in the June, 1965 *Road & Track*, wherein he described the convertible as "a rorty little car..." that "should be popular among those who like to zig along twisty roads." Henry concluded his story saying, "All in all, lovers of Fiats will welcome these little GTs, or for that matter anyone will who likes to experience that happy Italian feeling." I always thought that happy Italian feeling had more to do with a bottle of Lambrusco and a comely *signorina*, but I defer to Mr. Manney in all matters Italian.

The 850 Spider needed some two years to get through the immigration process and made its appearance in America in 1967. *Road & Track* road tested an early 1968 model in April of that year and our summary described it as an "attractive, nicely finished small-engined sports car... good handling, moderate performance... low price." The 1968 Spider had one significant difference from the previous year's model, a reduction in engine displacement from the original 843 cc to 817. This was a simple response to the new U.S. emission standards; because the 850 Spider engine now displaced less than 50 cubic inches, it was exempt. It did retain the crankcase recirculation system that was used in the 1967 engine for controlling crankcase emissions. The overhead-valve inline 4-cylinder engine was rated at 52 bhp at 6,200 rpm in 1968, whereas the 1967 Spider engine produced closer to 55 bhp, according to some sources, although Fiat claimed no difference.

The road testers were quite impressed with the Spider's styling, describing it as one of the most beautiful designs ever seen on a small car: "Its carefully fashioned Bertone lines were admired by everyone who saw the car, and more than one owner of a small-displacement British roadster cast covetous eyes upon it. The lovely body is matched by a good-looking and comfortable interior.... The top is of excellent design, easy to raise and lower and nicely hidden by a flush body panel when down. Fit is extremely good and no drumming or flapping was experienced."

In measuring acceleration, our enthusiasm was diminished somewhat as the 850 Spider required 20.0 seconds to move from rest to 60 mph and the quarter-mile time was 21.7 seconds at 62.0 mph. But with a list price of $2,109 and incredibly flat cornering capability, we concluded that, "The Fiat can be flung about enthusiastically, giving an exceedingly high fun-per-dollar quotient. The Spider gives every indication of maintaining its appeal over a long period of time."

In the October 1968 *Road & Track*, we compared the 850 Spider to three other basic sports cars: the Austin-Healey Sprite, the Datsun 1600 and the Triumph Spitfire. The Fiat gave a very good account of itself in the matchup, with virtually all the negative remarks about it resulting from its small, rear-mounted engine and modest power: "For around-town traffic where the indirect gears can compensate in some degree, the Fiat is lively, responsive and good fun. Out on the highway, however, the engine whirs out a lot of revs, far more than any of our drivers felt comfortable with. With the top down, as one described it, you have the feeling that an engine is chasing you and having to work hard to keep up."

By the time of that comparison test, the 850 Spider had undergone some subtle changes. The flush-mounted headlights were repositioned and uncovered, the front fender line was revamped to meet U.S. safety regulations, and the metal cover under which the top was stowed had been revised. An optional bolt-on hardtop was available.

For the 1970 model year, the 850's engine was given a longer stroke and displacement went to 903 cc with a small gain in bhp to 58 at 6,400 rpm. This larger engine had been in 850 Spiders in other parts of the world in 1969, but it took an extra year to get the emission controls worked out for the U.S. Also new for 1970 was the fixed-hardtop model known as the 850 Racer, the subject of a road test in April. The horsepower gain resulted in slightly quicker acceleration, with 0-60 now done in 17.9 seconds compared to the previous 20.0, and the quarter-mile figures were 21.0 seconds at 64.0 mph versus the earlier 21.7 seconds at 62.0 mph. But the car was still rated a modest performer.

The welded-on, vinyl-covered top of the Racer was given mixed reviews — it made for a cozy coupe with more luggage space behind the seats, but the vinyl covering was deemed illogical over steel, de-emphasizing the blending of the upper and lower body forms which was nicely done otherwise.

In that same April 1970 *Road & Track*, we presented an Owner Survey report on the 850 Spider from 1967 through 1969 models, and showed that more than 10 percent of the owners had troubles with instruments, the electrical system, body parts and the cooling system, while 5-10 percent mentioned problems with upholstery, carburetion, rain leaks, gearbox, cold starting, front brakes, engine oil leaks and the clutch. Only 70% of the 850 owners in the survey said they would buy another, a percentage that is somewhat below average. However, many 850 owners were buying the car because of its low price and expected to move up to something fancier. Our Owner Survey concluded, "And if the reliability record of the car is not impressive, it's probably because too many 850 owners are trying to extract American-style highway performance from what is essentially a stylish in-town runabout."

Our final word on the 850 Spider came in August 1971, when the diminutive Italian was named to our list of The Best Cars in the World, 1971, as the winner of the Best Sports / GT, Under $3,000.

Buying a Used 850 Spider

The item that tops the list of things to look for is rust. In January 1979, the National Highway Traffic Safety Administration (NHTSA) notified Fiat of its initial determination that a safety-related defect existed in 850 Spiders because of excessive rusting. In March 1979, an agreement was reached between NHTSA and Fiat for the recall of the 1970-71 850 Spiders, which got under way in July 1979.

This doesn't mean that every 850 Spider is a rusty hulk, but that you should be aware of the problem and make a thorough inspection of the body. Take the car to a garage where a hoist is available and inspect underneath, or if that's just not practical, wear your old clothes, grab your flashlight and crawl under the car. Bring along a small hammer and use it to tap lightly on various components, listening for a dull thud (suggesting rust) or a metallic ring (indicating healthy metal). Lift up the floor mats, check under the seats, look beneath the trunk mats and all around the panels within the engine compartment and fenders. Fiat says the rust troubles resulted from assembly problems in models up to 1971, so it may be that a badly corroded car doesn't reflect owner neglect, but why take the chance?

The 850's engine, whether 843-, 817- or 903-cc displacement, must be considered less than optimally sturdy — after all, that's not much displacement for any automobile engine, especially in pre-55 mph America. As a result, the redline for all the engines is above 6,000 rpm, and most drivers agree that you have to keep the revs above 4,000 to extract any sort of sporting performance. It's no surprise that head gaskets and valves can give trouble more often than with most engines. Low compression is a sure sign of trouble; also, large deviations in the

1968 Fiat 850 Spider

readings among the four cylinders may mean the head is warped. A single experience of engine overheating can warp the 850's cylinder head.

Conclusion

The Fiat 850 Spider has much to recommend it as a Used Car Classic: inexpensive to buy, available in sufficient numbers, offering great driving enjoyment and very thrifty with fuel. The flip side is that body rust is a problem, and unlike several older British sports cars, the engines are not tractor-derived workhorses that go on forever. The secret to being happy with the 850 is to recognize its limitations. The engine is small and works very hard most of the time. Thus the rule is to keep one step ahead of it, checking oil level, coolant level, etc., with much more regularity than you would other cars. The Fiat 850 Spider is lovely to look at. It can also be lovely to drive and a pleasure to own if you are the kind of person who takes pride in working on a car, maintaining it and caring for it as a valued possession. If you're the type of driver who wants easy upkeep and who has no interest in tinkering, it's best to stay away from the 850 Spider.

Owner Impressions

My Fiat 850 Spider, a 1967 model with the original 843-cc, lightly desmogged engine and (I believe) more attractive flush-headlight front end is now more than twelve years old and has more than 142,000 miles on it. In the April 1970 *Road & Track* feature "After the New Wears Off" (published in conjunction with an 850 Owner Survey), I described its first 39,066 miles. Then, the low cost of gasoline (premium averaged 34.9 cents per gallon) and the minimal amount of repairs meant an overall cost per mile of only 5.4 cents (at 31.2 mpg, about 1.1 cents went for fuel), while the first two years' depreciation, amounting to approximately $700, was a significant portion. Today, considering the relative rarity of a 1967 Spider and my car's still near-new condition, the car has appreciated beyond its original price, so repair expenses (totaling just under $3,000 in the subsequent ten years and 103,000 miles) and the tripled cost of fuel have combined to make its overall running cost about 5.6 cents per mile. Considering inflation, it's much cheaper to own than ever.

But that's enough objectivity. It was a subjective purchase in the first place, and the reason I've kept it (and kept it up, which has sometimes been a fairly demanding effort) all these years has been its continual pleasure value. For practicality, I've also had a 1972 Audi 100LS 4-door (itself now a veteran at 150,000 plus miles) and a 1979 Dodge Colt Hatchback (Mitsubishi Mirage). Aesthetically, I think the 850 Spider is one of the best-looking sports cars ever designed (Giugiaro, of course), and while current automotive styling is much more angular, the 850 Spider is still sufficiently taut in form to have an effective, aggressive appearance, especially with the 5-inch-wide Cromodora 3-spoke alloy wheels and Michelin XWX tires I've mounted, which widen the stance to full body width. (I've

1968 Fiat 850 Spider interior

always thought Fiat deliberately designed its sports models with room for more tire section.)

Its handling is distinctly improved, as well: although the car is no skidpad wonder by today's standards, I think it would do relatively well in the slalom. I run nearly equal tire pressures front and back (24 and 26) as I want better front-end adhesion and am willing to cope with the car's inherent oversteer, now manageable with the bigger tires. Incidentally, the current Michelins, mounted at 112,000 miles, are only the fourth set of tires the car has had. Next time around, I'd like to put on Pirelli P6s. Maybe the P6 is too much tire and too expensive for this kind of car — it's certainly not a high-performance machine — but when the time comes, the decision will be subjective, I'm sure.

While there have been a number of options for Spider owners wanting more performance, I have never seriously considered going in that direction (sometimes, when climbing a steep hill, such thoughts do hold sway). The car is a modest runabout with a lot of potential for top-down fun in nice weather, and I've left it at that. But "leaving it at that" has still meant a certain amount of engine repair, mainly head gaskets (three) and valve jobs (two), and one bottom-end rebuild, performed effectively by my son Kevin as a project in high-school auto shop. (For the overall cost-per-mile purposes, a regular professional repair cost was computed.) Now a new cylinder head is finally called for, as currently available premium fuel (about 93 octane) doesn't do the job after two millings.

Nevertheless, I've always driven the car hard, usually 5,000 and often 6,000 rpm on acceleration and (before the legislated limit) cruising at 70 mph. When the Spider was new, the *Road & Track* engineering editor didn't think the 850 was adequate for U.S. driving conditions. He was probably right about uphill performance, but my experience has refuted the rest, and now U.S. driving conditions favor this kind of car more than ever. The revs-per-mile figure of 4,425 isn't too great on the ears, but the main noise complaint now is an increased final-drive howl. That will be a future replacement, although the rest of the original transaxle is holding up well: I've accepted the departed second-gear synchros as normal wear after 142,000 miles and I'm willing to double-clutch. Along with the engine rebuild, I had to replace the water-pump assembly. Fiat 850 cooling systems aren't overly effective and the car will run hot if it isn't kept in good order, meaning a clean radiator and proper fan-belt tension.

The greatest traumas have not been the car's fault, but the results of damage inflicted from without. After five years of minor dents and chips, collected from other bumpers and doors in the Fiat's proximity, I had the car repainted and the top replaced. But the car's worst moment occurred about eighteen months ago, when it was sideswiped while parked and nearly totaled. The whole left side was caved in, including the door and both fenders, the left rear wheel and tire were destroyed and

Brief Specifications

	1967 850 Spider	1968 850 Spider	1970 850 Racer
Curb Weight, lb.	1640	1640	1690
Wheelbase, in.	79.8	79.8	79.8
Track, f / r	45.6 / 47.7	47.1 / 49.2	47.1 / 49.2
Length	148.9	148.9	148.9
Width	59.0	59.0	59.0
Height	48.0	48.0	48.0
Engine type	pushrod inline 4	pushrod inline 4	pushrod inline 4
Bore x stroke, in.	2.56 x 2.50	2.52 x 2.50	2.56 x 2.68
Displacement, cc	843	817	903
Horsepower, bhp @ rpm	52 @ 6200	52 @ 6200	58 @ 6400
Torque, lb-ft @ rpm	45.6 @ 4000	45.6 @ 4000	47.7 @ 4000

Performance Data From Contemporary Tests

0-60 mph, sec.	NA	20.0	17.9
Standing 1 / 4 mile, sec.	NA	21.7	21.0
Average mpg	NA	30-35	31.0
Road test date	NA	4-68	4-70

Typical Asking Prices

1967-1973 850 Spider	$1,000-$2,000
Typical engine-rebuild price	$1,000-$1,500

the rear suspension was all but torn off as well. But it was repairable and the offending party's insurance company covered it, even though I elected to put in the additional sum for a complete new paint job (can't stand mismatching panels!), still in the original dark green. So it again looked like new, and still does, stock throughout except for the Nardi wood steering wheel (a bit archaic in appearance these days and cracking a little too), the Sebring Mach I fender mirror (perfectly shaped for the car) and the Cromodora wheels. And I've kept all the original equipment, too.

The Spider has continued to be enjoyable, a willing runner and super economical. Replacement parts, especially for the short-run 1967-to-early-1968 series with the 843-cc engine and original nose, have not been exactly waiting on the shelves at local Fiat dealers, but they've all come from Fiat of North America headquarters in New Jersey within a reasonable time and at reasonable prices. The car is easy to work on and any conscientious repair shop can handle it.

My 850 Spider has always been used as a runabout, for going to work, doing errands or just open-air pleasure driving. It has had a few fairly long trips, to Northern California, Arizona and Nevada, and I'd trust it anywhere (unless the valves and head gasket were getting on toward 50,000 miles, in which case they ought to be done first!). I plan to keep my 850 Spider indefinitely; I'm biased, of course, but it seems I couldn't run a better-looking car for less money. —*Jonathan Thompson (February 1980)*

ITALY

Fiat 124 Sport Coupe and Spider

1968-1972

Inexpensive Italian sports cars of the first order

by Thos L. Bryant

Spinning off two sports cars from a boxy, 4-door sedan may seem like a feat best left to Merlin the Magician, but Fiat did it quite nicely in 1966; and the cars, the 124 Sport Coupe and Spider, have carved niches in the driving enthusiast's arena. The Spider was the first-born, making its European debut in late 1966, while the Sport Coupe followed in early 1967. American Fiat devotees were forced to wait a year, however, as it wasn't until early 1968 that the 124 Sport models were ready for the U.S. and able to meet our safety and emissions standards. The Spider is still in production but the Sport Coupe was discontinued after the 1975 model year.

Design and Engineering

The 124 sedan provided the chassis and drivetrain (with a major engine modification) for the 124 sports cars, and its handling characteristics were so good that little alteration was needed for the conversion to the Spider and Sport Coupe. The obvious changes were in the bodies, with Fiat's in-house designers taking charge of the Sport Coupe and Pininfarina styling the Spider. The roadster model was built on a shortened wheelbase (89.8 inches compared to 95.3 for the Sport Coupe and 124 sedan) and was fitted with a 5-speed gearbox as standard equipment. Initially, the Sport Coupe used the same 4-speed transmission found in the sedan, with the 5-speed an option; however, all U.S. coupes were equipped with the 5-speed from 1969 on.

The 124 sedan's body / frame was of unit steel construction, and this same design was used for the Sport Coupe with an entirely new body laid over the platform. Although the Coupe is 3.3 inches longer overall and 8.3 inches wider, its design resulted in a car with less interior space than the sedan, slightly less trunk room and 3.1 in. less height. For the Spider, however, it was decided to shorten the platform and reduce the wheelbase by 5.5 in. in order to build structural stiffness into the floor of the roadster. This was done by adding undersill box-section reinforcements and a box-section cross-member at the rear, and by making the wheel housing structures more rigid. The result is a shorter car that weighs some 160 pounds more than the sedan-derivative — but then the Sport Coupe is 20 pounds heavier than the Spider.

The entire suspension system, brakes and driveline of the 124 sedan went unchanged in the Spider and Sport Coupe with the exception of the final drive ratio, which became 4.10:1 (4.30:1 in the sedan), and the track width, which grew by half an inch with the substitution of 5-inch rims. The spring rates were raised 19 percent at the front and 14 percent at the rear; the coil springs were shortened a bit to make the sports cars lower, and the front anti-roll bar diameter increased from 20 to 21 mm. Finally, the clutch diameter was increased from 7.4 to 7.9 inches.

The big change for the Spider and Sport Coupe was the engine. The 124 sedan engine displaced 1,197 cc and was of overhead-valve design with pushrods and rocker arms. (There was also a 1,438-cc version, which came later and was used in the 124 Special sedan.) For the sports cars, Fiat increased the bore from 73.0 to 80.0 mm, increasing the displacement to 1,438 cc, and discarded the existing valve gear, opting for a double-overhead camshaft design with a toothed-belt drive (the first production car to use a toothed belt for twin-overhead cams). With the twin-cam design came new pistons, a special carburetor, different manifolds and revisions to the cooling and lubrication systems.

The 124 sports models' new cross-flow cylinder head was made of aluminum alloy (as was the sedan's) with pent roof combustion chambers. Fuel and air were mixed in a single 2-barrel Weber 34 DFH1 carburetor with a vacuum-operated secondary butterfly and manual choke and throttle controls.

The new cylinder heads and the increased displacement meant a marked increase in output, as the 124 sports cars are rated at 96 bhp at 6,500 rpm compared to 65 at 5,600 for the 124 sedan, and torque was 83 lb-ft at 4,000 rpm versus 70 at 3,800. Our initial reaction to the 124 sports models' torque was that it was rather meager at any speed.

The 124 suspension system (common to the sedan, Spider and Sport Coupe) has unequal-length A-arms, coil springs, tube shocks and an anti-roll bar in the front, while at the rear there's a live axle on trailing arms, Panhard rod and coil springs. Our first road test (*Road & Track*, July 1968) characterized the 124s as "outstanding," and went on to say, "They handle in a typical Italian fashion, with moderate body roll, a lot of understeer, an intimate relationship of feel between tires and steering wheel and ultra-light steering. The tires are small (165-13) radials and thus the absolute cornering bite isn't great, but these cars are tremendously stable and predictable through any corner and we'll guarantee they will make a better driver out of any novice."

Along with the excellent suspension design, the Fiat 124s could also boast 4-wheel disc brakes, an oddity in cars in their price class, and worm-and-roller steering with road feel as good as any other comparable rack-and-pinion equipped sports car.

Accommodations in both models rated quite high with our road testers, with the Coupe offering sufficient leg and head room in the rear for two adults, while the Spider could carry the two front passengers in comfort and an occasional third person

1968 Fiat 124 Spider

1968 Fiat 124 Sport Coupe

in the small seat behind the individual front seats. Both versions have identical instrumentation but the dash layouts are different. The Spider's dash is made of beautifully polished wood, while the sport coupe makes do with simulated wood. In the 1968 road test we praised the easy-to-read instruments and described all controls as being within easy reach. The roof and window design of the Sport Coupe afforded greater outward vision than just about any other closed car we could think of, while the Spider was given excellent marks for the design of its folding top that was (and still is) a model of simplicity that other manufacturers would do well to study.

This road test concluded, "There's no denying that the Fiat 124 Sports are extremely attractive cars, enjoyable to drive, and highly practical. Both are pleasant to look at too. Our only major criticism is that their on-the-road performance is not quite up to their looks, and we would respectfully suggest that Fiat consider making the 125 (1,608-cc) version of the dohc engine, which develops 100 lb-ft torque, standard equipment for the American market."

It was three years before Fiat increased the engine displacement and put the 1,608-cc twin-cam engine in the 124 Sports, and the 1971 models develop 104 bhp at 6,000 rpm and 94 lb-ft torque at 4,200 rpm. Considering that the 124 Sports' design was then five years old, it's interesting to note our comments about the Sport Coupe in a July 1971 comparison test with the Datsun 240Z, Opel GT, MG BGT and Triumph GT6 Mk 3: "The Fiat deserves more popularity. At nearly $200 less than the Datsun with comparable equipment, it did so well in our comparison test that it scored nearly as many points.... Its 4-cylinder engine, the smallest of the group, is nevertheless a most satisfying bit of machinery: quiet, very smooth for a 4-cylinder, and willing to rev happily to its 6,500-rpm redline. And the 5-speed gearbox is the best gearbox in the group.

"In road behavior the Fiat scores at the head of the group. Its steering is the most precise, its handling the best; it really shines at high speed in contrast to the Datsun, for it isn't blown about by sidewinds and can negotiate high-speed dips and humps without a hint of losing its composure." High praise, indeed, for a 5-year-old car being compared with the new 240Z. At the time of that test, the 124 Sport Coupe had a basic price of $3,292, up some $300 from its U.S. introductory price ($2,924). The Spider had started at $3,226 in 1968 and by 1972 the price was $3,692.

Buying a Used 124 Sports

In compiling the information for a Used Car Classic, I always seek expert advice from an enthusiast familiar with the particular car being covered. My source for Fiats is a dandy — Jim Weager. He has owned, worked on and raced in Fiat 124s and knows the cars well.

Starting with the engine, Weager characterizes the 1.5 (1968-70) and 1.6-liter engines (1971 and 1972 models) as "good, strong, durable engines," with few inherent problems, although early 1968 models did seem to have occasional valve guide weaknesses that resulted in burned valves. Buyers should look for oil leaks and find few if any with two exceptions: Around the rear cam tower covers some oil may leak out and drip along the flywheel housing and onto the exhaust manifold; the second common leakage problem occurs around the oil sending unit located near the oil filter. The early 124s were equipped with mechanical fuel pumps that seemed to wear out after approximately 40,000 miles, and this is usually signaled by the engine missing when accelerating at high speeds.

The 124 Sports' gearboxes are worthy of the designation "stout", although the throwout bearing has a tendency to get noisy after 20,000 miles or so, according to Weager. Also, many drivers don't take the trouble to pause briefly in neutral while shifting and failure to do so can often damage or weaken the synchronizers. Gear clashing during shifts *may* indicate rather rough treatment by a previous owner. The rear axle bearing seal may leak and coat the rear wheels with oil. If that's the case, chances are good it's the axle seals as the brakes themselves rarely display any leakage tendency, although they do seem to squeal on almost every 124.

The front end should rarely be a problem, Weager says, and if there is something wrong it usually indicates the car has been hit. The steering box can weaken with mileage and age, however, resulting in loose play in the steering wheel. Another potential front-end problem on the earliest versions concerns the ball joints, which have grease fittings on the top that are often neglected during servicing. This is not a load-bearing joint, and the car can go thousands of miles without giving any trouble even though neglected in this area. But Jim had the experience with his early 124 Spider of having the ball joint slip out and punch into the fender well. He learned from the experience that if the ball joints are making noise while the car is being driven, it's a good idea to consider replacing them. Also, many cars have a howl in the rear end coming from the ring and pinion gears; Jim's advice is to live with it **as it** does not cause any major problem and doesn't warrant replacing the gears.

Rust can be a serious problem with these Fiats. The rocker panel on the Spider is made of three metal pieces, and as a result there are corners, nooks and crannies where water can be trapped and eventually cause rust. Also, the floor area can get wet from water seeping in from the box-channel support member to the fender inner liner and then into the door sill area. There are drain plugs in the sill area but, as with many older cars, they are often plugged by debris. Fender rust is not a general complaint of Spider owners, but the Sport Coupe can't boast as good a record and prospective buyers of the closed 124 model should pay close attention to fender inspection. Also, the coupes have a tendency to rust at the corner of the top where it meets the rear fender line because the rear vent wings collect

1968 Fiat 124 Spider instrument panel

water; and many coupes have rust problems along the base of the windshield.

The 124 Spider has one of the easiest to use and most efficiently designed tops of any roadster, but water can leak around the latches at the top of the windshield — Weager says he tried all sorts of fixes for this problem and eventually just learned to live with it. The identification plate on the top of the cowl on early 124s was affixed to the car with hollow rivets that allowed water to leak down into the fuse box and cause shorts in the electrical system, but later cars were equipped with solid rivets and the problem was solved.

Weager and other Fiat 124 Sports owners we talked with were enthusiastic about their cars, and their main theme was the fun-to-drive aspect. As each person thought back over the history of his or her car and noted whatever problems had occurred, each still concluded: "I just love driving the car."

Driving Impressions

Marge Stevens is one of those people we read about but rarely ever meet: She won a car, a Fiat 124 Spider in a raffle in 1969. The car now has just under 55,000 easy miles on it, and Mrs. Stevens takes great pleasure in driving the car daily. Several years ago, she loaned it to her daughter for two years while the girl was going to college, but other than that hiatus, it's been hers since new. I have the feeling she wouldn't part with it for anything.

Over the 9-year period she has had the 124, Marge says it has been remarkably trouble-free, and she can only recall a problem with burned valves about a year ago, a starter solenoid that gave out and a new driveshaft that was installed some three years ago. The driveshaft went bad because she was car pooling during the energy crisis with two men, and the regular carrying of three adults evidently was simply too much weight.

Driving the 1969 Spider for even a limited time gave me a glimpse of why all the 124 owners I talked with are so pleased with their cars. The 1,438-cc engine fires up readily, and while it's admittedly a bit low on torque, it does offer lively performance. In combination with the excellent 5-speed gearbox, the engine makes spirited driving or easy loping a pleasure.

The chassis is one of the best I've encountered in doing these Used Car Classics reports, especially for a roadster, with ride and handling characteristics to please the most demanding driver while giving the nonenthusiast ample comfort — and no surprises. On bad pavement with ripples and small irregularities, the Fiat 124 Spider is a moving testimonial to Italian (and more specifically, Fiat) know-how in designing suspensions. Although the springing is relatively soft, there is plenty of suspension travel and the damping is firm.

There is moderate body roll during cornering, considerable understeer and a sensitive and pleasing amount of feedback through the steering wheel as to just what's going on with the front tires. In really fast driving, the 124 Spider displays excellent transient response through turns and sticks to the road impressively. At the risk of offending other nationalities, I'd have to say that when it comes to building sports cars that handle every driving situation with dash and competence, the Italians are up front. In its price class, the Fiat 124 is second to none.

— *Thos L. Bryant (November 1978)*

Owner Impressions

As a member of the *Road & Track* editorial staff, I drive 75 to 100 cars a year (I think the record was five between 8:00 and 10:00 a.m.), and I'm always pleasantly surprised when I return to my 1971 Fiat 124 Sport Coupe. Its looks please me, outward vision is excellent, the seating position is just right for me, the instrumentation is complete and, best of all, it is great fun to drive. Also, the clock is still keeping correct time.

When readers ask us which cars they should buy, we try to find out what their particular needs are. I had owned a 124 sedan and I appreciated it for its sensible use of space, but I was ready for something more sporty. The choice was down to the 124 Spider or Sport Coupe. As I had a St. Bernard puppy and would have only one car, I chose the Coupe.

The order was placed: red paint, optional alloy wheels and air conditioning by Frigidaire. I picked it up the night of June 3, 1971, and with the outdoor lights playing on the brand new paint, I couldn't have been more pleased. The dog was a little bit

Brief Specifications

	1968 124 Coupe	1968 124 Spider	1972 124 Spider	1972 124 Spider
Curb Weight, lb.	2110	2090	2220	2180
Wheelbase, in.	95.3	89.8	95.3	89.8
Track, f/r	53.0/51.8	53.0/51.8	53.0/51.8	53.0/51.8
Length	162.0	156.3	162.3	156.3
Width	65.8	63.5	65.8	63.5
Height	52.8	49.2	52.8	49.2
Engine type	dohc inline 4	dohc inline 4	dohc inline 4	dohc inline 4
Bore x stroke, in.	3.15 x 2.81	3.15 x 2.81	3.15 x 3.15	3.15 x 3.15
Displacement, cc	1438	1438	1608	1608
Horsepower, bhp @ rpm	96 @ 6500	96 @ 6500	104 @ 6000	104 @ 6000
Torque, lb-ft @ rpm	83 @ 4000	83 @ 4000	94 @ 4200	94 @ 4200

Performance Data From Contemporary Tests

	1968 124 Coupe	1968 124 Spider	1972 124 Spider	1972 124 Spider
0-60 mph, sec.	11.3	11.9	12.4	NA
Standing 1/4 mile, sec.	18.6	18.3	18.6	NA
Average mpg	24.0	25.0	22.1	NA
Road test date	7-68	7-68	7-71	NA

Typical Asking Prices

1968-1972 124 Sport Coupe	$1,500-$2,500
1968-1972 124 Spider	$1,500-$2,500
Typical engine-rebuild price (both models)	$1,500-2,000

bigger by then but he fit. Of all the cars available then in my price range, it was the one I wanted the most and so far I haven't met one I could replace it with. And what a buy!"Wood-rim steering wheel, 5-speed gearbox, disc brakes all around, tachometer standard, and with the options it came to $3,500.

The air conditioning was a bad choice. I could only use it on moderately warm days because otherwise it would cause the engine to overheat, even though it had a larger fan. The biggest problem was that in the rewiring, the electrics got screwed up and the car would spit fuses at me! This happened regularly but after several trips to the air conditioner installer, it was sorted out. However, I never felt good about using the a/c and recently had it removed. In 1971 an imported car owner who insisted on air conditioning was taking chances.

One time a friend and I took the Coupe from Los Angeles to Phoenix to attend a convention. Halfway there, I discovered my friend only drove automatics so I completed the 500-mile trip and at the end of it, I wasn't overly fatigued. On one leg of the trip the car got 31.0 mpg, the best it has ever done.

Another time it went with me to Ensenada and we camped on the beach. It's made numerous trips over the Ortega Highway, a favorite twisty mountain road of *Road & Track* staffers. But mostly it has been an around-town, in-between-test-cars car. It has 41,500 miles on it now. The St. Bernard fills up the entire back seat and if he is along there is no rear vision. The exhaust system has been replaced, ditto the fan belt, tires and one battery. The trunk's rubber molding fell off early on and was never replaced. The passenger's wind wing latch came unglued so it can't be opened. The window molding was replaced. The glass in the outside rearview mirror fell out because the plastic banding gave up and that was replaced. The hood support rod got tired and a new one was installed.

By 1976 the paint had gotten dull, there was a rust spot or two, and there were some dings from parking lot encounters. So the Coupe was treated to a new paint job.

The last time the Coupe went in for service, the gearbox and engine were pronounced healthy and strong. The interior is perfect — the seats look like new. A brisk run to the office in the morning is just as much fun as it was seven years ago and many of the new sports/GT cars I drive don't measure up to it in enjoyment per mile. — *Dorothy Clendenin (November 1978)*

GREAT BRITAIN

Jaguar XJ6 Series One and Two
1969-1979

I was driving the freeway the other day in my own Jaguar — not an XJ6 but a 1961 MK 2 sedan — when I came up behind a lovely E-type roadster, top down, with an equally lovely young lady at the wheel. She saw my car's leaping-cat hood ornament in her rearview mirror and gave a friendly wave. I flashed my lights in acknowledgment, and then she did an extraordinary thing: she motioned for me to pull over at the next offramp.

Now when you're an unattached male and a lady in an E-type commands you to stop, you obey. Henry Manney's famous line about the Jaguar E-type being the "greatest crumpet collector known to man" came to mind. Only this time could it be that the crumpet in the Jag was trying to collect me?

No such luck; she only wanted to admire my MK 2. And furthermore, she wondered, did I know a good mechanic? Jaguar owners are always looking for good mechanics.

Jaguars are frequently held up as paradigms of automotive unreliability. And until recently when John Egan put Jaguar's house in order, the reputation was not undeserved. (Egan is Jaguar's managing director and England's answer to Lee Iacocca.) People who bought new Jaguars in years past can usually recite a litany of problems, from bad brakes to roily radiators. If owners of new Jaguars went through all this tribulation, then buying a 5- or 10-year-old used Jaguar would seem to make as much sense as buying a vacation condo on the beach in Beirut.

Ah, but that's the thinking of a practical and objective person, not a Jaguar owner. You see, few cars can capture a person's heart, imagination and wallet like a Jaguar. They have a seductive charm that beguiles not only fellow Jaguar enthusiasts like my lady friend on the freeway, but innocent bystanders as well. When I drive my aging Jag sedan, little girls wave at me, grandmothers smile at me and truck drivers give me the thumbs-up sign. Owners of XJ6s tell me they too routinely receive spontaneous compliments on their cars.

Somehow the late Sir William Lyons, the founder of Jaguar Cars Ltd. and the man responsible for the styling of every Jaguar from the classic SS100 to the XJ6, imbued all his cars with a uniquely universal appeal. Jaguars are, in a word, romantic. And we all know that romance isn't necessarily practical or objective.

In fact, when people are smitten by romance, they tend to deny their lover's deficiencies. As Gilbert Burck once explained so well in a *Fortune* magazine article titled, "Confessions of a Jaguar Owner," rationalization is a prerequisite to loving an older Jaguar too. Regarding his Jaguar's mechanical demands, Burck wrote, "for like all personal accidents since the world

Affordable romance

by Peter Bohr

1978 Jaguar XJ6L

1969 Jaguar XJ6

began, (they) afforded a never failing topic of conversation and even became a mark of distinction. And I, like the engineer's apprentice in Mark Twain's 'Life on the Mississippi,' developed an ability to talk of gaskets and overhead camshafts in an easy and natural way that doubtless made my friends wish I was dead. I began to look forward to some other mishap.... For gossakes, any old pile of Detroit iron runs more or less trouble-free. What's the use in having an elegant, distinctive car if you can't also have some trouble with it?"

Indeed, true Jaguar lovers seem to thrive on adversity. Burck, who penned those words in *Fortune* twenty-nine years ago, still owns his 1955 MK 7 saloon. And the membership chairman of the Jaguar Owners Club of Southern California says that most of the club's 300 members own two or more Jaguars. One member, a friend of mine, owns four, none of which are currently running. He drives a Porsche as his everyday car. But then Ferdinand Porsche — yes, that Porsche — drives a Jaguar XJ sedan as his everyday car because, he says, "it's so sensitive."

Evolution of the XJ6

Not only is the XJ6 Jaguar's most successful sedan ever, it is also the last car designed by Sir William Lyons. Throughout the 1960s, Jaguar offered a varied selection of sedans. There was the esteemed compact model, the MK 2, which became somewhat less compact when it received an enlarged trunk and independent-rear suspension. This irs MK 2, called the S-type, was later restyled and renamed the 420. Jaguar's flagship of the 1960s was the MK 10, a rather bulbous sedan. It too was face-lifted and renamed, becoming the 420G, the "G" standing for "grand."

The XJ6 is the direct descendent of these two cars and ended up replacing them both in Jaguar's model line-up. The XJ6 is evolutionary rather than revolutionary in that it inherited most of its running gear from the 420, including the renowned XK engine, a design that dates back to the late 1940s. In overall size, the XJ falls midway between the 420 and the 420G. At just under 4,000 pounds, it's no econo-box to be sure. But its low profile, little taller than a Porsche 911, gives it an unmistakably sporty air.

The XJ6 was first introduced to this country in 1969 in what is now called Series One form. Then, as in the very latest Series Three cars, every XJ6 came to us colonials with a full compliment of features that were optional in its home market, things like an automatic transmission, air conditioning, power windows and the largest version of the venerable dohc 6-cylinder engine, the 4.2-liter unit.

In our road test of the Series One car, we were as enthusiastic about the XJ6's ride and handling as we were about its dramatic styling and luxurious walnut-and-leather interior. The XJ6 shared its independent rear suspension with the E-type sports cars. And because Jaguar engineers were able to keep road noise to a minimum through the use of a combination of sophisticated rubber mountings and a special suspension sub-frame adapted from the 420G, they were able to use unusually wide radial tires, which otherwise would have caused too harsh a ride. The big Dunlops, specifically designed for the XJ6, not only gave the car a hunky appearance, they contributed greatly to the car's outstanding cornering ability.

We were less impressed, however, with the light feel of our test car's rack-and-pinion power steering, and with the ventilation / heating / air-conditioning system. In sum, we found the XJ6 "a strange and wondrous car... one of the most beautiful sedans in the world, and certainly one of the best handling and best riding ones... combining excellence, graciousness and tradition with a look and feel of speed and sportiness in a way absolutely no other car even approaches. But in some respects... it seems to have been developed in a vacuum."

Although automotive technology has moved at a dizzying pace over the last decade and a half, an XJ6 still compares favorably with the best automotive designs of the 1980s in terms of ride, handling, silence and refinement. Moreover, Jaguar engineers have honed the design and attempted to correct its early deficiencies over the car's long production run.

The Series One cars, built through 1973, had two significant modifications. In 1972, the York air-conditioning compressor was replaced by a quieter GM compressor. And in 1973, Jaguar started to ugly up the bumpers by putting big rubber overriders in front.

It was also in 1973 when the XJ12 made its American debut. The combo of the XJ body and chassis with the exotic 12-cylinder engine from the E-type made for a formidable automobile in more ways than one. While its performance was daunting, so was its fuel consumption. Unfortunately, the Western world was on the eve of the age of fuel shortages, and the XJ12 never did become a best seller in this country, though the model was available through 1979. The special virtues and vices of 12-cylinder Jaguars are best left to a future Used Car Classic.

The Series Two XJ6s came in 1974, with a number of changes inside and out. The front grill was shallower to accommodate a new rubber bumper. Inside, Jaguar dropped its long-standing practice of placing the minor instruments in the center of the dash, with an awesome-but-confusing row of switches underneath. Instead, all the instruments were now clustered around the speedometer and tachometer in front of the driver, while light and windshield-wiper controls were moved from rocker switches to stalks on the steering column.

Especially welcome changes were made in the heater and air conditioner. The old unit was replaced by an automatic "climate-control" system. A temperature sensor sends a signal to a servo motor that drives a camshaft, which then regulates the amount of heating and cooling. Most important, the new system supplies one-third more refrigerated air. A change from

1975 Jaguar XJC

1976 Jaguar XJC interior

a Borg-Warner model 12 automatic transmission to a BW model 65, a new padded steering wheel and ventilated front disc brakes were other notable Series Two modifications.

In addition, 1974 saw the first of the long-wheelbase XJ6s. The idea, taken from Mercedes-Benz, was to give the rear-seat passengers more leg room by adding extra inches to the wheelbase. In the Jaguar's case, four inches were inserted behind the front door line, and the XJ6 became the XJ6L. Both short- and long-wheelbase XJ6s were available in 1974, though the former are rather rare as most buyers preferred the extra room of the XJ6L. The 4-door, short-wheelbase car was dropped in 1975, replaced by a new 2-door coupe called the XJ6C. Aside from having a shorter roof, just two doors and a rather vulgar vinyl top, it was identical to the short-wheelbase XJ6. Since it was more expensive than the 4-door XJ6, we couldn't really see the point of the car then, and we still don't. Sir William wanted pillarless construction: i.e., he wanted the front and rear window to fit flush against each other with no post in between. The absence of the pillar gives the coupe an elegant, airy look, but it made a tight, quiet seal very difficult. The XJ6C was discontinued after 1977.

The Series Two cars remained in production until mid-1979, when they were replaced by the model currently on sale in Jaguar showrooms, the Series Three. The Series Two cars didn't remain untouched during their 5-year production run, however. The bumpers, front and rear, were revised several times. The simple but somewhat anachronistic manual choke was changed to a more complicated automatic choke in 1975. More significantly, the addition of catalytic converters, exhaust gas recirculation and other pollution control equipment began to take their toll on the Jaguar's performance and fuel economy. So for 1978, the twin Zenith-Stromberg carburetors were dropped in favor of a Lucas/Bosch L-jetronic fuel injection system. Horsepower then rose 15 bhp, and EPA fuel consumption figures improved by 1 mpg to 16 mpg.

Between 1969 and 1979, the years of the Series One and Two cars, base prices jumped more than threefold, from a little under $7,000 in 1969 to more than $24,000 in 1979. But even the latter seems cheap compared to the $32,000 pricetag on a 1985 XJ6. And why are recent XJ6s considered better, more reliable cars? In fact significant mechanical changes to the Series Three cars were few. Most of the changes came in the form of refinements to the body, seats and instrumentation. Reliability improved primarily because John Egan has insisted on proper quality control, not only from his own workforce, but from Jaguar's parts suppliers as well.

When you consider that even a late Series Two XJ6 will cost less than half the price of a new Series Three model and is essentially the same car, the older Jag can be quite a bargain. Which brings up the question of which among the early XJ6s are most desirable.

Many Jaguar aficionados prefer the compactness of the short-wheelbase and the simple chrome bumpers of the Series One cars. The 1972 is the best choice here because it has the improved air-conditioner compressor, yet doesn't have the ugly front bumper overriders of the 1973 Series One car.

But if an effective air conditioner or heater is important to you, you'd better stick to a Series Two car. Most Jaguar experts like the advantages of the 1978-79 models' fuel injection. The 1975-77 XJC, despite our reservations, is considered "collectible" because there are so few of them.

Selection and Care of a Jaguar XJ6

It takes a special breed of cat, so to speak, to own a Jaguar. The Jaguar owner must be willing to abandon the traditional American notion of automobile maintenance, or I should say, lack of it. You can't abuse a Jaguar like you can a Toyota or Ford and get away with it.

Yet many people have tried. Because Jaguars are so appealing and because they've never been especially expensive to buy relative to other cars of equal sophistication, over the years many people have purchased the cars who can't afford to maintain them properly, in which cases the Jags rapidly degenerate into problem-prone heaps. Then there are those who get so fed up with a Jaguar's demands that they stuff a Chevy motor under the bonnet (more on this later).

Actually when a Jaguar is maintained by the book as Sir William and his engineers intended, it can be a reliable car. Really. We know of early XJ6s that have provided thousands of trouble-free miles. My own father drove a 1971 XJ6 nearly 150,000 miles before the head had to be removed for "decoking." And as one respondent wrote about his XJ6 in a 1978 *Road & Track* Owners Survey, "Like my Alfas and Coopers before it, proper driving and service have yielded excellent reliability; 100,000 miles now and the most major service has been new cam cover gaskets."

Thus finding a used XJ6 that's had a life of loving care is your best hope of having a reasonably trouble-free car. A prepurchase inspection by a knowledgeable Jaguar mechanic is a must. I asked Ken VanDorn, service manager at California Coventry Ltd., and Alan Woodward, co-owner of West Coast British Cars, (both shops are in Costa Mesa, California) what a complete prepurchase inspection should entail.

An engine compression test is a good beginning. If anything's wrong here, the repair bill could be steep. A complete overhaul of an XJ6 engine will cost between $3,500 and $5,000. A cylinder-head rebuild could cost $2,500.

The transmission should be checked for smooth operation. Woodward says the Series One has a tough old box, but the lighter duty model 65 on the Series Two isn't so durable. A transmission rebuild is about $1,100.

Repairing the inboard rear disc brakes can be time-consuming, and if the rotors need replacing, expect an $800 bill. The power-steering rack is a frequent source of trouble; VanDorn says misguided mechanics often overfill it with grease and blow the seals, which leads to serious leaking and failure.

The complex climate control system on Series Two cars should also be carefully checked. Switch the temperature control from hot to cold and listen for the whirring sound of the servo. If you don't hear anything, expect to spend $750 or more. All the U-joints should be checked for excessive leaking (though they all seem to leak some). Exhaust systems on Series One cars were especially prone to rust unless upgraded to stainless steel, and early on Series Two cars, alternators and the power-window switches were often troublesome.

Then there's the matter of a Jaguar's cosmetics. Mark Mayuga, president of the Jaguar Owners Club of Southern California, says early Series Two XJ6s had a problem with cracking paint. A proper respray requires that the old paint be stripped, an expensive proposition. Refurbishing the seats and interior trimmings of more mundane cars is usually a minor expense compared to major mechanical repairs. But restoring a Jaguar's wonderful Old World interior, with its Connolly hides and polished timber, can become very costly as well.

So as you shop the classifieds, bear in mind that a $3,500 XJ6 won't be a bargain if you have to pay $5,000 for an engine rebuild, $2,500 for paint, $3,000 for a new interior; and $2,000 to repair the suspension, brakes and steering. But if these prices horrify you, also remember you can largely avoid them by being careful about buying a used XJ6 in the first place, and by maintaining the car correctly after you buy one.

As for the latter, Bill Brady, a dapper Scot who repairs Jaguars and Rolls-Royces in his shop, Bonnet to Boot in Woodland Hills, California, suggests that any new owner of an old XJ6 immediately replace all cooling system hoses and rod or recore the radiator. There are eleven or thirteen hoses, depending upon the year of the car, and they cost about $200, but replacement is good insurance against leaks and ruptures so frequently suffered by XJ6 owners. The cooling system is probably the most frequent source of trouble on an older XJ6, and a serious bout of overheating can cause the head gasket to blow or the aluminum cylinder head to warp.

In addition, overheating can cause the steel valve guides pressed into the head to slip out to the point where they're ground away by the rotating camshafts. Early Series Two cars are most likely to develop the slipping-guide problem, and many of these cars have had their guides pinned in place so they're unable to move.

Once you've found the right XJ6, make a standing appointment with your Jaguar mechanic just as you would with your dentist or haircutter. Every 3,000 miles have the oil and filter changed. Every 24,000 miles completely flush the transmission fluid (don't just top it off). Flush the cooling system annually and always refill it with a 50/50 solution of water and coolant to prevent electrolysis. Replace the cooling system hoses again in two years. If you have a fuel-injected XJ6, replace the fuel-injection system hoses as soon as you buy the car and then again in three years. Change the brake pads before they grind down the rotors. Rub a little Lexol or Hide Food into the leather every couple of months. According to Ken VanDorn, following this sort of preventive maintenance regimen at his shop will cost about $1,000 to $1,200 a year (assuming you drive 12,000 to 15,000 miles).

No, it's not inexpensive to keep a Jaguar purring. But then who said romance was cheap?

Conversion or Perversion?

Conversion is not a phenomenon limited to politics and religion. Jaguar XJ owners frequently engage in the practice as well.

Chucking out the vintage 6-cylinder Jaguar engine and the lackluster Borg-Warner automatic transmission of an XJ6 and replacing them with a Chevy V-8 and GM Turbo Hydromatic would seem to make for an ideal marriage. You'd then have one of the world's best-looking automobile bodies and the most capable chassis combined with one of the most dependable powertrains.

But engine swaps are tricky business, trickier than they might appear at first blush. It's not just a question of room in the engine bay. There are plenty of possible complications, like compatibility of the cooling system, the electrics and the instruments, not to mention the handling quirks that might develop as a result of different total weight and different weight distribution.

Nevertheless, when I have advised readers to avoid buying "bastardized XJ6s," i.e., ones with Chevrolet power plants, in the past, I've received a number of grouchy complaints from happy "Jagolet" owners.

So I decided to investigate the matter. I contacted INTER-JAG in Huntington Beach, California, one of several shops in Southern California that do a booming business in swapping Jag engines for Chevy engines in XJ sedans. I turned to INTERJAG because several independent mechanics had mentioned their high-quality work.

1974 Jaguar XJ6 Series Two interior

First, service manager Larry Miller told me that if you bring your XJ6 to INTERJAG for a conversion, it will cost you $5,500. That says one thing right away: a conversion isn't a money-saving way to avoid an XJ6 engine rebuild. A first-rate conversion will cost as much as a first-rate rebuild of the Jaguar engine and transmission.

For $5,500, you will receive a blueprinted Chevy 350 engine and a Turbo Hydromatic 350 transmission, fully installed on a new set of engine and transmission mounts, with new exhaust manifolds and head pipes, air conditioning fittings and hoses, heater hoses and clamps, engine wire loom, drive shaft, spark plug wires with heat shield and hardware. You will also receive a shift linkage adapter, a speedometer adaptor and cable, a new custom-built radiator, shroud and fan with new hoses, clamps and coolant recovery system and a new air cleaner cover. The front end of the car will be readjusted and realigned in order to compensate for the Chevy engine's lighter weight (about 500 pounds less). For $1,500, INTERJAG will give you a kit that includes everything but the engine and tranny — you supply those plus the labor, of course.

I list all this to show that doing the conversion properly entails much more than just unbolting one engine and bolting in another. One reason I advised XJ buyers to avoid converted cars is that there are lots of $2,500-butcher jobs on the market, and unless you're sophisticated enough to know the difference, you might buy a car that will cause you no end of trouble.

If you have your XJ properly converted, you can expect the advantages of quicker acceleration, less expensive maintenance for the engine (a Chevy water pump costs a fraction of what a Jag water pump costs) and the availability of service for the powertrain in any isolated burg around the country. Fuel economy, at 14 to 15 mpg, isn't significantly different from the stock XJ6.

Brief Specifications

	1972 XJ6	1978 XJ6L FI
Curb Weight, lb.	3885	3980
Wheelbase, in.	108.8	112.8
Track, f / r	58.0 / 58.6	58.2 / 58.8
Length	189.5	200.5
Width	69.6	69.8
Height	52.8	54.1
Engine type	dohc inline 6	dohc inline 6
Bore x stroke, mm	92.1 x 105.9	92.1 x 105.9
Displacement, cc	4235	4235
Horsepower, bhp @ rpm	186 @ 4500	176 @ 4750
Torque, lb-ft @ rpm	240 @ 3750	219 @ 2500
Suspension, f / r	ind / ind	ind / ind
Brakes, f / r	disc / disc	disc / disc
Steering type	rack and pinion	rack and pinion

Performance Data From Contemporary Tests

0-60 mph, sec.	10.7	9.6
Standing 1 / 4 mile, sec.	17.1	17.7
Average mpg	15.2	17.5
Road test date	2-72	12-78

Typical Asking Prices

1969-1973 Series One XJ6	$4,500-$6,500
1974-1979 Series Two XJ6, XJ6L	$5,500-$14,000
1975-1977 XJ6C	$9.500-$12,500
Typical engine-rebuild price (all models)	$3,500-$5,000

What you should remember, however, is that you still have a car with the stock Jaguar differential, steering rack, instruments, electrical accessories (window switches, windshield-wiper motors and the like), brakes and suspension. According to our 1978 Owner Survey, these components gave as much trouble as the engine, if not more. So if you live in Coon Rapids, Iowa, miles from the nearest Jag repair shop, the local Chevy dealer may be able to fix your converted XJ's engine, but what about its leaky steering rack?

Sorry, but I remain the purist. To me, the beautiful dohc inline-6 that has proven itself in Jaguar sports cars on race courses around the world since 1949 is one of the XJ6's attributes, not one of its deficiencies. If you want a Chevy engine, then buy a Camaro in the first place. — *Peter Bohr (May 1985)*

GREAT BRITAIN

MGA *1955-1962*

Little treasure

by Peter Bohr

The purists were aghast. The new MGA, introduced at the Frankfort Auto Show in September 1955, didn't look anything like its predecessors. Since the Midget of 1928, MG sports cars had always had flat-front radiators, delicate sweeping fenders and "square-rigged" bodies. Instead, the MGA was a contemporary car, not a throwback to the days of Evelyn Waugh's *Brideshead Revisited*. But to the purists, the MGA's envelope body was a reckless step toward modernity.

That sort of conservatism persisted for many years. While an active cadre of enthusiasts promoted the MG T-series and pushed their prices to dizzying heights, interest in the MGA languished. As recently as five years ago, you could buy a running MGA for considerably less than $1,000, while basket-case TDs were selling for five times that amount.

There's no question that the MG T-series positively ooze creamy English charm. And certainly the immortal TC, as well as the TD and TF that followed, deserve credit for introducing us colonials to the delights of sports cars. But in sales figures, the T-series cars were only the forerunners to the MGA invasion that was to come. Purists aside, the public embraced the MGA, expecially the American public. Between 1955 and 1962, MG's Abingdon factory built 101,081 MGAs, more than double the entire production of the T-series. The MGA was the first sports car from any car maker in any country to break the magic 100,000 mark. And better than 80 percent of the MGA production was exported to the U.S.

1960 MGA 1600

1958 MGA 1500 Coupe

It's no wonder then that the MGA became something of a fixture at the local drive-in theater or hamburger stand during the 1950s. With its streamlined styling, knockoff wire wheels and wide, wide whitewall tires, the MGA fit right in there with Elvis Presley, ducktail haircuts, 1957 T-Birds and other artifacts of that happy decade. In a 1955 road test, our editors concluded, "If you look over the MGA with a critical eye, drive it and note the price tag — you will probably ask the same question we do: How are they going to supply enough cars to meet the demand?"

Since then, the MGA has aged gracefully. Controversially modern in 1955, the car has a charm all its own today. Thanks to the current 1950s revival, and thanks to the enthusiasm of the members of the North American MGA Register, the car has gone from black sheep of the MG family to something of a rising star. Prices are climbing, and more and more MGAs are being carefully restored. But there are still plenty around in various states of repair, and it's still possible to find a bargain. All this makes the MGA a natural for our Used Car Classic Series.

Evolution of the MGA

The MGA might have gone into production instead of the TF had Donald Healey not approached BMC management first with his new 100 model. Syd Enever, one of the automotive industry's great engineers, had actually designed the basic MGA body for use on a LeMans racer in 1951. The following year Enever refined the styling and designed a new chassis. The car, known by the factory code name EX175, was essentially the MGA's prototype. However, BMC management (MG had become a part of the BMC group in 1952) decided to concentrate its resources on the new Austin-Healey. The TD was face-lifted and became the TF, while the EX175 was shelved. But when flagging TF sales became inpossible to ignore in mid-1954, MG received permission to break with the past and proceed.

More than just the MGA's styling was new. Aside from the front suspension (independent with lever-arm shock absorbers) and the steering (rack-and-pinion) little else was carried over from the T-series. The extremely strong box-section frame was taken directly from the EX175. But unlike the prototype that used the TD drivetrain, the MGA has the so-called Austin B-series engine, a hardy 4-cylinder unit that was used in several BMC sedans including the Magnette. The gearbox, also from the Magnette, has a nonsynchronized first gear. The live rear axle, yet another component from the Magnette, is located and suspended by semi-elliptic leaf springs, and, like the front suspension, uses lever-action shock absorbers.

Most of the body is steel, but to save weight, MG made the hood, doors and trunk lid of aluminum. The cockpit is certainly cozy, and the seating position is surprisingly low. All but the tallest people will find plenty of leg room, although there's not much space around the pedals for the driver's feet. In the usual British roadster fashion, the placement of the shift lever is ideal,

and there's a full complement of handsome, readable instruments. Unfortunately, the folding top is also typically
British: it requires an abundance of patience as well as physical
dexterity to erect or stow away.

Overall, the MGA is considerably smoother and more refined than the TF. And because of improved aerodynamics, the
MGA's efficiency is higher. A 1955 MGA has a top speed 10 mph
greater than a TF, yet its weight and horsepower are unchanged.
Throughout its production run the MGA was also reasonably priced
with a U.S. price tag of $2,195 in 1955, rising to $2,485 in 1962.

The MGA really didn't change much over its life span,
though there were four official models and one unofficial model
and each of them was available in two body styles. The roadster
with soft top and side curtains was the usual configuration. A
detachable fiberglass hardtop was an option for the roadster, but
in 1956 MG decided to go a step further. Copying the concept of
Jaguar's successful XK120 coupe, the company gave the MGA a
permanently fixed steel hardtop. With roll-up windows and a
fully carpeted interior, the snug little coupe is slightly more luxurious than the roadster.

The 1500 was the first model, and was sold until the summer of 1959. Altogether some 59,000 MGA 1500s rolled off Abingdon's assembly line. The second model, the 1600, was MG's
answer to its competitors in the sports-car market, expecially to
Triumph's TR3. With Lockheed front disc brakes and an increase of nearly 100 cc of engine displacement, the MGA 1600
has much improved braking and quicker acceleration. The 1600
was also the first truly 100-mph MGA, a noteworthy fact in the
late 1950s, when top speed enjoyed the priority that fuel
economy holds today.

Though never officially called the MK I, the 1600 of 1959
was superseded by the 1600 MK II in mid-1961. Except for revised taillights and several badges that say 1600, the 1500 and 1600
MK I look identical. However, the 1600 MK II has a recessed
grille that distinguishes the model from the two previous
models. In addition, the MK II has yet another type of taillights,
and another increase in engine displacement, from the MK I's
1,588 cc to 1,622 cc. The MK II was around for little more than a
year before the MGA was replaced by the MGB. Altogether, production of the 1600 MK I and MK II totaled some 40,000 cars.

The 1500 and the two 1600 models were MG's bread and
butter between 1955 and 1962. But there were two variations on
the MGA theme that have since come to be highly valued by collectors. The MGA Twin-Cam of 1958 was an official model built
alongside the 1500 and later the 1600. The distinguishing
feature of the Twin-Cam is, of course, a dohc engine. Though
based on the block of the standard MGA pushrod engine, the
Twin-Cam engine's alloy cylinder head was all-new. The
1,588-cc unit produced an impressive 108 bhp compared with
79.5 for the 1600 MK I. But from the beginning, the Twin-Cam's
engine developed a nasty reputation for heavy oil consumption

and burned pistons. When the compression ratio was lowered from 9.9 to 8.3:1 in 1959, reliability improved. Nevertheless, by the following year the company had had enough, and the Twin-Cam was dropped after a total production of slightly more than 2,000.

The dohc engine was the most important feature of the model, but there were several other modifications. In additon to a slightly different suspension and steering arrangement, the Twin-Cam carried 4-wheel Dunlop disc brakes and knockoff pressed-steel disc wheels. It appears that when the Twin-Cam engine met its demise, there was a store of the other components left over. Consequently, about 350 of the usual pushrod engines were installed in what were otherwise Twin-Cam cars, and these were called DeLuxe versions. While DeLuxe versions of both the 1600 MK I and MK II were built, they were never classified as official models.

Although not in the same league as those lengthy scrolls from Detroit car makers, the MGA's list of options did offer some interesting items. It's hard to believe today, but a heater was an option. Other popular items included telescoping steering wheel, tonneau cover, fog lights, radio and oil cooler. An optional luggage rack was especially designed to distribute weight over a broad area of the relatively soft aluminum trunk lid. Perhaps the most important option to people buying old MGAs today is wire wheels. They enhance the appearance and value of an MGA.

1961 MGA 1600 MkII interior

MGAs came in what we called "a veritable rainbow of color choices." Well, maybe that was a bit of hyperbole, but 1500 models were available in red, white, black, light green and light blue, with red, black, gray or green Connolly leather-covered seats. However, in place of the light blue, the 1500 coupes came in a special dark blue. The 1600s, both MK I and MK II, came in red, white, black, beige, light blue and light gray, with black, beige or red leather. There was no special color for the 1600 coupes, and British racing green was never offered.

Selecting the Right MGA

So among the various models, what's hot and what's not? MG fanatics are the only ones gallant enough to put up with a Twin-Cam's unreliability. Even so, their rarity makes them quite valuable. The rear disc brakes of a DeLuxe version are desirable, but once again it's primarily the rarity of the 1600 DeLuxe cars that makes them coveted by MG fanciers.

Your best choice is probably a 1600 MK I or MK II, preferably with wire wheels. Red or white are the most popular among the original colors. Roadsters are much more common than coupes, so coupe prices tend to be higher. A Twin-Cam or DeLuxe coupe is, of course, the rarest of the rare. A coupe is safer in a rollover and offers better weather protection. But the floorboards (yes, Virginia, MGAs have genuine wooden floorboards!) of all MGAs let uncomfortable amounts of engine heat into the passenger compartment. As a consequence, coupes can become mighty hot in the summer.

Regardless of the model you fancy, no MGA is a spring chicken anymore. Even the youngest, a 1962 model, is twenty-two years old, while the oldest is nearing thirty. But fortunately MGAs were built tough. Oh, sure, the electrical system is protected only by two fuses and the cooling system is marginal. But the MGA's frame is massive enough for a bulldozer. And the MGA's heavy gauge sheet metal makes the body of today's typical import look like it's built of kitchen foil. This heft gives you a fighting chance to find a decent MGA.

We asked two experts for tips on inspecting MGAs. Lee Dudacek is a Jaguar mechanic by profession and drives a 1600 roadster around Southern California as his everyday car. Gene McClelland owns an MG repair shop in Costa Mesa, California, appropriately called "McClelland's Garage" (MG). Both begin an inspection with a careful search for rust. Lee says the rear ends of the rocker panels are often the first spots to corrode. If they're sound, move on to the rest of the rocker panels (run your hand behind the panels as well) and the fenders. Open the doors and check the jambs; if the hinges or the lock seem to flex, the chassis supports may be rusted away — a very serious problem. Lift up the carpets and check the side chassis rails that support the floorboards. Take off the panel behind the seats and look at the two battery boxes (the MGA uses two 6-volt batteries instead of a single 12-volt). Finally, open the trunk lid and check the trunk floor for rust.

If the car passes rust inspection, Gene then likes to examine the front tires, which can indicate the condition of the front suspension. When the inside edges are rounded off, either the bushings or the front shocks may need replacement. Lever-arm shocks are about $65 apiece. There should be zero play in the steering wheel. If not, the problem might just be worn tie-rod ends. But if the rubber boots on either side of the rack are cracked or missing, you'd better expect a bum rack and pinion (about $350).

A pushrod MGA engine should have compression readings of 120 psi on each cylinder. Gene charges between $1,000 and $2,000 for rebuilding the engine. To replace the clutch, the engine must be removed; clutch parts and installation run between $300 and $400. Overhauling the transmission is costly. If the tranny seems especially noisy, plan on spending as much as $1,000 for repair.

The rear end and rear shocks seem to last forever. But the brakes will often give trouble, especially if the car has been sitting for six months or longer. If the handbrake lever pulls up eight clicks or more, the rear brakes, at least, may need work. A complete brake system overhaul is about $300.

Then there's that old British-car bugaboo, the SU carburetor. The MGA has a pair of them. When the engine idles either too high or erratically, you should suspect worn throttle shafts. Rebuilding a pair of SUs costs about $175. Then once they're set up, both Lee and Gene urge you to "leave 'em alone." Says Lee, "When a car isn't running right, people immediately head for the carbs. Nine times out of ten, it's an electrical problem or perhaps burned valves." On the subject of electrics, the vacuum advance mechanism in the distributor of an old British car like the MGA often freezes. That, of course, results in pretty ragged high-end performance.

As for overheating, another common problem of older British cars, MGAs in warm climates often lose their cool. If the radiator, hoses, thermostat and water pump are all in good order, and the car still makes tea on warm days, Gene would suspect faulty ignition timing. If that's okay too, Lee suggests several fixes. First, there's plenty of room in front of the radiator for an electric cooling fan. Second, you could add an oil cooler. Third, you could replace the standard 2-row radiator with a 3-row unit; this requires a little body work, however. And as a last resort, you can remove the front grille. "The grille was cleverly designed to direct air away from the radiator," says Lee.

Finally, there's the subject of parts. Happily, most MGA parts are easy to obtain, and at a reasonable cost, too. We have to put in a plug here for Moss Motors, Ltd in Goleta, California. Moss specializes in parts for old British sports cars. Their wonderfully detailed catalogs can serve as parts manuals. Moss will supply anything for an MGA, from precut leather upholstery kits to original badges. Though Moss is perhaps the best known of the firms in the British car-parts business, there are several other good ones; check Road & Track's classified advertising section.

Driving Impressions: Tales of Two MGAs

It was an emotional response, pure and simple. Why else would I buy a tired 23-year-old British roadster with a pull-type starter switch, a horn button in the middle of the dash, and a ride reminiscent of a Conestoga wagon? Talk about a lack of modern features, this baby doesn't even have sun visors or roll-up windows, let alone a climate-control system or one of those little computer voices to remind you to get fuel or fasten your seatbelt. The only climate control system on my MGA is a soft top with an opaque rear window, and the only voice is the little one in my head that says, "Wow! This thing is fun to drive!"

Undoubtedly some MGA owners really think their cars are practical. Yes, MGAs do turn in 25 or 30 mpg of petrol. They do have quick and light steering, a wonderfully precise gearbox, decent road-holding and a forgiving nature that wouldn't let even the most ham-fisted driver get in trouble. And indeed, MGAs are ruggedly durable and relatively inexpensive to buy or repair.

But come on — you can say much the same about a Toyota. No, we love MGAs because the little dears seem to tug at our emotional strings. For one thing, an MGA is among the best-looking sports cars of the 1950s; its lines are as clean and smooth as a baby's bottom, unmarred by door handles or even a trunk handle. The car also has a certain tossibility that encourages its driver to speed up through the corners and zip around the behemoths that block traffic. And, of course, there's the MGA's nostalgia value. It's a reminder of a time when chrome was plated over metal, not plastic; when seats were made from the hides of cows, not Naugas; when instruments were just instruments, not imitation video games.

In fact, I suspect nostalgia plays the largest role in the purchase decision of many MGA buyers. In my case it takes me back to the days of high school and a fellow named Richard. Richard was a senior and drove a pristine but unoriginal British-racing-green MGA with wire wheels. I was a sophomore and drove a Schwinn. Richard was class president and a hunk. I was... well, it doesn't matter. But I certainly didn't have an MGA and all those girls. Richard and his MGA were an unbeatable combination when it came to attracting the school's most beautiful girls.

So eventually there I was, another baby-boomer in his thirties, with a little disposable income and a memory. What to do but buy the car I couldn't have back in high school? My 1960 1600 cost $2,000. On the way back from the seller's house I had to pull over every ten miles and add water to the percolating radiator. And when I stopped, I had to make sure the MG pointed downhill; a compression start was the only choice as the batteries were too weak to turn the starter motor. But we made it. After a new radiator core, new batteries, a new muffler and a carburetor rebuild, I had a decent, driveable MGA. The clutch slips badly enough so that it's a real adventure going up even a modest incline. And the car could use new paint and some front tires. But, boy, is it fun. And, yes, girls of all ages love it. Maybe Richard wasn't such a hunk; it was just his MGA.

Ken Palmer is another victim of MGA nostalgia. Ken's is a classic case dating back to his boyhood in a small farm town in Iowa, of all places. Among the Ford sedans and Chevy pickups of his neighbors, there was a red TD. "How could one ever achieve an MG?" he wondered. By working construction jobs during college and saving $900, he found his answer with a 6-year-old 1957 MGA. He graduated with it, did a stint in the air force with it and honeymooned in it.

Seven years ago, fond memories of that car led Ken to search for another. But this time he wanted a rare MGA. His 1962 MK II DeLuxe was delivered to him on a trailer. Except for the tattered interior, the frozen clutch and the vestiges of a paint job, it was certainly worth the $1,000 he paid. Many dollars and hours of labor later, Ken's DeLuxe became a black beauty.

When Ken drove up in his car, with its distinctive knockoff disc wheels and set-in grille, my poor MG wanted to hide in the garage with its tailpipe between its shock absorbers. Resplendent in its gleaming paint and red leather interior, the DeLuxe has nearly every factory option, including a rare close-ratio gearbox and competition seats. "The seats are monumentally

Brief Specifications

	1955 1500	1959 1600	1961 1600 Mk II	1958 Twin-Cam
Curb Weight, lb.	2020	2050	2050	2200
Wheelbase, in.	94.0	94.0	94.0	94.0
Track, f/r	47.5/48.8	47.5/48.8	47.5/48.8	47.9/48.9
Length	156.0	156.0	156.0	156.0
Width	57.3	57.3	57.3	57.3
Height	50.0	50.0	50.0	50.0
Engine type	pushrod inline 4	pushrod inline 4	pushrod inline 4	dohc inline 4
Bore x stroke, in.	2.87 x 3.50	2.97 x 3.50	3.00 x 3.50	2.97 x 3.50
Displacement, cc	1489	1588	1622	1588
Horsepower, bhp @ rpm	68 @ 5500	79.5 @ 5600	90 @ 5500	108 @ 6700
Torque, lb-ft @ rpm	77 @ 3500	87 @ 3800	97 @ 4000	104 @ 4500
Transmission	4-speed	4-speed	4-speed	4-speed
Suspension, f/r	ind coil/live leaf	ind coil/live leaf	ind coil/live leaf	ind coil/live leaf
Brakes, f/r	drum/drum	disc/drum	disc/drum	disc/disc
Steering type	rack and pinion	rack and pinion	rack and pinion	rack and pinion

Performance Data From Contemporary Tests

0-60 mph, sec.	14.5	13.3	12.8	9.9
Standing 1/4 mile, sec.	19.6	19.0	18.7	18.1
Average mpg	30.0	28.0	28.0	19.5
Road test date	12-55	10-59	9-61	11-58

Typical Asking Prices

1955-1962 1500, 1600, 1600 Mk II	$2,000-$7,500
1958-1960 Twin-Cam	$4,500-$10,000
1960-1962 1600 DeLuxe, 1600 Mk II DeLuxe	$4,500-$10,000
Typical engine-rebuild price (all models except Twin-Cam)	$1,500-$2,000

uncomfortable," says Ken, "but they're wonderful at car shows." Indeed, Ken's car took first in its class five years ago at the North American MGA Register's national meet.

But the best goodie of all is under the bonnet: a Judson supercharger. Though not a factory option (Judsons were made in Conshocken, Pennsylvania), they were a popular add-on in the late 1950s. *Road & Track* tested a 1500 MGA with a Judson in 1958 and found about a 25-percent boost in both torque and horsepower with little sacrifice in fuel economy. The big advantage, says Ken, is improved high-gear flexibility.

The Judson certainly comes in handy when Ken decides to scale Mount Baldy, a 4,500-foot mountain resort behind his West Covina home in Southern California. The car has no problems making it up the grades. Nor does Ken have any qualms about taking the DeLuxe each year on an 800-mile round trip to the Monterey Historic Car Races. But Ken and I both are reluctant to use our MGAs as everyday commuter cars. It's not that the cars couldn't take it, once I fixed my car's clutch, that is. It's just that Southern-California-style commuting involves a lot of tedious stop-and-go freeway driving in warm weather, which is not the MGA's forte. Better to have an enclosed Toyota with air conditioning and a good stereo.

MGAs are, instead, meant for open roads, preferably twisty ones. They're a perfect weekend toy, a perfect escape device, a perfect antidote to the usual sensory-deprivation machines that populate America's highways. They're just right for chasing girls or chasing memories. That's why Ken Palmer wouldn't take even $15,000 for his car. As for my car, make me an offer. No, on second thought, a driveable MGA in my garage is one of the few things that would give me more pleasure than a certificate of deposit in my bank.   — *Peter Bohr (March 1984)*

GREAT BRITAIN

MGB 1962-1974

*A lot of fun
for very little money*

by Thos L. Bryant

"The sports car connoisseur will find in this latest MG challenger all that he has been looking for. . . ." Those are the opening words of the British Motor Corporation's (now British Leyland) sales brochure for the MGB when it was introduced in late 1962. The B was the newest in a long line of sports cars from Morris Garages, the original firm named for the founder, Sir William R. Morris. It succeeded the MGA which had been in production for seven years and established a sales record never previously equaled by any sports car: 100,000 cars.

The MG octagon made its initial appearance in 1923, when a Morris Oxford chassis of the period was fitted with a Hotchkiss engine and went out into the world of competition. MG was a name to be reckoned with in automobile racing until 1935, when the program was allowed to terminate because the management felt that it was no longer achieving sufficient research and development information from the racing program.

MGs arrived in the United States after World War II, the forerunners of an invasion of sports cars from abroad. In the late 1940s and early '50s, the sight of an MG TC, or the slightly more modern looking TD model, was enough to stir the heart of many red-blooded American youngsters who dreamed of some-day owning one. It seems to us that much of the affection we still feel for MG cars is the result of those early days of youthful dreams of traveling briskly down our favorite country road behind the wheel of a TC or TD with the top down and the wind whistling over, around and through us.

The MG TD was followed by the short-lived MG TF model with a larger engine and more rakish lines, but still the original and what we thought of as traditional MG styling. In 1955,

1963 MGB

1967 MGB GT

1969 MGB

however, the Old World gave up the struggle to maintain tradition, and the MGA was born with its more modern styling based on various racing and experimental car designs and using the B-series engine with a displacement of 1,489 cc. In 1959 the engine displacement grew to 1,588 cc, which lasted until 1961, when it was again increased, this time to 1,622 cc. The MGA was produced until June 1962, when it gave way to the MGB.

The MGB was an almost totally new design inside and out. Not only was the styling a departure, but perhaps the biggest news was that the traditional ladder-type frame had given way to unit-body construction.

The engine was a continuation of the B-series engine but further expanded to 1,798 cc by enlarging the cylinder bores but with no increase in stroke. The crankshaft and block casting were strengthened to handle the increased displacement and power output. Horsepower was now 94 bhp at 5,500 rpm and the compression ratio dropped from 9.4:1 to 8.75:1.

Although the B featured a new Borg & Beck diaphragm-spring clutch for lighter effort, it continued to use the A gearbox with its nonsynchromesh first gear. *Road & Track*, along with other automotive journals, lamented the lack of an all-synchro gearbox, but it was not until the 1968 model that this became available.

The final drive ratio for the MGB was 3.91:1 rather than 4.10:1 as in the A but there was also a change to 14-inch wheels from 15, so there was little difference with the higher final drive. Acceleration was still brisk and performance good. Overdrive was an extra-cost option that many MGB owners wished they had ordered after driving their cars awhile and discovering that they were churning along at 3,340 rpm at 60 mph.

In terms of accommodation, the B is a vast improvement over the A, with considerably more hip room, more comfortable seats with a seatback adjustment and gobs of legroom. Headroom in the roadster is also quite good, and most road tests and reports on the car commented on how good the visibility was even with the top up because of the large plastic rear and quarter windows.

In October 1965, BMC introduced the MGB GT, a closed 2-seater with a spacious coupe body and easy access from the rear through a large liftback. The GT was essentially the same as the roadster in its mechanical details, with the exceptions of stiffer springs front and rear to take care of anticipated heavier loads and the addition of an anti-roll bar in front. MG felt that the GT would fill a gap in the market for those who wanted the performance of a sports car with the comfort and security of a closed car.

Both the B roadster and the GT are relatively simple and straightforward cars, which is part of their charm. The suspension is nothing fancy; it features a live rear axle with leaf springs and A-arms with coil springs up front. The drivetrain is neither unusual nor exotic. What these cars offer is driving pleasure for the enthusiast along with a reasonable degree of reliability and, with the roadster especially, a lot of fun.

Selecting An MGB

Even by 1962 standards the MGB was not an avant garde car such as the Jaguar E-type, for instance. Few people then would have guessed that the MGB would live on for eighteen years. And frankly, it probably shouldn't have. By the mid-1970s, the B was not merely outdated, it was becoming something of a joke. To meet U.S. regulations, British Leyland (the parent company of MG) seemed to take the cheapest and most inelegant way out in nearly every instance. It was as if the company said, "You Yanks want padding on the dash? We'll give you padding — lots of ugly plastic plastered all over the beautiful old metal dash. You want 5-mile-per-hour bumpers? You got 'em — big grotesque cowcatchers tacked on to both ends. And you say the bumpers aren't high enough? O.K., we'll just jack up the suspension; so what if the car resembles a pickup truck?" And that wasn't all. Smog control equipment sapped power as well. In 1970, the MGB's engine put out a lively 92 horsepower. By 1975, it had been reduced to a measly 63 horsepower.

When the last MGB rolled off the line in Abingdon in October of 1980, the poor car was so emasculated and defaced that it was nothing but a parody of itself. If the Old World charm of an MGB appeals to you, you'd be best off looking for a 1967 or earlier model, or, as second choice, a 1968-74 model, one with chrome bumpers. A pristine MGB from the 1960s won't be much cheaper than a more recent one. But all MGs are good buys now because they are currently at the bottom of the depreciation curve.

What to Look for

The first decision facing the MGB buyer is rather an obvious one: roadster or GT. The former offers much of the historical MG flavor of driving: top down, wind in the face, sky above and hassles with the top. The latter is snug and warm no matter what the weather and gives the owner extra carrying capacity for parcels and luggage but not people.

1962 MGB interior

As with most cars, the MG is susceptible to rust. The areas to check thoroughly are the rocker panels, above the rear wheel openings, along the seams on the top of the rear-quarter panels and front fenders, around the front turn-signal and parking-lamp assembly and the floor area of the cockpit.

Many MGs will show signs of the infamous "MG crack." This is a quite noticeable crack on the doors starting at the rear post of the vent windows and running down toward the bottom of the door, usually extending about six inches. It is not just a crack in the paint but in the metal itself in many cases, and it is more prevalent in the roadsters than in the GT models.

The convertible top comes in two configurations: the traditional roadster-type, stow-away top is detachable from the erector-set-like supports so that the whole apparatus can be removed and put into the trunk; the fold-down top folds into the luggage compartment behind the seats.

Both types suffer when improperly folded and a car of this vintage will likely have had its top replaced. The plastic windows have a tendency to discolor and crack with age, seriously inhibiting rearward visibility.

The B-series engine is quite robust. It was strengthened in 1965 and later models with the change from three main bearings to five, so you may want to consider a 1965 or later car. All MGBs delivered to the U.S. were equipped with external oil coolers mounted in front of the radiator. A weak point of the engine, especially the 5-bearing model, is the head gasket between the number three and four cylinders. If a head gasket is going to go, it will probably be in that area. You should always have a compression check performed on the car before agreeing to purchase it.

Another problem that crops up on MGBs is cracked cylinder heads resulting from overexuberant mechanics applying too much torque on the bolts or following an improper tightening sequence, so this is also a must for examination.

Brief Specifications

	1962 Roadster	1966 GT
Curb Weight, lb.	2080	2308
Wheelbase, in.	91.0	91.0
Track, f / r	49.2 / 49.2	49.2 / 49.2
Length	153.2	153.2
Width	59.9	59.9
Height	49.4	49.8
Fuel Capacity (gal)	12.0	12.0
Engine type	pushrod inline 4	pushrod inline 4
Bore x stroke, mm	80.3 x 89.0	80.3 x 89.0
Displacement, cc	1798	1798
Compression ratio	8.75:1	8.8:1
Horsepower, bhp @ rpm (net)	94 @ 5500	98 @ 5400
Torque, lb-ft @ rpm	107 @ 3500	107 @ 3500
Gearbox	4-speed, non-synch 1st gear	4-speed non-synch 1st gear
Final drive ratio	3.91:1	3.91:1

Performance Data From Contemporary Tests

0-60 mph, sec.	12.5	13.6
0-90 mph, sec.	34.5	37.2
Standing 1 / 4 mile, sec.	18.5	19.6
Average mpg	26.5	23.0
Road test date	11-62	5-66

Typical Asking Prices

1962-1974	$1,500-$3,500
Typical engine-rebuild price	$1,500-$2,000

1972 MGB interior

Valve noise is common and is a result of loose settings for rocker clearance given by the factory.

Getting the SU carburetors to work together is of vital importance in terms of the MGB's performance. Many MG owners have tried different jet sizes but most have come back to the factory stock size as it really works best. Balancing and coordinating the operation of the two carburetors, not modification, is the best answer for performance and economy.

In the area of emission controls, the pre-1968 MGBs had only the PCV to contend with, but proper maintenance of the PCV is very important. If the rubber diaphragm inside the valve is the least bit brittle or cracked, it will pull oil from the sump and pass it through the induction system, producing a large amount of smoke from the exhaust. If in doubt, change the valve; do not pull the head off to do a valve job without checking the PCV first.

Pre-1968 cars without synchromesh may have damaged first gears and this should be checked out. Also, you'll often find that the synchro in second gear has deteriorated or disappeared. Many enthusiasts do not mind this overly much and feel it gives them good practice at double-clutching.

Overdrive was available as an option on the MGB models, and if you can find one it is well worth having. It makes the B a much more pleasant highway cruiser. However, make sure it's operating properly because repairing it is expensive.

MG suspension design is not the most modern in the world, but it does get the job done. In examining an MGB, check the condition of the lever-arm shock absorbers by pushing down on each corner of the car. If the car bounces quite a bit, you can be certain the shocks are badly worn.

Look at the shock bodies too, and if they show signs of leaking they are no good and should be replaced, no matter what the owner may tell you. Lever-arm shocks cannot be disassembled and repaired, they must be replaced. Koni makes a kit for the rear suspension that adapts regular tube-type shock absorbers to the B. The potential buyer should also check the wheel bearings and the condition of the rear leaf springs. These springs have been known to break periodically, and you should be aware of their condition before you purchase a car.

MGBs, like their predecessor MGs, came with a choice of wire or disc wheels. Most enthusiasts know the perils of wire wheels and the cost of keeping them in good shape and will recommend going for the discs. Also, if you are planning any sort of competition with the car, such as slaloms or gymkhanas, disc wheels are stronger and safer. If you must have the wire wheels or the car you want has them, they should be checked by someone who knows about wire wheels, and spokes should be replaced if they are bent or broken. The application of a little spray paint can make them look as good as new.

MGBs generally tend to run cool and they will start quickly as long as the temperature is no lower than 0 degrees F. The oil pressure should register 55-60 psi or thereabouts, fluctuating somewhat at a stop.

All things considered, the MGB is probably an excellent choice in these times. It offers relatively economical driving with a minimum of fuss over tune-ups and valve adjustments, straightforward handling characteristics and reasonable performance. Replacement parts are easily attainable through specialty companies like Moss Motors, Ltd., in Goleta, California, and are not terribly expensive. The motoring enthusiasts who are looking for an inexpensive form of entertaining driving should find the MGB fills their needs quite nicely.

Driving Impressions

We wanted to drive a 1967 MGB as '67 was the last year MGBs were made without an overabundance of emission-control equipment. We were aided in our search for a suitable car by the Long Beach MG Club of Southern California, one of the largest and most active MG clubs in the U.S. They put us in touch with member Joe Heinz, who is the proud possessor of a '67 B he purchased new in Europe.

Joe came to our offices in Newport Beach one gorgeous afternoon, and we took his car out for a spin down Pacific Coast Highway, running along with the top down, the sun warming us and the wind providing just the right amount of exhilaration.

The car has accumulated slightly more than 94,000 miles over the years and has won several concours d'elegance. Thus far Heinz has avoided having any major work done, and his service records show such relatively minor entries as a new head gasket in June 1970, rebuilding the brake master cylinder in November 1971 and so on. Joe is a strong believer in preventive maintenance and has had his car serviced about every 2,000 miles throughout his tenure as owner.

Having disposed of a 1968 MGB roadster little more than a year ago, I found the Heinz car quite familiar and comfortable upon entry with all the switches, gauges and controls in the proper places. The engine fired up immediately on the first turn of the starter motor and belied its 94,000 miles of operation, running smoothly and quietly.

Even for my portly, over-six-foot frame, the B is quite spacious and there is an abundance of leg room. The pedals are well-situated for heel-and-toe downshifting and the shift lever is correctly located with relatively short throws. The car moves out quite briskly and revs freely up to about 4,500 rpm, where it begins to feel a bit strained. Joe's B roadster is not equipped with the optional overdrive unit; maintaining a high cruising speed for any length of time can be a rather noisy and tiring experience.

The handling and cornering characteristics of the B are satisfyingly normal and predictable and it's quite an easy car for the novice sports-car driver to manage. I have long maintained that an MG is a near ideal choice for the first-time sports car buyer because it is relatively simple and straightforward, yet offers a good deal of motoring fun for the dollar. The suspension is on the firm side and there is a stiff-legged feel to the car on bumpy and irregular surfaces.

My memories of the MGB with the top in position are that it is one of the coziest cars imaginable, especially on a rainy night. Certainly the convertible top is not entirely free from leaks, but it does a good job of keeping wind and rain out and does not encroach much on usable headroom except during entry and exit. The Heinz car has the top that folds down into the boot rather than the totally removable type; however, with the roll bar the top will not fold down properly so Joe has to remove it entirely, which is quite an operation.

It was great fun to be at the controls of an MGB again and the experience gave rise to feelings of regret at having sold mine. Although it is not an especially sophisticated or exotic automobile, it does present the driver with a good deal of pleasurable driving, which is more than can be said about many cars.   — *Thos L. Bryant (September 1975)*

U.S.A.

Trans-Am Pony Cars
1967-1971

by Allan Girdler

The subjects of this article are the production versions of domestic pony cars homologated for the original Trans-Am races, a series that lasted from around 1966 through 1971. They are primarily the Camaro Z-28, Mustang Boss 302, AAR (All-American Racers) Barracuda 340 and T / A (Trans-Am) Challenger. Earlier Barracudas are included with some reservations, the Javelin SST gets honorable mention and a couple other models get short shrift, in due course.

This survey is predicated on the writer's belief that these cars can be considered sports cars, in the American manner. They consist of high-performance packages fitted to stylish cars based on passenger sedans. They are relatively big, not especially refined and offer maximum bang for the buck. They have speed and quickness equal to anything one is likely to meet on the open road, and they handle with more grip and agility than they've been given credit for. They can be maintained by anybody with the standard two thumbs. They are becoming collector's cars.

Against these virtues are balanced two stigmas: humble origin and low original price. These cars have been unappreciated for both reasons. Trans-Am cars are among the best

Camaro Z-28,
Mustang Boss 302,
Barracuda 340,
Javelin SST,
Cougar 302 Eliminator and
Firebird Trans-Am
at their sporting best

190

sports cars American makers have produced. They are the last of an era and the best of that era.

First, some semiflexible parameters. Pony cars — the name comes from the Mustang, of course — began as family compacts in fancy dress. Some grew into big lumps, some evolved into pleasant touring cars, and some died while others survive as subcompacts in fancy dress. During this period the Barracuda and Mustang nameplates appeared on three body shells, the Firebird and Camaro on two. Challenger and Cougar were actually Barracuda and Mustang under the badges. Further, the same bodies for most of these cars came with anemic 6s and as drag-racing projectiles like Hemi-powered 'Cudas and single-overhead-cam 427 Mustangs, faster than cannonballs and about as easy to control. We are not, therefore, talking about just any 1967 Camaro, 1968 Mustang or 1970 Barracuda. We want the special Trans-Am package.

The secret weapon for us fanciers of secondhand-but-potent performance cars is homologation. Because the Trans-Am was for production cars, the race cars had to be direct descendants of actual cars sold to the general public. The Z-28s and Boss 302s now on the roads are street-legal versions of competitive racing sedans.

We draw our lines for this article around the makes and models at the top of these road-racing packages; high-performance pony cars with tuned small-block V-8s and better-than-normal brakes, suspensions and transmissions.

In 1966, first year of the series, the Trans-Am pony cars raced each other in class and lost overall to smaller GT cars like the Alfa GTA. By 1970 they were cornering with competition Porsches and beating big-motor Corvettes, head to head. I call that progress.

Z-28 Camaro

There are those who say the Z-28 wouldn't have existed except for the Trans-Am races and vice versa. That is, if the SCCA (Sports Car Club of America) hadn't been assured of Chevrolet's interest, they wouldn't have tried a professional series for domestic sedans.

One can readily believe that. The early races were won by Ford Mustangs and Dodge Darts, with engines of less than the 305-cubic-inch limit. Late in 1967, not long after the Camaro itself appeared, there came a Camaro option known as Z-28. (There was nothing mystical about the number, by the way. Chevy had options Z-27 and Z-29, neither with any competition potential, in the same catalog.)

The first Z-28 was the most complete and in many ways the most honest road racing sedan ever. Chevrolet took the crankshaft from the old 283 and put it into the 327 block for a legal and tidy 302 cubic inches. Atop the block went cylinder heads and such from the semirace Corvette engine.

The car itself got a beefy 4-speed manual transmission, stronger springs and shocks, a control rod for the rear axle, front

1968 Chevrolet Camaro Z-28

disc brakes, special linings for the rear brakes and a quick steering kit. SCCA didn't allow any body changes and the Z-28 came stock with a rear deck lip spoiler.

Neatly avoiding various regulations, the optional 1967 cold-air induction and steel tubing exhaust headers were delivered in the car's trunk with installation instructions.

On one hand, Chevrolet wanted some of these cars in public hands. California had emissions regulations that year and ten cars were built for that state, with air pumps and each car dyno-tuned to run properly and be legal. On the other hand, Chevrolet didn't want mass sales. The Z-28 was not mentioned in the ads or the literature, and there weren't many sold in 1967; 730 is the best figure I can get.

The word got out, though, and the 1968 Z-28 was sold over the counter. The cold-air system and headers became a dealer-installed option and the camshaft was one step milder. The quick steering got an optional power assist, much more pleasant for normal driving.

For 1969 the Z-28 got a 4-wheel disc brake option, although neither the writer nor anybody I know has ever seen a Z-28 sold through normal channels with this feature. My guess is it was done to get Corvette brakes onto the racing cars. Real production cars got GM's variable-ratio, power-assisted steering; the cold air entered through a raised section of the hood, and there was a new grille for the original body. In sum, the racer became a sporting and popular production car and lost a few rough edges in the process.

The 1970-1/2 Camaro had a completely new body. And — surely to accommodate more manufacturers — the SCCA allowed destroking of production engines down to the 305 limit. Naturally, Chevrolet dropped the 302 engine and substituted the 350 cubic-inch Corvette engine known as the LT-1. It had more power, more torque and less fuss. It also allowed the use of the then-new GM 3-speed automatic transmission, suitably valved and calibrated for the high-revving engine. They also tamed the camshaft timing again and put in more insulation and sound-deadener. It had the same stiff suspension, though, and was very much a performance car, right down to the 15 x 7 wheels, 60-series tires, rear spoiler and lots of stripes. The 1970 Z-28 was as close to a mild-mannered racing car as the industry has come.

In 1971 General Motors struck a great blow for public relations and dropped compression ratios. The Z-28 lost power and performance. The mild-mannered racing car became a mild-mannered car with racing heritage and so it has remained.

Boss 302 Mustang

Because Chevrolet's racing was done in secret, it had to be honest. Ford's racing was ever so public, and it took a while before Ford sold what Ford raced. One gets the impression the factory never really believed in the private-owner / sporting-driver concept, preferring factory teams on one side, cheering customers on the other and nothing in between.

1969 Ford Mustang Boss 302

Mustangs came with performance versions of the 289 right from the start and while they were equipped with stiffer suspensions and front disc brakes, high-performance Mustangs from 1964-68 don't meet the spirit of our group. There was a 4-barrel 302 and a full-race tunnel-port 302, but the latter didn't derive from the former. The SCAA took a lot of heat and dished out a lot, too, over the homologated tunnel-port engines not actually being available.

Ford got straight in 1969 with the Boss 302, a true Trans-Am car and a complete package: Ford did a Chevrolet with a short-stroke crank inside a new and strong block, topped by special (although not tunnel-port) cylinder heads, giant carburetor and properly shaped exhaust headers. Ford seems to have begun with the racing version, then eased off on tune until the lighter Mustang could match the original Camaro Z-28. The Boss 302 has a little less power and a lot more torque than the Z-28 302.

The car came as a fastback only, 4-speed manual transmission only, quick steering with or without power assist, stiffer springs and shocks, front discs and limited-slip differential. The front spoiler was standard and the rear lip an option. Ford built the same car with slightly altered front sheet metal through 1970.

In 1971 Ford followed Chevy again, with a Boss 351 in a new and different body. Didn't work, though. The car was clumsy and didn't have the power gain it showed on paper, so the Boss 302 from 1969 or 1970 is the only honest Trans-Am model Mustang.

AAR Barracuda 340 and T / A Challenger 340

These models begin with some exceptions to the rules. Chrysler began making the thinwall and excellent 340-cubic-inch V-8 in 1968, but because the factory wasn't willing to turn out a special engine, or more likely couldn't afford it, the 340 didn't get into the Trans-Am until 1970.

The 1968-69 Barracuda and an occasional Dodge Dart do receive honorary eligibility though. What Plymouth and Dodge did before 1970 was build nicely balanced packages for their fastbacks, coupes and convertibles, with the 340 engine, good automatic or manual transmissions, front disc brakes and handling packages.

Because Ford and Chevrolet did more in the line of race-based pony cars, they also did less for their standard production models. A 1967 Camaro with 307 V-8 and 2-speed automatic is a slug and a sponge, while a 340 Barracuda is a nicely sized package with the speed of a Z-28. And you can have a convertible, in case that's important.

With the early Barracudas and Darts the 340 is easy to find and the Formula S or GTS handling package generally comes with the engine. Chrysler reckoned that what was good enough for Richard Petty was good enough for everybody else, and so front drum brakes are all too common with early 340s. If it matters, take a careful look first.

1970 Plymouth Barracuda 340-S

The actual certified Trans-Am pony cars came from Plymouth and Dodge as the AAR 'Cuda 340 and / or T / A Challenger 340 — same body and mechanical specs all the way through — in 1970, the year of the legally reduced displacement.

It was a new body for both nameplates, and both divisions used improved cylinder heads, an extra beefy block so that 4-bolt mainbearing caps could be installed for racing and three 2-barrel carburetors for the highway (but not the track as they were illegal there). Decorations, i.e. stripes, emblems and spoilers, were of course provided.

While the earlier cars were economy sedans with muscle added, the 1970 Barracuda and Challenger pony cars were in effect an intermediate with the center chopped from the wheelbase. The car itself was heavier and the added weight was in front, alas, while the interiors were smaller than before. Barracuda and Challenger both tended to understeer. The sporting versions conquered this, well, mostly, through rear anti-roll bars and larger tires in back — G60 versus E60 in front. The AAR and T / A were coupes only, although the standard 340 with good suspension and brakes was fitted to Barracuda and Challenger convertibles during 1970 and 1971. Like Ford, both Plymouth and Dodge held onto the performance engines and higher compression ratios through 1971, when GM's lead became too much to resist. The Barracuda and Challenger offer the best chance for a least-used car, so to speak.

Javelin SST

Full points, first, for honest effort. American Motors saw the value in competition early on, and when the Javelin came out in 1967, AMC signed up a professional team and went racing, without much success. In 1970 AMC signed up Roger Penske and Mark Donohue and won, first just races and then the series title, although by that time the other factories had decided if they couldn't win, they wouldn't play and poor AMC had nobody worth bragging about beating.

The racing Javelins were good race cars; their limitation for our purposes was that they weren't very much Javelin. The basis for the engine was the AMC 360-cubic-inch V-8, a good example of what the British call a "cooking engine," well-suited to daily life but not to competition. Traco built the racing engines and eventually achieved both competitive power and reliability. It didn't come easy. The guys in the shop sharing a wall within Traco's dyno room painted their side with warnings: *Stand Well Back*. It seemed like a Penske / Traco / AMC 305 went BANG every half hour during the winter of 1969-70.

Two problems here: One is that while the Javelin SST was a perfectly nice car with 360 V-8, 4-speed transmission, front discs and stout springs, it was not much like the racing Javelins. Second, there has been no mystical transference. Even when AMC won the series title, the enthusiasts decided Mark Donohue could make a winner out of anything. Unfair, perhaps, but so is life.

Collectors are not scouting for clean and authentic Javelins, so while you can expect to buy low, don't expect to sell high.

Cougar 302 Eliminator

Now we come to barely honorable mentions. Mercury's Cougar was Ford's Mustang with extra trim and floss and sheer dead weight. There was a Cougar with the honest 302 engine, 4-speed transmission, handling package and brakes, so one cannot throw the whole thing out, even though the Eliminator name reveals that Mercury believed the youth market to be the drag market.

What you got with the 302 Eliminator was the same engine and related bits trying to haul 400 extra pounds; more paint, less punch. Quoting a man in the used performance-car business, people buying Trans-Am pony cars know what they are looking for. A 302 Eliminator sells for $1,000 less than a Boss 302, which tells you enough right there.

Firebird Trans-Am

Firebird from 1967 to the present is a Camaro body with Firebird badges on the outside and Pontiac running gear inside. In 1969 Pontiac offered a Firebird model with a great snorting 400-cubic-inch, drag-tuned engine. (The same year homologation papers were filed making the outright false claim that Firebirds came with 302 Chevrolet Z-28 engines in Canada).

1970 Pontiac Firebird Trans-Am

The 1970 Trans-Am Firebird, the new and current body, had the same ill-tempered engine, a stiff and responsive suspension and the damnedest assortment of fender flares, front scoops and lips and rear trim tab. A private team — well, private as far as the record shows — raced the 1970 model with a destroked but actually Pontiac engine. The cars were far off the pace.

In fairness, the later Trans-Am Firebird was an entertaining slalom car; lots of opposite lock, howling tires and that sort of thing. The lumpy fussiness of a cooking engine tuned beyond its expectations probably has an appeal in some quarters.

Even so, the Trans-Am Firebird is denied full membership in this group on grounds that Pontiac snatched up the name without playing the game.

Price Structure

A large share of a Trans-Am pony car's value is an illusion, an image. The owner pays for heritage and history along with performance and transportation.

There's also a bit of guilt by generalization, i.e., Z-28 owners tend to be either maintenance perfectioninsts or boy racers. Used Z-28s seem to be super clean or to have gone 100,000 miles at 7,200 rpm, every shift a speed shift and every brake application enough to flat-spot the tires. Much the same for Barracudas with the added hazard that 'Cuda racers haunted the drag strips. The Boss 302 crowd appears more clubby, more apt to rally and slalom and more apt to maintain fairly carefully as they drive fairly hard. Ergo, Boss 302 Mustangs tend to be in good shape but not perfect shape.

Also we must consider rarity: as the 1967 Z-28 is rarest and closest to race-ready, so it has a higher asking price than a 1969, which in turn does better than the 1968 because the 1969 has more visible racing options (like the raised carb intake).

In sum, a good Z-28 has a higher asking price than a good Barracuda, and may be either higher or lower than a Boss 302. And given equal condition and mileage, any of these will out-price a Firebird or Javelin because the latter cars aren't completely race-based cars.

The prices shown here, then, are but a loose guide. When you actually get down to bidding on, say, a 1967 California-certified Camaro Z-28, only one for sale in your area, it's worth what the owner wants, what you're willing to pay, or something in between.

Driving Impressions

Z-28 302: Honest, direct and fierce are the words that leap to mind. The early Z-28 was mighty close to being race-ready as delivered. Insulation is minimal, and there is a constant clatter of solid lifters, *whoosh* of carburetor intake, drumming from the exhaust pipes and the odd, tinny rattle of steel headers. Clutch, brake, steering and gearshift all require effort and are quick. Everything is done in short, firm motions, and there's no doubt when the clutch is engaged or the transmission is in gear.

This car is something of a struggle around town, as one wrestles with the steering and gets tired of shoving down on the clutch and heaving the lever from one gear to the next. The engine does not appreciate being nursed. There is little torque below 3,000 rpm and while the 302 will lug, it sounds unhappy.

My, is it ever quick. Something shared by all these high-compression engines is sharpness of response and smoothness of power application.

Driving the Z-28 302 with *brio* is especially rewarding to those of us accustomed to a stiff suspension. Thunder into a turn, put the wheel just so. The Z-28 braces itself against the road and the driver can do as he pleases, cranking in more lock for tight turns, booting the tail out with power, whatever the situation calls for. One quickly forgets the annoyance of rowing around town. The Z-28 302 is rough, noisy, demanding but so what?

Z-28 350: The later model is a different car. As mentioned, the rules allowed Chevrolet to start with a larger engine tuned more for street use, in turn permitting automatic transmission and power assist for the steering.

The 1970 Z-28 gained 200 pounds and the handling package was mostly stronger anti-roll bars with relatively softer springs, resulting in a better ride with equal cornering stance. There was more insulation as well, and the Z-28 350 is as quiet as the Z-28 302 is raucous.

Switching from early to late Z-28s is, in all practical ways, a clear gain. The newer car is faster and more tractable, the steering is as quick and much lighter. Clutch and gear change are identical. The different suspension technique does give the 1970 car more understeer at low speeds and it takes, say, up to 6 / 10s, in racing terms, before the later Z-28 stops trying to plow off the line.

Incidentally, road tests from 1970 show the 4-speed Z-28 doing the standing quarter-mile in 14.50 seconds while the automatic, same driver (me), same track turned 14.51. You don't lose much with the automatic, in other words.

If there is a loss from early to late, it's emotional. The newer car is easier to drive, giving better performance and equal handling with less effort, less fuss. The earlier models are more like racing cars, that's all.

Boss 302: Ah, the virtues of lightness. Getting equal performance with a lighter car allowed Ford to tune its 302 for mid-range power, and the Boss 302 feels and drives more like a standard high-performance engine. The idle is bumpy but once above that, ample torque all the way to "six thou," which is where the ignition's rev limiter takes over. The Boss 302 is a neat little engine.

Loud, though. The entire car is loud, with great gusts of

Brief Specifications

	1968 Z-28 Camaro	1969 340-S Barracuda	1969 Boss 302 Mustang	1970 Z-28 Camaro	1970 Trans-Am Firebird	1970 AAR 340 Barracuda
Curb Weight, lb.	3355	3470	3260	3580	3960	3630
Wheelbase, in.	108.0	108.0	108.0	108.0	108.0	108.0
Track, f / r	59.9 / 59.5	57.7 / 55.6	58.5 / 58.5	61.3 / 60.0	61.6 / 60.3	59.7 / 60.7
Length	184.6	192.8	187.4	188.0	191.6	186.7
Width	72.3	69.6	71.8	74.4	73.4	74.9
Height	50.9	52.7	50.3	50.5	50.4	50.9
Fuel Capacity (gal)	18.5	18.0	20.0	18.0	17.0	19.0
Engine type	pushrod V-8	pushrod V-8	pushrod V-8	pushrod V-8	pushrod V-8	pushrod V-8
Bore x stroke, in.	4.00 x 3.00	4.04 x 3.31	4.00 x 3.00	4.00 x 3.48	4.12 x 3.75	4.04 x 3.31
Displacement, cu in	302	340	302	350	400	340
Bhp @ rpm, SAE gross	290 @ 5800	275 @ 5000	290 @ 5800	360 @ 6000	345 @ 5200	290 @ 5000
Actual bhp*	320	300	280	350	350	310
Torque, lb-ft @ rpm	290 @ 4200	340 @ 3200	290 @ 4300	380 @ 4000	430 @ 3400	345 @ 3400
Gearbox	4-speed	4-speed	4-speed	4-speed	4-speed	4-speed
Final drive ratio	4.10:1	3.91:1	3.91:1	4.10:1	3.91:1	3.55:1

*Based on engine tests, reliable-if-confidential reports and the author's secret chart which reveals actual power through the use of quarter-mile speed and test weight.

Performance Data From Contemporary Tests

0-60 mph, sec.	7.4	7.1	6.9	6.5	6.3	7.0
0-100 mph, sec.	14.2	15.6	16.0	15.1	14.7	14.7
Standing 1 / 4 mile, sec.	14.85	14.93	14.85	14.50	14.51	14.50
Average mpg	12-15	13-16	12-14	12-15	11-14	14-16
Road test date	7-68	11-68	9-69	5-70	6-70	7-70

Typical Asking Prices

Camaro Z-28, Mustang Boss 302, Barracuda 340, Javelin SST, Cougar 302 Eliminator, Firebird Trans Am	$4,000-$12,000
Typical engine-rebuild price (all models)	$1,800-$2,500

howling and thrashing. The ride is as bumpy as the idle, because the shocks and spring rates are quite stiff for the car's weight. There was one choice of steering ratio — fast — and the option was power assist or not. Purists in 1969 frowned on power assist and most didn't order it. They were wrong. If there's a choice, take the booster.

Bumpy or not, the Boss 302 is delightfully sporting when driven hard. It takes a firm stance, goes where it's pointed; mild understeer with power oversteer as close as your right foot.

Okay, it's a noisy little devil. One can't draw street conclusions from race records but the Mustang *did* beat the Camaro head-to-head in 1970 and the impression in 1976 is that the Boss 302 is... well, it's heresy but the Boss 302 feels like an improved Z-28 302.

Barracuda 340-S: In exchange for being the least powerful and least quick of the models in the Trans-Am pony car group, the 340-S is the least demanding.

The 340 provides enough torque to climb practically anything. Controls are light and precise, perhaps even too light in the case of the brakes, which demand a delicate toe else you lock the wheels. And there are those who say the steering has too much assist and filters out the road feel, although my ex-

---

WEST GERMANY

Porsche 912/911

1965-1971

by Joe Rusz

Don't get me wrong. I love the British, the Italians and even the Americans. In fact some of my best friends are Jaguars, MGs, Alfas and Corvettes (you are what you drive). They're all fine cars and everything that *Road & Track*'s Used Car Classic reports claim they are. But let's forget the rhetoric and say that when putsch (Freudian slip?-Ed.) comes to shove we all know the best automobiles are still built in Germany and that of their lot the best GT machines are Porsches, specifically the 901 series. (Speak for yourself, Joe — Ed.)

Here are cars that have caught the fancy of every true motoring enthusiast who lusts after what Porsche calls, "driving in its purest form." It doesn't take a movie of questionable merit nor an actor who probably doesn't know an Aston Martin from a hole in the ground to make the public and the cogniscente aware of the Porsche. Its history, merits and track record speak for themselves and in case you haven't been listening too closely, Porsche GTs have won the Camel GT, the Trans-Am, the European GT Championship plus countless other races and rallies. Although the autos involved have usually been much-

How to enjoy Porsche performance, styling and economy at a fraction of the cost of a new one

1970 Porsche 911T

perience is this becomes less true with practice. The automatic transmission is excellent.

AAR 340 'Cuda: Let the record show that late in 1969 the author went to Detroit, inspected and drove the new 1970 Barracuda, then rushed home and snapped up a 1969 Barracuda. It's my opinion that the AAR 340 'Cuda (and T/A 340 Challenger), while genuinely homologated and factory-backed Trans-Am pony cars, are less appealing than the older cars.

Nothing wrong with the 3-carb 340, which has more power without more temperament. The 340 engine was pretty much the same from 1968 through 1971. The Torque-Flite automatic transmission is great and the massive 4-speed manual transmission shifts with surprising ease. Equal points in those departments.

But the 1970 models weighed more and were more nose-heavy. The normal high-performance 340 Barracuda and Challenger don't handle as nimbly as the earlier cars, and compared even less well against the Z-28 and Boss 302. The AAR and T/A models are competitive, but they got that way through great whacking rear anti-roll bars and oversize rear tires. While they will do what you want, they gotta be forced into it.

— *Allan Girdler (March 1977)*

---

modified versions of production Porsches — Carreras, the *ne plus ultra* of Porsche grand touring machines — the point is that beneath the flared fenders, wide wheels, spoilers and 3-liter engine lies the basic type 901, a car that has changed little since its debut at the 1963 Frankfurt Automobile Show. Which is just the point we're trying to make, i.e., where looks and performance are concerned, the early-model 901-series Porsche is not much different from the current crop of high-priced boulevard racers. And that, dear reader, is what makes the 1965 through 1971 911 and 912 perfect Used Car Classics.

Before launching off in earnest on the merits of the early Porsches, let's clarify Porsche's model numbering system. All things Porsche — from engines, to transaxles, to complete automobiles — are assigned a project number dating back to the founding of Dr. Ferdinand Porsche's design facility in the early 1930s. Thus the first Porsche was model 356, the early Spyder a 550 and our present GT star the 901. Unfortunately, the 901 model designation never got past the prototype stage, because at about that time Peugeot laid claim to all three-digit model numbers with a zero in their midst (104, 204, etc.), and Porsche, forced to substitute another number (at least in so far as production cars were concerned), chose "1". Thus the 901 with its 6-cylinder engine became the 911, while the 4-cylinder model, introduced one year later, became the 912. (Incidentally, Porsche design number 912 was assigned to a much more awesome project, the 12-cylinder racing engine that powered the 917.) In spite of their dissimilar model numbers, the 911 and

1966 Porsche 912

199

912 are nearly identical. The differences lie in their engines, instrumentation and accessories, which are more elaborate in the 911.

The 911

The first of the 901-series Porsches, the 911 is the car that dazzled the crowds at Frankfurt. In its original form it was equipped with a single-overhead-cam, 6-cylinder engine, 5-speed transmission and 4-wheel disc brakes; quite a performance package in those days and even today. The early engines displaced 1,991 cc and produced 130 bhp DIN. With a bore of 80 mm and a stroke of 66 mm, these tiny powerplants powered all Porsche sixes until 1970, when the bore was increased to 84 mm.

At the time of its introduction, the 911 was intended to be a top-of-the-line Porsche designed to replace the 2-liter dohc Carrera four. Hence the many standard-equipment items such as 5-speed transmission, 6-cylinder engine, etc. One year later Porsche began having second thoughts about pricing and for 1966 (the first 911s went on sale in '64 in Europe), the 4-speed, which had been developed for the 912, was offered as standard equipment on the 911, while the 5-speed became an option. The 1966 911 differed little from the '65 model. The engine was still rated at 130 bhp, although in mid-production the bothersome Solex 40, PI-series, dual 3-barrel carburetors were replaced by Weber 40 IDAs of the same configuration.

In 1967 Porsche offered, in addition to the 911 and 912S, a 911S. The normal 911 engine was virtually identical to its predecessors and rated at the same 130 bhp. The stellar attraction of the '67 model year was the S (for Super), an option-laden Porsche that could cruise at 140 mph. A higher compression ratio (9.8:1 vs 9:1), wilder cams and larger carburetors (Weber 40 IDSs) all helped to produce 160 bhp DIN in a 1,991-cc engine that was structurally identical to its normal stablemate. A noteworthy addition to the '67 model line was the Targa, a convertible coupe featuring a built-in roll bar, foldable roof and removable rear window. It was available as a 911 or 912.

1967 Porsche 911 Targa

The 1968 model year saw Porsche reach the nadir (no, not Ralph) of performance. It was the beginning of bureaucratic bungling in the U.S. and Porsche got caught with its guard down and its emissions up. It certified only two engines, the 912 4-cylinder and the normal 130-bhp version of the sohc six. The air injection pump was pressed into service and the normally smooth running powerplants were suddenly subject to countless maladies. In addition to the 912, Porsche offered the 911 and the 911L (for Luxus), a gussied-up version of the basic 911. The difference was mostly cosmetic with fancy interior and forged alloy wheels included as standard equipment. Distinguishing characteristics included add-on side reflectors (the only time they were used), wide headlight bezels with no glass covers, new door handles and restyled VDO gauges. Also new that year was Porsche's semiautomatic, 4-speed Sportomatic transmission. Europe was not subject to emissions-control regulations at that time and in the Old World the S model was still available. Human nature being what it is (sneaky and determined), a few '68 S models snuck into the U.S. in spite of the emissions embargo.

By 1969 (or more accurately, fall of '68), Porsche had cleaned up its act, so to speak, and was again offering U.S. buyers a full line of Porsches, including a 912, 911T, E and S. The air pump was gone as were the ugly side reflectors. Available for the first time was a Bosch timed-flow fuel-injection system that was nearly identical to the unit used on racing Porsches of that era. Porsche had developed a new model whose E designation referred to its being equipped with *Einspritzung* (fuel-injection). Needless to say, the S was also injected that year. The E was meant to be an in-between Porsche, a Porsche to grow on, that offered many of the S model's features (wheels, trim, etc.) without its handicaps (a very high-strung engine). The E powerplant, though injected, was detuned to develop 140 bhp DIN by virtue of a 9.1:1 compression ratio and milder cam timing. By contrast, the S with its 9.9:1 compression ratio and performance goodies produced 170 bhp DIN. Also available was the 911T (T for touring), a model that had been introduced in Europe in the previous year. The T was the so-called "stripper six," offering many of the benefits of the more luxurious 911s without the stigma of high price. The T engine had the same displacement (1,991 cc) as the E and S, but featured Zenith 40 TIN carburetors, 8.6:1 compression ratio and even milder cam timing that resulted in an output of 110 bhp. The T engine also had a cast-iron (vs forged) crankshaft — an austerity move to lower the production cost of that model.

Although an impressive engine lineup made 1969 a noteworthy year for Porsche, changes in the chassis and body produced the most distinguishing characteristics that season. A 2.25-inch lengthening of the wheelbase improved handling, while a slight flaring of the fenders refreshed the coupe's looks. Electric defroster wires were added to the rear window, and the Targa's plastic back window was replaced with glass. Additionally, flow-through ventilation was added and the wing windows eliminated on the coupe but not the Targa.

Following on the heels of the 901's chassis / body change came a displacement increase in the 1970 model year. After five years of make-do with the original 1,991-cc powerplant, Porsche upped the bore by 4 mm and produced a 2,195-cc engine that offered an across-the-board horsepower increase for the T, E and S. Although engine components remaining otherwise unchanged, horsepower zoomed upward to 125, 155 and 180 bhp respectively. The 912 with its 4-cylinder pushrod engine was dropped from the line-up.

For 1971 the model line remained unchanged. Although there were cosmetic updates (paint, etc.), engines, drivetrains and body styles were identical to the previous year's models.

The 912

Introduced at the 1965 Frankfurt Automobile Show, this "more economical" version of the 901 was designed to offer the new car's many benefits to budget-minded buyers. It cost about $1,700 less than the cheapest 911 and its 1,582-cc pushrod four developed 90 bhp, just enough to give the model a 115-mph top speed. Both 4- and 5-speed transmissions were available with the 912 from the very outset. In most other respects the 912 was identical to the 911. It shared the same body and chassis, the same (or at least similar) running gear and a comparable interior. Early 912s had the most basic instrumentation (tachometer, speedometer, fuel and temperature gauges), but in '67 the model began to share the 911's more elaborate gauge layout and electric clock. The 912, a reliable though gutless poor-man's Porsche, sold well. Its simple 4-cylinder engine (based on the old 1600SC powerplant) featured dual Solex P-11 carburetors, was easy to maintain and, unlike the more complex sohc 6-cyl, could be serviced by almost any VW mechanic, or even by its owner. Unfortunately, Porsche scuttled the 912 at the end of the '69 model year and gave the public the 914. But for 1976 only, Porsche brought back the 912 powered by the 2-liter 914 engine, and called it the 912E.

Synopsis: The Models and Their Features

Where used 911s / 912s are concerned the best bargains and in some cases the best finds are among the early models. The bargains are the '66 / '67 911s (get one with Webers if possible), which are capable of outperforming more expensive machinery Herewith, a synopsis.

1965: The first year for the 901, publicly called the 911. Few cars were built and all used the 6-cylinder, 1991-cc 130-bhp engine. Solex carbs, 5-speed. Rare.

1966: First U.S. 901s, equipped with 4-cylinder (912) and 6-cylinder (911) engines. Available with 4- or 5-speed transmissions. Early 911s feature Solex carbs but later models use Webers. Some good bargains here.

1967: Best of the early years. Bugs ironed out and cars reasonably trouble-free. Models available: 912, 911, 911S, the last a somewhat peaky runner not well-suited to 'round-town motoring. Targa introduced and offered with all engines. Soft plastic rear window bothersome but retrofit kit available using solid glass window. Most popular and often expensive, 912 Targa.

1968: Worst year for U.S. models, at least where engines are concerned. Air pump noisy, troublesome. Only 912 and 911 engines available (no S) in U.S. L model has deluxe trim, wheels, etc. Targa has optional solid glass rear window. Sportomatic offered with 911.

1969: Good year and thus very popular. Four models (912, 911T, E, S), fuel injection (E, S), longer wheelbase, flared fenders, new ventilation. Last year for the 912, making this a very desirable model. Most desirable Porsche of the crop, the '69 912

Targa. T model with Webers also popular.

1970: Few major changes except for engine. Displacement increased to 2,195 cc ups horsepower for all models and makes the S the fastest of the 911s up to this time (143 mph top speed). Good year even though T model reverts to Zenith carbs.

1971: Same as '70. Entire model line virtually unchanged except for minor details. Some T engines Weber equipped, although Zeniths prove trouble-free.

What to Look For

As a Porsche owner for many years, I feel quite knowledgeable about the marque. But in order to ensure thoroughness I called upon several Porsche dealer / service people for advice. Here's what they said you should look for:

Rust. Lots of it to be found on Midwestern and Eastern cars, sometimes even on Southern and Western Porsches. Salt used on snowy streets is a culprit that can eat its way through the best automobile bodies. Porsches are especially susceptible because there are many areas that can trap salty water and just plain moisture. The result is rust, both inside and outside. Rocker panels are the most obvious places, as are bottoms of doors, fender seams and parts of the substructure. Because of the 901's unibody design, rust in the substructure can cause the suspension to collapse. Also, look for rust around the headlights, taillights, upper and lower door edges and where the side windows meet the body.

Defective heater boxes. These are the beauties that get heat into the cockpit. They use air from the cooling fan passing over hot exhaust manifolds to do the job. They'll rust internally and / or externally, and the danger is carbon monoxide in the cockpit. Very expensive to replace, so give a close look. Turn on heater control while engine is running to see if there are internal leaks.

Axle shafts. Early cars ('65 and '66) use Nadellas with conventional universal joints without protective boot — a perfect opportunity for crud to get in. Later models use Loebro constant velocity joints (covered, better) and are preferable. Conversion can be made on early models but it ain't cheap.

Muffler. Insist on the stocker. Flow-through types (high-performance, they say) are noisy, sure-fire cop catchers (ask the man who owns one). Stock exhaust works as well and is quiet. But look for rust.

Oil reservoir leaks, corrosion. On 911s only, because they use dry sump oil system. Tank located in right rear fender well with lines running to engine. Look for leaks there and in tank itself.

Worn chain tensioners (911 only). You can't see the devils but they're around. Located at the rear of the engine in the flat area under the carb bodies, these hydraulic tensioners keep the camshaft drive chain taut. When worn they allow chain to whip and can result in cams slipping a cog (bad trouble). Characterized by a rattle or growl that is most noticeable when engine is

1969 Porsche 911S interior

cold or during cold-weather operation.

Gearbox synchros. Especially prevalent on 5-speed gearbox where low is the first to go with second following suit. Noticeable when downshifting into low while car is rolling (at low speeds, please). In second, noticeable on quick upshifts. Faulty synchros, though bothersome, can be lived with, especially considering the expense and the hassle involved in their replacement (engine must be removed).

Rear camber misalignment. Excessive negative or positive rear camber causes wheels to lean in or out (depending on setting), resulting in premature tire wear. For racing some experts recommend a considerable amount of negative camber to improve stability, but for street use and for good tire life a little bit of negative or positive camber goes a long way.

Faulty hydropneumatic front suspension ('69 and '70 911E only). Standard equipment on E models, optional on Ts, these hydraulic struts replaced the usual front torsion bars. Said to provide a softer ride and some degree of self-leveling, the devices are fine if struts have not collapsed. Many owners of Es and Special Ts change over to torsion bars, a conversion that is slightly more expensive than repair of the original unit. Later model Es ('71) reverted to torsion bars as original equipment.

In spite of what seems like a demanding maintenance program, Porsche 901-series automobiles are reliable machines that can bring years of driving pleasure to their owners. Chances of finding a good used model are better than average because, as a rule, Porsche owners care about their cars. And the best part is that by buying a used 901, you'll be getting the performance and styling of a late-model Porsche at a fraction of the cost.

Driving Impression

Can one evaluate his own automobile and still give an objective opinion of its performance? Yes if, like myself, that person drives more than forty different automobiles per year and is willing to concede many of them (the Mercedes 450SE, BMW 530i and Ferrari 308 to name a few) are exciting machines. But we're talking about Porsches, and I'll put things in proper perspective by saying that my 1967 911 is as exciting to drive today as it was that first afternoon when I drove it off the dealer's lot in Long Beach, California. Mine is a basic 911, equipped with a 5-speed, AM / FM / SW Blaupunkt radio and chrome wheels. At present there are nearly 98,000 miles on the odometer and thanks to my conscientious maintenance schedule (tune-ups every 6,000 miles, oil changes every 4,000, wash every week), the car still looks new in spite of some slightly oxidized paint (the Germans were not known for their paint in those days). After its recent engine rebuild (blown cylinder head gasket), my rejuvenated Porsche should go another 98,000 miles if I decide to keep it that long.

If you've never driven a 901-series Porsche let me say that you're in for a treat. The pedal location and angle, steering position and dash layout are testimonials to Teutonic engineering. The shifter, which (as they say) falls readily to hand, is of the hot-knife-through-soft-butter variety — very smooth. The sohc 6-cylinder engine fires up readily, and after warm-up revs freely to its 6,800-rpm redline. I consider the engine one of my Porsche's strong points. Because of its lack of emission controls

Brief Specifications

	912	All 911s
Curb Weight, lb.	2140	2380 (1)
Wheelbase, in.	87.0 (2)	87.0 (2)
Track, f / r	53.8 / 52.5	53.8 (3) / 52.5 (4)
Length	163.9	163.9
Width	63.4	63.4
Height	52.0	52.0
Fuel Capacity (gal)	16.4	16.4
Engine type	pushrod flat 4	sohc flat 6
Bore x stroke, mm	82.5 x 74.0	80.0 x 66.0 (5)
Displacement, cc	1582	1991 (6)

(1) S model lighter

(2) Wheelbase increased to 89.3 in. 1969

(3) 54.1 with alloy wheels

(4) 53.3 with alloy wheels

(5) 84 mm bore 1970-71 (6) 2195 cc 1970-71

Performance Data From Contemporary Tests

	1965 911	1966 912	1967 911S	1968 911S Sportomatic	1969 911E	1970 911S	1971 911T Sportomatic
0-60 mph, sec.	9.0	11.6	8.1	10.3	8.4	7.3	9.1
0-100 mph, sec.	23.7	34.0	20.0	26.0	22.5	19.7	27.0
Standing 1 / 4 mile, sec.	16.5	18.1	15.7	17.3	16.0	14.9	17.2
Average mpg	16.5	24.0	17.5	17.5	18.4	15.0	19.8
Road test date	3-65	2-66	4-67	2-68	1-69	3-70	4-71

Engine Horsepower & Compression Ratio

Model	Horsepower (DIN)@ rpm	Compression Ratio
912 (1966-69)	90 @ 5800	9.3:1
911 (1965-68)	130 @ 6100	9.0:1
911S (1967-68)	160 @ 6600	9.8:1
911T (1969)	110 @ 5800	8.6:1
911E (1969)	140 @ 6500	9.1:1
911S (1969)	170 @ 6800	9.9:1
911T (1970-71)	125 @ 5800	8.6:1
911E (1970-71)*	155 @ 6200	9.1:1
911S (1970-71)*	180 @ 6500	9.8:1

*Engine displacement of all engines increased to 2195 cc in 1970.

Typical Asking Prices

1965-1971 912, 911		$5,000-$10,000
Typical engine-rebuild prices:	912	$1,800-$2,500
	911	$4,000-$5,000

(legal in that era), it is still capable of 16-second quarter-mile times and 130-mph top speeds. Few new cars can offer the same advantages.

Handling is something that Porsches are both famous and infamous for. A 911 can be driven quickly by almost anyone, but to drive it well takes a trained driver. Because of the 911's rear weight bias, the car oversteers very strongly, especially the early model with its skinny tires and wheels. Lesson one in the Porsche driver's handbook: keep the power on when cornering. Otherwise a spin or at least some wild tail wagging is inevitable.

Silent running is not my Porsche's forte and there is wind and engine noise to contend with. The former can be subdued quite effectively by installing 1974-'75 door rubber, but the latter must be accepted unless one cares to install sound deadening material in the back seat (it's been done). Early Porsche engines, mine included, are peaky runners that prefer engine speeds above 3,000 rpm and respond to the driver's demands at 4,500 rpm or more. No wonder they are noisy. Yet in spite of their speeds, these small displacement powerplants, free of smog controls, pull strongly while delivering 19 mpg in city driving and 26 mpg in highway use. However they do require premium fuel.

The most enjoyable aspect of the 911 is its styling, which I think will never grow old. Porsche seems to think so too, because they are still using the same basic design.

— Joe Rusz (December 1975)

WEST GERMANY

Porsche 914 and 914/6 1970-1976

Somehow it seemed more important in 1970 to distinguish between the Porsche 914s and the *real* Porsches, i.e., the 911 and 356 models. The 914 was treated rather rudely by most Porsche enthusiasts in the U.S., and for years there were many Porsche clubs that refused to open their doors to 914s. In Europe, it was sold under the combined name Volkswagen-Porsche 914, but the U.S. distributor wanted no part of that moniker, although it did signify the joint marketing agreement signed by the two German automakers. Now, the controversy over whether or not the 914 is truly a Porsche has lost much of its steam, particularly in light of the unveiling of the 924, 944 and 928. Nonetheless, there are those who continue to disparage the 914. The prospective Used Car Classic buyer who is status conscious may want to consider selecting another sports car. But if measuring yourself against someone else's yardstick isn't as important as driving fun, read on.

Cheap Porsche or expensive VW, the driving fun is abundant

by Thos L. Bryant

1974 Porsche 914

1970 Porsche 914/6

1975 Porsche 914

The first public viewing of the mid-engine 914 and 914/6 came at the Frankfurt Auto Show in the autumn of 1969. The considerable interest in a new model from Porsche, the first of the modern sports cars with such a layout, was tempered by the car's styling. Criticisms focused on the car's slab sides and pinched-fender front end. On the other hand, the rear styling was rather more acceptable, and the Targa-style removable roof was applauded as an efficient blend of open and closed motoring. The interior appointments were quite plain compared to the 911 models, and the less-than-luxurious seats came in for considerable criticism, although they actually did provide reasonable lateral support and fair comfort. As with *real* Porsches, there was abundant head, leg and elbow room in the 914.

A differentiation was made by most Porsche enthusiasts between the 914 and the 914/6 — the latter being more acceptable as nearly the real thing. Whereas the 914 used primarily VW running gear and powertrain, the 914/6 (which came to the U.S. some three months after the 914) was built with more pieces out of the Porsche parts bin. It was assembled at Zuffenhausen, the Porsche plant outside Stuttgart, while the 914 was put into finished form at the VW plant in Wolfsburg.

The 914 had VW's flat-4 from the 411LE sedan and Bosch electronic fuel-injection. This 1.7-liter (1,679-cc) powerplant produced a fairly modest 85 bhp at 4,900 rpm and 103 lb-ft torque at 2,800, resulting in performance that was characterized as somewhat disappointing. In our initial road test (April 1970), we measured a 0-60 mph time of 13.9 seconds and a quarter-mile capability of 19.2 seconds at 70.0 mph. The transaxle was a 5-speed manual, which some observers felt was a bit pretentious for the engine's performance, and both fourth and fifth gears were overdrive ratios (0.927 and 0.708:1, respectively).

The 914/6 is considerably more powerful than its sibling and features larger brakes, wider wheels and tires and more instrumentation. The engine was from the 911T, a 2.0-liter (1,991-cc) opposed-6, rated at 125 bhp at 5,800 rpm and 131 lb-ft torque at 4,200. In our July 1970 road test we stated that it "is such a beautiful, strong engine that it transforms the 914 back into a real Porsche — say what you will about the chassis, the 4-cylinder version still comes off as a VW." In hard numbers, the 914/6 demonstrated that 2.0 liters, properly done, could be enough as it sped from 0-60 mph in 8.7 seconds and romped through the quarter-mile lights in 16.3 seconds at 83.0 mph — just a few ticks slower than the 911T's time of 16.0 seconds.

The testers of the day were even less enchanted with the wisdom of a 5-speed in the 914/6, pointing out that the 911T was able to manage quite well with a 4-speed gearbox. They did acknowledge that the shift linkage in the 914/6 was "much better than the vague operation we experienced with the 4-cylinder. There's a different engine layout to pass the linkage around as well as the fact that Porsche assembles the 914/6 (the whole car) while VW builds the four." An automatic gearbox, the Porsche Sportomatic, was also offered but very few buyers elected that option.

In discussing the handling attributes of the 914, our initial skidpad number was a disappointing 0.723g. The report added, however, that "its transient characteristics — the way it responds when you first steer it into a turn or change the throttle opening in the middle of a turn — are excellent. Initial response to a steering input is utterly without delay, a feature we expect with a central engine; body roll is so slight as to go unnoticed. And what happens when the driver lifts his foot from the throttle in a hard corner — this is the trickiest thing about rear-heavy cars — is simply a mild tuck-in of the front or, at the extreme, a smooth breakaway of the rear. Even if the driver does something stupid (like stabbing the brakes) after finding himself in a corner going too fast, the 914 does nothing violent and control can be recovered easily."

Very few changes were made to the 914 and 914 / 6 for 1971 (the 4-cylinder car's interior and trim were made slightly fancier). That year marked the end of the line for the 6-cylinder model after a production run of some 3,107 cars. Porsche cited price resistance (it cost almost as much as a base 911), and complications from increasingly stringent emissions regulations as reasons for putting the 914 / 6 to rest.

For 1972, the 914 / 4 sailed on alone with little alteration: The ventilation system was improved by adding fresh air ducts at each end of the dashboard, the quality of the carpeting was upgraded, and the passenger's seat was finally made fully adjustable, something that should have been done from the beginning. By 1973, U.S. emissions standards were beginning to affect seriously the 1.7-liter engine's performance: The 49-state version was now showing 76 bhp with the original compression ratio of 8.2:1, but in the crucial California market, even tougher standards meant special tuning that resulted in an output of 69 bhp and a compression ratio of 7.3:1 — scarcely in keeping with the car's image and price (the base price had risen from $3,595 in 1970 to $4,749 for 1973). To counter this situation, Porsche (or VW) introduced the 2.0-liter, 4-cylinder version that boasted 91 bhp at 4,900 rpm. The 914 2.0 package also included more attention to interior appearance, a center console that housed a voltmeter, clock and oil temperature gauge, forged alloy wheels and front and rear anti-roll bars.

Outside, the 1973 models were fitted with rubber bumper guards that marked the first major exterior change since introduction. The next year, federally required safety bumpers gave the 914 its only significant change in appearance. The anemic 1.7 engine gave way to the 1.8-liter (1,795-cc) that was a 50-state engine and produced 76 bhp. The 2.0-liter was unchanged except for emission controls that reduced its output to 88 bhp.

That year (1974) also marked the "boutique" approach to marketing cars, and 914 buyers could select from a wide variety of new paint colors and special graphics. There was another change in bumper design for 1975 (and many observers found this treatment the most visually pleasing of all), but otherwise the 914 continued unaltered. A front spoiler could be ordered as an option and fitted below the front bumper, and the alloy wheels were now optional on both the 1.8 and the 2.0.

The 914 line came to an end with the 1976 model year — some 2,686 versions of the 2.0 were built that year, but in May production was halted. *Road & Track*'s Motor Sports Editor Joe Rusz noted in his book, *Porsche Sport 1976/77*, that the "914's life was short but prolific. It was the most popular Porsche ever sold — 83,841 units (U.S.) in seven years. And it was controversial — a Porsche to some, a Volkswagen to others. Ironically its successor, the front-engine 924, seemed destined for the same life of controversy."

Buying a Used 914

Engine compartment fires are the first thing many people think about in considering Porsche 914s. There was a serious problem with rupturing fuel lines (often caused by the battery tipping over or coming unfastened and leaking onto the fuel lines that were just below the battery's platform in the engine bay). A car that shows evidence of such a fire may be a reasonable purchase, but you must ascertain whether the fire was sufficiently serious to have damaged or weakened the car's frame.

With the help of more than 300 *Road & Track* readers who completed our 914 Used Car Classic Questionnaire, we've gained a comprehensive picture of the major areas of concern in seeking the 914 of your dreams. As with most sports cars there are those examples that have been driven into the ground and those that have been accorded kid-glove treatment. For some reason a lot of 914s were not well cared for, but this means that there is a fairly good supply of spare parts available in wrecking yards around the country where 914s have been laid to rest.

The 914 is no exception to the pervasive used-car rust problem. The cowling between the top of the front fenders and the windshield are prone to rust, as are the rocker panels and the bottoms of the doors and the sills. The rear suspension pickup points and the passenger's floor, along with the area where the roof pillar joins the body, are other locations where rust takes hold. A Richmond, Virginia, owner wrote that he had rust spots around the windshield, fenders, doors, sills and headlights despite garaging his car and rarely driving in snow.

The pop-up headlights can be a problem in 914s, and they are not inexpensive to replace. If the car has suffered front-end damage, the price of repairs may be prohibitive unless you're a competent do-it-yourselfer. The valance panels under the front and rear ends are susceptible to damage from parking lot bumpers, snowbanks, and whatever debris one may happen upon, and it's relatively common to see 914s being driven without them, unsightly though that may be.

Inside there aren't too many serious problems with the 914, thanks in large part to the original simplicity of the design. The carpeting, particularly in the earliest models, is prone to wear. Also, it's not uncommon to find the window cranks broken, but these are VW parts and are readily available, as are the switches, knobs and levers.

In looking over the mechanical problems reported by our questionnaire respondents, we find that the fuel line difficulties previously mentioned are among the most common. Many owners have resorted to aircraft-quality fuel lines to prevent rupturing. As with other air-cooled Porsches, there is also the frequent problem of exhaust system heat exchangers wearing out, and replacement isn't cheap. Other relatively common problems are broken clutch cables, door handles and instrumentation failures.

As is true of other Porsches and most German cars, the parts and repairs for the 914 and 914/6 are rather expensive. Because of its exclusivity and performance advantage, the 914/6 is considered a more desirable car. Existing examples are usually kept in good condition and will be offered for sale at fairly high prices. But, as one Pittsburgh, Pennsylvania, owner noted, "What a fun car — you have to drive it to believe it!"

Driving Impressions

Jeff Zwart, photographer extraordinaire, whose work ap-

Brief Specifications

	1970 914 1.7	1970 914/6	1976 914 2.0
Curb Weight, lb.	2085	2195	2250
Wheelbase, in.	96.4	96.4	96.4
Track, f/r	52.6/54.1	53.6/54.4	52.8/54.4
Length	156.9	156.9	164.4
Width	65.0	65.0	65.0
Height	48.0	48.0	48.0
Engine type	pushrod flat 4	ohc flat 6	pushrod flat 4
Bore x stroke, in.	3.24 x 2.59	3.15 x 2.60	3.70 x 2.80
Displacement, cc	1679	1991	1971
Horsepower @ rpm	85 @ 4900	125 @ 5800	84 @ 4900
Torque @ rpm	103 @ 2800	131 @ 4200	97 @ 4000

Performance Data From Contemporary Tests

	1970 914 1.7	1970 914/6	1976 914 2.0
0-60 mph, sec.	13.9	8.7	12.7
Standing 1/4 mile, sec.	19.2	16.3	19.2
Average mpg	25.5	21.3	26.5
Road test date	4-70	7-70	1976 S&GT*

*1976 R&T Guide to Sports & GT Cars

Typical Asking Prices

1970-1971 914/6		$7,000-$10,000
1970-1976 914/4		$2,500-$5,500
Typical engine-rebuild prices:	914/6	$4,000-$5,500
	914/4	$2,000-$3,000

pears in our pages and on our covers from time to time, is the second owner of a 914 / 6 that was picked up at the factory by the original buyer. The flared fenders are steel and were a factory option but not a widely advertised one and thus rather rare. Jeff has owned the car for twelve years and says he prefers its handling to that of the 911 he formerly owned. His car is also fitted with the aftermarket Richie Ginther suspension kit that included Teflon bushings, special coil springs in the rear and a 22-mm front torsion bar.

With more than 130,000 miles on it and the engine never apart, Jeff characterizes his car's performance as still brisk but showing signs of tiredness. In my brief time at the wheel, I found it quick and exciting, with plenty of mid-range torque and lots of top-end speed. The 5-speed gearbox is beginning to exhibit synchro wear, but it gets the job done, albeit with a feeling of long distance between the shift lever and the gearbox itself.

The handling characteristics of the 914 have always been entertaining, and it's a car that can be driven quickly on first acquaintance. It has the proverbial "on-rails" feel and a marvelous responsiveness that encourages you to press on, faster and faster in the corners. Jeff added Scheel seats to his car, and while they do offer greater support, they also take away a bit of the roominess.

The controversy about the 914 will probably continue as long as the car itself is on the road — is it or is it not a real Porsche? I suppose each person has to answer that question for himself, but the fact is the 914 and 914 / 6 are great fun to drive. And isn't that the basis for selecting a sports car?

— *Thos L. Bryant (July 1982)*

GREAT BRITAIN

Sunbeam Alpine and Tiger

Initial rumors of a new sports car from Sunbeam, a division of Britain's Rootes Group, began to circulate in 1958, and the following year the Alpine was introduced to the motoring press. The Alpine name had been attached to an earlier Sunbeam 2-seater in 1953, but that car had not been a success and was short lived. The second Alpine bore no resemblance to its predecessor, nor, for that matter, to the rest of the Rootes line of cars (Hillman-Rapier-Singer), but it did make extensive use of existing Rootes components.

The new Alpine went on sale in the autumn of 1959, using Rapier's 1.5-liter (1,494 cc) 4-cylinder engine in slightly modified form. The cylinder head was changed to cast aluminum and the valves were inclined to improve combustion-chamber shape. The Alpine's engine also differed from the Rapier engine by using twin carburetors and a strengthened cylinder block.

The Alpine 1.5-liter engine was rated at 83.5 bhp at 5,300 rpm and in our road test of the new car (May 1960), it delivered a 0-60 mph time of 15.2 seconds. The standing-start quarter mile was covered in 20.6 seconds with a trap speed of 68.0 mph. These figures were recorded with the standard 4-speed gearbox and 3.89:1 final drive ratio. A Laycock de Normanville overdrive unit was available as an option (0.80 reduction) and with this extra came a final drive ratio of 4.22:1, resulting in quicker acceleration and a top speed in overdrive near the 100-mph mark.

Our road test of the Alpine praised its driving characteristics: "Driving the car is great fun for anyone who likes the sports-car feel. There is ample room for your feet and everything seems right. The engine has a solid healthy note and the transmission is one of the best we've used in a long time. The control lever travel is short, the feel is accurate and positive, the synchromesh (on second, third and fourth) is effective and the ratios are well chosen for all-around use.

"The clutch action is light, though the throttle pedal is not. On moving off, the throttle needs considerable pressure, due to its stiff spring, to avoid stumbling, and second-gear starts are not possible. This is fine as far as we are concerned, since we believe everyone should have the experience of learning the use of a properly spaced 4-speed transmission. The Alpine's third and fourth gears may be treated like a dual high gear: one for zip and one for economical cruising at low engine speeds."

1959-1967
Comfort and sportiness combined

by Thos L. Bryant

Among the foremost attributes of the Alpine is its comfortable ride, which attracted many Americans previously put off by sports-car ride harshness. We rated the ride "extraordinarily good for a car of this size and category" and concluded that it struck an excellent compromise between softness and stability. The Alpine is not quite as nimble as some of its competitors of the time and the steering is a bit slow (3.3 turns lock to lock), although it gives good control.

All in all, the Alpine was designed with the American market uppermost in Rootes' plans — a personal car with a soft ride, wind-up windows rather than sidescreens, proper ventilation of the cockpit and other creature comforts. Traditionalists among the sports-car movement had some rude comments about these features, but the car was a success and in many ways was a sneak preview of the sports cars of the future.

Later Series

Slightly more than a year after the introduction of the Sunbeam Alpine, the Alpine Series II was announced. As our road test (October 1961) pointed out, the external appearance was unchanged.

The most important improvement with the Series II was the engine: "Officially, the changes here have been very minor: a change of cylinder bore (from 79 to 82 mm) gives a trifle less than a 100-cc increase in displacement (1,592 cc) and the two Zenith carburetors have 30-mm instead of the previous 28-mm throats. Power and torque are changed very little from the Series I car and, indeed, the engine feels de-tuned. The effect of these changes is seen in the performance figures; the top speed is not much better, but the standing quarter-mile has been improved by 1.3 seconds and the medium-speed-range road performance has been considerably enhanced." In fact, still with a 3.89:1 final drive ratio, the Series II Alpine sped from 0-60 mph in 14.0 seconds versus 15.2 seconds for the earlier car. Changes in handling and ride characteristics were nil and our road test of the Series II Alpine concluded, "it is still a good car for the money."

Sunbeam debuted the Series III Alpine in 1963, and while the major components and body panels remained virtually the same, there were again a number of relatively minor changes to the car that resulted in significant improvements. Underneath, the third rendition was still using unequal-length A-arms, coil springs and tube shocks for the front suspension (adapted from the Hillman Husky), while the rear was suspended by a conventional live axle carried on semi-elliptical leaf springs. However, the previous rear lever shocks were replaced by telescopic shocks. To keep tooling costs within reason, the Alpine's unitized body/chassis was also borrowed from the Husky. By welding on the cowl, fenders, etc, the torsional stiffness of the Alpine's open body was improved, but this also added weight.

Another Series III change was a division of the car into two models, the Sports Tourer (with folding soft top) and the GT

1963 Sunbeam Alpine

1964 Sunbeam Tiger

(which had a removable hardtop but no folding soft top), with minor engine specification differences between the two. The Sports Tourer 4-cylinder engine was equipped with Zenith Type 36 WIP3 carburetors, mesh-style air cleaners and produced 88 bhp. The GT engine had Type 36 WIA3 carburetors with large, silencer-type air cleaners, and a different exhaust manifold and, as a result, developed only 80 bhp. It was quieter and smoother though.

The latest edition of Alpine's gearbox also came in for refinement with the use of close-ratio gears, although synchronization was unfortunately not added to first gear. The revised gear spacing resulted in a better match between the transmission ratios and the engine's torque and horsepower characteristics. Nevertheless, the Series III tested in the September 1963 issue of *Road & Track* (the 80-bhp version) couldn't match the acceleration figures of its predecessors: 0-60 mph now took 18.1 seconds and the quarter-mile time was 22.2 seconds at 66.0 mph. The Laycock de Normanville overdrive was still available as an option (reduction was now 0.78 versus the earlier 0.80), but the axle ratio remained 3.89:1 with or without the overdrive.

Again, the big changes were in the interior, and somehow that's not too surprising in a car that was designed with comfort as a primary objective. The location of the fuel tank and spare tire restricted trunk space in previous Alpines, but in the Series III the fuel containers were relocated to the rear fenders (6.8 gallons in each fin, fed from a common filler on the right rear fender). The spare tire was positioned upright at the front of the luggage compartment. As a result, trunk space was effectively doubled.

Driver and passenger were given all-new accommodations in the Series III, although the basic package remained the same. The seats received heavy side bolstering for greater lateral support, new foam cushions over elastic webbing gave the right amount of firmness, and the seats had a greater range of adjustment fore and aft as well as in seatback angle. The entire seat could also be moved vertically (only an inch or so) and the lower seat cushion could be tilted to suit the angle of the occupant's legs. Additionally, the Alpine had a telescoping steering column and the hanging clutch and brake pedals could be set in two different positions. The Alpine was truly remarkable in providing a great variety of adjustments so the driver could tailor the driving position to fit his particular stature.

Although we lamented the loss of performance in the Series III Alpine GT model tested in 1963, the car's handling seemed better than ever: "The Alpine's ride and handling are exceptional. The car will glide along as smoothly as a 2-ton sedan, and yet does not bob and sway. When pressed, the Alpine's springing seems to stiffen, and it suddenly turns into a pure sporting machine with quite good road adhesion (something it has not always had) and confidence-inspiring stability."

The Series IV Alpine debuted in the summer of 1964 and for the first time there were differences in the body's styling: The rear fender line was lowered and squared off to do away with the high-pointed fenders of previous editions, and the grille opening was now split by a single crossbar rather than four. Also, the fuel filler cap was now a snap-top affair.

The biggest news, however, was that the Alpine had been fitted with an optional Borg-Warner Type 35 automatic transmission. This 3-speed gearbox had been used previously in Rootes' Hillman Super Minx and featured a console-mounted shift lever in the Alpine. Our road test of the Series IV with automatic (November 1964) noted that "because the torque of the 1.6-liter Alpine engine is modest (93 lb-ft at 3,500 rpm), the 3-speed automatic adds absolutely nothing to the performance of the car. With the accelerator pressed to the floor, the Alpine shifts at about 5,000 rpm. At the shift, there is a noticeable change in engine note and a conclusive drop in revs." The testers of the day went on to say that the performance was adequate but not neck-snapping and suggested the automatic would probably take about a second longer to run through the quarter-mile than the 4-speed car. In fact, the quarter-mile time for the automatic was 21.0 seconds at a speed of 67.0 mph and 0-60 mph took 16.5 seconds.

Of equal, or perhaps greater import, was the fact the Series IV now used the 90-bhp engine in both the GT and Sports Tourer versions of the car. The lower horsepower engine (80 bhp) that had been fitted to the hardtop GT was dropped, which was good news for Alpine enthusiasts. Other alterations included a change from a mechanical tachometer to an electric unit and extended-interval oil changes. Otherwise, the Alpine Series IV continued to be a comfortable, good handling sports car with adequate power, excellent driving position, vacuum-assisted brakes (front disc / rear drum) and a decent-sized trunk. One objection we registered against the Series IV was a softening of the suspension, which turned an excellent riding car into one that had a tendency to float over uneven surfaces at high speeds.

For 1966, Sunbeam made another significant change in the Alpine line: the Series V was fitted with a 1,725-cc engine that gave 99 bhp at 5,500 rpm and 103 lb-ft torque at 3,700 rpm. The new engine had the same external dimensions as the previous 1,592-cc powerplant, but now there were five main bearings rather than three and the stroke was longer. The 1,725 engine was fitted with a pair of Stromberg CD carburetors and a finned oil cooler was standard equipment. A final drive ratio of 4.22:1 with or without overdrive was available, although the standard ratio remained 3.89. Acceleration was improved (our test car was equipped with the 4.22 rear end but no overdrive — *R&T*, March 1966) with the larger engine; the Series V would go from 0-60 mph in 14.0 seconds and cover the quarter mile in 19.3 seconds at a speed of 70.5 mph. The 1966 road test concluded that the Alpine "has retained the virtues of the previous versions and added a few new ones which assure that it continues to be one of the most civilized of the contemporary sports cars. We like it."

Sunbeam Tiger

The Tiger I is a Series IV Alpine with a Ford 260-cubic-inch V-8 engine that produces 164 bhp at 440 rpm and 258 lb-ft torque at 220 rpm — certainly more than enough for a car with a test weight of 2965 pounds.

We first road tested the Tiger for the November 1964 issue, and the staff was generally impressed with the car. Our test car would accelerate from rest to 60 mph in 7.8 seconds and run the quarter-mile in 16.0 seconds at 84.9 mph. The road test of the Tiger also included mention of the 245-bhp version of the engine, which was to be optional, but our feeling at the time was that this was overkill. We summed up the Tiger: "We have registered our enthusiasm on several occasions in the past for the Ford V-8 engine and the superb all-synchro 4-speed transmission which goes with it. When these units are installed in a car such as the Alpine, which combines good sporting characteristics with all the comforts of home, the result cannot fail to please — particularly at only $3,500."

The Tiger uses the same suspension as the Series IV Alpine but with considerably stiffer springs to compensate for the extra weight of the larger engine. The result is a ride that is firm, but nonetheless well controlled and comfortable. The Tiger's steering is rack-and-pinion rather than the recirculating ball of the Alpine. This change was dictated by the need for more clearance at the front end where the V-8 took up a lot of space.

In 1965, the Tiger II appeared with some changes. By this time, Chrysler had acquired the Rootes Group. Because Chrysler didn't have an engine of its own that would fit the Tiger, the company wisely elected to stay with a Ford V-8, though not without some abashment. However, Chrysler did change over to a 289-cubic-inch Ford V-8, which raised the bhp figure to 200 at 4,400 rpm. The more powerful engine dictated a larger clutch and wider-spaced gearbox ratios. The rear suspension was modified with the addition of track bars, an alternator replaced the generator, and an oil cooler was added in front of the bottom of the radiator.

Outside, stripes were laid along the flank of the Series II, an eggcrate grille replaced the single horizontal bar, and stainless steel trim moldings around the fender cutouts and body sill were added. Also, the small emblem that said "Powered by Ford 260" was quietly replaced by one reading "Sunbeam V-8." Inside, the steering wheel was raised a touch to give more thigh room, and vents were added to bring fresh air into the cockpit.

The Tigers (both I and II) are not the most nimble cars in the world, as we concluded in our road test of the Series II: "The Tiger II doesn't take kindly to being flung around. It's a car with dignity and asks to be driven that way. That doesn't mean slow-

1959 Sunbeam Alpine instrument panel

ly, necessarily, but that there's sufficient power on tap to embarrass the incautious. But if you treat it right, respecting it for what it is, the Tiger II can offer driving pleasure of a very high order."

The 4-cylinder Alpine was sold alongside the Tiger. But when U.S. government safety and emissions standards went into effect in 1968, both models were discontinued.

Buying a Used Alpine or Tiger — What to Look for

In setting out to find a good example of either an Alpine or a Tiger, there are some particular factors to keep in mind, as with any marque. For help in this area, I turned to Tony Inzana, who lives in Northern California. Inzana owns a 1967 Tiger II, an Alpine Series I and a 1965 Series IV Alpine. Just to show that he is a truly devoted aficionado of Sunbeams, he also has a Sunbeam-Harrington LeMans coupe, which he bought as a wreck and has restored.

The Alpine and Tiger can be considered well-built cars. The 4-cylinder Alpine and the V-8 Tiger engines are as sturdy as anything going if properly maintained and not abused. Many Tigers have suffered from owners either modifying the 289 or 260 engines or, in some cases, installing a 302 V-8. Inzana says he wouldn't touch any of those. The Tiger was not a hot rod; it was an excellent sports / GT car that could cruise at high rates of speed all day. Unfortunately many buyers have not realized this and have treated their Tigers as cars to be hopped up. As with any make, this multiplies the chance of trouble later. Tony says, in fact, he would look for a car with an engine that had never been taken apart, just to be on the safe side. If it should need major work, he would at least know from where he was starting.

A couple of items peculiar to the Alpine engine are a tendency for the lower crank pulley to start to wander with age, which causes the oil seal to leak around the timing chain cover — the leak is not a result of a faulty gasket but is coming from the pulley seal. Also, oil leaks around the Alpine's aluminum cylinder head are relatively common and not cause for undue concern.

With the Tiger, the increased weight of the V-8 engine often causes the A-arms to weaken at the top, and it's almost impossible to detect such a condition without dismantling the front end. This is especially true on cars with wider-than-normal tires and / or aftermarket shock absorbers installed. This condition can often be presumed present on cars that show obvious signs of having been driven hard. Another condition to look for, says Inzana, is motor mounts that have loosened with age, which can lead the exhaust system to move around and perhaps destroy hangers and brackets with regularity. Another possible trouble area in the Tiger is the camshaft timing gear; it was made of synthetic material and can become a problem on high-mileage cars. If an owner is going into the mechanicals to make other repairs, Tony recommends converting this item to steel.

The Alpine's 4-speed gearbox is one of those traditional

British units that is durable, stout and able to withstand heavy-handed driving up to a point. That's not to say they're un-breakable, however, and prospective buyers should be aware that replacement parts for the transmission (and the rear end) can be very difficult to find. Inzana added that he probably wouldn't touch either an Alpine or a Tiger with a bad rear end. The Tiger's 4-speed is also noted for being strong and shouldn't give too many problems if the car hasn't been abused. As with Ford Mustangs of the 1960s, the Tiger's reverse gear is selected by pulling up on two prongs on the shift lever. The reverse gear lock-out cable is frequently damaged or broken in cars that have not been perfectly maintained; this is another hard-to-find part.

The front-disc / rear-drum brake arrangement used by Sunbeam was quite acceptable for the Alpines but doesn't in-spire a great deal of confidence among Tiger owners. Be that as it may, Tony cautions against brake conversion jobs. Some owners have tried to convert to Ford Pinto brakes, and Inzana says he has seen a few cars with Jaguar E-type rear discs added, but always with less than outstanding results.

He feels it's better to stay with the brakes the manufacturer installed, maintain them in first-rate condition and recognize their limitations.

Sunbeam did a good job of undercoating the Alpines and Tigers. There aren't any particularly vulnerable rust areas, although early Alpines had a flat floor beneath the seats and moisture didn't always drain well from that area. Later, seat wells with drain plugs were incorporated into the design and this problem was alleviated. On the Tiger, the rubber channel for water runoff inside the fresh-air vent can deteriorate, allow-ing the water to drain into the passenger compartment. But in all, these Sunbeams are generally impressive in construction and durability.

Driving Impressions

It was one of those partly cloudy, fresh and breezy days that I think of as normal for Northern California when I visited Tony Inzana at his home in Danville. As both a Tiger and Alpine owner, Tony seemed a logical choice for help in preparing this report, and I couldn't have found a more knowledgeable nor willing accomplice. After spending time shooting the photos and talking about the cars, the fun began: driving them.

It had been many years since I had driven either Sunbeam. My oldest brother owned an Alpine in the 1960s and I was occa-sionally permitted a turn at the wheel. My last exposure to a Tiger had been in contemplating the purchase of one from a used-car dealer in Santa Barbara, California, in 1970. (I didn't.)

I started with the Alpine, a Series IV model that Tony had bought while still in college. He has maintained it very well over the years and still drives it regularly. The Alpine is one of the most comfortable sports cars ever, especially for taller drivers. There is space for legs, elbows, etc, and little of the

Brief Specifications

	1960 Alpine I	1963 Alpine III	1966 Alpine V	1964 Tiger I	1967 Tiger II
Curb Weight, lb.	2200	2185	2220	2565	2560
Wheelbase, in.	86.0	86.0	86.0	86.0	86.0
Track, f/r	51.2/48.7	51.2/48.7	51.0/48.5	51.0/48.5	51.8/48.6
Length	155.0	155.2	155.3	156.0	156.0
Width	60.5	60.5	60.5	60.5	60.5
Height	51.7	52.5	51.5	51.5	51.5
Engine type	pushrod inline 4	pushrod inline 4	pushrod inline 4	pushrod V-8	pushrod V-8
Bore x stroke, in.	3.11 x 3.00	3.21 x 3.00	3.21 x 3.25	3.80 x 2.87	4.00 x 2.87
Displacement, cc	1494	1592	1724	4262	4737
Horsepower (gross) @ rpm	83.5 @ 5300	80.2* @ 5000	99.0 @ 5500	164 @ 4400	200 @ 4400
Torque @ rpm	89.6 @ 3600	92.0 @ 3600	103 @ 3700	258 @ 2200	282 @ 2400

*The Sports Tourer version with different carburetion developed 88.0

Performance Data From Contemporary Tests

0-60 mph, sec.	15.2	18.1	14.0	7.8	7.5
Standing 1/4 mile, sec.	20.6	22.2	19.3	16.0	16.0
Average mpg	24.0	23.5	26.0	20.0	19.0
Road test date	5-60	9-63	3-66	11-64	9-67

Typical Asking Prices

1959-1967 Alpine	$1,500-$4,000
1964-1967 Tiger	$5,500-$10,000
Typical engine-rebuild prices: Alpine	$2,000-$3,000
Tiger	$1,800-$2,300

semiclaustrophobic effect of many earlier British sports cars. There is ample seat adjustment, and it's hard to imagine any driver not being able to find a comfortable driving position.

The 4-cylinder Sunbeam engine is a willing performer, and the exhaust note of almost every Alpine I've ever heard is musical — a sharp *brraaaapp* as one goes up through the gears adds just the right touch. The Alpine is not terribly quick, and the suspension is a bit softer than I like for very hard cornering and sharp maneuvers, but the balance and harmony of the car are extraordinary. It may not be quite as exhilarating as some sports cars of its day, but for everyday use and driving long distances, it's excellent.

I then moved on to Tony's Tiger II, which he has owned for five years. He's gone through the engine and rebuilt the front end as well as adding a number of small improvements and personal touches to the car. Frankly, the Tiger is where my heart lies. Probably as a result of my growing up in Southern California in the late 1950s and early 1960s, I like hot rods and performance cars. True, the Tiger is not a hot rod, but performance it does have. The Ford 289 emits a low rumble from the tailpipes, quite in contrast to the Alpine's sharper note, and despite the heavier front end, the car handles very nicely.

One of the problems with a Tiger is that it's almost impossible to refrain from putting your boot into the throttle at any opportunity. It responds so smoothly and quickly. There's a bit of a growl (it had to come up sooner or later) and things happen. No pussyfooting around with this car — except that the brakes are marginal, so the novice driver has to be wary of coming up too quickly on slower cars or obstructions. The Tiger has to be managed and controlled, rather than thrown around with alacrity. Nevertheless, the fun factor is quite high.

— Thos L. Bryant (July 1978)

GREAT BRITAIN

Triumph TR2, TR3 and TR4 1953-1967

Ample driving fun for not very much money

by Thos L. Bryant

Triumph is a name in transportation circles that dates back to the late nineteenth century when Sigfried Bettman emigrated from Germany to Great Britain and began building bicycles. His shop in Coventry soon segued to motorcycle production and after World War I the first Triumph motor cars arrived. In the 1930s the company grew under the direction of Claude Holbrook, managing director, and Donald Healey, later to gain fame with the Austin-Healey, as technical manager.

While other British car makers were gaining reputations in racing, Triumph concentrated its efforts in international rallying and enjoyed some success. In the late 1930s, the Dolomite Roadster, designed by Walter Belgrove, made its debut and was a success as a sporting tourer, but by 1938 nothing could stem the tide of financial ruin for Triumph and the following year the company went bankrupt. (The motorcycle portion of the business, by the way, had been sold off in 1938 to company-founder Bettman who had been retired for some years.) What was left of the automobile business was sold to Thomas Ward, Ltd., of Sheffield, but World War II came along, the factory was destroyed in air raids, and it all just about vanished.

At the conclusion of the war, Sir John Black's Standard Motor Company bought the use of the Triumph name and little else from Ward. The only remaining link with the prewar company was the presence of stylist Walter Belgrove, who had been at work in Standard's planning office during the war and was now given the task of coming up with another Triumph. The 1800 Roadster was Triumph's first postwar car, and it bore a remarkable resemblance to the Dolomite Roadster Belgrove had designed in 1938. The 1800 was not a smashing sales success, but it did keep the Triumph name alive through the rest of the 1940s.

1956 Triumph TR3

Sir John Black had come to the decision in 1945, when he bought the Triumph name that he wanted to get into the sports-car field. Some five years later, after the 1800 Roadster had about run its course, Belgrove was again called on to come up with a new design, this time for a true sports car. The result was the Bullet, which was a disaster and never went into production. Black was not prepared to give up yet, however, and in early 1952, he gave orders to have a new sports car designed and built in time for the Earls' Court auto show in October of that year.

The Triumph engineers were able to meet the deadline, and the car aroused some interest at the show, but chief chassis engineer Harry Webster was not satisfied with the car. He, along with Ken Richardson who had been hired from BRM, spent the next six months putting it right and the Triumph TR2 made its first public appearance in March 1953. The car was programmed to fill the gap between the small MG and the larger Jaguar cars, and it did just that. Another key to success was Black's realization that the British home market was not large enough to support the car, so he looked to America as a vital market. His timing was excellent as the sports-car boom was just getting underway here in the former colonies.

Triumph TR2

As with many British sports cars, the TR2 was a mixture of old and new. The engine was adapted from the Standard Vanguard sedan, and the displacement was reduced from 2,088 cc to 1,991 so that the TR2 could compete in under 2-liter race and rally classes. The Vanguard's 92.0-mm stroke was retained while the bore was reduced from 85.0 to 83.0 mm by using new cylinder liners. The cylinder head was modified to give a compression ratio of 8.5:1, and new manifolds were fitted so that twin SU carburetors could take the place of the single Solex unit used with the Vanguard. The result was a basically sturdy and dependable engine that was more finely tuned to give 90 bhp at 4,800 rpm versus the original 65 bhp at 4,200 rpm of the Vanguard.

Engine power was transmitted through a 4-speed gearbox with Laycock de Normanville electric overdrive available as an extra-cost option. Synchromesh was applied to second, third and fourth only. The rear axle was adapted from the Triumph Mayflower sedan and was of the semifloating hypoid variety. The final drive ratio was 3.70:1.

The TR2's suspension system was rather simple at the rear with a live axle located by semi-elliptical springs and tube shocks. The independent front suspension consisted of A-arms, coil springs and tube shock absorbers. The result, according to our road test of the TR2 (*R&T* April 1954), was quite respectable: "Roadability, ride and handling qualities are difficult to measure in specific units. In these three categories, however, the TR2 rates well in comparison with other sports cars in a wide size and price range. It is not the best — but it is above average. A very moderate roll angle was probably the car's outstanding virtue, and a steering geometry that came very close to being neutral (neither under- nor oversteer) was a criticism — but a condition that some drivers might prefer."

The steering system was of cam-and-lever type and was quite quick, requiring only 2-1/4 turns, lock to lock. However, the turning circle of 32 feet was not exceptional for a car of that size. Our original road test of the car pointed out that at speeds up to 90 mph the car felt secure and was easy to control.

The TR2 was a definite step up for the sports-car owner who was driving an MG TD for example, as the interior appointments were considerably more refined. *Road & Track* reported that "the general quality level of the car, inside and out, is of British standards. The plastic trim is of good quality and the dash panel layout is neat and efficient. Top, side curtains and tonneau cover (which is included with the car) are of a special, heavy, rubberized material color-keyed to complement the car. Top shape is neat and efficient appearing and unlike some other sports cars, removes completely from the bows for storage in the trunk or behind the seat. The bows fold flat behind the individual bucket seats. Side curtains feature zipper flaps for signaling and cigarette-butt discarding, but should a driver neglect to leave the zipper open, entrance (with the top up and curtains in) is difficult because of the handleless doors. The curtains also need that individual adjustment required of weather protection of this type. The test car was drafty and the wind spread the gap between side curtain and windshield post during the high-speed runs."

1956 Triumph TR3 interior

The TR2, at a test weight of 2410 pounds, accelerated from 0-60 mph in 12.2 seconds and achieved a best time through the quarter mile of 18.1 seconds (18.4 seconds average for several runs) and we noted that "the TR2 will out-drag any stock American car, from a standstill." This lively performance was not delivered at the expense of fuel economy either, as our test at a steady cruising speed of 70 mph in direct drive resulted in 32 mpg. Using overdrive and cruising at 75 to 80 mph, the figure improved to 34 mpg. And all of this at a price of $2,448, POE!

Triumph TR3

Two years after the introduction of the TR2, the Triumph people debuted the TR3. This model was not actually a new car but rather an improved version of the TR2, with some worthwhile refinements. Our initial road test of the TR3 (*R&T* June 1956) was quite laudatory in this regard: "The fact that the basic car remains the same is a credit to the Standard Motor Co. Ltd., of Coventry, and speaks volumes for the original design — one which has proved exceedingly sound and reliable both in normal driving usage and in competition."

The refinements of the TR3 included a fiberglass hardtop ($150 extra), with improved side curtains and plexiglass windows. There was also a new optional rear bench seat that was far from spacious but in a pinch could accommodate human beings. The loud, rappy exhaust note of the TR2, which had caused some problems for owners in areas where the police were not terribly understanding, had been toned down for the TR3, while still retaining a satisfyingly healthy note. The grille had been redone and the cavern-like opening was gone, replaced with a crosshatch design metal grille that was flush with the opening.

Under the hood, improved carburetion and better port alignment increased the bhp figure from 90 to 100 at 4,800 rpm. The torque, however, grew by only 1lb-ft (to 117.5) so acceleration times for the TR3 were nearly identical with those of the 2. The TR3 tested did not have the optional overdrive of the earlier Triumph, and as a result the fuel economy for the later car suffered by about 2 mpg, but still offered a range of 26-32 mpg.

When it came to stopping power, the 1956 road test report had these comments: "One highly commendable feature of the Triumph has always been the brakes, which have stood up well in severe competition usage. This year (1956) they are even larger. Lining width has been increased, an especially good idea, since rubbing speed of large-diameter drums is an important factor in deterioration. Applying 10-inch brakes, such as on the TR3, at 100 mph is equal to applying 12-inch brakes on a similar car at only 82.5 mph, in terms of rubbing speed. (In these two examples, fpm at lining is 3510.)" The following year, the TR3 became the first British car in volume production to be fitted with front disc brakes as standard equipment.

The 1956 version of the car had a list price of $2,599 and our concluding remarks of the report summed up the TR3 quite well: "The new version is a thoroughly likeable car, whatever the uses it may be put to... At its basic delivered price, the TR3 offers a package so tempting that no tentative sports-car buyer, bankroll notwithstanding, can afford to overlook it."

Late in 1957, Triumph updated the car and gave it a new designation as the TR3A. The changes included outside door handles (finally!), a handle on the trunk lid, and reinforced front bumpers to help stave off less considerate parkers. Also, the 3A's grille was wider and there were some interior detail improvements. By the way, the 3A designation was not made by Triumph officially; it just came into being as a convenient way to differentiate the newer TR3s from the older ones.

The last of the TR3 line was the 3B which was built for only one year, 1962. Some 2500 to 3000 examples of this car were produced and all were destined for the U.S. market. The plan was that they would all have the new fully synchronized gearbox and the 2.2-liter engine of the TR4, which had been introduced in the autumn of 1961. There is some confusion, however, because a few hundred of the Bs were built with the older transmission of the 3A. (British Leyland says those TR3Bs with the smaller engine have a serial number that begins with TSF1, while those with the larger engine start with TCF1L or TCF1E.)

The TR3 series officially came to an end in 1962, although

there may be some 1963 cars. This is because in those days it was permissible for a manufacturer to retitle leftover cars at the end of a year if there were no differences in the car. More than 75,000 TR3s were built over the years, compared to about 8600 TR2s.

Triumph TR4

There will probably be a number of TR2 and 3 enthusiasts who will object to a Used Car Classic report that lumps in the 4 with those earlier cars. There is a distinct difference, but the TR4 was based on the TR3 chassis and drivetrain, making it a natural progression in the Triumph's evolution.

1962 Triumph TR4

The formal introduction of the TR4 in 1961 came at a time when sports cars were beginning to be bought by people who, although enthusiasts, saw no reason to put up with uncomfortable cars. The new Michelotti-designed Triumph was lower, rather squared off, and without many of the awkward angles of its predecessors. The engine had been bored out to 2,138 cc, and the transmission offered synchromesh on all forward speeds. For the more effete, there were roll-up windows, increased trunk space and a softer ride.

1962 Triumph TR4

The performance of the TR4 was somewhat improved, with the larger engine developing 105 bhp at 4,750 rpm and 128 lb-ft of torque at 3,350 rpm. We tested it for the February 1962 issue, and the result was a 0-60 mph time of 10.5 seconds and a quarter-mile run of 17.8 seconds at 77.2 mph, more than half a second faster than the TR3. One of the more significant changes on the 4 was the replacement of the cam-and-lever steering box with rack-and-pinion steering. Our road test report on the TR4 described the effect of the change: "The new steering is very light — almost 'dead' in fact — and it is certainly direct, but the steering action is twitchy, every little nudge of the wheel producing a disproportionate change in direction. To the car's credit, it should be said that the effect was noticeable mostly at low speeds; the steering action at 70 mph was all that one could ask."

That report also summed up the 4 nicely: "Our staff never reached unanimity of opinion regarding the TR4. Some thought it was very worthwhile despite its obvious shortcomings — others were not convinced. If experience with earlier Triumphs can be counted on, the TR4 should be a very reliable car, and it is an enjoyable vehicle to drive. The TR4 offers excellent performance at a moderate initial cost and a sporting driver would search for a long time to beat the combination. And, in spite of our criticisms of the car, ('we don't think the improvements are as great as should have been made') we think Standard-Triumph has a real winner here, if production can keep up with demand."

In 1965, the TR4 was updated with optional independent rear suspension and a newly designed top that could be raised and lowered by one person with a minimum of fuss. The irs used semi-trailing A-arms, coil springs and lever shocks. This combination resulted in improved handling, especially over choppy surfaces, and a great increase in ride comfort. There was a drawback, however, in that the softness of the rear suspension gave it a tendency to bottom rather easily because of the short amount of suspension travel available.

The TR4A continued until 1968, when it was replaced by the 6-cylinder TR250 in the American market. That year marked the advent of the new U.S. federal emission control regulations, and Triumph correctly reasoned that they could best maintain performance by going to a 6-cylinder engine.

What to Look For

We had conversations about these Triumphs with two of the most knowledgeable people around when it comes to the marque: Mike Cook of British Leyland and Harry Barnes, who has been restoring Triumphs for some time and is considered one of the experts in that field.

Triumph TR models, like many early British sports cars, are generally characterized by stout, durable engines, transmissions and running gear. All the 4-cylinder TRs have wet-sleeve engines so repairs are usually less expensive as there is little or no wear on the block itself. The main bearings rarely go and the rod bearings are almost as durable. The valves usually give few problems but the rings and pistons can be weak. The timing chain cover seals have a tendency to deteriorate with age and cause an oil leak at the front of the engine; this is not a major problem, however, as the seals are easily replaced. Also on the TR2, 3 and early 4s, the front gearbox seal will often be worn out, producing an oil drip down onto the bellhousing; again, not a major problem.

On all TRs, one of the first items to scrutinize is the front suspension. The potential buyer should look for play in the

Brief Specifications

	1954 TR2	1956 TR3	1962 TR4
Curb Weight, lb.	2070	2090	2200
Wheelbase, in.	88.0	88.0	88.0
Track, f/r	45.0/45.5	45.0/45.5	49.0/48.0
Length	151.0	150.3	155.0
Width	55.5	56.5	57.5
Height	50.0	50.5	50.0
Engine type	pushrod inline 4	pushrod inline 4	pushrod inline 4
Bore x stroke, in.	3.27 x 3.62	3.27 x 3.62	3.39 x 3.62
Displacement, cc	1991	1991	2138

Performance Data From Contemporary Tests

	1954 TR2	1956 TR3	1962 TR4
0-60 mph, sec.	12.2	12.0	10.5
Standing 1/4 mile, sec.	18.4	18.4	17.8
Average mpg	30.0	28.0	25.0
Road test date	4-54	6-56	2-62

Typical Asking Prices

1953-1967 TR2, TR3, TR4	$2,500-$6,500
Typical engine-rebuild price (all models)	$1,500-$2,500

front end, being sure to check the lower pivot points as well as the steering arms. An immediate check of the front wheel bearings is also standard procedure, because these bearings give no warning that they are going bad; they just fail, which can lead to more serious problems. The steering box on the TR2 and 3 allows considerable room for adjustment, so if a car is marked by very heavy steering, the cure may lie in this area. The whole front end and steering system is somewhat complex and a major repair of the front suspension is costly.

On the TR4A with irs, the splines on either side will loosen with age, producing a clunking noise at the rear. There is apparently no repair; you just learn to live with it. The lever-type shocks can blow their seals and take in crud that mixes with the lubricant. It is sometimes possible to take the shocks off, pump them until all the old lubricant is emptied, and then refill them with automatic transmission fluid or Castrol R-40. If that doesn't work, the alternative is to replace the shocks.

Rust is always a big bugaboo with older cars and the TRs are no exception. The buyer should be sure to lift up the carpeting and look for rust in the floor area, and to make the effort to look underneath the car for rust in the seat pans. Another spot to check is behind and below the battery box where acid splash can often cause rotting.

A few other random items to note: a short in the electricals often stems from the dimmer switch; cracked wheels are not rare, and these should be carefully examined; failure of the electric Laycock de Normanville overdrive is usually a result of the dash switch going bad or a break in a very fine wire that goes from the overdrive's solenoid to the wiring harness. Many TR2s and 3s may have a tooth off the first gear cluster because it lacks synchromesh.

Owner Impressions

It wasn't until I had a son of my own that I finally realized why my father let me have the TR4. He is far too intelligent a man to have believed that line about the TR ultimately being a more reasonable vehicle for me than the 1957 Chevy that was getting me through my senior year at the University of Wisconsin.

Being a practical man, I'm sure my father had his doubts about the car and fully expected a call from me some Sunday, saying I was standing in a phone booth on the edge of a pasture holding the more precious parts of the engine's innards in my left hand. He probably would have been right were it not for the second character in my short narrative, Dick McKee. I don't know how many people reading this would remember Dick — except perhaps for Augie Pabst and Bob Tullius — but they would recall him for the wonders he could work on a Triumph engine.

Lord knows, he kept my TR running and that was no small task. You see, my TR4 was of dubious repute. If you looked way down in the engine compartment, you'd find — I swear — purple paint. Local sports-car salesmen knew the car's history well and could tell of it being towed in with still another body panel crunched.

Well, it looked pretty good to me when I bought it and, besides, I wouldn't have known what to do with a straight TR4 if I'd owned one. But I did know enough to enjoy the car and with a good McKee tune on that 4-banger, I could outrun any TR I went up against. The only effect of the car's checkered past was that I had to rebolt the transmission to the frame once a month.

Triumphs were always known as the sturdiest of the middle-priced sports cars, and mine never did let me down. Why, with my cheap Atlas tires and a $12 battery (Pirellis and DieHards were years away) I was king of the early morning dew as I cut through the Ektachrome green hills of Wisconsin's beautiful spring of 1966.

The trick was to put the tonneau over the passenger's side, turn the heat to max and trap it under that little tent. You could drive like that on a frosty morn in a T-shirt and the inside was toasty warm. Of course, the interior was never the same after I left the half-empty bottle of unprocessed apple cider in the backseat on a hot day... with the top up. Blew the damn stuff all over the inside.

My father sold my TR4 after the Army finally got me, but I happened to see the car a year later while home on leave. I wish I hadn't; it was rusted to junk.

I recently heard that Dick McKee died; his heart finally gave out. I don't think I ever thanked him for putting up with my questions and my TR4 and helping put enough solid automotive enthusiasm in my head to convince me to pursue a career in this business and save me from what would un-doubtedly have been a much duller life.

— *John Lamm (October 1976)*

GREAT BRITAIN

TRIUMPH TR6

1969-1976

Hunky, traditional British roadsters   **by Peter Bohr**

1972 Triumph TR6

Remember the Austin-Healey 100-6/3000, the so-called Big Healey? What veteran sports-car nut doesn't? Over the years various automotive writers described it as a "handsome brute," a car with "Churchillian steadfastness," and "a rough, solid, lovable bastard."

In 1967 British Leyland retired the Big Healey rather than subject it to the indignities of American emission and safety regulations that were about to come into effect. Aficionados of British sports cars grieved because BL had no replacement.

Or so everyone thought. BL did actually replace the Healey—in 1969 with Triumph's TR6. No, Donald Healey had nothing to do with the TR6, and BL never exactly touted the TR6 as the Healey's successor.

But think for a moment: what made the Big Healey such a charmer? It was of course a two-seat convertible (those tiny rear seats couldn't *really* accommodate people). The Healey 100-6/3000 had a rugged 6-cylinder engine with gobs of torque. And the Healey had a distinctive, hunky body. Well, all the same things are true for the TR6. Moreover, a Big Healey and a TR6 are just about equal in size and weight.

Today, Big Healeys are hot items in the used-car market. Decent examples are fetching $8000-$10,000, and sometimes more. Meanwhile, Triumph TR6s are languishing in the gray matter of the market. They're not dirt cheap, but very nice TR6s are only about a third the price of a good Austin-Healey 3000.

The TR6 may never reach the Big Healey's rather dizzying price heights, at least not in the near future. But considering the TR6's basic similarities to the Healey, it's a good bet that these Triumphs won't get any cheaper than they are now. And that makes them a perfect subject for a Used Car Classic.

Family Ties

When R&T's editors first got a look at the TR6 in early 1969, they were a little disconsolate. "We've been hoping for an all-new sports car from Triumph for some time, but what they've done is updated the old one again," the editors wrote in a road test. They added, "If Triumph were to put an all-new car on the market (a TR7?) the car would probably be too good to be true."

Ha! When the all-new TR7 did come in 1975, it was such a dud that it eventually killed the Marque. From the TR2 through the TR6, Triumph had wisely, as it turned out, followed a policy of slow evolution.

The TR6 is a direct descendent of what is perhaps the quintessential Triumph sports car, the TR2/TR3. With its pug nose, bulging headlights and doors cut so low that passengers could reach down and scrape their knuckles on the pavement if they were so inclined, the TR2/TR3 has a unique, funky look. Like other British sports cars of the 1950s, the TR2/TR3 was an assemblage of components from sedans. The Standard Vanguard contributed its 4-cylinder engine, the Standard Flying Nine its frame, and the Mayflower its independent front suspension and live rear axle.

Odd-looking or not, the TR3 (which is only a slightly refined version of the TR2) was a smashing success in the sales rooms, on the race track and on rally courses. This bulldog of a car earned Triumph a reputation for toughness that remained with the marque until the TR7. The TR3, incidently, was also the first high-volume production sports car to use front disc brakes.

Nevertheless, by the early 1960s sports-car buyers wanted a little less funk and little more creature comfort—like roll-up windows. The TR4 has a more modern, squared-off body, but it's a TR3 under the skin. The TR4's mechanical changes were few, notably a fully synchronized transmission and a rack-and-pinion steering system.

The TR4 was a winner too, but by 1965 Triumph needed to give the car an edge on the competition, in particular the Austin-Healey 3000 and the MGB. (At this time Leyland-Triumph had yet to merge with British Motors Corporation, the builders of the Healeys and MGs.) High-tech cars like

Jaguar's E-types used independent rear suspensions, so Triumph gave irs a go on the TR4, which then became the TR4A.

Triumph's gambit to add sophistication to its flagship sports car was a noble but poorly executed idea. Like Banquo's ghost, handling and maintenance problems haunted every irs-equipped TR, from the TR4A through the TR6. Ten years later, Triumph exorcised irs and gave the TR7 a live axle.

All this is somewhat puzzling because Triumph was no stranger to irs. Prior to the TR4A, the company had given its sedan irs, and even the TR4's baby brother, the Spitfire, had a primitive swing-axle irs. The TR4A's setup was adapted from Triumph's 2000 sedan, and used semi-trailing wishbones with coil springs and lever shocks. The TR4's chassis was reshaped to incorporate a bridge that supported the differential and mounting points for the coil springs.

"When the going gets rough, the TR's independent rear suspension...is less happy than most such systems," we stated in a road test. "The frame rails actually run underneath its axles, severely limiting suspension travel in the rebound direction. The result is a strange combination of softness in the bounce (up) direction and super-control on the rebound."

The TR's evolution continued in 1968 as the TR4A became the TR250. This was the first year of U.S. emission standards. Rather than fool with the old 4-banger, Triumph decided a new version of the 2-liter inline 6-cylinder engine from the 2000 sedan and GT6 would be just right for the TR. This engine was stroked to 2.5 liters, and in carbureted U.S. form, produced 111 bhp. (In the mother country, the TR250 was called the TR5 and had troublesome Lucas fuel injection.)

There was only a 6-bhp increase over the 4-cylinder's horsepower, but the 6-cylinder's torque—152 lb-ft at 3000 rpm versus the 4-banger's 128 at 3350—and smoothness were real advantages.

1969 Triumph TR6

Bruce McWilliams, then Executive Vice President for Leyland-Triumph of North America and now an automotive marketing consultant, recalls that he was horrified when Triumph tossed the new engine into the old TR4A and pushed it out the door. Together with a factory engineer, he brought a TR250 prototype to his New York state country home where they spent a day getting the car to at least *sound* different from the old 4-cylinder TR4A. "We stuck broom handles up the exhaust pipes and experimented with different baffling until we got that special throaty roar characteristic of the 6-cylinder TR6s," he says. Broom handles!—hard to imagine in this age of computer-aided design, isn't it?

Triumph also gave the TR250 a revised interior to conform with new U.S. safety rules. Protruding knobs and switches were eliminated, while soft visors and a breakaway mirror were added. Triumph also changed the high-gloss finish on the wood dash to a flat finish, and from chrome bezels around the instruments to black bezels.

To McWilliams' relief, the TR250 lasted only a year until the newly styled TR6 was ready. R&T's editors may have been disappointed that the TR6 had a front suspension little changed from the TR3, a gearbox from the TR4, a chassis and irs from the TR4A, and an interior from the TR250, but they were (and we still are) enthusiastic about the car's styling.

Indeed, the German firm of Karmann, commissioned by Triumph to style the TR6, did a remarkable job. Triumph insisted that Karmann use the TR4/5/250 floor, cowl, doors and inner panels. The firm had to design the car, have it approved and then manufacture the new body tools in a mere 14 months.

Karmann cleaned up all that was superfluous about the older TRs. The TR6's chopped tail and crisp front end turned the somewhat frumpy TR4/5/250 into a virile, lean machine. New, wider 5 1/2-in. wheels gave the TR6 a more aggressive stance. Together with a new front anti-roll bar, they also improved high-speed cornering. Other modern touches included larger taillight assemblies, flat-black paint on the transom and throne-type seats. Triumph also offered a most attractive removable hardtop for the TR6.

Despite the improvements however, there was still no doubt that the TR6 with its separate-body-and-frame construction and its narrow cockpit was about as avant-garde as a Conestoga Wagon. "There's nothing wrong with the TR6 that a good chassis wouldn't cure," the pundits said.

But devoted Triumph fans liked the car just fine. With its facelift and lusty 6-cylinder engine, the TR6 was updated just enough to seem fresh and to satisfy U.S. regulations without sacrificing the rough 'n tumble, wind-in-the-hair qualities of a traditional British roadster. This partially explains why the TR6 continued to sell well for two years after the introduction of the "modern" TR7.

1974 Triumph TR6

By the time the TR6 went to market, Leyland-Triumph, BMC, Jaguar, and Rover had all been thrown together in a giant melting pot called British Leyland. From 1969 through 1977, BL went on to sell some 94,000 TR6s. Bruce McWilliams calls the car a "fantastic money spinner" for British Leyland and says that dealer gross profits on the car were five times the national average.

BL only put token engineering and advertising efforts into the TR6 after its introduction. Of course the car had to meet increasingly stiff U.S. emissions rules, and it acquired exhaust gas recirculation and an air pump along the way. The engine's compression ratio was also dropped from 8.5:1 to 7.75:1 in 1971. But power held up well even in the last few years of production and remained a little more than 100 bhp. The pleasant chrome bumpers grew rubber tits in 1974, and at the same time BL added a fiberglass front spoiler. Overdrive, always an option on TRs, became standard on the TR6 in 1974. In both appearance and performance, the TR6 survived the perils of

American regulation during the 1970s far more gracefully than its BL stablemate, the poor emasculated and uglified MGB.

TR6 Selection Tips

The Triumph TR6 is a car with definite strengths—and weaknesses. The TR6's engine, transmission and brakes are exceptionally stout, in the tradition of the TR3. That's assuming owners provide a modicum of normal maintenance. However, that's a big assumption. Folks who buy these relatively inexpensive cars are often too penurious or impoverished to provide even routine care. "We've opened up some TR6 transmissions and they've smelled like something died inside," says Dick Enfantino, a Triumph specialist in San Jose, California.

I asked him to share his wisdom regarding the TR6's mechanical pitfalls. At the top of his worry list is the rear end and, as you might expect, the independent rear suspension. Unusual clunks, whines and vibrations from the aft end of a TR6 can indicate all sorts of problems. For one, the differential mounts are fragile, and either through stress or corrosion they often break. The fix involves rewelding the pins that hold the rear end to the mounts. There are also four U-joints that frequently pack up, especially if they haven't been greased regularly. Replacing all four costs about $200, parts and labor.

Then there are the wheel bearings. Because of their peculiar design, they're difficult to replace. And finally there's the differential itself. Under hard use it isn't always able to handle the torque of the 6-cylinder engine.

Even if all the components in the rear of a TR6 are in good order, the car can still seem poorly suspended. When the clutch is dumped at a standing start, the car first points skyward and in the next moment seems headed into the pavement before settling down to a level attitude. To mitigate this up-and-down syndrome, he suggests converting the archaic and oh-so-British lever shocks to tube shocks. Adding a pair of stiffer rear springs, a rear sway bar and a larger front sway bar will also noticeably improve a TR6's road manners. Such a package costs under $500.

The rack-and-pinion steering mounts are another TR6 weakspot. If the steering doesn't feel as positive as it should, broken rubber mounts could be the problem.

Triumph used both Borg & Beck and Laycock clutch assemblies. It's vital that worn components be replaced with new components from the same manufacturer. That is, a Borg & Beck pressure plate shouldn't be installed on a car with a Laycock clutch, a point often overlooked by backyard mechanics. It costs about $120 for parts and $200 for labor ($250 for cars with overdrive) for a complete clutch replacement. TR6 transmissions are generally unbreakable, but if one goes bad, expect to pay $500 for a rebuilt unit and again $200-$250 for labor.

Should a TR6's engine need rebuilding, rebuilt units are available—long blocks with everything but the carburetors— for about $1,700. Installation will cost another $500.

There's always the danger of terminal rust lurking in an older car. One, and perhaps the only, advantage to the TR6's separate body and frame is the relative ease of repairing either collision or rust damage. Replacement panels are available and are easily installed. Moreover, a badly rusted body won't affect the structural integrity of the car as it will on a car of unibody construction.

However, check the usual rust-prone spots: the rocker panels, fenders, floors and inside the trunk. If the body shows much corrosion, check the frame very carefully, especially at the various suspension mounting points. A car with a frame that's beginning to resemble Swiss cheese isn't good for anything but the scrap heap. Because there are plenty of doggy TR6s around, it's smart to be fainthearted about buying a TR6 until you're certain it's sound. A good TR6 is a bargain at current prices. But if you sink a small fortune into a restoration job, your chances of recouping your investment are slim.

Brief Specifications

	1969 TR6
Curb Weight, lb.	2360
Wheelbase, in.	88.0
Track, f/r	50.2/49.8
Length	156.0
Width	58.0
Height	50.0
Engine type	pushrod inline 6
Bore x stroke, mm	74.7 x 95.0
Displacement, cc	2498
Horsepower, bhp @ rpm	106 @ 4900
Torque, lb-ft @ rpm	133 @ 3000
Transmission	4-speed manual w/optional overdrive
Suspension f/r	ind/ind
Brakes f/r	disc/drum
Steering type	rack and pinion

Performance Data From Contemporary Test

0-60 mph, sec.	11.6
Standing ¼ mile, sec.	18.2
Average mpg	18.0
Road test date	2-69

Typical Asking Prices

1969-1976 TR6	$2,500-$4,500
Typical engine-rebuild price	$2,200-$3,000

Driving Impressions

I met John Yerger and his TR6 on a blistering summer afternoon. How hot was it? John, a factory representative in Southern California for Jaguar, had a unique perspective. "On a day like this ten years ago," he said, "I would have been hiding from irate owners of boiling XJ12s."

From their cumbersome ragtops right down to their optional wire wheels, TR6s have all the hallmarks of a vintage British sports car except for one: they're not prone to overheating. On such a day, I was thankful for that.

John bought his TR6 brand new in 1972 for $4100. Some 75,000 miles have passed beneath it since then, including six coast-to-coast trips. Through it all, the car has been remarkably reliable. Now John's everyday car is of course a new Jaguar, and the TR6 is reserved for weekends.

To my eye, the TR6's styling hasn't lost its excitement after all this time. John's car isn't concours-ready. But the original coat of maroon paint still shines, the tan vinyl upholstery is holding up well, and there isn't a speck of rust anywhere. Like a favorite pair of shoes, John's TR6 is comfortably broken-in, but has plenty of miles left in it.

Both John and I have lanky physiques, and the TR6 gave us all the legroom we needed. A more corpulent couple would certainly rub shoulders in the car's narrow, cozy cockpit. The TR6's passengers sit upright on shapeless squabs, and the steering wheel practically kisses the driver's chest. More endearing is the piece of genuine timber across the dash, the well-placed gearshift lever, and the complete set of easily readable instruments.

Unfortunately, John has fiddled with his car's exhaust system, and when I goosed the accelerator pedal I was given a nasty rasp rather than the throaty roar that Bruce McWilliams had worked so hard to achieve with his broom sticks. Though the sound wasn't typical TR6, the muscular engine pulled smartly without the slightest fuss.

The notchy gearbox and servo-assisted brakes worked just fine. But oh what a clutch! It's said that the TR6, like the big Healey, is a hairy-chested man's car, and the heavy clutch is testimony to the notion. Even Arnold Schwarzenegger's left leg would get tired after slogging through rush-hour traffic in a TR6. Apparently John's car wasn't peculiar in this respect; when the TR6 was introduced automotive scribes complained about the stiff clutch, too.

Cruising along on smooth roads in the TR6 was delightful. With the top down and the transmission in high gear, the engine sounded relaxed and there was so little wind buffeting that John and I could talk normally. But then we encountered railroad tracks, followed by a few potholes. That silly irs lost its composure and the ride degenerated into something more akin to a century-old donkey cart than an automobile from the 1970s.

Handling was also a mixed bag. At lower speeds, when I asked the car to turn, it seemed to answer "What?" and then understeered ferociously. But at 50 mph or so, the steering lightened up and the response became more neutral.

Yes, Triumph's TR6 can be a cantankerous beast. But cheerfully accepting privation is part of the Traditional British Sports Car Experience. Although John has considered selling his TR6 several times, "the thought always left quickly," he says. After all, a young fellow like John needs relief from all that luxury of a Jaguar XJ6, and the TR6 is a perfect diversion.

—Peter Bohr (March 1987)

GREAT BRITAIN

Triumph Spitfire and GT6

1962-1970

Incomparable cars in their price classes

by Thos L. Bryant

Leyland Motors took over the Standard-Triumph Company in late 1960 and saved it from death. While S-T was doing fairly well with overseas sales of the Triumph TR3A sports car, the British home market was seriously depressed by a credit squeeze. The result was that fewer than 650 TR3As were sold in the U.K. in 1960, and, amazingly, less than 100 in 1961.

One of the early moves following the Leyland takeover was the revival of a small sports-car project that the S-T management had commissioned Giovanni Michelotti to design. It was to be competitive with the Austin-Healey Sprite and soon-to-come MG Midget: a sports car that would be less expensive than the TR3A and the upcoming TR4. Michelotti designed what would eventually become the Spitfire, but his prototype arrived at the S-T Coventry facility when the company's finances were near rock bottom, so the prototype was pushed into a corner and tucked away. The new Leyland management resurrected the program in short order, and in late 1962 the Triumph Spitfire 4 made its debut.

A design parameter for the Spitfire was that it be based on the Triumph Herald chassis and running gear, but Triumph aficionados are quick to point out that the sports car is *not* simply a Herald with a roadster body. The chassis was a backbone design, as was that of the Herald. But it was designed around a wheelbase 8.5 in. shorter than that of the Herald, and the only common parts were suspension mountings and supports.

The Spitfire has a double Y-type frame with the front Y accommodating the engine and the rear Y tying in with the frame-mounted differential and independent rear suspension. The irs feature of the Spitfire was a major selling point because it was the only car in its price class that didn't use a rigid rear axle. The Spitfire uses swing axles and a single transverse leaf spring.

The irs does give the Spitfire decent ride characteristics. However, at a spirited pace, the swing axles live up to their name and swing, producing more wheel hop and jacking than most road testers cared for, as we pointed out in our first Spitfire test (April 1963):

"When pressed along at racing speeds, however, the picture changes a bit. The back of the car lifts and the wheels begin to pull under, which sends the car skating sharply outward. The Spitfire's quick, precise rack-and-pinion steering makes it easy to catch the car before the situation gets out of hand, but it is impossible to get around a race course very rapidly in a series of swings and slides. Also, on tight corners the inside rear wheel lifts completely clear of the road and spins free, making acceleration out of the turn very leisurely indeed."

It wasn't long before aftermarket camber compensators were being sold to Spitfire owners who wanted to improve the high-speed handling characteristics. Replacing the original 3.5-inch-wide wheels and the 5.20-13 tires with wider ones (preferably radial tires) also made a big difference and brought more stability to the rear end.

1967 Triumph Spitfire

The Spitfire's front suspension was adapted from earlier Triumph cars and had been well proven through usage in a variety of racing cars. It's a fairly simple design with A-arms, coil springs, tube shock absorbers and an anti-roll bar, all of which work well together.

1967 Triumph GT6

Engine and Gearbox

The best adjective for describing the Spitfire's 4-cylinder engine is rugged. It dates back to the Standard Eight sedan of 1954, but there were a number of changes over the years. In its initial stage, the engine was 803 cc, but it grew to 948 cc in the Herald and later to 1,147 cc in that model and later in the Spitfire. In the Herald or 1200, the engine generated 43 bhp at 4,500 rpm, but the Spitfire develops 63 at 5,800 through altered valve timing and carburetion (twin SUs).

The Mark 2 Spitfire (1965-67) engine received a slight horsepower boost (to 67) through a revised camshaft and a 4-branch exhaust manifold. The next update came in 1967 with the introduction of the Mark 3. Engine displacement increased to 1,296 cc and the Spitfire engine was now based on the 1300 Triumph instead of the 1,147-cc unit used before. The gross horsepower rose to 75 at 6,000 rpm, but the following year, U.S.-version Spitfires suffered their first encounter with emission controls and the bhp figure sagged to 68 at 5,500 rpm, where it remained through the term covered by this report.

The gearbox is a relatively simple affair with synchro on second, third and fourth gears. An electrically operated overdrive on third and fourth gears was offered as an option in late 1963, and while it did not improve performance, it did improve the already impressive fuel economy. The Spitfire went into production with a single dry-plate Borg & Beck clutch, but this was replaced with a larger, diaphragm-type unit on the Mark 2s.

General Comments

From its introduction in late 1962, the Spitfire was a welcome addition to the small sports-car range, with such features as the independent rear suspension, front disc brakes, roll-up windows, pleasing Michelotti styling and an affordable price ($2,199 list in 1963). The Mark 2, introduced in 1965, was little changed except for a new extruded-aluminum grille, a "Mark 2" emblem on the rear deck lid and vastly improved upholstery material and seat padding. The Mark 2 price rose only slightly, to $2,249 list, and continued to sell at a good pace (Mark 1 sales from 1962 to 1965 were almost 46,000 and more than 37,000 Mark 2s were sold from 1965 to 1967).

The Mark 3 (1967-70) represented more sweeping changes in the evolution of the model. The already-mentioned larger engine was complemented by better braking through the use of slightly larger calipers on the front discs, and the build-it-yourself convertible top with separate frame was replaced with a lift-over-and-clamp top that was infinitely easier and more convenient to use. The most notable exterior change was a new front bumper that gave the Spitfire the appearance of a shark with a bone in its teeth because it split the grille opening horizontally. The Mark 3's list price took another small jump, to $2,373, but it was still a good buy in terms of value received and in comparison with competing sports cars such as the MG Midget III with its $2,255 price tag.

Triumph GT6 and GT6+

It didn't take long for some enthusiasts to start thinking and talking about a 6-cylinder Spitfire, and, in fact, conjecture about such a car began as soon as the Spitfire 4 was introduced. The decision makers at Triumph were not terribly keen on the idea because their production facilities were stretched to the limit. But it was bound to happen. Michelotti was given free rein to design a fastback body for the Spitfire and what became the GT6 appeared in 1966. The engine was the pushrod 1,998-cc unit from the Triumph 2000 sedan, developing 95 bhp at 5,000 rpm. It was mated to an all-synchro gearbox, which had been developed for the Triumph Vitesse. The new, stronger transmission was deemed necessary to handle the additional torque load of the 6-cylinder engine, as was a stronger rear-end assembly to handle the 3.27:1 final-drive ratio in place of the 3.89:1 Spitfire ratio. So, a new case and stronger half-shafts were fitted to the GT6.

The suspension for the new car was little different from the Spitfire and not everyone was impressed with swing-axle rear suspension on a car with the torque of the GT6. The British motoring press by and large found the suspension arrangement unsatisfactory, complaining that it was too soft and that it produced unacceptable handling characteristics. Triumph's response was that the suspension's softness was designed for

American customers, pointing out that more than 90 percent of the company's sports cars had been exported to the U.S. and Canada since 1945.

Our road test of the GT6 (April 1967) gave the car high marks: "We approach any car with conventional swing axles with a little apprehension but we found that the GT6 could not be faulted on its handling." Also, "...one gets the feeling that the car has a degree of oversteer that can be enjoyed and utilized by a moderately skilled driver while never crossing up an unskilled one. The GT6 corners flat, too, and doesn't seem to want to lift its inside rear wheel in violent low-speed maneuvers."

The GT6 also impressed us with many of its other features, and our conclusions about the car were quite enthusiastic:

"In summary, the GT6 is a smaller package that incorporates many of the same qualities that make the Jaguar E-Type such an exhilarating car. It is smooth; it has good torque, low noise level and agility as well as stability in its handling. It's a great improvement over the Spitfire 4 from which it descended. Not that the Spitfire 4 was bad, it's just that the GT6 is so much better. It has no parallel and it's worth the money."

1969 Triumph Spitfire

So, the GT6 was quite a pleasant car, in our opinion, and certainly worth the list price of $3,039. There was an optional Laycock de Normanville electric overdrive available from the car's inception, and U.S. models of the GT6 came with wire wheels and Dunlop SP-41 radial-ply tires as standard equipment. The GT6 Mark1 continued in production until 1968, with nearly 16,000 examples being built during its two-year life span.

The GT6+ (that was the U.S. moniker; in England it was known as the Mark 2) was built from 1968 until 1970, and the total production was just over 12,000 units. The new model featured increased performance and a different rear suspension system. The 2-liter engine was bumped up to 104 bhp at 5,300 rpm (instead of the previous 95 at 5,000) through installation of a new camshaft with more lift and greater overlap, plus slightly larger intake and exhaust valves. Another change was replacement of the generator by an alternator.

The new rear suspension retained the transverse leaf spring but replaced the swing axle with double-jointed shafts that were located by the spring at the top, a wide-based lower arm and a radius arm. The new arrangement diminished the camber changes and unsettling jacking and tuck-under characteristics of the earlier model. Another alteration worthy of note was a reduction in the seat height to provide more head room for taller drivers who had found the original GT6 uncomfortable. The GT6+ models also featured a full range of U.S. safety equipment of the period and raised bumpers both front and rear that did little for the styling but were considerably more practical. And amazingly, the list price had risen only $6 (to $3,045) over the original GT6 two years earlier. The trick was the replacement of the previously standard wire wheels with less expensive steel discs.

Our summary of the GT6+ (February 1969) was a query: "Where else can you get a 6-cyl, 100+-mph coupe with a proper chassis, good finish and Jazzy looks for $3,000? Nowhere *we* know of."

Buying a Used Spitfire or GT6 — What to Look for

In conversations with owners, it appears there are few quirks to keep in mind when searching for a Spitfire or GT6 to buy. The rugged 4-cylinder engine (and the 6-cylinder from the GT6) is dependable and durable in the manner of British sports car engines of the era. One expert we talked to said he couldn't think of any special engine weak points to check, and after further thought added, "You should look for oil leaks around the timing cover seal and things like that, but no more so than with any used car you'd think about buying."

One of the points that did come up is the transmission tunnel cover, which is fiber rather than metal — it can wear out and crack. This will allow noise and fumes into the cockpit and may make you think the gearbox is bad because of the noise level. Because the Spitfires covered here did not have synchro on first gear, the prospective buyer should be aware that an unskilled driver might have damaged that gear, so listen carefully for undue noise while driving the car in first. Also, a Spitfire that has been raced may leak oil from the gearbox tailshaft housing, but that condition rarely occurs with a car that has not been campaigned.

Another item that deserves careful inspection is the front ball joints. The grease boots there can wear out and leave no reservoir of lubricant for the ball joints. While we're at the front of the car, we should mention that the hinges for the large hood / fender section can come loose but don't normally wear out or break. There are rubber bumpers at the junction of the hood and cowl that serve to keep the hood assembly from rattling, and these can come off, giving you the impression of an unsound, vibrating front end.

At the rear end, there can sometimes be a clunking noise that would indicate the U-joints between the swing axle and the differential are worn and should be replaced. Underneath the car rust coming out of the U-joints is an indicator that this problem will crop up soon if it hasn't already. Otherwise, if the engine, gearbox and differential are quiet, that's a good indication that the car is in good shape as the Spitfire drivetrain components are quite durable.

We don't care to go into a long dissertation on the shortcomings of Lucas electrical parts, but the buyer should be aware that these can cause some problems in older cars. Also, one man who is familiar with Spitfires said that generator brushes seem to wear out every 25,000 miles or so.

Because of their designs, the Spitfire and GT6 don't seem to be as prone to rust damage as other British sports cars, especially along the rocker panels. Apparently the body and the double Y-type frame result in fewer nooks and crannies for trapping water, although floor rust in front of the seats can be a problem with the convertible if the carpeting gets wet frequently.

The prospective purchaser of a Spitfire should give a lot of thought to suspension modifications if he or she is planning to engage in spirited driving, racing or slalom activities. For normal touring, as we said, the Spitfire handles quite well and the independent suspension soaks up bumps and uneven surfaces with efficiency. But, the swing-axle rear suspension does have its limitations. Replacing the shock absorbers with stiffer units (such as Konis), adding a camber compensator, re-arcing the rear transverse leaf spring or putting on the transverse spring (known as a swing spring) from the Mark 4 Spitfire models (1973-on) will make a big difference. Although the Mark 4s have a wider track, the swing spring will fit earlier models with the narrower track.

Owner Impressions

My twin brother and I pooled our meager resources to buy what eventually became my Spitfire when we graduated from college and went our separate ways. We bought our powder-blue Triumph on June 15, 1964, a date I know is correct, not because it sticks in my memory, but because I still have the original bill of sale — which probably says a lot about the way I still feel about the car. We paid cash, exactly $2,358, and that price included a heater (you mean it wasn't standard?), pushbutton AM radio, tonneau cover, bias-ply white walls (we were too naive to know about radials in those days), seatbelts (which weren't standard equipment back then), an outside mirror and $8 in sales tax. Can you imagine just $8 in sales tax?

Choosing the Spitfire wasn't a hasty decision. We shopped around, read all the sales brochure hype and pored over every magazine article we could find. And even back then we considered the Sprite and Midget somewhat old-fashioned compared to the Spitfire. After all, what other sports car in its price range could boast of roll-up windows? Yes, emotion played a large part in the choice of the Spitfire.

In a sense my interest in things automotive, which had been brewing for the past two or three years, blossomed with the purchase of that car. I discovered the joy of open-air motoring and the euphoria of sliding around corners on the twisty back roads of Long Island and Connecticut, and also the heart-stopping limitations of swing axles. The car turned me into an avid reader of magazines like *Road & Track* and *Sports Car Graphic* and words such as gymkhana, rally, heel-and-toe, driving gloves, Vilem B. Haan, MG Mitten and SCCA became part of my everyday vocabulary. I helped form my college sports car club and was turned on to racing by watching the NASCAR stockers and Ferraris, Alfas, Cobras, Gran Sport Corvettes and even Spitfires go roaring around Bridgehampton Raceway. My Spitfire and I discovered Lime Rock Park tucked away in the picture-book countryside of northwest Connecticut and to this day it's still my favorite race track.

The Spitfire taught me mechanics. It's an easy car to work on, and I learned how to synchronize the throttles on the twin SU carbs by listening to the hiss in the intakes using a length of 3-mm tubing (I know it looks dumb but it works), how to change points and adjust timing and dwell, how to set valve clearances and how to bleed brakes and change disc brake pads. It also taught me the eccentricity of Lucas electrics.

It didn't stay stock very long. I mentioned the words Koni and camber compensator long and loud enough that for Christmas 1965 both items appeared under the tree. This was followed by a rollbar (No, Dad, I'm not going to race it. The car's a lot safer to drive on the street with a rollbar. You wouldn't want me hurt if it rolled over, would you?) and a set of narrow Goodyear Blue Streaks for gymkhanas. The rollbar and a Bell helmet were all I needed to attend a touring school (something like an SCCA Solo I driver's school) at Bridgehampton, an event that only whetted my appetite for racing, a luxury my limited finances didn't allow at the time.

1969 Triumph GT6 interior

Then came a summer job with Ford and a cross-country (well it seemed like cross-country to someone who'd never been west of New Jersey) 700-mile trip to Detroit. This was a trek the Spitfire was to repeat more times than I can recount during the next three years, and it faltered only twice: Once in the middle of Pennsylvania during a bitterly cold and rainy post-Thanksgiving drive back to Michigan, the track for the passenger window unbolted itself and the window disappeared into the door. (Damn, and to think I bought it for those roll-up windows.) Then there was the time the power fell way off and even the slightest incline felt like Mt. Everest. A compression check uncovered the problem: zero compression in number three. That's when I first began to suspect British craftsmanship. How do you think your head would feel if someone stuffed in an intake valve where an exhaust should be? I bitterly complained to British Leyland and received the expected satisfaction — none. "So sorry, old chap, but it lasted 30,000 miles, you know."

The Spitfire didn't take kindly to the cold and snow of Detroit winters, venting its unhappiness by giving me the cold shoulder... and cold hands and feet and every other part of my body. Even with the radiator fully blocked off, the heater wouldn't generate enough warm air to defrost a gnat's eye. That and the fact I was working for Chrysler at the time resulted in the purchase of a used 1966 Formula S Barracuda, relegating the Spitfire to the confines of an unheated garage until warmer weather arrived.

This turn of events made the idea of converting the Spitfire into a "real" race car more than just idle chatter between one of my roommates and me. Several months later, after following the gospel according to Kas Kasner, the transformed Spitfire was ready for its first SCCA driver's school. A less-than-accomplished racer screwed up, and the Spitfire rolled over and died. Most of my friends were ready to write off the car. But not

Brief Specifications

	1963-1965 Spitfire 4 & Mark 2	1967 Mark 3	1967 GT6	1969 GT6+
Curb Weight, lb.	1555*	1680	1970	1975
Wheelbase, in.	83.0	83.0	83.0	83.0
Track, f / r	49.0 / 48.0	49.0 / 48.0	49.0 / 48.0	49.0 / 49.0
Length	145.0	147.0	145.0	147.0
Width	57.0	57.0	57.0	57.0
Height	47.5	47.5	47.0	47.0
Engine type	pushrod inline 4	pushrod inline 4	pushrod inline 6	pushrod inline 6
Bore x stroke, in.	2.73 x 2.99	2.90 x 2.99	2.94 x 2.99	2.94 x 2.99
Displacement, cc	1147	1296	1998	1998
Horsepower (gross)	63*	75	95	95

*curb weight for Mark 2 is 1630 lb; horsepower is 67

Performance Data From Contemporary Tests

	Spitfire 4	Mark 2	Mark 3	GT6	GT6+
0-60 mph, sec.	15.5	15.0	13.6	12.3	11.0
Standing 1 / 4 mile, sec.	20.8	20.4	19.3	18.8	18.0
Average mpg	30.0	27.0	23.0	24.0	24.0
Road test date	4-63	6-65	9-67	4-67	2-69

Typical Asking Prices

1962-1970 Spitfire	$1,500-$2,500
1966-1970 GT6	$1,500-$2,500
Typical engine-rebuild prices: Spitfire	$1,500-$2,000
GT6	$2,000-$2,500

I. The body was wasted but the Spitfire's separate body / frame design allowed me to literally unbolt the body from the frame and replace it with a less than pristine 1963 shell I bought for $150 and bondo-ed, primed and spray-painted Chrysler-Hemi orange in my backyard. The Rolling Stone, as the Spitfire was referred to by the unbelievers among my roommates and friends, rode again.

Soon after it left Detroit for the last time, hitched to a makeshift tow bar attached to the Barracuda's rear bumper for the long haul to California and my job with *Car Life* magazine. The Spitfire thrives in Southern California's sunny clime. It doesn't get driven very much these days because I'm usually too busy driving the *Road & Track* test cars to have much time for it. But it's still an automotive high to put the top down and get behind the wheel of a car with a responsive high-compression engine, even if that engine only displaces 1,147 cc. Then I blast down the coast highway or along one of the twisty roads running through California's coastal hills with the relatively unsilenced exhaust throbbing in my ears, being jounced all around by the Spitfire's nimble handling (but barely streetable) competition suspension.

The body's not much to look at and someday I may get around to fixing it. But one thing's pretty sure. I'll probably have that Spitfire forever. —*John Dinkel (September 1977)*

WEST GERMANY

Volkswagen Karmann-Ghia

1956-1974

*A sleeper today,
a keeper tomorrow?*

by Thos L. Bryant

1967 Volkswagen Karmann-Ghia

The Volkswagen Karmann-Ghia was unveiled to the world at the European auto shows in the fall of 1955, but I must confess that my appreciation of this coachbuilt car is quite recent. I'm not unique in this tardiness, however, as many car enthusiasts in the U.S. cast only cursory glances upon the Karmann-Ghia during its production lifetime. There are at least two reasons for this myopic view: The admittedly handsome body concealed mundane Volkswagen drivetrain and running gear, and the Karmann-Ghia was produced in sufficient numbers (nearly a half-million from 1956 to 1974) to make it seem a common car. With so many of them populating the roads, and with performance that differed very little from the Beetle, it's not surprising that the K-G has languished in the backwaters of the car-collecting rush.

However, if the historical pattern of U.S. automotive phenomena — i.e., popular fads and crazes begin in California and then sweep eastward — means anything to you, you'd be well advised to go buy at least one K-G. You see, lots of Johnny-come-latelies have turned the Karmann-Ghia, particularly the convertible, into the popular "in" car in the beach areas of Southern California.

Our first road test of the car appeared in April 1956, and we called it the Ghia-Karmann Volkswagen, giving top billing to the designer and putting the coachbuilder second. That may have been more logical, but it never caught on. Our first impression of the Karmann-Ghia was that it held nearly universal visual appeal: "It is, as the French would say, *une poupee vivante* (a living doll). As can be seen from the accompanying photos, the car's lines are low, beautifully balanced and ornament free."

The interior of the inaugural K-G was also praised for its touch of custom coachwork and quality of the fit and finish, although the relatively low seating position did draw some criticism. Outward vision was characterized as exceptionally good.

Beneath the lovely skin, the K-G was pure Volkswagen: "As might be expected, therefore, the K-G drives, feels, and sounds pretty much like the sedan," said the road testers of 1956. And despite the car's weight, 120 pounds greater than the Beetle, its improved aerodynamics provided less susceptibility to crosswinds and quicker acceleration: 0-60 mph in 28.8 seconds, whereas the Beetle had never bettered 30.0 seconds for that run.

According to the data panel accompanying that road test, the list price for the K-G was $2,475 (but the East Coast POE price was $2,395), which seems a bargain by any standard for a car that was virtually handcrafted. Nevertheless, the K-G was not lavished with praise in our report: "When all is said and done, what does the VW K-G amount to? The overall performance improvement, we feel, is negligible. For nearly $1,000 more than the sedan, then, the customer is acquiring a very pretty body." However, some dealers were quoting two to four years for delivery, so clearly there were those who immediately recognized the Karmann-Ghia's virtues.

Two years later, in the fall of 1957, Karmann exhibited the convertible version of the K-G at the European auto shows, and by 1958 that model was available in the U.S. to complement the hardtop coupe. It is remarkable, and perhaps indicative of the low interest the K-G held for most enthusiasts, that *Road & Track* never did a road test of the convertible version during the sixteen years of its life span in the U.S. It is essentially the same car with the notable exception of the folding top, a marvelous mechanism that provides unusually effective sealing against the elements thanks to the care taken in its design and construction.

In 1958, Volkswagen made its only significant change to the sheet metal of the K-G: the front fenders were slightly raised and the headlights were moved upward; also, the front air scoops were made slightly wider and a small override bar was added to the front and rear bumpers. There were to be no further exterior changes of note until 1972, when U.S.-mandated heavy bumpers were added, giving a bulky look to each end of the sleek little car. Also, the rear taillights would grow into relatively enormous units taking up much of the vertical surface of the rear fenders.

1956 Volkswagen Karmann-Ghia

In March 1962 we conducted a road test of the latest version. The 1,192-cc flat-4 engine's output had been raised from the original 36 bhp to 40 bhp in 1960. This may not seem to important, "but it represents an 11-percent increase, which made the difference between barely adequate performance and that which is very satisfactory." Curiously, however, the 0-60 mph time for the 1962 K-G increased to 30.0 seconds from the 28.8 seconds of 1956, even though the curb weights listed in the respective data panels are within 10 pounds of each other.

One unusual aspect of the 1962 Karmann-Ghia was that its list price was *less* than that of the 1956 model: $2,295 versus $2,475. Fuel consumption continued in the 30-35 mpg range in 1962, and sales were in the area of 9,000-10,000 K-Gs per year in the U.S. As time went by, sales climbed dramatically, reaching a peak of more than 38,000 in the U.S. in 1970. The K-G's popularity reached its zenith at that time, however, as the following year sales were less than 24,000. By 1974, the last year for the Karmann-Ghia, Americans bought fewer than 8,000.

After our March 1962 K-G test, we ignored the VW sports car in our road tests until April 1973, when the K-G took part in a track test of nine showroom stock sports cars. (We did publish

1962 Volkswagen Karmann-Ghia

a European road test of the Karmann-Ghia 1500 based on the VW Variant, but the car was never officially sold in the U.S.) In the interim, a number of changes had been made to the K-G. In 1966, the ubiquitous VW 1,285-cc engine was introduced to the car, raising the output to 50 horsepower and in 1967 the displacement went to 1,493 cc and the horsepower rose to 53. For the last four years of its life, 1971-74, the K-G would boast a modest 60 bhp from a displacement of 1,584 cc. Most experts look upon 1967 as the most significant year of change for the Karmann-Ghia, not only for the upgrade to the 1,493 engine, but also because the interior trim was improved, the final-drive ratio was changed from 4.37:1 to 3.88, the rear track grew by 2.0 inches to 52.7 inches, a rear camber compensator was added, and the electrical system converted from 6-volt to 12.

In the 1973 nine-car comparison test at the race track, the Karmann-Ghia was outclassed in acceleration, but it was noted for having "a good ride and proper steering, and it can be driven on the ragged edge without incident and with drama...." By that time the K-G's 60 bhp propelled it to 60 mph from a standing start in 17.5 seconds, while the quarter-mile run was managed in 21.2 seconds at a speed of 65.5 mph. Compared to the early models, the newest K-G was rather quick, but compared to most other cars on the road it was lacking in power.

Selecting a Used K-G — What to Look for

We tabulated Used Car Classic questionnaires from 175 Karmann-Ghia owners and found them an enthusiastic lot, with only twenty-two saying they would decline to buy another. Their ownership experiences give us some expected guidelines for the potential purchaser of a K-G. The first thing to look for — and this is the cardinal rule with nearly every car in this series — is rust. K-Gs suffer from this affliction as badly as any. The unibody construction means that replacing panels and pieces may not be easy, so a careful inspection could save time, money and heartbreak. The rocker panels, rear quarter panels, bottoms of doors, rain gutters, heater boxes, headlight buckets and floor pan are all areas that can give way to the ravages of rust. Also, within the rear engine compartment, rust can get started in hard-to-see places, such as beneath the battery. So take the time to look and don't be afraid to get your hands dirty scraping aside grease and grime in this area.

Poor sealing and insulation around doors and windows contribute to the rust problem, according to the owners surveyed, one of whom claimed that his car "rusts from the in- side out." The original seals were well done by Karmann, but over the years they will deteriorate, and few owners will take the time or trouble to replace them until it's much too late.

Potential K-G buyers are cautioned to check the quality of the car's front end. Many owners assert that the inadequate bumpers (pre-1972) make for dings and dents in the noses of the cars, and the more serious ones can be expensive to put right. There are also a number of chrome trim pieces on the exterior of the K-G, and replacing these items can be costly and time-consuming — because they can be hard to come by.

Interior upholstery is another area that K-G owners find troublesome, but the wear and tear level seems about normal. The earliest K-Gs came with cloth upholstery rather than vinyl, and it didn't wear as well. However, there are so few examples of early K-Gs available in the U.S. that this shouldn't be a cause for concern. The padding around the dash has a tendency to crack and come apart, expecially near the radio, the owners tell us, and this was variously attributed to Texas sun, New Hampshire cold and Colorado altitude.

The pre-1967 models with the 6-volt electrical system came under fire from their owners, and it's clear that the change to 12 volts was timely and needed. Otherwise, from a mechanical standpoint, the K-G is basic VW and the same rules apply. The drivetrain is reliable and durable, and with normal care and maintenance, it should provide many miles of trouble-free driving. As for the convertibles, the top is a marvelous piece of engineering, but it can suffer from wood rot in the bows, as well as eventual deterioration of the fabric. The Karmann-Ghia may be one of the real sleepers among Used Car Classics, as long as you keep in mind that the performance is modest. But for a hand-finished coachbuilt car that won't cost an arm and a leg, the K-G is an excellent choice.

Driving Impressions

One of the first things you notice upon driving a K-G is that the pedals are offset to the right of the seat because of wheel-well intrusion and space considerations based on the difference between the Beetle body and the Ghia's. There is a slightly awkward feel to the resulting driving position. This sensation will go away after some time at the wheel, but nearly everyone who has owned a K-G will mention this quirk.

Because the running gear and drivetrain are strictly VW Beetle, the K-G doesn't exhibit any tremendous power and yet it does *seem* quicker. At the upper end, the Ghia's more efficient aerodynamics will contribute to some improvement, but I'm certain that the difference is primarily an optical illusion produced by the K-G's styling.

I spent some time talking with Norm Batchelder, proprietor of Mesa West German Automotive in Costa Mesa, California. Norm knows as much about VW cars as anyone I've ever met, and his shop is constantly jammed with VW products of every description awaiting normal service, general repair or total restoration. When I asked him about buying a used Karmann-Ghia, his first thought was about the bent noses mentioned by a number of our survey respondents: "It's so common I can't remember the last time I saw a Ghia without some bodywork having been done up front." Norm said that if he were buying a used one, he would choose one that had not been restored because he'd want to see what he was getting. Also, he said lots of Ghias have been lowered or otherwise customized, and that

Brief Specifications

	1956	1962	1973
Curb Weight, lb.	1760	1750	1960
Wheelbase, in.	94.5	94.5	94.5
Track, f / r	50.8 / 49.2	51.4 / 50.7	51.3 / 52.7
Length	163.0	163.0	165.0
Width	64.2	64.2	64.3
Height	52.4	52.4	52.0
Engine type	pushrod flat 4	pushrod flat 4	pushrod flat 4
Bore x stroke, in.	3.03 x 2.52	3.03 x 2.52	3.36 x 2.72
Displacement, cc	1192	1192	1584
Horsepower (gross) @ rpm	36 @ 3700	40 @ 3900	60 @ 4000
Torque @ rpm	56 @ 2000	64 @ 2400	72* @ 2800

*SAE net rating

Performance Data From Contemporary Tests

	1956	1962	1973
0-60 mph, sec.	28.8	30.0	17.5
Standing 1 / 4 mile, sec.	23.6	22.7	21.2
Average mpg	30-35	30-35	NA
Road test date	4-56	3-62	4-73

Typical Asking Prices

1956-1974 Karmann-Ghia Coupe	$1,500-$3,500
1958-1974 Karmann-Ghia Convertible	$2,500-$5,000
Typical engine-rebuild price	$1,100-$1,500

1958 Volkswagen Karmann-Ghia interior

he would stay far away from those cars.

Batchelder talked about the Ghia being a fun car to drive, with good handling characteristics, much like a Beetle, of course, and with slightly better fuel efficiency because the improved aerodynamics. Like a lot of car enthusiasts, though, Norm doesn't give the Ghia rave reviews, finding the performance disappointing for his taste. He did acknowledge, however, that it is easy to add performance items, such as dual carburetors, because there's considerably more room in the engine bay than in the Beetle's.

In summing up the K-G as a car to own, Norm said, "Just remember, everything on a Ghia is expensive except the running gear." While that is true in regard to finding and purchasing parts for the body (and the top in the case of the convertibles), the Karmann-Ghia does offer a lot of coachbuilt excellence at a very affordable initial price. The exclusivity factor that often attracts car enthusiasts to a particular model is virtually nonexistent with the Ghia, but it can be a fun car to drive and relatively inexpensive to keep running. — *Thos L. Bryant (November 1982)*

SWEDEN

Volvo 122-S and P 1800

1959-1972

You probably don't know the names Assar Gabrielsson or Gustaf Larsson and there's really no reason why you should. But, they were the founders of AB Volvo in 1924 and thus the originators of the Swedish car industry. Gabrielsson was a management expert at SKF, a Swedish ball bearing manufacturer, and Larsson was a young engineer with a considerable interest in automobiles. After three years of hard work, they produced their first car in April 1927, a touring car with a 28-bhp 4-cylinder engine.

Twenty-some years later, the first Volvos arrived in America. These were the 444 models, and everyone went around commenting on how cute they were and how they resembled, from the rear, a 1946 Ford. Well, the 444 was in production in 1944, so perhaps this was another case of our ethnocentricity getting in the way of the facts. However, the 444 and later the 544, which appeared in 1958, proved to be popular among enthusiasts and the Swedish car manufacturer was off and running in the U.S.

122-S

In 1956, Volvo showed the 120 series to the press in Sweden, and the reaction was quite favorable to the new design. In Europe the car would become known as the Amazon, but in the U.S. the moniker was 122-S. It took two years for the 122-S to make the journey to the American market, and in the September 1959 issue of *Road & Track* there appeared a laudatory road test report on the car: "And a refreshing new car it is, too: pleasant looking, easy (and fun) to drive, economical and durable in the extreme. It is also refreshing to find a company that actually does something to make its product safe for the occupants, and does it without asinine statements that the public won't buy safety."

Our report went on to say, "...the newest import is a handsome car in a reserved way, with no evident ostentation or gaudiness." Also, "...a close examination of the car, along with many miles behind the wheel, brought favorable comments from every tester and rider. Design, construction and general quality are obviously excellent, and there is a pervasive feeling of durability."

The early 122-S is powered by a 1,586-cc engine, which had been used in the 444 since 1956. In the 122-S, the engine, designated the B-16, produces 85 bhp at 5,500 rpm and 87 lb-ft torque at 3,500 rpm. In Sweden, the B-16 engine could be pur-

Used sporting cars for people who think

by Thos L. Bryant

1962 Volvo P 1800

1959 Volvo 122-S

chased with a single carburetor and detuned output of 60 bhp, but the export model has twin SU carburetors. All of the motoring press was enthusiastic about the performance capability of the 122-S, saying the 4-cylinder engine was extremely flexible and one of the most free-revving pushrod engines around; and pointing out, too, that the car's performance was one of its outstanding attractions, especially considering that it was a family 4-seater. Our road test in 1959 showed a top speed of 92.0 mph and a 0-60 mph time of 16.2 seconds. Certainly not breathtaking performance, but admirable for a 4-door sedan with a 4-cylinder engine.

Safety features included optional shoulder belts and such standard items as padded instrument panel, dished steering wheel and a collapsible steering column. The package tray on the passenger's side was also designed to collapse under impact, and the sun visors are thickly padded — all of this long before governmental regulations came into being.

The suspension design of the 122-S was carried over from the 444 and 544: coil springs and tube shocks all around with A-arms and an anti-roll bar in front, while at the rear there are trailing arms and a Panhard rod for lateral location of the live axle. This combination works very well, and we noted in our original test report that "corners can be taken with gusto, though with considerable body roll and squealing of tires...." We also noted that the ZF steering was precise and transmitted good road feel to the driver, although it seemed slower than its 3.2 turns lock-to-lock would indicate.

For 1962, Volvo added a 2-door sedan to the 122-S line and increased the engine displacement to 1,780 cc. Power rose from 85 bhp to 90 at 5,000 rpm and the torque went from 87 lb-ft to 105 at 4,000 rpm. The increased displacement of the B-18 engine was accomplished by an increase in the bore (from 3.13 to 3.31), while the stroke remained the same as in the B-16 engine. At the same time, disc brakes were now standard on the front instead of drums all around as on the earlier models, and a 12-volt electrical system replaced the 6-volt setup. The new B-18 engine was reported by Volvo to have greater fuel economy as a result of increasing the number of crankshaft bearings from three to five, full machining of all combustion chambers and two additional intake ports that gave direct induction to each cylinder. Our tests, however, didn't support the factory claims. We reported that the 122-S with the B-16 engine delivered 24-27 mpg (R&T, September 1959) while the B-18 engine delivered 21-26 mpg (R&T, May 1962). The larger engine did show an improvement in performance, however, as the acceleration time from 0-60 mph dropped from 16.2 seconds to 14.5.

The new engine was also used in the P 1800, which had been introduced just shortly before the 122-S 2-door, so let's take a look at that model.

P 1800

The P 1800 was designed in 1959 and introduced in late

1961 as a 1962 model. It shares the same suspension and engine with the 122-S, but it has 10 more horsepower (100 @ 5,500 rpm vs 90 @ 5,000) as a result of different carburetion. The body was designed by Frua of Italy, and the first couple years' production was built in England with the drivetrain components being shipped over from Sweden. Late in 1964, production was transferred to the Volvo factory in Sweden.

We tested the P 1800 in February 1962 and made the following comments about its performance: "All cars of this type that come our way for test get a thorough wringing-out on twisty roads and there the Volvo, despite its weight and soft ride, gave a fine performance. There is a dreadful amount of lean while cornering, but the driver can't feel it inside the car and it doesn't seem to affect the handling. Bends, fast or slow, can be taken with *elan* — just a touch of steadying understeer being present at all times."

We also noted that the P 1800 was not meant for sprinting and that it would take a drubbing in acceleration from less expensive cars, but went on to say, "In doing that for which it was intended, fast steady cruising, the P 1800 is superb and it gave us the impression it would run forever at near maximum speed."

1962 Volvo P 1800 interior

With production of the 2+2 coupe in Sweden, the car became known as the P 1800S. The basic changes were a revised interior including new seats, less fancy wheel covers and a boost in the bhp figure to 115 at 6,000 rpm. Despite the increased horsepower, performance was virtually unchanged (0-60 mph in 13.9 seconds for the 1800S vs 13.6 seconds for the original P 1800), and it was more or less a case of Volvo continuing with what they considered a basically good car that needed only refinement. By the time of the *Road & Track* road test of the 1800S (August 1966), our staff had become less than enthralled with the styling of the car: "...staff opinions on the 1800S styling were generally unenthusiastic, with low marks going to the chromium sweepspear and the semi-finned rear fenders, both cliches of a bygone American era."

In 1969, the 1800 engine jumped from 1,800 cc to a full 2 liters with fuel injection. The car was designated the 1800E, and there were other important changes as well, including 4-wheel disc brakes, Michelin radial tires, aluminum alloy wheels and a strengthened gearbox. The eggcrate grille was replaced by a simpler and more attractive one composed of horizontal bars, but the basic styling was the same.

The 2-liter, fuel-injected engine gives the 1800E greatly improved performance, lowering the 0-60 mph time to just over 10 seconds. The 2-liter engine was also used in the sedans of the day, but only the 1800 received the fuel injection and thus had 12 more bhp and 7 more lb-ft torque than the carbureted Volvo engine at no increase in engine speed. Our comments in the road test of the 1800E (February 1970) went like this: "The engine, noted for its durability rather than refinement — it's neither mechanically smooth nor quiet in the coupe — has good low-speed torque as well as the ability to pull nicely all the way to its 6,500-rpm redline, and in overdrive the car will now do an honest 115 mph. The 0-60 mph and quarter-mile times are quite respectable too, putting the 1800E into the same class with such cars as the Alfa 1750, BMW 2500 or Mercedes 280SL. Furthermore, the engine runs cleanly without any trace of emission-control leanness symptoms and uses very little more fuel than the earlier test car."

Our 1970 test shows we were quite favorably impressed with the new gearbox: "The hefty lever on the new gearbox gives one an impression of unbreakability that is borne out by the gearbox itself; we manhandled the box unmercifully in the acceleration tests and found it capable of taking the fastest slam shifts without a crunch."

In summarizing the 1800E in 1970, we noted that — while the car was up to date in performance, handling and braking — the styling, accommodations and use of available space had fallen off the pace of cars at that time, and called on Volvo to design a new model.

Buying A Used Volvo — What to Look For

The engines, from the B-16 to the B-18 to the 2-liter B-20, are workhorses. *Road & Track* printed an Owner Survey covering the 1800, 122-S and early 144 Volvos in the March 1969 issue and not a single car in that report had required an engine overhaul. We were impressed by that and said in the survey, "...we're going to project 110,000 miles as an average life between overhauls in a Volvo." When searching for a good, used Volvo then, chances are the engine will not require major work, but it should be checked over anyway, and preferably by someone who knows Volvos well.

Some of the early 122-S models came with a 2-speed automatic transmission that was, frankly, terrible. We don't recommend purchasing these used models with automatic gearboxes because of diminished performance. The 4-speed manual gearboxes found in other models have proved nearly indestructible.

We should point out that on nearly all the early 1800 coupes, the overdrive unit shared a common oil reservoir with the gearbox. The Laycock de Normanville overdrive used 30W engine oil for lubrication, and many owners never bothered to check the oil level. The result was that they fried the overdrive. So, perhaps the first question to ask in examining an 1800 is, "Does the overdrive work?"

Unlike many of our Used Car Classic subjects, Volvos have not been prone to body rust problems. Not to say that it never occurs, but it's not especially common. However, we should mention the early 1800 coupes had an annoying tendency to leak water through the cowl vent in front of the windshield. Volvo is quick to point out that this was a problem on those cars that were built in England. Often, this is a result of the deterioration of the rubber molding around the vent hatch, or the drain tubes that allow excess water to run out of the vent opening may be clogged.

Our 1969 Owner Survey indicated that: many 1800 coupe owners found the instruments rather unreliable; cooling system problems could occur in all models; 122-S cars tended to have window-winding problems; and 10 percent of those responding to the survey reported oil leaks from the differential and gearbox. The survey also showed that 12 percent of the cars had clutch difficulties.

By and large, it would be safe to say that the Volvo models covered in this Used Car Classic have few major problems.

Driving Impressions

I was about half way through this project when I looked out the window into the parking lot one day and spotted a good-looking 122-S. Joe Bergman is the assistant managing editor of *Sea* Magazine, one of our companion publications, and he owns the 122-S described here.

Joe bought the car, a 1968 model, in Indianapolis in the fall of that year. He is the original owner and has racked up more than 104,000 miles on his Volvo. Through the years he has replaced the clutch and universal joints once and installed hydraulic clutch cylinders three times. Other than that, only routine maintenance has been necessary.

I borrowed the 122-S one morning for a drive along Pacific Coast Highway. My first impression was one of solidity: the body, chassis, engine and gearbox all have a solid, unbreakable feel. The steering is slightly heavy by today's standards and that too adds to the overall impression of durability.

The performance characteristics of the 122-S are not startling, but it is a fairly responsive car. The braking ability I would call adequate although not superior. Hard cornering produces lots of body roll, but once you get used to that and press on, the car actually corners quite well.

P 1800 Impressions

Peter Alper is the advertising manager for Volvo of America's Western Division, and he provided a considerable amount of expert help in the preparation of this report. In addition, Peter owns a 1963 P 1800 and he brought it by for us to drive. Peter's Volvo is not typical, but we thought it would be of interest to discover what can be done to build a street racer. Alper bought his P 1800 four years ago for $200 and took it home on a trailer. "It was junk," according to Peter, "and I knew it was going to be a total rebuild operation." The first step was installation of a 1973 B-20 (2-liter) engine in place of the B-18. The new engine was given an Iskenderian VV71 camshaft and tubular pushrods, Volvo Competition Service (VCS) lightweight lifters, VCS exhaust header, intake manifold and dual Solex carburetor set up. Peter had the head redone, too, but kept the stock ignition system because he feels it's better than anything else he could add. A new 4-speed gearbox and rebuilt overdrive

Brief Specifications

	1959 122-S	1962 P 1800
Curb Weight, lb.	2225	2430
Wheelbase, in.	102.4	96.5
Track, f/r	51.7/51.7	52.0/52.0
Length	173.0	173.0
Width	63.5	67.0
Height	59.2	51.0
Fuel Capacity (gal)	11.9	11.9
Engine type	pushrod inline 4	pushrod inline 4
Bore x stroke, in.	3.125 x 3.15*	3.31 x 3.15
Displacement, cc	1586*	1780

*122-S engine displacement was increased to 1780 cc by increasing the bore from 3.125 to 3.31 in 1962.

Performance Data From Contemporary Tests

0-60 mph, sec.	16.2	13.6
Standing 1/4 mile, sec.	20.0	19.0
Average mpg	25.5	24.5
Road test date	9-59	2-62

Typical Asking Prices

1959-1968 122-S	$1.500-$3,000
1962-1972 P1800, 1800S & 1800E	$2,500-$5,000
Typical engine-rebuild price (all models)	$1,400-$1,800

unit along with VCS heavy-duty clutch and pressure plates also went in, as did VCS rally springs at the rear end.

There have been a number of other modifications and changes including a Volvo 140-series sealed cooling system, Bilstein shock absorbers, IPD (specialists in Volvo handling and performance parts, 2762 N.E. Broadway, Portland, OR 97232) front and rear anti-roll bars, 7-inch wide American Racing wheels, Pirelli CN36 radials, a custom front air dam and lots more. Peter estimates he's getting 165 bhp from the engine and says the car will do an honest 125 mph.

Driving this P 1800 has almost nothing to do with what you would experience if you went out looking for one to buy, but it is great fun and damned exciting. As you would guess, it has more acceleration than you can normally use, and Peter's alterations to the suspension have brought about dramatic changes in the handling. In the final production years of the P 1800, our road test reports were critical of the car's outdated feel: the suspension was too soft, the performance was not crisp and so on. Alper's modifications show that these problems can be overcome and the car converted into a strong performer.

—Thos L. Bryant (February 1977)

Short Takes

ITALY
1978-1979 Alfa Romeo 2000 Spider Veloce

The Alfa 2000 Spider's design dates to 1966 but, in fact, is the same basic car that's still available in Alfa Romeo new-car showrooms for about $14,000. By sports-car standards of the 1960s, the car's well-controlled live rear axle gave better-than-average handling. But today, in sheer cornering power, a Honda Civic CRX, a VW Rabbit GTI and similar cars of humble econobox origins clearly outclass the Alfa. Moreover, the Spider's relatively primitive suspension gives a fairly harsh ride compared with cars of more recent design.

The Spider also suffers from the Italian-driving-position syndrome. Or, more precisely, the Spider driver suffers. With an awkwardly-positioned accelerator pedal and a long reach to the steering wheel, many Americans find the Spider uncomfortable on long-distance voyages.

Then there's the styling. Pininfarina's original design included a sloping rear end to harmonize with the sloping front end. But for no apparent reason, the tail was chopped in 1971. The strange gouge along the sides, the elimination of the headlight covers (illegal in the U.S.) and the ponderous 5-mph bumpers are blemishes on an otherwise handsome profile.

With all these gripes, you must wonder why we like the Spider. Well, the car's virtues more than compensate for its deficiencies. The aluminum dohc engine, refined over the past thirty years, still sings a uniquely sweet song. As for the transmission — oh, rapture! Shifting is crisp, quick and precise. In this age of front-wheel-drive cars and contorted linkages, transmissions like the Spider's are an endangered species. And the 4-cylinder Spider engine delivers good fuel economy.

Of course, the Spider is an open car, and that alone makes us partial to it. The top is marvelously easy to raise or tuck away. And we must confess that despite all our nitpicks about the styling, we've warmed to its looks over the years. One tends to become inured to the peculiarities of old friends.

Like fine wines, some vintages of Alfa Romeos are better than others. The best years were a function of how gracefully Alfa engineers managed to pull the Spider through the web of ever-tightening U.S. emissions standards. In 1976 and 1977, the Spider engine was strangled by various modifications and lost a good deal of performance compared with early 1970s cars. But in 1978, exhaust-system changes brought performance back up to snuff. And beginning with the 1978 cars, Alfa spruced up the

1979 Alfa Romeo Spider 2000

1978-1979 Alfa Romeo Spider Veloce

Specifications	Spider Veloce
Curb weight, lb.	2430
Engine type	dohc inline 4
Displacement, cc	1962
Transmission	5-speed manual
Suspension, f / r	ind / live
Brakes, f / r	disc / disc
Steering type	worm and roller

Performance Data

20-60 mph, sec	10.0
Stopping distance from 80 mph, ft	282
Standing 1 / 4 mile, sec @ mph	17.6 @ 78.5
Fuel economy, mpg	27.5
Road test date	5-77

Typical Asking Prices

1978-1979 Spider	$3,500-$6,500
Typical engine-rebuild price	$2,000-$2,500

Spiders by offering a new palette of interior and exterior color schemes, leather upholstery and a tan or a black top. So, Alfa lovers, seek a 1978 or 1979 Spider and enjoy a modern classic.

— *Peter Bohr*

WEST GERMANY
1969-1974 BMW 2800CS / 3.0CS

1971 BMW 3.0CS

Any BMW has some appeal to driving enthusiasts. But of all the BMW models built since World War II, probably only four are guaranteed to get the pulses of true BMW enthusiasts beating: the M1 exotic car, the 507 sports car of 1956, the 2002tii and the 2800CS / 3.0CS coupes. The M1 was never officially exported to this country though a few have been privately imported and modified to meet U.S. laws. The 507 is very rare and correspondingly expensive. The 2002, of course, established the BMW name in the U.S. and examples are easy to find on the used-car market. However, the tii is a faster, less common, fuel-injected version. Unquestionably it's our favorite 2002 rendition, and good ones can fetch $6,000 or more.

But the real bargain is the 2800CS of 1969-71 and the 3.0CS of 1972-74. However, it's rapidly becoming more difficult to find decent CS coupes for less than $10,000. So, as the hucksters say, you'd better act fast. That's because folks are discovering that the CS coupes may just be the best all-around BMWs ever sold in this country. True, there's a successor to the 2800CS / 3.0CS, the 633CSi. It's certainly a nice car, but it's also longer, heavier and decidedly less sporty than the earlier coupes.

The 2800CS / 3.0CS is brilliantly versatile. When you need to transport family or friends, it's a luxury sedan. When you feel like tearing up a mountain road, it's a sports machine. Few cars manage such a magical combination of high style and high performance with a high level of comfort. The car's lines are quietly elegant and timeless. Its engine is incredibly smooth. Its capable chassis gives it handling to match many sports cars. Yet its wood-and-leather interior is more akin to a Rolls-Royce than an MG.

There's little difference between the 2800CS and the later 3.0CS. The 3-liter car has better brakes (the 2800 has drums in the rear and the 3.0 has discs all around) and a larger engine, which provides more low-end torque. Although the 2800 requires premium fuel, it gets a little better fuel economy than the 3.0CS. The 1972 3.0CS models have weak cooling systems (see profile on the 2500, 2800, 3.0 and Bavaria for more detail), and the 1974 models have heftier but uglier bumpers. So that makes the 1973 3.0CS perhaps the best of the bunch. But unfortunately, all these CS coupes turn into heaps of iron oxide with just a whiff of moisture. So finding a rust-free example from any year is all that truly matters. It seems that fast-buck artists are buying these cars in Germany for $2,000 to $3,000, shipping them to

1969-1974 BMW 2800CS / 3.0CS

Specifications	3.0CS
Curb weight, lb.	3175
Engine type	sohc inline-6
Displacement, cc	2985
Transmission	4-speed manual
Suspension, f / r	ind / ind
Brakes, f / r	disc / disc
Steering type	worm and roller

Performance Data

0-60 mph, sec	10.0
Stopping distance from 80 mph, ft	282
Standing 1 / 4 mile, sec @ mph	17.2 @ 82.5
Fuel economy, mpg	17.0
Road test date	7-73

Typical Asking Prices

1969-1974 2800 / 3.0CS	$8,000-$14,000
Typical engine-rebuild price	$3,000-$4,000

the U.S., throwing on a quick paint job and selling them for high prices. You can often identify these recent imports because they may have speedos that read in kilometers per hour, and they'll rarely have leather upholstery or air conditioning. Invariably they turn out to be riddled with rust and to have led hard lives on the *Autobahnen*. So if an early CS is in your future, caveat emptor.

— *Peter Bohr*

U.S.A.
1970-1973 Chevrolet Camaro

We don't think it's an overstatement to call this Camaro the best-looking American car of the 1970s; in fact, the car could be included among the best-styled American cars of any decade. This is not to say that it's an especially original design. Any Ferrari fan can spot the similarities among the Camaro and a couple of legendary cars from Maranello.

The Camaro is certainly larger and less space-efficient than it could be. Nevertheless, the second-generation model lasted for more than twelve years, far longer than the very first Camaro, introduced in 1967. Its styling remained virtually untouched over the years except for the addition of hefty bumpers in 1974. Though GM did an admirable job integrating the bumpers, our favorite models remain the 1970-73 cars with the cleaner-looking chrome bumpers.

Detroit's cars are to automobiles what Whoppers are to hamburgers: You can have them your way. Domestic automakers' options lists are dizzying to buyers familiar with fully-equipped European or Japanese cars, and the Camaro list was no less daunting. Engine alternatives ranged from modest inline 6-cylinder units to gas-guzzling V-8s, though as the decade progressed the largest engines available declined in horsepower. A buyer also had his choice of close- or wide-ratio 4-speed manual transmissions, or a 3-speed manual or a 3-speed automatic. However, most Camaros left the factory with a V-8, an automatic and power-assisted steering and brakes. Many also had air conditioning. There was a plethora of other options, including a limited-slip differential, handling packages and various sorts of gingerbread/trim pieces. All this makes buying a used Camaro akin to buying something from a grab bag. But if you come across one of the high-performance Z28s, or perhaps an SS350 with the sport suspension option, you'll have a proper handling car with plenty of acceleration.

Like the little Datsun 510, many older Camaros seem to be either clapped out and ready for some loving care or jacked-up, hot-rodded monstrosities. And like many older cars, Camaros are prone to body corrosion. If you're fortunate to find a well-maintained, relatively stock, rust-free older Camaro, you won't have to worry much about its reliability.

1971 Chevrolet Camaro SS

1970-1973 Chevrolet Camaro

Specifications	Z-28
Curb weight, lb.	est. 3700
Engine type	pushrod V-8
Displacement, cc	5735
Transmission	3-speed automatic
Suspension, f/r	ind coil/live leaf
Brakes, f/r	disc/drum
Steering type	recirculating ball

Performance Data From Contemporary Tests	
0-60 mph, sec	7.5
Stopping distance from 80 mph, ft	295
Standing ¼ mile, sec @ mph	15.5 @ 90.0
Fuel economy, mpg	12.3
Road test date	4-72

Typical Asking Prices	
1970-73 Camaro	$1,500-$3,000
1970-73 Camaro Z-28	$4,500-$5,500
Typical engine-rebuild price	$1,800-$2,500

Overall, the Camaro's mechanical and electrical components had few if any major problems.

— *Peter Bohr*

ITALY
1978-1979 Fiat 124 Spider / Spider 2000

1979 Fiat Spider 2000

1978-1979 Fiat 124 Spider / Spider 2000

Specifications	Spider 2000
Curb weight, lb.	2365
Engine type	dohc inline 4
Displacement, cc	1995
Transmission	5-speed manual
Suspension, f/r	ind coil / live coil
Brakes, f/r	disc / disc
Steering type	worm and roller

Performance Data

0-60 mph, sec	10.6
Stopping distance from 80 mph, ft	170
Standing 1/4 mile, sec @ mph	18.1 @ 77.0
Fuel economy, mpg	21.0
Road test date	1979

Typical Asking Prices

1978-1979 Fiat 124 Spider	$2,500-$3,500
Typical engine-rebuild price	$1,500-$2,000

Just think back a decade and a half to the cars we could buy then. Among all the Buicks, Fords and Dodges, how many could go on sale today as new cars and not be laughed off the showroom floor? Not many, we'll wager. Yet the Fiat Spider seems just as handsome today as it did then.

This is testimony to the Fiat's Pininfarina styling, as well as to good engineering when the car was first designed. Though this Fiat is Italian, the overall concept is traditional English roadster: two seats, convertible top, rigid rear axle and a front-engine/rear-drive arrangement. The dash is even genuine polished wood and the instruments have highly legible white-on-black faces. But that's as far as the similarities go, for the ride is comfortable, the top can be raised and lowered with one hand and the whole car has a civilized feeling unmatched by any MG or Triumph of the late 1960s.

The Spider really didn't change much in all those years. It received big ugly bumpers in 1975, and the dohc engine went through several displacement permutations: from an original 1,438 cc in 1968 to 1,608 cc in 1971, a slight decrease to 1,592 cc in 1973, an increase again in 1974 to 1,756 cc, and a final increase to 1,995 cc in 1979. With the 1979 displacement increase, Fiat decided to drop the "124" name, and called the car the Spider 2000 instead.

We like the 1971-73 models because these cars had the larger engines but weren't terribly strangled by emission control devices. These earlier models are typically Italian in that they beg to be wound up to 5,000 or 5,500 rpm. By contrast, the later Spiders seem happiest under 4,500 rpm. Nevertheless, by 1978 Fiat had improved the Spider, especially the electrical system, enough to make the 1978-79 versions good buys.

As with the Alfa 1600/1750/2000 series, some of our staff members prefer the coupe version (which was discontinued after 1975) to the Spider. And like the Alfa Spider and GTV, both Fiat 124s share the same suspension and drivetrain. Those who like the enclosed car particularly prefer the cleaner styling of the earliest coupes, the 1968 through 1970 models.

Yes, we recommend the Fiat Spider despite all those bad jokes about reliability. It's true, Fiats aren't the most rugged cars ever to come down the road. Their interiors seem to fray easily, their engines frequently drip oil and their oddball electrical systems try the patience of owners and mechanics alike. The early 124s' mechanical fuel pumps are given to problems, as are the front-end ball joints and rear axle bearing seals. In addition, Fiats are notorious for rust. But as with most cars, Fiats will return enjoyable motoring in exchange for a little loving attention to regular maintenance.

— *Peter Bohr*

ITALY
1974-1980 Fiat X1/9

When Fiat's X1/9 made its American debut in 1974, the car was as up to date as tomorrow's news. After nearly 13 years, that's no longer true, but neither is the X1/9 ancient history. With a mid-mounted engine, independent rear suspension, 4-wheel disc brakes, a lift-off targa top and styling reminiscent of its big brother, the Ferrari 308/328 GTS, the X1-9 is among the most modern of all our used sports cars. It's also still sold in the new-car market, though it's now called the Bertone X1-9.

When you first approach the X1/9, your reaction might well be, "Gad, what a tiny devil!" But just wait until you're settled inside. Unless you're a pro basketball player, you'll find the interior surprisingly spacious. There's also room enough for a couple of passenger's worth of luggage in two compartments, one up front and another one behind the engine.

The diminutive X1/9 proves you don't have to drive a behemoth to have a comfortable ride, thanks to the car's excellent springing, damping and wheel travel. The car has good transient handling characteristics too. Unlike some rear-heavy cars, there's no abrupt change in attitude even when lifting your foot off the throttle in a turn. Unlike the Fiat 124s, the more modern X1/9 exhibits little body roll.

The main drawback to an older X1/9 is that it was a Fiat, suffering the usual Fiat annoyances like flimsy upholstery, paint that fades quickly, and failures of things like hood-release cables. None of these render a car immobile, but it does tend to make Fiats look dilapidated before their time. On the other hand, in the mid-seventies when the X1/9 was introduced, Fiat had begun to take precautions against rust.

Beware of X1/9s with wide aftermarket wheels, a common sight. The wheel bearings, weak in pre-1979 cars, are easily overstressed by larger wheels and will fail every 10,000 to 20,000 miles. It's also important to change the X1/9's camshaft belt regularly, just as it is on Fiat 124s.

Unfortunately air conditioning on X1/9s built before 1979 isn't worth a piece of pasta. It won't blow much cold air when it works, and when the compressor fails, expect a $500 repair bill if you intend to restore the system's mediocrity.

But don't worry. Most other parts aren't costly and they are

1980 Fiat X1/9

1974-80 Fiat X1/9

Specifications

Curb weight, lb.	2045
Engine type	sohc inline 4
Displacement, cc	1290
Transmission	4-speed manual
Suspension, f/r	ind/ind
Brakes, f/r	disc/disc
Steering type	rack and pinion

Performance Data

0-60 mph, sec	16.3
Stopping distance from 80 mph, ft	280
Standng ¼ mile, sec @ mph	20.4 @ 66.5
Fuel economy, mpg	26.0
Road test date	6-76

Typical Asking Prices

1974-80 Fiat X1/9	$1,500-$3,000
Typical engine-rebuild price	$1,400-$1,800

in good supply even though Fiat did pull a disappearing act in this country.

With hot little CRXs, Fiero GTs and MR2s around today, the Bertone X1/9 faces stiff competition in the low end of the new sports-car market. But in a contest for the most modern sports car for the least money, a $2500 used X1/9 wins.— *Peter Bohr*

WEST GERMANY/U.S.A.
1971-1977 Ford Capri 2600/2800

1972 Ford Capri 2600

You want bargains? We got a bargain. How about a genuine *Autobahn* cruiser with a slick gearbox, fine handling, outstanding brakes and one of the smoothest yet most economical engines around? There are also plenty from which to choose, and spare parts, at least those for the engine, are as near as your local Ford or Mercury dealer. All this for much less than $2,000, and even less than $1,500 if you're lucky. Such a deal.

The Capri was conceived as a Mustang for Europe by Ford management following the pony car's sales triumphs in the U.S. during the late 1960s. It does indeed look like a scaled-down Mustang, but that's as far as the similarities to the American car go. The Capri has many of the virtues we've come to associate with German cars, especially a feeling of solidity and overall quality. Moreover, it's comfortable and easy to drive.

However, it's important to realize that not all Capris were created equal. The first Capri to come to our country was the 1600 model of 1970. Though every Capri sold in the U.S. was built by Ford of Germany, the 1600 used a 4-cylinder engine taken from Ford's British Cortina. These early Capris were quite underpowered, even when equipped with a larger German-made, 2.0-liter 4-cylinder engine available a year later. Worst of all, both the 1600 and 2000 Capri proved remarkably troublesome.

But all that changed in 1971, when Ford blessed the Capri with a 2.6-liter V-6 engine. In addition to the larger engine, the 2600 carries full instrumentation (including a tachometer) and wider tires. The V-6 is a real sweetheart. It provides excellent acceleration, fuel economy of better than 20 mpg and a delightful exhaust note. Besides that, it seems to run forever with little fuss. All the same praises can also be sung for the enlarged version of the engine, the 2800, introduced in 1974. That same engine, incidentally, lived on in American-built Ford and Mercury cars even after the demise of the German Capri in 1977.

Our Owner Surveys show that the V-6 Capris have a good overall record of reliability: with the possible exception of front-end alignment and wheel bearing problems, there are no consistent major maladies. There are a number of nig-

1971-1977 Ford Capri 2600/2800

Specifications	Capri 2800
Curb weight, lb.	2685
Engine type	pushrod V-6
Displacement, cc	2792
Transmission	4-speed manual
Suspension, f/r	ind coil/live leaf
Brakes, f/r	disc/drum
Steering type	rack and pinion

Performance Data

0-60 mph, sec	10.6
Stopping distance from 80 mph, ft	273
Standing 1/4 mile, sec @ mph	18.0 @ 77.0
Fuel economy, mpg	19.5
Road test date	7-75

Typical Asking Prices

1971-74 Ford Capri 2.6	$1,000-$2,500
1976-77 Capri II 2.8	$2,000-$3,500
Typical engine-rebuild price	$1,400-$1,600

gling problems, however, such as faulty instruments and alternator / voltage regulator ills. Body parts are becoming harder to find. Drivetrain parts are readily available.

—Peter Bohr

ITALY / U.S.A.
1971-1974 Ford / DeTomaso Pantera

To be absolutely candid, exotic mid-engine cars are impractical. Ford / DeTomaso Panteras, Ferrari 308s, Maserati Meraks and Boras, and even Lotus Esprits are perfectly ridiculous as everyday commute-to-work, run-to-the-store vehicles. The whole lot of them tend to be noisy, cramped, ponderous to drive in heavy traffic and vulnerable to parking-lot damage. They're also fuel inefficient (except for perhaps the Lotus) and they're certainly no good for carrying several business associates or bags of groceries. No, for normal day-in, day-out driving, you'd be far more prudent to buy a Z-car or a Mercedes SL.

So what are exotic cars good for? For blowing the cobwebs out of your mind. For feeling your oats if you're young. Or for feeling young again if you're old. They're for uncongested roads passing through wide open spaces. They're for car enthusiasts who demand the ultimate in acceleration, top speed and cornering power, and who don't give a hoot about practicalities. And of course, they're for those daring characters who are unafraid to make a statement, for driving one of these exotics is like a middle-aged gentleman walking down the street with a trashy blond on his arm — he feels a little conspicuous, but he knows there's a good time to be had.

1971 Ford / De Tomaso Pantera

Just as there's a pecking order among automobiles in general (sports cars being the most desirable, wheezing econo-boxes the least), there's a hierarchy among exotic cars as well. Most rabid car nuts like to think they were born to drive a Ferrari or maybe a Maserati. The Ford DeTomaso Pantera, however, falls several notches down the list; after all, the Pantera's engine is nothing but a Ford — built in Cleveland of all places. Nothing very exotic about that!

Of course exotic-car lovers who also have a shred of practicality left in them will quickly point out that having Detroit iron under a zoomy Italian body has certain advantages. Instead of shelling out $1,000 to tune up a Ferrari, you can take your Pantera to the local gas station and have the job done for $49.95. If your Pantera's engine should need major work, you won't have to wait for sanctified parts from Modena; just run down to Pep Boys and grab some stuff off the shelf.

The Pantera's engine may be prosaic, but make no mistake, in every other respect it's a thoroughbred Italian exotic car. Beneath the showy steel body, there are big magnesium wheels, a five-speed transmission, all-independent suspension, four-wheel disc brakes and, of course, the mid-engine layout. The car will do 0 to 60 mph in little more than 7 seconds and has a top speed near 150 mph.

The Pantera, like other exotic cars, even has a convoluted history behind it. The DeTomaso part of the car's name comes from Alessandro DeTomaso, an energetic industrialist, race-car driver, designer and modern-day Renaissance man. Originally from Argentina, DeTomaso settled in Italy, where he drove for Maserati and later went on to build his own race cars. In the mid-1960s, DeTomaso designed a nice chassis that was to be propelled by a Ford V-8. He turned to Ghia, one of Italy's famous *carrozzeria*, for a body. It just so happened that Giorgetto Giugiaro was in the employ of Ghia, having left Bertone but not yet opened his shop, Ital Design. The young Giugiaro whipped up one of his own usual magnificent designs — the car that became the Mangusta.

DeTomaso then bought Ghia and began building Mangustas. About this time DeTomaso met Lee Iacocca, then president of Ford, and the two became friends. Iacocca decided that a Ford-powered Italian exotic car was just what his company needed to brighten its image, so Ford bought a large share of DeTomaso Automobili. In 1971 a revamped Mangusta, called the Pantera, began appearing in selected Lincoln-Mercury dealerships. The car sold for an amazingly low $9,800.

The price was certainly right and the Pantera looked as terrifically zoomy as any Italian exotic, but unfortunately it was terrible to drive. *Road & Track* found the seating position impossible, the engine noisy, the gearshift recalcitrant, and the braking sometimes uncontrollable. DeTomaso and Ford set about making the car right, and by 1973, the Pantera was a decent product, replete with style, excitement, and an affordable price tag. However, by the end of 1974, Ford tired of exotic cars and stopped selling the Pantera.

Someone looking for an older Pantera should be most concerned about rust; it will show up along the rocker panels, the rear fenders and along the inner fender wells in the rear. As with the Porsches, heavy corrosion can seriously weaken a Pantera because the body and chassis are one unit. The engine is an easy-to-fix Ford, so the only other major component to worry about is the German transmission. A bad one is expensive to replace — about $3,500, though it can be rebuilt for considerably less.

— *Peter Bohr*

1971-1974 Ford / DeTomaso Pantera

Specifications	Pantera L
Curb weight, lb.	3205
Engine type	pushrod V-8
Displacement, cc	5763
Transmission	5-speed manual
Suspension, f / r	ind / ind
Steering type	rack and pinion

Performance Data

0-60 mph, sec	7.6
Stopping distance from 80 mph, ft	256
Standing 1 / 4 mile, sec @ mph	15.6 @ 94.5
Fuel economy, mpg	10.5
Road test date	1974

Typical Asking Prices

1971-73 Pantera	$16,000-$23,000
Typical engine-rebuild price	$1,800-$2,300

GREAT BRITAIN
1961-1971 Jaguar E-Type

From the cozy cockpit in the rear to the extremely long hood, this Jag looks sleek and potent. It's undoubtedly the ultimate in road going phallic symbols. Even the interior is sensual, though perhaps not as much as the XJ6. But E-Types do have soft leather seats and lots of switches and knobs to fondle.

And the E-type isn't just another pretty shape. There's performance to match. Early E-Types are honest 150-mph cars. Even the later cars, though burdened with pollution-control equipment, could manage 120 mph or so. E-Types may be vintage cars today, but that sort of performance is still exciting. And though aluminum engines, fully independent suspensions and 4-wheel disc brakes are fairly commonplace on cars now, these were usually components reserved for exotic cars in the 1960s. But the E-Type had them all.

From its beginning in 1961, the E-Type was available as either a 2-place coupe or convertible with a trunk. For the first four years, it had a 3.8-liter 6-cylinder engine and an archaic transmission with a stump-puller first gear. Then in 1965, the engine was enlarged to 4.2 liters and the old gearbox was replaced by an all-synchromesh unit with more useful ratios. In 1966, Jaguar introduced a stretched 2+2 version. A big change came in 1971, when a V-12 was stuffed into the 2+2 chassis.

In looks, the E-Type didn't age gracefully. Over the years it became more cluttered, and in 2+2 or V-12 form, longer and fatter. But from a standpoint of function, the seats, brakes, headlights, cooling and electrical systems all improved. Each E-Type fancier has a favorite year, though many prefer a 1967 model because the car had matured by then but was yet to be saddled with pollution controls.

We think 2-place coupes are especially good values now. For one reason, convertibles generally sell for more than $12,000 if in good condition, while a decent coupe can be yours for around $9,000. For another, the early 2-place coupe is perhaps the most beautiful of all the E-Types from a purely aesthetic point of view. By contrast, we consider the 2+2 bulbous (if you want a 4-passenger Jag, find a MK 2 or XJ6). As for the 12-cylinder E-Types, as one editor said, "If it doesn't look like an engine, I don't want it." Indeed, the V-12 may be an exciting piece of machinery, but all its components and associated plumbing are mighty intimidating, not to mention its insatiable thirst for petrol.

Which brings us to the question on the tip of everyone's tongue: Aren't these old Jaguars about as reliable as a drunk on New Year's Eve? Alas, our own Owner Survey conducted in 1969 confirmed the sad truth. Whether it be a 3.8 or a later 4.2

1961-1971 Jaguar E-Type

Specifications	E-Type Coupe
Curb weight, lb.	2900
Engine type	dohc inline 6
Displacement, cc	3781
Transmission	4-speed manual
Suspension, f / r	ind / ind
Brakes, f / r	disc / disc
Steering type	rack and pinion

Performance Data

0-60 mph, sec	7.4
Stopping distance from 80 mph, ft	NA
Standing 1 / 4 mile, sec @ mph	15.6 @ 91
Fuel economy, mpg	17.0
Road test date	4-64

Typical Asking Prices

1961-71 E-Type coupe	$6,000-$14,000
1961-71 E-Type convertible	$9,000-$18,000
Typical engine-rebuild price	$4,000-$5,500

1968 Jaguar E-type

model, the list of problems is daunting. (See the profile on the XJ6 for more detail.) But keep in mind that these are complex cars and one should expect more (and expensive) maintenance. Unfortunately, an E-Type coupe sold for $5,900 in 1964. It's unfortunate because it meant many people could afford the initial price, but not the maintenance. Consequently, many of the cars deteriorated rapidly, even when relatively new. And now, years later, well... if you buy one, consider yourself a risk seeker.

But you know what? Our Owner Survey also showed that despite all the problems, a surprisingly large number of owners intended to buy another Jag. Just goes to show you that when passion is involved, logic can go out the window. And there's no more passionate seducer than an E-Type.　　— *Peter Bohr*

GREAT BRITAIN
1973-1976 Jensen-Healey

When the Austin-Healey 3000 roadster went out of production in 1967, a lot of its fans on this side of the Atlantic were deeply saddened. Among them was Kjell Qvale, a British-car distributor in San Francisco. But energetic Qvale did more than shed tears; he decided to build a replacement.

Of course Qvale needed a factory, so he bought venerable Jensen, one of the tiny specialty car makers so often found in England. Donald Healey, creator of the 3000, and his son conceived the chassis of the new car while the folks at Jensen designed the body. The little company didn't have the wherewithal to build its own engine, so Qvale turned to Lotus for its modern, all-aluminum, dohc 4-cylinder engine. With that, the Jensen-Healey was born in late 1972.

Though the Healey name is attached to it, the newer car is quite unlike the Austin-Healey 3000. The older car was a rough, tough beast with a distinctively handsome body. Though also a two-seater, the J-H by contrast is a comfortable, soft-riding car with a less than exciting body.

1975 Jensen-Healey

Predictably, its lack of styling pizzazz didn't thrill the marketplace. This, together with labor problems at the factory, spelled doom for the Jensen-Healey after little more than three years of production. The big, Chrysler-powered Jensen Interceptor, the only other car built by the company, was still in demand, but Qvale was losing too much money to continue. Altogether, some 8,000 roadsters reached the U.S. before Jensen went into receivership. In a last-ditch effort in 1976 to make the car more attractive, the company sent 400 enclosed GT versions of the Jensen-Healey to the U.S. These had such luxury trimmings as air conditioning and power windows.

The Jensen-Healey is a traditional British sports car with the engine up front and a live, rigid axle in the rear. But despite this pedestrian suspension, the J-H isn't terribly upset by rough roads. The car also feels unusually stable, primarily because of an especially wide track. And the rack-and-pinion steering gives light, quick and accurate response.

Because Jensen was a small concern without acres of automated assembly equipment, much of the body was hand-made. Handwork can be exceptionally fine if accomplished craftsmen wield the tools; though the J-H is no Aston Martin, the workmanship is good. The cockpit is roomy, and there's space behind the two seats, in addition to the trunk, for packages. But while the old 3000 had the traditional leather seats and a broad expanse of walnut across the dash, the J-H has mostly plastic.

The convertible top is certainly British traditional — that is, a terrible chore to lower and raise and not very efficient in keeping out the elements. It can't match those of other contemporary mid-1970 sports cars such as the Fiat 124 Spider.

The Lotus engine, however, is anything but traditional, notably because there are four (not just two) valves per cylinder, two inlet and two exhaust. Though obviously more complicated, the sixteen valves are highly efficient, both in terms of exhaust emissions and fuel economy. The eight inlet valves pull in torrents of air through a pair of Stromberg carburetors, making the engine quite noisy. But it's also strong: putting out 140 horsepower, the engine propels the car to 60 mph in under ten seconds.

It's a durable machine, but if the cam belt should break, watch out! Though the belt (which drives the two overhead camshafts) doesn't break especially often, it's a disaster when it does. The arrangement is such that the pistons will crash into the valves, bending everything out of shape. The belts should be replaced regularly as a precautionary measure.

The prospective J-H buyer should look for either a late 1974 or 1975 model, or for one of the rare 1976 GTs, all of which will have 5-speed transmissions. Most 1974 and all 1973 cars have 4-speeds, which had trouble with the gearshift lever spontaneously popping out of second and third gears. Early models (1973) are also more prone to rust.

For any car whose maker has long departed, spare parts can be a primary worry. Fortunately for Jensen-Healey owners, parts availability is no problem, though they tend to be expensive. A company called Jensen Parts and Service, which still exists in England, supplies everything through three U.S. distributors to keep the cars going. Of course engine parts are also available from Lotus, and the brakes (made by Girling) and electrical components (by Lucas) are common to several British sports cars.

— *Peter Bohr*

1973-1976 Jensen-Healey

Specifications	Jensen-Healey
Curb weight, lb.	2155
Engine type	dohc inline 4
Displacement, cc	1973
Transmission	4-speed manual
Suspension, f / r	ind / live
Steering type	rack and pinion

Performance Data	
0-60 mph, sec	8.1
Standing 1 / 4 mile, sec @ mph	16.2 @ 87
Fuel economy, mpg	17.5
Road test date	1973

Typical Asking Prices	
1973-76 Jensen-Healey	$3,500-$7,500*
Typical engine-rebuild price	$2,000-$3,500

*Highest prices for 1976 GT

WEST GERMANY

1971 Mercedes-Benz 300 SEL 3.5, 1972-1973 280 SE/SEL 4.5 and 300 SEL 4.5

1972 Mercedes-Benz 280SEL 4.5

1971 Mercedes-Benz 300SEL 3.5, 1972-1973 280SE/SEL 4.5 and 300SEL 4.5

Specifications	280SEL 4.5
Curb weight, lb.	3775
Engine type	sohc V-8
Displacement, cc	4250
Transmission	3-speed automatic
Suspension, f/r	ind/ind
Brakes, f/r	disc/disc
Steering type	recirculating ball

Performance Data

0-60 mph, sec	11.2
Stopping distance from 80 mph, ft	320
Standing 1/4 mile, sec @ mph	18.1 @ 78.5
Fuel economy, mpg	11.5
Road test date	11-71

Typical Asking Prices

1971 300SEL 3.5	$6,000-$9,000
1972-73 280SE/ SEL 4.5 & 300SEL 4.5	$4,500-$8,000
Typical engine-rebuild price	$4,500-$6,000

What's the most confusing thing you can think of? Your federal income tax return? The instructions for your new personal computer? Perhaps, but *we* can think of few things more confounding than the Mercedes-Benz model nomenclature of the late 1960s and early 1970s. However, if you're searching the classified ads for a 280- or 300-series sedan of that vintage, expecially one with a 3.5- or 4.5-liter V-8, you'd better know why one 280SE sells for $50,000 and another for $5,000. So let's sort out the models.

In 1966, Mercedes introduced a conservative, pleasant-looking, 4-door sedan with a 2.5-liter 6-cylinder engine. If the car had a carburetor-equipped engine, it was called a 250S, and if it had fuel injection (*Einspritzung* in German), it was called a 250SE. In 1968, with the 6-cylinder engine's displacement at 2.8 liters, these cars became the 280S and 280SE. So far so good.

In 1967, when Mercedes added four inches to the wheelbase and gave the car a self-leveling suspension that used airbag springs instead of metal ones, they called the 2.8-liter, 6-cylinder, car the 300SEL (the L indicating a longer wheelbase). Then in 1968, Mercedes decided to build its own version of a muscle-car by dropping the huge 6.3-liter, fuel-injected V-8 from the 600 limo into the 300SEL. This amalgam was called the 300SEL 6.3 and was built through 1972. It's one heck of a car, and well-preserved specimens usually sell for more than $10,000.

Now things really get confusing. For 1970, Mercedes came up with a completely different V-8, a 3.5-liter engine. They put this V-8 into the 300SEL and called it the 300SEL 3.5. During the same year, the 3.5-liter V-8 was also placed into a large 4-passenger coupe and convertible, models that dated back to 1961. These cars were called the 280SE 3.5 Coupe and the 3.5 Convertible. Today they're very popular with the Beverly Hills set, and convertibles in particular can change hands for astronomical prices — as much as $50,000.

Then in 1972, the regular 4-door 280SE, the 280SEL and 300SEL received a V-8, but a 4.5-liter engine. It was really the same 3.5-liter V-8 as in the 1971 300SEL 3.5, but with increased stroke. The change in displacement was necessary because of power-robbing emissions controls, but a 1971 3.5-liter car was actually quicker and much more fuel-efficient than the 4.5-liter cars. All these cars were finally superseded by the new 450SE and 450SEL in late 1973.

The cars we're recommending here are the 300SEL with

265

either a 3.5-liter or a 4.5-liter V-8, and the 280SE/SEL with 4.5-liter V-8s. Both the 300SEL 3.5 and 4.5 are quite rare; Mercedes sold less than 3,500 from 1971 to early 1973. However, the 280SE/SEL 4.5 cars are plentiful because Mercedes sold nearly 21,000 of them during that time. But remember, whether it's a 300- or 280-series car, it will look just like the 6-cylinder 250S/SE of 1966.

These Mercedes are dignified but rather old-fashioned looking. Their suspension, with low-pivot swing axles, is out-of-date too.

So why do we like these V-8 Mercedes sedans? First, the smoothness of the V-8 engine makes these cars magnificent highway cruisers. The 3.5/4.5 engine is typically Mercedes in that it's built with prolonged high-speed *Autobahn* cruising in mind. The engines are tough; mechanics tell us 150,000 miles between overhauls is the norm, which is about 50 percent more than the distance for most engines. Finally, there's the outstanding workmanship and attention to detail that every Mercedes-Benz seems to possess. The Mercedes is imbued with quality that never goes out of style.

Bear in mind that these cars have been on the road for a dozen years or so and that they're complex and very expensive to repair. So just search extra hard for a well-maintained car, and you'll have one of the best examples of the Mercedes-Benz marque at a bargain price.

— Peter Bohr

WEST GERMANY
1972-1979 Mercedes-Benz 350SL/450SL

The reputation of Mercedes-Benz in the United States is the envy of all other automakers. Certainly Ferrari and Porsche are held in high esteem by the general public, but their cars are also sometimes considered to be playthings for the wealthy rather than serious transportation. Perhaps that other Teutonic wunderwagen, BMW, comes closest to matching the Mercedes image, though in many circles the BMW is only thought to be the next best thing to a Mercedes. Ask the fellow on Main Street, U.S.A., to pick the all-around best-engineered automobile and chances are he'll name the car symbolized by a three-pointed star. Mercedes-Benz automobiles are believable. They're solid. They're dependable. They're good investments.

1979 Mercedes-Benz 450SL

They can also be rather dull, unfortunately. For one thing, their very popularity makes them tedious. Consider Mercedes' 450SL. An SL in West Los Angeles or Palm Beach is about as distinctive as a pinstriped suit at a bankers' convention. As an automotive representation of nouveaux riches, the SL has become a cliche of the first order.

1972-1979 Mercedes-Benz 350SL/450SL

Specifications	1974 450SL
Curb weight, lb.	3730
Engine type	sohc V-8
Displacement, cc	4520
Transmission	3-speed automatic
Suspension, f/r	ind/ind
Steering type	recirculating ball

Performance Data

0-60 mph, sec	10.2
Stopping distance from 80 mph, ft	289
Standing 1/4 mile, sec @ mph	17.7 @ 81.5
Fuel economy, mpg	14.5
Road test date	1974

Typical Asking Prices

1972-79 350/450SL	$14,000-$30,000
Typical engine-rebuild price	$4,500-$6,000

But there is another reason for their dullness — corporate philosophy. Mercedes engineers leave nothing to chance. Even the most minute details of design are carefully developed. Mercedes works slowly to get everything right the first time; totally new models are thus infrequent. Gimmicks are taboo, and styling is conservative. Technically, Mercedes-Benz cars are nearly faultless. What's so bad about that, you ask? Refinement, precision, function-over-form and perfection-carried-to-an-extreme are all well and good in a workaday sedan. But in a sports car, a little quirkiness or a little flamboyance (not too much mind you) adds personality. Sports-car drivers usually want to become involved with their cars, and in this respect choosing a sports car is not unlike finding a lover. Would you find it easier to love a predictable perfectionist or a spontaneous romantic?

There's no question about it, the Mercedes SL has a host of attributes. Let's start with creature comforts. The heating, air conditioning and ventilation systems are on a par with Cadillac (and no company does better in this area than GM). The controls are handy and well marked. Standard equipment on the SL includes cruise control, power windows and power radio antenna. The standard power steering is perhaps the best in the world, giving just the right amount of road feel without overboosting.

What about ergonomics? It would take a peculiar body not to be comfortable in an SL. All the instruments are logically arranged and easy to read. The relationship between the driver's seat, pedals, gearshift lever and steering wheel should satisfy people of almost any stature. The seats are firm, but not too firm, and give plenty of support. And the ride, well, it would please your grandmother.

The SL's big V-8 engine is smooth and quiet, more befitting a luxury sedan than a sports car. That's not surprising since the same engine is used in Mercedes' luxury sedans. The convertible top and the removable hardtop are both easy to operate, and both provide superb weather sealing. And with either top, the visibility is outstanding, especially by sports-car standards.

And then there's the Mercedes' legendary quality of construction and reliability. Even the underside of the dash is neatly finished off. The doors shut with a precise "clink" rather than a harsh "clunk." The materials are all first-rate, including the leather on the seats. And you can count on a Mercedes to take you where you need to go in almost any conditions outside of a flood. Finally, durability and long-lasting quality make the SL one of the best sports-car investments around.

But, alas, comfort, convenience and durability don't add up to excitement. There's just not much about the SL to please the right side of your brain. The styling, though dignified, is rather heavy and ponderous. It lacks the grace and agility of contemporary Italian sports-car design or even of older sports cars like the Porsche 911. The SL's handling is safe and predictable, but it doesn't grab the corners any better than a Fiat Spider or a VW Scirocco. Even quietness can be boring if you appreciate the sound of a healthy exhaust note from a sophisticated engine. And perhaps worst of all, in this country the SL has only been available with an automatic transmission — not very sporting at all.

The car began as the 350SL 4.5 in 1972, which replaced Mercedes' previous sports-car model, the lovely 280SL. Mercedes has traditionally designated its models according to engine size. Hence, 450SL refers to the car's 4.5-liter engine, while the "SL" refers to "Sport Light" cars. By that tradition, the 350SL was a meaningless designation because the car had a 4.5-liter V-8 engine. Consequently, the name was changed to 450SL in 1973.

Of course Mercedes-Benz has never offered bargain-priced cars. Quality frequently costs more, and Mercedes quality is no exception. But when you consider that a 1972 350SL was priced at slightly more than $10,000 when new, and that a nearly identical 1985 380SL costs four times as much, you wonder if Mercedes' management hasn't become a little greedy. However, exorbitant price tags only seem to reinforce Mercedes' high-status image in this country.

More than anything else, the Mercedes reputation is based on the vaultlike solidity of their cars. Mercedes-Benz bodies and engines hang together long after those of other marques are heaped in the junkyard. A 450SL with a minimum of maintenance should go 180,000 miles before needing a complete overhaul. This sort of longevity is truly remarkable.

Mercedes SLs may be exceptionally long lived, but they are also exceptionally costly to repair. Replacing a 450SL's engine with a factory-new short block (the bottom half of the engine) and an overhauled cylinder head could cost $6,000. These prices are right up there with exotics like Aston Martin and Maserati.

— *Peter Bohr*

WEST GERMANY
1968-1973 Opel GT

The Opel GT is an international smorgasbord. Its body was made in France. Its drivetrain was German. It was assembled in Germany by Opel, a subsidiary of America's General Motors. And in the U.S. it was sold by Buick dealers.

The Opel GT's main appeal is that it appears to be a pint-size Mako-style Corvette, the model sold until 1983. The Opel GT has the same flashy lines, including the Vette's familiar swooping front fenders and retractable headlights. Both cars also went on the market in 1968, but the Opel had a much briefer life, lasting only through 1973.

1968 Opel GT

Styling aside, the Opel GT is more the antithesis of the Cor-

1968-1973 Opel GT

Specifications

Curb weight, lb.	2110
Engine type	sohc inline 4
Displacement, cc	1897
Transmission	4-speed manual
Suspension, f/r	ind/live
Brakes, f/r	disc/drum
Steering type	rack and pinion

Performance Data

0-60 mph, sec	11.9
Stopping distance from 80 mph, ft	277
Standng ¼ mile, sec @ mph	18.4 @ 74.0
Fuel economy, mpg	25.9
Road test date	7-71

Typical Asking Prices

1968-73 Opel GT	$1,500-$2,500
Typical engine-rebuild price	$1,100-$1,500

vette than a mini-replica. People assume that because the Vette has a fiberglass body the Opel has one too. The Opel actually has a steel body made by the French company Brissonneau and Lotz. Among the Opel GT's attributes is its solid, rattlefree construction and its high quality finish.

The Opel GT could be ordered with an automatic transmission. But the Opel's standard 4-speed gearbox is a fine unit, as is its dead-accurate rack-and-pinion steering.

We asked Rick Graham of Huntington Beach, California, a founding member of the Opel Motorsport Club AG, for his thoughts on Opel GTs. That nemesis of old cars, rust, is a serious Opel GT problem too, according to Rick. As for mechanical problems, the major one is carburetion. Rick suggests changing from the stock Solex carb to a Weber; he says there's a smog-legal one available.

Then there's the matter of parts. "The only thing you'll get out of a Buick dealer," says Rick, "is a belly laugh." Most parts can be found in junkyards or through one of a few independent suppliers. The club publishes an annual directory of parts sources. Body pieces, interior trim and the pop-up headlight mechanisms (they're operated by muscle power with a hefty lever) are the most difficult parts to come by.

The Opel GT is eye-catching like a Corvette, but it doesn't perform like one. It's a gelding wishing it were a stallion, but a cheerful gelding nonetheless.

— *Peter Bohr*

JAPAN
1975-1979 Toyota Celica

Toyota's Celica is one of those Cinderella stories everyone finds so charming, unless, of course, he happens to work for another car maker. Once upon a time back in 1971, Japan's largest automobile manufacturer presented its first Celica to America. Unfortunately, the sporty little coupe was a rather awkward product without the performance or handling of Datsun's fabulously successful 240Z, introduced just a year earlier. But soon the Celica became a winner too, as people began to realize that it had virtue all its own. Maybe it wasn't a real sports car, but it had adequate performance, acceptable handling, plenty of comfort for two, an inexpensive price tag and, most impressive of all, it was darn-near bulletproof.

Well, almost. There was a slight problem with the engine; it tended to fry its valves, a malady that seemed to get worse each year as emissions regulations tightened. In 1974, Toyota modified the cylinder head of the 18R engine, which solved the problem. But a year later the company replaced the 18R engine altogether with the larger 2.2-liter 20R, a sturdier, more modern engine. We like the 1975-79 Celicas because they have the improved engine.

With the exception of a Liftback model introduced in 1976,

1974 Toyota Celica GT

and an extensive face-lift in 1978, the Celica's styling changed relatively little over the decade. Most of us at *Road & Track* prefer the look of the traditional notchback to the hatchback version. The notchback gives better rear headroom besides. We also like the crisper, more European styling of the 1978 and later cars.

Japanese cars in general are known for having a full complement of standard equipment, and the Celica is no exception. Even the standard ST models carry such goodies as reclining bucket seats, full console, clock and tachometer. The GT versions improved on the list with a 5-speed transmission, AM/FM radio and some fancier interior features. The 5-speed, however, became standard on both the ST and GT versions in 1978.

As we mentioned before, these Toyotas earned a reputation for exceptional reliability, once the valve burning was fixed. Consequently the used-car shopper looking at older Celicas need not worry about chronic problems. Toyotas even seem less rust-prone than other cars, particularly other Japanese cars. Though you can't expect true sports-car-like handling with a Celica, if you add a set of high-quality shock absorbers and radial tires, you'll have yourself an economical yet entertaining sporty car.

— *Peter Bohr*

1975-1979 Toyota Celica

Specifications	GT Liftback
Curb weight, lb.	2505
Engine type	sohc inline 4
Displacement, cc	2189
Transmission	5-speed manual
Suspension, f / r	ind coil / live coil
Brakes, f / r	disc / drum
Steering type	recirculating ball

Performance Data	
0-60 mph, sec	10.4
Stopping distance from 80 mph, ft	270
Standing 1 / 4 mile, sec @ mph	18.1 @ 77.5
Fuel economy, mpg	26.0
Road test date	1-78

Typical Asking Prices	
1975-79 Celica	$1,000-$2,500
Typical engine-rebuild price	$1,300-$1,900

WEST GERMANY
1975-1979 Volkswagen Scirocco

Occasionally greatness can spring from humble origins. In this case it's the VW Scirocco. Some call it nothing more than a gussied-up Rabbit; true, the two cars are brothers under the sheet metal. But in no way should the Scirocco be diminished as a real GT just because it's closely related to a ubiquitous econo sedan.

The little Scirocco has that elusive balance found in a proper sports car. The ride is taut, but not uncomfortable; the engine gives spritely performance, while the brakes are capable enough to match this. And despite its front-wheel drive, the Scirocco exhibits relatively little understeer and has cornering power to match the likes of Porsche 924s and Mazda RX-7s. In sum, it's highly tossible.

It's also a very modern package with its front-wheel drive. Moreover, master stylist Giugiaro is responsible for the Scirocco's handsome shape. Although you'll never confuse it with Giugiaro-designed Alfas, Lotuses and Maseratis, the car is a prime example of the designer's now-famous "wedge" shape.

The displacement of the Scirocco's engines has fluctuated over the years, beginning as a 1.5-liter unit in 1975 and increasing to 1.7 liters in the later versions. But despite the changes, power output always remained in the 70-75 bhp range. Although in the first two years, 1975 and 1976, the cars had car-

1975-1979 Volkswagen Scirocco

Specifications	Scirocco
Curb weight, lb.	1950
Engine type	sohc inline 4
Displacement, cc	1475
Transmission	4-speed manual
Suspension, f / r	ind coil / ind coil
Brakes, f / r	disc / drum
Steering type	rack and pinion

Performance Data	
0-60 mph, sec	10.4
Stopping distance from 80 mph, ft	240
Standing 1 / 4 mile, sec @ mph	18.0 @ 77
Fuel economy, mpg	29.0
Road test date	2-78

Typical Asking Prices	
1975-1979 VW Scirocco	$1,500-$3,000
Typical engine-rebuild price	$1,600-$1,800

1975 Volkswagen Scirocco

1978 Volkswagen Beetle Convertible

buretors, all Sciroccos from 1977 on have fuel injection.

We like the 1978 and 1979 model years because these two are relatively new cars and are available on the used-car market for $5,000 or less. Later Sciroccos show many improvements over earlier ones. And it's a good thing too, for the 1975-76 cars (the first two years of production) are, to be uncharitable, dogs. The most notable failing of the cars is weak valve-stem seals that lead to heavy oil consumption. The malady was severe enough for VW to recall 1979 and earlier Sciroccos. A different kind of seal seems to solve the problem. But the early cars were also plagued with carburetor-related driveability troubles and poor quality control on body parts and interior fittings. Cars built after June 1977 (check the plate attached to the driver's door ledge) not only had fuel injection, which cleared up the driveability problem, but seem to be better constructed as well. Sciroccos are all new enough so that many on the used-car market will have air conditioning. Because the Scirocco's electrical system is rather weak to begin with, some mechanics advise prospective buyers to avoid the added complication of non-factory air conditioning units. Factory air conditioning has neater wiring.

It seems that when VW came up with the Rabbit and Scirocco as replacements for the trusty Beetle and Karmann-Ghia, they sacrificed reliability for handling. Even so, the Scirocco in particular is such an exuberant car that we can't resist recommending it.

— *Peter Bohr*

WEST GERMANY
1956-1979 Volkswagen Beetle Convertible

What? A Beetle among Ferraris, Jaguars and Porsches? Surely we jest. Well, perhaps just a little. But you may recall that the British victors after World War II dismissed the Beetle as a joke, too. They left the car and its tooling to the vanquished Germans, and by 1972 the Beetle had become the world's best-selling car, breaking Ford's Model T record.

Okay, so the Beetle isn't much in the performance or handling department. Even in its later life as a "Super Beetle," its 0-60 mph time of around 18 seconds and its lateral acceleration figure of about 0.6g seem laughable today. Its rear-end weight causes notorious oversteering, and its tall body makes the Beetle a handful in gusty sidewinds. All Beetles have 4-wheel independent suspensions, but even so the ride is bouncy and harsh. And finally, the Beetle's air-cooled flat-4 engine makes quite a racket.

The Beetle has its vices all right, but the car is also celebrated hither and yon for three virtues: fuel economy, an unusually high standard of workmanship and an unmatched

1956-1979 Volkswagen Beetle Convertible

Specifications	Super Beetle
Curb weight, lb.	1970
Engine type	pushrod horiz- opp 4
Displacement, cc	1584
Transmission	4-speed manual
Suspension, f / r	ind / ind
Brakes, f / r	drum / drum
Steering type	worm and roller

Performance Data

0-60 mph, sec	18.4
Stopping distance from 80 mph, ft	353
Standing 1 / 4 mile, sec.	21.1 @ 63
Fuel economy, mpg	28.7
Road test date	3-71

Typical Asking Prices

1956-1979 Beetle Convertible	$3,500-$6,500
Typical engine-rebuild price	$1,100-$1,500

reputation for long life and easy service. Beetles usually manage fuel economy in the high 20s or low 30s. Their quality of assembly is always superb; their doors are so airtight that it's reputed Beetles have been driven into lakes and floated. As for durability, only the exhaust valves are occasionally a problem, and with regular maintenance and moderate driving, nothing ever seems to go wrong.

When you take those virtues and add to them a convertible top, you get a practical car with pizzazz. Not beauty, mind you, but a funky kind of charm. Unlike most convertibles that have some sort of compartment where the top stows away when it's down, the Beetle's ragtop just piles behind the back seat, looking for all the world like an old English perambulator — you almost expect to see a nanny pushing the car along.

Actually the Beetle's convertible top is anything but a "rag" top; similar to the top on a Mercedes or Rolls-Royce convertible, the Beetle's isn't just a single layer of material, but has an exterior layer, a headliner inside and padding in between. Very fancy, and very expensive to replace.

During the nearly quarter century that VW sold the Beetle in the U.S., from 1956 to 1979, the company bragged that almost everything in the car was refined over the years, except its basic styling, of course. The changes were so great that late-model VWs share virtually no parts with the earliest VWs, though they look the same. Important changes include more powerful engines in 1961, 1966, 1967, 1970 and 1975. Suspensions were also upgraded several times over the years, with the swing axles eliminated in 1969 and the trailing arm front suspension replaced on the Super Beetle in 1971.

But because Beetles changed so relatively little in appearance, prices for convertibles are determined more by a car's condition than anything else. Beetle convertibles are so popular that fully restored cars from the 1960s frequently sell for more than $5,000. The early cars have the advantage of less smog equipment and are truer to the Beetle's simple nature. The Mac-Pherson struts of the later models also seem to be more troublesome than the earlier type of suspension. However, you're probably best off looking for a 1975-79 car just to beat the wear and tear of old age. Lift the floor mats and check for rusty floors (a result of leaky tops). In addition to the fabric, check the condition of the wooden bows that form the top. Regardless of which year you choose, you'll find a Beetle convertible to be a fun, funny car — and that's no joke.   — *Peter Bohr*